Andrew Leith Adams

Monograph on the British Fossil Elephants

Andrew Leith Adams

Monograph on the British Fossil Elephants

ISBN/EAN: 9783337815912

Printed in Europe, USA, Canada, Australia, Japan

Cover: Foto ©Andreas Hilbeck / pixelio.de

More available books at **www.hansebooks.com**

THE

PALÆONTOGRAPHICAL SOCIETY.

INSTITUTED MDCCCXLVII.

LONDON:

MDCCCLXXVII—MDCCCLXXXI.

THE BRITISH FOSSIL ELEPHANTS.

The Monograph on the British Fossil Elephants will be found in the Volumes of the Palæontographical Society issued for the years 1877, 1879, and 1881.

DATES OF PUBLICATION.

PAGES	PLATES	ISSUED IN VOL. FOR YEAR	PUBLISHED
Title-page	—	1881	May, 1881
1—68	I—V	1877	February, 1877
69—146	VI—XV	1879	May, 1879
147—265	XVI—XXVIII	1881	May, 1881

MONOGRAPH

ON THE

BRITISH FOSSIL

ELEPHANTS.

BY

A. LEITH ADAMS, M.A., M.B., F.R.S., F.G.S.,

PROFESSOR OF NATURAL HISTORY IN THE QUEEN'S COLLEGE, CORK.

LONDON:

PRINTED FOR THE PALÆONTOGRAPHICAL SOCIETY.

1877—1881.

PRINTED BY
J. E. ADLARD, BARTHOLOMEW CLOSE.

BRITISH FOSSIL ELEPHANTS.

CORRIGENDA AND ADDENDA.

Page 26, line 28, *for* in inches *read* in 6 inches.

  ,,   47 ,, 12, Table, *for* x 9 x *read* x 8 x.

  ,,   47 ,, 13, ,, *for* x 19 x *read* x 21 x.

  ,,   47 ,, 17, *for* x 24 x *read* x 22 x.

  ,,   57 ,,   3, *after* *E. antiquus* *add* Plate XVII, figs. 2 and 5.

  ,,   62 ,, 24, *for* more apart *read* more convergent.

  ,,   71 ,, 35, *for* Alwick *read* Atwick.

  ,,   76, note 4, *for* care *read* cave.

  ,,   92, line 6, *for* Hyæna, Horse, Irish Elk, and Rhinoceras, October 6th, *read* with tooth of Ox, 21st October, 1870.

  ,, 121 ,, *for* Dawson *read* Dowson.

  ,, 125, Table, under head of x 21 x lower molars, *for* 1 *read* 2.

  ,,   ,,   ,, under head of x 24 x upper molars, *for* 5 *read* 6.

Plate XII, fig. 2, *for* Penultimate *read* Ultimate.

THE

PALÆONTOGRAPHICAL SOCIETY.

INSTITUTED MDCCCXLVII.

VOLUME FOR 1877.

LONDON:
MDCCCLXXVII.

MONOGRAPH

ON THE

BRITISH FOSSIL

ELEPHANTS.

BY

A. LEITH ADAMS, M.B., F.R.S., F.G.S.,

PROFESSOR OF ZOOLOGY IN THE ROYAL COLLEGE OF SCIENCE, DUBLIN.

PART I.

DENTITION AND OSTEOLOGY OF ELEPHAS ANTIQUUS (*Falconer*).

Pages 1—68; Plates I—V.

LONDON:

PRINTED FOR THE PALÆONTOGRAPHICAL SOCIETY.

1877.

MONOGRAPH

ON THE

BRITISH FOSSIL ELEPHANTS.

ELEPHAS ANTIQUUS.

I.—INTRODUCTORY.

THE history of the discovery of the remains of the Elephant described in this Memoir has been narrated by Dr. Falconer in his masterly essay on 'The Species of Mastodon and Elephant occurring in the Fossil State in Great Britain.'[1] It seems important here, however, to indicate certain points in connection with the discovery. Up to the year 1844 all remains of Elephants met with in the Tertiary formations of the British Islands were considered to belong to the *Elephas primigenius.*[2] At that time Dr. Falconer was engaged in arranging and describing the rich harvest of Tertiary Vertebrata collected by himself, Sir Proby Cautley, Mr. Fraser, and others, in the Tertiary beds of the Sub-Himalaya and river deposits of Central India. During the preparation of the 'Fauna Antiqua Sivalensis,' which began to be issued during the following year, he was struck with the resemblance between molars from India and certain teeth of Elephants found in the Norwich Crag and deposits of the Thames Valley; moreover, it seemed to him that the molars from the Thames Valley agreed with similar teeth discovered by Nesti in Tuscany as far back as 1808. It is asserted, however, by Dr. Falconer that at that time he was not sufficiently conversant with the foreign specimens; inasmuch as, instead of connecting the Norwich Crag molars with those from the deposits of Tuscany, he made a mistake and correlated the molars from the Thames Valley and the latter under the name *Elephas meridionalis* of Nesti, whilst to the owner of the teeth from the older British strata he gave the name of *Elephas antiquus.* This mistake, unfortunately, was perpetuated in the representations of the two species published in the 'Fauna Antiqua

---

[1] 'Journal Geological Society of London,' vols. xiii, xiv, and xxi, reprinted in the 'Palæontological Memoirs of the late Dr. Falconer,' vol. ii.

[2] Owen, 'British Fossil Mammals,' p. 232.

1

Sivalensis ;' it has, however, been fully pointed out by himself,[1] and corrected in the descriptions of the plates.[2] It may be further stated that the so-called *Elephas priscus* of Goldfuss, which Dr. Falconer considered was represented by certain molars from the Thames Valley,[3] was subsequently withdrawn by him in consequence of more extended researches establishing these teeth as being only a variety of the grinder of *Elephas antiquus*.[4]

In connection with the discovery and description of the species of Elephant under consideration, I have to observe that the first portion of Dr. Falconer's essay on the British Mastodon and Elephant referred to, was published in 1857, and the second part, after his death, in 1865.[5] The latter is so far imperfect that it does not contain the description of the entire dentition of the *Elephas primigenius*, nor any observations on the *Elephas antiquus*, which, however, in the form of note-book entries, have been published by the editor of his Memoirs.[6] These jottings of the author appear, however, to have been written prior to the latest impressions he had formed with reference to the characters of certain molars in foreign museums, which on more matured experience he conceived did not belong to *Elephas antiquus*.[7]

The flood of light thrown on the study of fossil Proboscidians by the late Dr. Falconer shines nowhere more clearly than on the molars of British fossil Elephants ; inasmuch as, through the splendid discoveries made by him in the Tertiary formations of India, he received the impressions which led him to apply his inductions to European forms, and with what measure of success his masterly expositions amply show. It is to be regretted, however, that he has left no detailed account of the *Elephas antiquus* beyond " note-book entries " and a few impressions dispersed throughout his various essays. With the view, therefore, of supplying a desideratum in fossil zoology, I have attempted to bring together the results of an extensive acquaintance with such proboscidian remains as appear to me to belong to this Elephant. I have also compared them, as far as opportunities would permit, with associated and allied teeth and bones of other forms of British and foreign Elephants.[8]

It may be observed here that to attempt to draw a sharp line between molars of one

[1] 'Pal. Mem.,' vol. ii, p. 108.

[2] Idem, vol. i, p. 438, *et seq.*

[3] Idem, vol. ii, p. 94, and ' Fauna Antiqua Sivalensis,' pl. xiv, figs. 6 and 7.

[4] Idem, vol. ii, p. 251 (Note 1).

[5] 'Jour. Geol. Soc. London,' vols. xiii, xiv, and xxi.

[6] Vol. ii, p. 176.

[7] 'Pal. Mem.,' vol. ii, p. 249.

[8] The illustrations in the ' Fauna Antiqua Sivalensis ' are here referred to whenever the original specimens have been examined by me. Of course, in comparing the figures with the text in that monograph the error in nomenclature pointed out above should be always borne in mind, and this will be best attained by having recourse to the description of the plates in the ' Palæontological Memoirs of the late Dr. Falconer,' compiled and edited by Dr. Murchison, F.R.S.

species of Elephant and another is impracticable in several instances; for example, although the ordinary true grinder of the Mammoth, *E. antiquus*, and *E. meridionalis*, can be easily distinguished when entire and the crown-sculpturing fully developed; still, there are varieties of crowns in these and other species barely distinguishable from one another. In making this statement I by no means desire to advance an opinion that the above-mentioned forms are mere varieties of one species of Elephant, such as is usually understood by the term species. At the same time, considering the conditions under which Pliocene and Pleistocene Elephants existed as compared with their living representatives, it seems to me that their dentitions and osteologies are likely to exhibit more extensive modifications; indeed, the variability in connection with the dental materials, here referred to *E. antiquus*, has no equal, as far as I am able to discover, in the dentition of either of the two recent Elephants.

In the 'Synoptical Table of the Species of Mastodon and Elephant' published by Dr. Falconer in 1857[1] he divides the Genus Elephas into the sub-genera Stegodon, Loxodon, and Euelephas, and characterises each sub-genus by certain dental peculiarities. The *Elephas antiquus* is included, along with *E. primigenius*, *E. Iudicus*, *E. Columbi*, *E. Armeniacus*, *E. Namadicus*, and *E. Hysudricus*, in the last sub-genus, which is split up into four groups, in the second of which he places the *E. antiquus* and *E. Namadicus*.

The definition of the sub-genus Euelephas by the author is—"Dentium molarium 3 utrinque intermediorum coronis lamellosa colliculis deinceps numero auctis, anisomeris, attenuatis, compressis. Præmolares nulli."

The dental characters common to the *Elephas antiquus* and *Elephas Namadicus* are —"Colliculi approximati medio leviter dilatati, machæridibus undulatis."

With reference to these distinctions, as peculiar to the *E. antiquus* and *E. Namadicus*, although general, they cannot be accepted as invariable, as is shown by the admission subsequently, by the author, of the loxodontine type of *E. priscus* as a variety of the above, and the absence of central dilatation in the "broad-crowned" variety of the *Elephas antiquus*. Indeed, central expansion and angulation, as will be shown in the sequel, are occasionally met with in certain molars of all or nearly all the living and extinct Elephants hitherto discovered; moreover, these, as well as the other characters, are shown in all the Maltese fossil Elephants which Falconer correlated with the Loxodontes,[2] but now from data I have furnished elsewhere they come closer to the Euelephas or the anisomerous ridge formula.[3]

The close affinities between *Elephas antiquus* and the *Elephas Namadicus* seem to have been the cause of Dr. Falconer first calling in question the teeth from British strata, which had been hitherto correlated with those of the Mammoth; indeed, looking to the figures and descriptions he has left behind him, it seems to me remarkable that he

[1] 'Pal. Mem.,' vol. ii, p. 14.   [2] Idem, p. 298.   [3] 'Trans. Zool. Soc. Lond.,' vol. ix, p. 36.

hesitated in considering these two Elephants different in any respects, at all events, as far as their dental materials are comparable.

The general characters of the molars of *E. antiquus* are differentiated as follows :— The crown is narrow in comparison with the length and the height. This is apparent in the "broad" and "thick-plated" crowns, and is pronounced in the more common British specimens, or, in other words, what is named the "narrow crown."

There is usually in upper, and almost invariably in lower molars a slight central expansion of the disk with or without a small angular dilatation (Plate III, fig. 1). The crimping or festooning of the enamel varies. It is excessive in many members of the long narrow crown, less so in the thicker plated variety, and often faintly indicated in broad crowns where the disks are packed close together and nearly parallel, with little or no mesial expansion. This latter description of molar has been often mistaken for that of the Mammoth and also of *E. meridionalis*. It is found with the Forest-bed remains on the Norfolk coast and elsewhere; indeed, unless in entire teeth there will be a difficulty in distinguishing well-worn fragments of all these forms. The broad crown is, moreover, the characteristic type of *E. Namadicus* and of many huge molars found in the Tertiary strata of Southern Europe.

The degree of "crimping," as it has been called, of the enamel on the worn disk, whereby this vertical plaiting presents an uneven aspect, varies very much in different forms of Elephants; and it is important in estimating the amount of crimping in any one instance to bear in mind that the same tooth will show considerable discrepancies in that respect according to the circumstances whether or not its crown is just invaded and the digitations of the laminæ are not ground down, or when half-worn or when nearly worn out. This is at once evident from the examination of a single plate. Again, the central expansion and angulation of the disk will be found also to be affected in the same way, so that only by abundant materials and by fully estimating these points can a satisfactory judgment of the characters of the tooth be formed.

The crown of the molar of the Elephant, considered in the light of a masticating apparatus, has been fully discussed by Dr. Falconer in his essay on the 'American Fossil Elephant.'[1]

The degree of crimping of the enamel, the thickness, configuration, and number of the laminæ, vary immensely in the different forms of elephants. The narrow and fluted disk of the Asiatic, and the wide rhomb-shaped and more sparsely crimped disk of the molar of the African Elephant, represent extremes—modifications of which are displayed by several distinct forms, including that now under consideration.

It has been asserted by Falconer and others that the fluted crown indicates a graminivorous diet, whilst the broad uncrimped disk suggests arboreal verdure, as exemplified by the African Elephant,[2] and perhaps to some extent these views may be

[1] 'Natural History Review' for January, 1863, and 'Pal. Mem.,' vol. ii, p. 277.
[2] Baker's 'Albert Nyanza,' vol. i, p. 275.

correct. At the same time, considering the smooth, narrow, and aggregated disks of the Mammoth and the Arctic distribution of the animal, and that, in all probability, pine and other trees of woody fibre constituted the staple food of the denizens of the boreal regions, it seems that the fluted enamel would have been better adapted for the attrition of the twigs of timber trees and such like evergreen forest vegetation of high latitudes.

The evidences on which the presence in Pliocene and Pleistocene deposits, both in Great Britain and elsewhere, of the so-called *Elephas antiquus* have been hitherto confined, as far as the former is concerned, to England and Wales, whilst molars, apparently undistinguishable from remains found in British strata, have been identified by competent observers from similar formations in Belgium, Germany, Spain, France, Switzerland, Italy, and Sicily.

Reverting to the distribution of the species in the British Islands, there is no evidence, therefore, as far as is known to me, of any remains of *Elephas antiquus* having been met with in Scotland or Ireland ; indeed, the cavern deposits of Kirkdale and Settle Caves of Yorkshire mark the northern limits at present. The molars on which its specific characters are chiefly established have therefore been discovered throughout England and Wales, from Yorkshire to the English Channel, and from Wales eastward to considerable depths on the sea-bottom of the German Ocean.

Stratigraphically the evidences of the existence of the species have been obtained from the pre-glacial deposits of the coast of Norfolk and Suffolk, and from more recent river and estuarine beds, and from cavern and fissure deposits. Before proceeding to an enumeration of the particular localities from whence remains have been determined, it appears necessary to observe that, although abundant traces of this form of Elephant have been met with in England, it would seem from exuviæ that the species was *par excellence* South-European ; at all events, negative testimony points to the fact that, whereas its congener, the Mammoth, has left unmistakable proofs of its residence in the boreal regions of the Old and New Worlds, not a single instance of the existence of the so-called *E. antiquus* has yet been adduced from any continent or locality north of the 54th parallel of latitude in North-Western Europe ; moreover, although there are cogent proofs of the Mammoth having ranged as far south as Spain and Central Italy, it would seem that the *E. antiquus* was the more common. At the same time, as in not a few instances in England, the elephantine remains of continental collections have been erroneously ascribed to the Mammoth. Indeed, little has been added since Falconer's time to our knowledge of the European distribution of the species I am now considering ; inasmuch as palæontologists have been slow to admit that the evidences furnished by the teeth were sufficient to separate the aberrant from the typical molar, which, until Falconer's differentiation, had been considered to be only varieties of that of the Mammoth.

It appears from the evidences adduced in connection with the Pre-glacial deposits of the east coast of England and the river deposits of Northern Italy that the *Elephas antiquus* and *Elephas meridionalis* were contemporaneous, whilst, on the other hand, as far as yet known, there is no positive proof that the Mammoth existed in England prior to the Glacial period, but it is assumed that teeth have been found in Scotland in peat underlying the Boulder-clay.[1]

Again, there is abundant evidence to show that the *Elephas antiquus* and *E. primigenius* were contemporaneous in Europe during the Pleistocene epoch, and that, at all events, the Mammoth survived up to the human period.[2]

As regards associated animal remains the *E. antiquus* has been met with in conjunction with nearly all the Pleiocene mammals usually considered Pre-glacial,[3] and it has been also associated with all or nearly all the Pleistocene fauna of the caves and river deposits of England and Wales.[4]

Molars and bones referred to *Elephas antiquus* have been washed ashore, dredged, or removed from the so-called "elephant and forest beds"[5] at various parts along the eastern coast—to wit, Happisborough (1, 2), Cromer (1, 2), Ostend (1, 2), Easton (1, 2), Clacton (1, 2), Southwold, Mundesley (1), Harwich (1), Felixstowe, Yarmouth (1), Bacton (1, 2), &c. Abundant dental and other exuviæ of this Elephant have been met with in the gravels and brick earths of the Thames Valley at various points, in particular at Grays Thurrock (1), Erith (1), Ilford (1), Slade Green (1), London (1), Brentford (1), Abingdon, Wytham, Henley Bottom, Ballart Pit, Culham (1), Oxford (1), &c.[6]

It has been determined also from similar deposits in the valley of the Ouse (1), at Cambridge, near Huntingdon (1), at Aylesford (1), Canterbury, Brackleshaun Bay (1), Copen Hall in Cheshire, Peterborough, Lawford (1), Rugby, Barrow-on-Soar, Lexden near Colchester, Stoke, Saffron Walden, Peckham in Surrey, Oundle (1) in Northamptonshire, Walton (1) in Essex.

Remains of *Elephas antiquus* have been determined from the following caverns and rock fissures of England and Wales:

In caves of Kirkdale, Victoria, Raygill, and North Cliff, in Yorkshire; Bleadon Cave (1), Mendip Hills (Falconer); Cefn, North Wales (Falconer); Bacon's Hole, Crow Hole,

---

[1] Bald, 'Memoirs Wernerian Society,' vol. iv, p. 64.   The remains discovered at Belturbet, in Cavan, Ireland, have been inferred to have been of the same age, 'Philosophical Transactions,' vol. xxix.

[2] 'Lubbock on the Origin of Civilisation,' p. 30; Tiddeman, 'Report on Victoria Cave;' 'Reports of British Association for the Advancement of Science,' 1874 and 1875; Busk, 'Journal Anthropological Institute,' vol. iii, p. 392.

[3] 'Falconer's Palæontological Memoirs,' vol. ii, p. 471.

[4] Dawkins, 'Jour. Geol. Soc. London,' vol. xxv, p. 210.

[5] See 'Jour. Geological Society,' vol. xxvi, p. 552, and vol. xxxii, p. 123.   The Rev. John Gunn, F.G.S., than whom no one is more entitled to an opinion on this point, asserts that from his large experience he is of opinion that remains of *E. meridionalis* and *E. antiquus* are met with in both of these beds, but that in the "Elephant Bed" the former prevails, whilst exuviæ of the latter elephant are more plentiful in the "Forest Bed."

[6] (1) Indicates the remains of *E. primigenius*, and (2) that remains of *E. meridionalis* have also been discovered in the same situation, although it is not established in all instances that the exuviæ were derived from the same beds.

Long Hole (1), Minchin Hole, Raven's Cliff, Spritsail Tor (1) in Glamorganshire (Falconer); Durdham Down (1) in Somersetshire (Falconer); Portland Fissure, in Dorsetshire (Busk); Castletown Bone Caves, Staffordshire (Dawkins).

II.—DENTITION.

The classification of Elephants, founded on the number of laminæ and the relative proportions and structure of the enamel, dentine, and cement, has received valuable exponents in the divisions instituted by Falconer into the sub-genera Stegodon, Loxodon, and Euelephas; moreover, believing in the persistency and uniformity of the characters of molar teeth through seemingly vast intervals of time as displayed in the Mammoth,[1] he formulated the colliculi in the successive teeth, and maintained their specific constancy within a moderate range of individual variation. He did not admit intermediate forms, and therefore viewed the dentition as broadly distinctive of species. It seems to me, after a critical examination of the dental materials of Proboscidea, that a rigorous adherence to numerical formulæ as regards the molars of Elephants in general and *Elephas antiquus* in particular as established by Dr. Falconer is incompatible with the results furnished by a close analysis of abundant specimens; indeed, as regards the very variable characters of the molars of the Elephant under consideration, it will be evident that they present very close affinities in all available characters to other teeth at present considered as belonging to distinct species, and consequently the susceptibility of mutation must be considered as an important etiological fact in the genesis of the species.

In estimating the number of ridges entering into the composition of a molar it has been the habit with several observers to eliminate the talon ridges, and only include the laminæ which arise from the common base. Now, as the proximal and distal ridges vary very much in size and configuration, it is apparent that the rejection of any single ridge however dwarfed or insignificant must greatly interfere with the accuracy of a ridge formula established from a large assortment of materials. I have, therefore, in the following included talon ridges at all worthy of the name, whether arising from the common base or from a plate.[2]

1. INCISORS.

I can find no reference anywhere to the milk incisor of *Elephas antiquus* either in museums or in published accounts. It seems to be unknown. Whether, therefore, like the

---

[1] Essay on the American fossil Elephant, 'Pal. Memoirs,' vol. ii, p. 252; also 'Natural History Review' for January, 1863.

[2] In giving the ridge formula I have carried out the method adopted by Dr. Falconer and others of making "*x*" represent the talon.

African and Maltese forms,[1] it was tipped with enamel or not remains to be shown. Indeed, the permanent tusk has yet to be identified, and this is the more remarkable considering the quantities of its grinders which are constantly discovered in British and European deposits. Professor Boyd Dawkins[2] and Mr. Davies[3] are disposed to believe that it was nearly straight; the latter describes a long tusk four feet two inches in length from ILFORD, and I have seen a similar straight or nearly straight tusk from WALTON in ESSEX, in the University Museum, Oxford; but considering how plentiful are the incisors of the Mammoth and the enormous quantities dredged up or exposed by the sea on our eastern coasts, it appears strange withal that only one description of tusk should turn up, that is, supposing the defensor of the *Elephas antiquus* differed very much in contour from that of the *E. primigenius*. The degree of curvature evidently varied in the latter, and no doubt as occasionally happens in the recent species, now and then an abnormality in the degree of curvature took place which would include probably the instances above mentioned. Moreover, the dimensions of full-grown incisors seem to vary considerably in what appear undoubted tusks of the Mammoth, and occasionally there are instances of much arcuation in defensors of the recent Elephants. There is a pair of tusks, No. 2753, in the Hunterian Museum of the Royal College of Surgeons of England of the Asiatic Elephant, fully as much curved as the usual tusk of the Mammoth, and I have seen similar examples of the African Elephant's incisor, whilst perfectly straight specimens are also not rare.

The enormous tusk from the pre-glacial deposits of the Norfolk coast in the Gunn Collection, Norwich Museum, has been considered by Falconer on account of its size and slight curvature to have belonged to *E. meridionalis*, the defensor of which, judging from the entire specimens in place in a skull at Florence, did not differ as regards contour from the generality in living elephants.

Dr. Falconer also refers to a tusk of *E. antiquus* eight feet in length from Bracklesham Bay, along with other remains of the same animal in the Chichester Museum. I find, however, that the latter specimen is broken in three places and otherwise considerably injured, so that its original contour cannot be determined with accuracy; but, judging from the fragments, I am informed by the curator Mr. Hayden that the degree of curvature does not appear to exceed that of the living species. Dr. Falconer also alludes to a tusk " seven feet long and rounded in section " in the museum at Syracuse,[4] but gives no further details with reference to its configuration.

In the Maltese fossil Elephants generally and in the largest form *Elephas Mnaidriensis*, with which and *E. antiquus* there is a very close dental and osteological assimilation, the permanent incisor partook of the configuration of the recent species.[5]

---

[1] Author, 'Transactions of the Zoological Society, London,' vol. ix, p. 8; and Falconer, idem, vol. vi, p. 284.

[2] Vol. xviii, Palæontographical Society, issued for the year 1864, 'Pleistocene Mammalia,' p. 35 (Introduction).

[3] 'Catalogue of the Pleistocene Vertebrata from Ilford,' p. 28.

[4] 'Pal. Mem.,' vol. ii, p. 198.   [5] 'Trans. Zool. Society of London,' vol. ix, p. 9.

2. MILK MOLARS.

Ante-penultimate Milk Molar.

The first milk molar, commonly called the ante-penultimate to distinguish it from the theoretical first, a pre-ante-penultimate milk tooth usually suppressed, is not common in collections.

There is a fragment of a left maxilla, No. 44,783, in the Palæontological Collection of the British Museum,[1] containing the ante-penultimate and penultimate milk grinders. The specimen, a late acquisition, was obtained with other elephantine remains by the late Mr. Bright from British strata, but the exact locality is unknown.

The ante-penultimate tooth is half worn; its sides are covered with a dense coat of cement, but the crown is entire and shows four ridges,[2] with the disks not sufficiently developed by wear to allow of their characters being fully ascertained. The ridges are thick, with more intervening cement than attains in the Mammoth. There are *two* fangs, a large posterior and a small anterior, which diverge at the distance of $\frac{4}{10}$ inch below the crown. The dimensions of this tooth are given in the following table, and reference will be made to the associated penultimate molar in the sequel.

Another detached unworn upper molar, No. 21,654, B. M., is represented, crown and profile, Plate I, figs. 1 and 1 *a*. It shows no trace of wear, and the fangs are not developed, consequently it must have belonged to a sucking calf or uterine individual. It is somewhat narrower than the last, and its greatest breadth is behind. The specimen is from the fluviatile deposits at GRAYS, ESSEX, so prolific in exuviæ of the Elephant in question. The thickness of the plates, the rugæ, and vertical ribbing on the enamel are diagnostic.

Two remarkably interesting and highly suggestive lower molars of this stage of the dentition were lately discovered in what are supposed to be pre-glacial deposits[3] in the VICTORIA CAVE, SETTLE, YORKSHIRE. Both have lost the extremities of their fangs, but are otherwise perfect, and appear to have belonged to the same individual. The fang of the left tooth being the more entire, I have selected it for illustration at Plate I, figs. 2 and 2 *a*. The crowns are narrow in front and broad posteriorly; the penultimate ridge

---

[1] For the sake of brevity the letters B. M. after a number indicate that the specimen is in the British Museum.

[2] The term "ridges" is applied throughout to all the enamelled laminæ of a tooth, including talons. The measurements here given, unless otherwise indicated, are in English inches and tenths of an inch.

[3] 'Second Report on the Exploration of the Settle Caves;' 'Report of the British Association for the Advancement of Science' for 1874. I am indebted to Mr. Tiddeman, F.G.S., for permission to represent the above teeth; he has been also kind enough to permit me to examine the other molars of *E. antiquus* lately discovered in the Settle Caves.

has four digitations with a small flattened posterior talon, the anterior talon being single and conical. There are altogether five ridges. Here, again, the thick plates with rugæ and ribbing of the enamel are well shown ; the crown displays faint traces of wear. The thickness of the ridges in all of these molars is out of proportion with that of the Mammoth, and is even thicker in comparison than in the same tooth of the Asiatic, but agrees in this respect with that of the African and Maltese fossil Elephants.[1]

It will be seen, moreover, that they are only slightly larger than the equivalent molars of the *Elephas Mnaidriensis* with which, and possibly the other forms of Maltese fossil Elephants, they agree in often possessing a compressed connate fang, at all events in lower ante-penultimate molars. Unfortunately the extremities of the fangs are wanting, but for the distance of $\frac{7}{8}$ths of an inch below the crown it is single, with a constriction down either side, forming two shallow grooves, which on a transverse section of the root divide the cavity into a large posterior and a smaller anterior hollow, equivalent to the posterior and anterior fangs in the upper molars (No. 44,783, B. M., just described). It would seem, however, that there was a bifurcation at *x*, fig. 2 *a*, inasmuch as the excentral depression is deeper at that point, and there is just an indication of a divergence on the anterior side close to the line of fracture. I think it likely, therefore, that the teeth may have been slightly furcate at the extremities of the fangs.

As compared with the lower ante-penultimate molar of the Asiatic Elephant, No. 2811 of the Osteological Collection, in the Royal College of Surgeons of England, it will be seen that the fangs diverge in the latter to form a large posterior and a smaller anterior fang. In connection with the connate condition of the fang I have been unable to ascertain if a similar condition exists in the same member of the series in the *E. meridionalis* and *E. primigenius*. Dr. Falconer makes no mention of the circumstance in describing their ante-penultimate molars ;[2] judging, however, from the alveolar socket in a mandibular ramus, No. 33,403, B. M., of *Elephas primigenius*, there is evidence of two pits. I believe, therefore, whether an abnormality or natural condition, it is clear, as demonstrated by the above specimens and the Maltese molars I have described,[3] that Mr. Busk's view with reference to the connate condition in the Maltese fossil molar, referred to by Falconer, has been thoroughly substantiated,[4] and thus, as far as evidence extends, the character establishes an important relationship between the *Elephas antiquus* and the Maltese forms. It will be interesting to notice how far the data will stand the test of further comparisons.

The ante-penultimate milk molar varies in length and number of ridges in *E. antiquus*, as will be seen is the case also in the other species wherever sufficient materials have been obtained for comparison ; and, as also obtains in this molar and in all members of the dental series, the maximum number of ridges is very generally found in the lower

[1] 'Trans. Zool. Soc. London,' vol. ix, p. 10, pl. i, figs. 3—6; and vol. vi, p. 286, pl. liii, fig. 2.
[2] 'Pal. Mem.,' vol. ii, pp. 114 and 161.
[3] 'Trans. Zool. Soc. London,' vol. ix, p. 10.   [4] Ibidem, vol. vi, p. 286 (footnote).

jaw. As far as data extend, the ridge formula of the first or ante-penultimate milk molar agrees pretty closely in all known fossil and recent species; the usual number in upper teeth varying from four to five ridges, and in lower from four to six. The largest known number occurs in the Asiatic and African Elephants and Mammoth. As will be seen by comparison with other species recorded in the following table, this member of the series in *E. antiquus* holds from two to three plates, exclusive of the fore and hind talon, in upper molars, and three plates and two talons in the lower jaw; but no doubt exceptions will turn up, as variability is a marked feature in the dental morphology of the species.

Table of Comparisons between the Ante-penultimate Milk Molars of Extinct and Recent Elephants.

	U. upper; L. lower.	Plates; talons x.	Maximum length and breadth of crown.	Remarks.
Elephas antiquus...	U	x 2 x	0·8 × 0·7	No. 44,783, B. M., p. 9.
	U	x 3 x	0·9 × 0·7	No. 21,654, B. M., pl. i, figs. 1, 1 a, p. 9.
	L	x 3 x	0·7 × 0·4	Right and left; Victoria Cave, Yorkshire, pl. i, fig. 2, 2 a, p. 9.
E. Manidriensis ...	U	x 2 x	0·5 × 0·1	'Trans. Zool. Soc. Lond.,' vol. ix, pl. i, fig. 3, p. 11.
	U	3 x	0·4 × 0·32	Ditto, vol. vi, pl.liii, fig. 2, p. 286.
	L	x 3 x	0·6 × 0·4	Ditto, vol. ix, pl. i, fig. 4, p. 12.
	L	x 3 x	0·55 × 0·3	Ditto, vol. ix, pl. i, fig. 5, p. 11.
E. Africanus[1]	U	x 3 x	0·9 × 0·6	Busk, 'Trans. Z. S. L.,' vol. vi, table, p. 307.
	U	x 4 x	0·9 × 0·68	
	L	x 2 x	0·8 × 0·6	
	L	x 4 x	1·0 × 75	
E. meridionalis ...	U	x 3 x	0·95 × 0·75	Falconer, 'Pal. Mem.,' vol. ii, p. 110.
	L	x 3 x	0·7 ×	Ditto, p. 114.
E. primigenius.........	U	4 x	0·8 × 0·7	Busk, 'Trans. Z. S. L.,' vol. vi, table, p. 307.

[1] The rare instance in collections of the first or pre-ante-penultimate milk molar is shown in the mandible of an African Elephant, No. 708 'Osteological Catalogue,' B. M., where a functionally developed first milk is seen on the left ramus in front of the ante-penultimate. The former is 0·6 × 0·4 inch in breadth, with a ridge formula of x 2 x, whilst the second milk holds the same number of ridges in a space of 0·85 × 0·6.

	U. upper. L. lower.	Plates; talons x.	Maximum length and breadth of crown.	Remarks.
E. Asiaticus[1]	U	x 3 x	0·7 × 0·5	Mus. Royal Coll. Surg. England.
	U	x 4 x	0·8 × 0·55	Busk, 'Trans. Z. S. L.,' vol. vi, table, p. 307.
	L	x 3 x	0·7 × 0·5	Mus. Royal Coll. Surg. England.
	L	x 4 x	0·75 × 0·45	Busk, 'Trans. Z. S. L.,' vol. vi, table, p. 307.

Affinities.—The first or ante-penultimate milk molar in the Mammoth is not, that I am aware of, represented in any collection, public or private, in Great Britain; and Dr. Falconer does not appear to have met with it, and surmises only as to its probable ridge formula,[2] so that his inferences are based on the strict concord which exists in the number of lamina of its successional teeth and of the Asiatic Elephant. It is of the utmost importance, however, with reference to *E. antiquus* and allied forms that comparisons should be drawn between the ante-penultimate milk molars in them and the Mammoth. It may be stated, as regards the teeth here referred to *E. antiquus*, that their discoveries in the fluviatile deposits at GRAYS THURROCK and in the VICTORIA CAVE, irrespective of dental characters, are additional evidence of their connection with *E. antiquus*, seeing that the former has produced more molars of this Elephant, than perhaps any single locality in England, and the latter has furnished remains of *E. antiqua* only. Judging from what is known of the dentition of the Mammoth, it seems to me highly probable that its ante-penultimate milk molar will show a higher ridge formula and much more attenuated ridges than in *E. antiquus.*

This molar in *E. meridionalis*, according to Falconer, is "a broad oval, narrowest in front and broadest in the middle," with "very wide disks" and "thick enamel plates" in the upper jaw, whilst the lower molar is "much smaller and more compressed in front," and "cusp-shaped," like the corresponding tooth of the Sewalik " *E.* (*Loxodon*) *planifrons.*[3]

The same tooth in the Maltese fossil Elephants is quite like that of the *E. antiquus*, but is of smaller size.[4]

The ante-penultimate in the African is rather more robust ordinarily, but does not,

[1] I prefer Asiatic to Indian as a general designation for the animal of Asia, including the Hindee, Sumatran, Burmese, and Cylonese Elephants, on the score that they are only varieties of one Continental species.

[2] 'Pal. Mem.,' vol. ii, pp. 159 and 161.

[3] 'Pal. Mem.,' vol. i, p. 21 (Note), vol. ii, pp. 110 and 114, and 'Fauna Antiqua Sivalensis,' pl. xii, figs. 1, 1 a, 1 b. The close affinities between the *E. meridionalis* and *E. planifrons* on the one hand, and the *E. antiquus* and *E. Namadicus* on the other, were repeatedly pointed out by Falconer.

[4] 'Trans. Zool. Soc. Lon.,' vol. ix, p. 12, pl. i, figs. 3, 4, and 5.

as far as the few instances I have examined, differ materially from the same tooth in *E. antiquus.*

The ridges in the Asiatic Elephant are ordinarily but not always more numerous; they are, however, more attenuated than I have seen in similar teeth of *E. antiquus.*

It will be apparent from the Table that the ridge formula of *x* 3 *x* is often present in all the forms of Elephants I have referred to, and that generally the diagnoses are not likely to be so easily determined as in successional molars.

Second or Penultimate Milk Molar.

This member of the milk series varies considerably in dimensions and number of plates; besides, the crown constituents bear different ratios to one another. A thick-plated crown of unusually large dimensions is remarkably well shown in a specimen, No. 47,408, B. M., from GRAYS, ESSEX, where this *thick-plated* variety is usually met with. The tooth in question holds *x* 6 *x* in a space of 3·1 inches, and is 1·2 inch in breadth in front, 1·4 inch at the middle, and 1·6 inch behind. Only four of the anterior ridges are ground down for a short distance. This upper molar might be fairly placed with the last of the milk series but for its low ridge formula.

A good example of the tooth is seen *natural size*, Pl. I, fig. 3. It is a lower molar, and also from GRAYS, but the crown is narrow and holds *x* 6 *x* in a space of 2·6 inches. It is No. 18,810 of the Palæontological Collection, B. M. The central expansions, angulations (the crown is scarcely sufficiently worn to develop the latter), and excessive crimping on the one hand, the distances between the ridges, and height of crown on the other, are characteristic features of *Elephas antiquus.*

Another very good example of this tooth is seen in the fragment of the maxilla containing the penultimate milk molar referred to at p. 9. The jaw holds the two teeth, *in sitú,* and is numbered 44,783, B. M. Here there is an entire penultimate molar, showing only a ridge formula of *x* 5 *x* in 2·5 inches, with a maximum breadth of crown of 1·1 inch. Three of the anterior ridges are invaded. The specimen, as before observed, is from the Bright Collection, but its precise locality is unknown, although doubtless from British strata.

A large lower molar, No. 21,655, B. M., from GRAYS, ESSEX, holds *x* 7 *x* in 3 inches, with a maximum breadth (posteriorly) of 1·3 inches.

Besides the above there are many other excellent examples of this member of the series in the National Collection.

An upper molar from the NORWICH CRAG, EASTON, SUFFOLK, holds *x* 6 *x* in 2·5 × 1·5 inches. The cement has been denuded in part from the plates, laying bare the *rugæ* so plentiful on the enamel of the tooth of *E. antiquus,* as compared with that of the Mammoth.

Another upper molar, No. 28,273, B. M., from Easton, likewise gives a similar number of ridges in 2·3 × 1·2 inches.

No. 27,991, B. M., from Clacton, although not entire, is a well-worn upper molar, and therefore distinctive as regards the crown pattern.

A well-worn upper molar, 40,952, B. M., from the cave of Raven's Cliff, Gower, has lost ridges by wear, leaving only six plates, which show the characteristic disk. The tooth is 2·3 × 1·4 inches.

The upper molar, 23,376, B. M., from Grays, is rather broad in front as compared with upper-jaw specimens; but perhaps in this instance the first true molar was also in wear at the same time, seeing that the latter preserves the anterior portion of the succeeding tooth from lateral detrition.

The upper tooth, 40,990, B. M., from Kent, is figured by Falconer;[1] and, although fragmentary, it is a good illustration of a molar commencing wear.

Among the recent discoveries in Victoria Cave, besides the aforementioned ante-penultimate, there were two instances of the succeeding members of the milk series, both of which I have carefully examined. The penultimate is a right upper milk molar more than half worn. The cement has been denuded from the enamel, displaying the profuse elevated rugæ to an unusual degree. There is a distinct pressure mark on the posterior talon. The large posterior fang is 1·5 inch in length by 1· inch in breadth. The stumps of the two central fangs are in front of it, and the anterior ridges, ground down to the common base, are supported on a broad anterior fang 0·8 inch in breadth. All the ridges are in wear, and there is an evident loss of the anterior talon, whilst the disk of the succeeding ridge is worn out anteriorly. Altogether the ridge formula is 6 x in 2·1 inches, with a maximum breadth of crown of 1·2 inch. The average thickness of the plates is about 0·3 inch. The disks show the central expansion with the pronounced crimping of their machærides, and altogether the characters of *Elephas antiquus*. To me the above is a distinctive instance of the penultimate milk molars of the Elephant in question.

I am thus particular in indicating these points inasmuch as, with the foregoing and others I will refer to in the sequel, there cannot be a doubt that the remains from Victoria, Raygill, and Kirkdale Caves fix the most northern limits of the *Elephas antiquus* in the British Islands and in Europe, at all events, as far as I have been enabled to determine.

The mandibular teeth are represented by No. 47,407, B. M., from Grays. The molar is entire and of the left side, with the cement denuded, showing the ribbing very clearly. It holds x 6 x in 2·9 inches. The plates are not thick, and the crown is long and narrow.

In the British Museum there is a fragment of a left lower ramus, containing an entire penultimate milk tooth, No. 21,310, see Plate V, fig. 2. It is from the Thames Valley

---

[1] 'Fauna Antiqua Sivalensis,' pl. xiv A, figs. 1 and 1 a.

deposits at ILFORD. The crown is little worn, therefore the sculpturing is not pronounced; in consequence, Dr. Falconer could not make up his mind with reference to its specific characters.[1] The ridges, however, are thick, the crown is narrow as compared to the height, and it holds $x\,6\,x$ in 2·7 inches, which are in favour of its connection with *E. antiquus*.

Two specimens in the National Collection, from BLEADON CAVE, in the Mendip Hills, each displaying a formula of $x\,7\,x$ in 2·3 inches, are very characteristic of the lower penultimate milk molar of *E. antiquus*.

Mr. Fitch, F.G.S., of Norwich, has in his possession two distinctive lower molars, right and left, from the FOREST BED at Cromer. They hold $x\,6\,x$ in 3 inches, and as usual are broad behind and narrow in front. The crowns are in full wear.

It is now well ascertained that all the determinable elephantine remains from KIRKDALE CAVE belong to *E. antiquus*, and not to *E. primigenius*, as was supposed prior to the differentiation of the characters of the former by Falconer. The tooth figured in the 'Reliquiæ Diluvianæ'[2] is, with others, in the Oxford Museum, and has been referred to by Falconer.[3] It shows the large ridge formula of $x\,8\,x$ in a space of only 2·65 inches, but as elsewhere observed, the highest ridge formula does not necessarily carry a corresponding length of crown.

I have been unable to obtain references to specimens of the penultimate milk molar of *Elephas antiquus* in foreign collections.

Affinities.—The second milk tooth in the Mammoth ordinarily holds a ridge formula equal to the higher expression here given in connection with *E. antiquus*. The contour of the tooth also in the former partakes more of an oval than an oblong shape; consequently, the crown is relatively broader. It is the case, however, that individual instances may occur when it would be difficult to give a decided opinion. I believe, however, that in any member of the dental series a well-worn crown, perfectly entire as to ridges, will in practised hands, indicate to which of the two Elephants it belongs. The compressed laminæ with no well-defined rugæ on the enamel, and therefore an absence of crimping of the disk of wear, the breadth of the crown, as compared with the height of the ridges, and the high ridge formula will ordinarily suffice as diagnostic of this tooth, and, indeed, of all members of the series in *E. primigenius*, as compared with the Elephant in question.

This tooth in *E. meridionalis* is distinguishable generally by its comparative broader crown, more massive laminæ, with the crimping more exaggerated than in *E. antiquus*, and ridge formula of only $x\,6\,x$;[4] but it must be freely admitted that even well-worn crowns may be found presenting characters barely distinguishable from the same in the second milk molar of *E. antiquus*, especially its *thick-plated* variety.

---

[1] 'Pal. Mem.,' vol. ii, p. 179.
[2] Plate vii, fig. 1.
[3] 'Pal. Mem.,' vol. ii, p. 179.
[4] 'F. A. S.,' pl. xiv n, figs. 1 and 3, and 'Ossemens Fossiles,' pl. xv, fig. 4.

There is no available example of the second milk molar of *E. Namadicus* to compare
with the teeth of *E. antiquus*.

In *E. Africanus* the second milk molar appears seldom to exceed a ridge formula of
x 6 *x*, but no doubt exceptional instances do occur. The open disk and absence of
pronounced crimping will ordinarily distinguish its teeth.

In *E. Asiaticus* the ridge formula is very much the same as in the Mammoth; and,
excepting in the absence of the central expansion and angulation, which, however, are
not always present in *E. antiquus*, there is little to distinguish individual second milk
molars in the two forms. I suspect, however, that it is rare to find a tooth of this
member of the series in the Asiatic Elephant with a smaller ridge formula than *x* 7 *x*.

The Maltese fossil Elephants represent in their second milk teeth all the characters
of *E. antiquus* in much smaller Elephants. At the same time, as I have shown,
individuals of the largest form (*E. Mnaidriensis*) possessed molars occasionally holding
x 8 *x* in 2·4 inches.[1]

The diagnosis of the second milk molar in *E. antiquus*, although ordinarily well defined
when the dental materials are well exposed, is not always easily determined. The tooth
is subject to considerable variety with reference to the number of ridges; indeed,
it seems futile to attempt to formulate an average. Dr. Falconer inferred that it
ordinarily held five plates and two talons.[2] From the materials here furnished it would
seem that *x* 6 *x* for the upper and *x* 7 *x* for the lower molar would be nearer the truth.

An analysis of the foregoing and of specimens mentioned by Falconer[3] and from other
sources, I find that the ridge formulæ in upper molars vary from *x* 5 *x* to *x* 7 *x* in
a space of from 1·9 inch to 3·1 inches, whilst in lower molars I find *x* 6 *x* to *x* 8 *x* in
from 2·5 inches to 3 inches.

Third or Last Milk Molar.

The well-known similarity between the last milk and first true molar must always
make it difficult to determine detached specimens of these teeth. In the *Elephas antiquus*
and other members of the sub-genus Euelephas the true molars, in particular mandibular molars, are usually more arcuated than in milk teeth, and the crowns are
broader.

The last milk molar of *Elephas antiquus* varies considerably in size and number of
ridges, so that the maximum dimensions may attain to those of the succeeding tooth, and
seeing that the ridge formula is about the same, there must of necessity be much
uncertainty in the diagnosis.

A very characteristic example of the upper molar of this stage of growth is seen,

[1] 'Trans. Zool. Soc. London,' vol. ix, pl. i, fig. 14, and p. 16; see also figs. 7 to 16.
[2] 'Pal. Mem.,' vol. ii, p. 176.   [3] Idem., vol. ii, pp. 177 and 179.

natural size, in Plate I, fig. 4. This palate specimen, No. 21,301, B. M., is the one referred to in Dr. Falconer's notes.[1] It is from GRAYS, and holds nine plates and two talons, *i. e. x* 9 *x*, in a length of 5 inches, the maximum breadth of crown being 1·9 inch. These teeth are matched by another pair, No. 21,068, B. M., and 21,318, B. M., from the same locality. Each tooth holds *x* 9 *x* in 4·8 by 1·7 inch, with an average thickness per ridge of 0·5 inch. Another upper molar, 27,914, B. M., from CLACTON freshwater deposits, is precisely like the foregoing in the number of ridges and length. It is scarcely necessary to dilate on the characters of these four examples. The angulation of the enamel of the disk so frequent in lower molars is not always present in the upper, but the tendency to central expansion is general, and, with crimping, narrow crown, and height of ridges, is very characteristic of the species.

The characters of the palate teeth are well seen also in the specimen in the Oxford Museum, alluded to by Dr. Falconer,[2] where *x* 10 *x* are contained in 5·3 inches. The tooth represented in the 'F. A. S.,' pl. xiv A, figs. 3 and 2 *a*, from SOUTHWOLD, holds 12—13 ridges in 5·5 inches. It is No. 8409 of the collection in the Geological Society of London. This tooth contrasts well as regards dimension with the upper-jaw specimens, figs. 3 and 3 *a* of the same plate, No. 18,789, B. M. The locality of the latter is unknown; it holds *x* 10 *x* in 6 inches. Dr. Falconer was uncertain whether to consider it as a large last milk or a small first true molar,[3] and the same doubts must be acknowledged by every experienced observer. There are imperfect upper molars, such as figs. 6 and 7 of pl. xiv A, 'F. A. S.,' the former from SUFFOLK, the latter from KENT; both are much worn and imperfect, so that they are of little use in establishing their positions in the dental series.

The mandibular teeth of this stage of growth are numerous; and wherever the jaw is preserved there is not much difficulty in assigning their proper places in the series.

In the fine collection in the British Museum there are seven excellent examples of the lower ultimate milk tooth. There is an entire lower molar in the Bright Collection, British Museum; the locality is unknown, but evidently from British strata; it holds *x* 11 *x* in a space of 5·9 inches. Like many beach specimens from the NORFOLK coast, it shows evident signs of rolling in the surf. The enamel is thin, and all the ridges excepting the last two are in wear. Similar specimens are numerous in the Layton Collection, also from the PRE-GLACIAL DEPOSITS of the EAST COAST. Thus No. 33,388, B. M., a right lower from HAPPISBOROUGH holds *x* 19 *x* in 5·6 inches. Here the ridges are broad, being each nearly 0·7 inch in thickness. No. 33,375, B. M., left lower from the same locality, like the last, shows evidence of rolling. It holds *x* 11 *x* in 5·8 inches; another tooth, 33,374, B. M., has *x* 12 *x* in 5·5 inches. These dredged specimens are further illustrated by No. 33,390, B. M., a right lower, with a formula of *x* 10 *x* in 5·9 inches, and an average thickness of each ridge of about 0·5 inch.

---

[1] 'Pal. Mem.,' vol. ii, p. 177. [2] Idem, vol. ii, p. 178. [3] Idem, vol. i, p. 442, and vol. ii, p. 180.

Specimens 33,387 and 33,389, B. M., are somewhat injured, but, with the above, demonstrate the typical characters of this stage of the pre-glacial specimens, which are supported by a tooth in a ramus, No. $\frac{9}{11}$ of the Jermyn Street Museum Collection ; it is marked from the "Forest Bed," and holds $x\,10\,x$ in 5·5 inches.

In the Norwich Museum and in the Collection of Mrs. Fitch there are several very characteristic instances from the same formation. The lower molar, No. 304 of the Gunn Collection, from the "Iron-pan Forest Bed," labelled by Dr. Falconer as having held $x\,10\,x$ in 4·4 inches, is a good example, although not quite entire as to length; whilst a rolled specimen containing $x\,10\,x$ in 4·5 inches, in Mrs. Fitch's cabinet, shows a seeming disposition to a crowding of the ridges and an unusual breadth of crown, such as will be shown in the sequel to characterise the *broad-crowned variety* of the ultimate true molar.

I have before me, along with the teeth already described from Victoria Cave, a right upper, possibly an ultimate milk molar, from the same situation. It is fractured perpendicularly in two places, and one of the three portions does not unite, so that there is probably a loss of one or more ridges. The tooth had just been cutting the gum, and shows broad pressure marks on the cement in front and on the top of the first ridge, where it had been impinging on the tooth in front. None of the ridges are invaded. The crown is broad in front and narrow posteriorly, like lower molars. The talons are very rudimentary, the anterior being inconspicuous, whilst the posterior is reduced to a small splint attached to the last plate. The tooth presents an unusual small ridge formula of $x\,8\,x$ in 3·6 inches, but this estimate is not to be relied on for the reason just observed. Looked on, however, as a molar of *E. antiquus*, there is the thickness of the collines, which average each as much as 0·4 inch in thickness ; the narrow crown, ribbing of the enamel, height of the main ridges, all favouring a belief that it belongs to this species. At all events, I have not seen a tooth of the Mammoth in any ways like it ; and, considering the evidence already adduced, I think the above molar, although small, may be justly referred to the last of the molar series of *E. antiquus*.

Another very perfect and highly characteristic left lower molar from Raygill Cave, in Lothersdale, Yorkshire, has also been kindly lent to me by Mr. Tiddeman. All the ridges are in wear excepting the posterior talon. The tooth is arcuated, and holds $x\,11\,x$ in 6 inches. Accompanying the above were four posterior collines of a larger molar, either the second or else the ultimate true molar. It is also marked Raygill Cave, and its plates show all the characters of *E. antiquus*.

Foreign specimens.—The upper molar from Maccagnone cave, Palermo, figured by Mr. Busk,[1] is doubtless the specimen No. 40,798 B. M., which was presented to the National Collection by Charles Falconer, F.G.S., after the death of his brother. The locality and position in the dental series are recorded in Dr. Falconer's handwriting on a

---

[1] 'Trans. Zool. Soc. London,' vol. vi, pl. liii, fig. 10, and p. 301.

ELEPHAS ANTIQUUS—MILK MOLARS.

label attached to the specimen. The tooth is not entire, there having been a loss of posterior ridges, leaving eight in a space of three inches. The worn crown is eminently characteristic of the species. This may be the "last upper milk molar" discovered by Falconer in the cave of Maccagnone, and which he failed to distinguish from the existing Indian Elephant[1] at the time, although it is clear from the label that he subsequently had cause to withdraw his previous decision. A third milk molar upper jaw, holding x 10 x in 0·118 m. or about 4·8 inches, is described and figured by Belgrand[2] as that of *E. primigenius*. It is from the gravel pits of Montreuil, near Paris, where remains of *E. antiquus* have been found, including the humerus and teeth I shall refer to in the sequel. The author considers this milk tooth to belong to the Mammoth ; but, as far as the figure and descriptions extend, it seems to me unquestionably that of *E. antiquus*.

A highly instructive instance of the last milk molar from the MACCAGNONE CAVE is represented by Baron Anca in the 'Bulletins of the Geological Society of France.'[3] I examined the above and other specimens in Anca's collections from the PALERMO CAVES in 1863. Dr. Falconer, however, in his paper on the 'Natural History Review'[4] seems to have considered the tooth in question, like the above, "undistinguishable from the existing Indian Elephant ;" whilst Lartet, who had also seen it in Anca's possession, was of opinion that it belonged to the last of the milk series of *E. antiquus*, and I arrived at the same opinion from an independent examination of the specimen. It is fairly represented in the plate referred to below. The crimping of the machærides in the specimen is, however, more pronounced than in the plate. The central expansion, angulations, ridge formula, and general character of the crown are undistinguishable from British specimens. It holds x 10 x in 4·8 inches.

Another specimen of apparently a well-worn last upper milk tooth, holding seven plates and a heel in 3 inches, and a third, also imperfect, were shown to me by Baron Anca. The latter specimen was nearly entire, and contained 10 x in 5 inches. Here, again, the crowns presented unmistakable characters of *E. antiquus*.

I am particular in noting these facts, more especially for the reason that teeth have been found in deposits in the basin of Palermo with such pronounced mesial expansions of their disks and other characters as to lead to the opinion that they belong to *E. Africanus ;* whilst another set from the caves in the same neighbourhood display peculiarities not referable to either, and more in common with the crown of the Asiatic Elephant or its fossil ally the *E. Armeniacus*.

Affinities.—The last milk molar of *E. Namadicus* is shown in plate 12 c, figs. 2 and 3, of the 'Fauna A. Sivalensis,' and holds 11 ridges in 5·5 inches. It is impossible to distinguish the above from lower third milk molars of *E. antiquus*.

[1] 'Pal. Mem.,' vol. ii, p. 250.
[2] 'Basin de Paris, Texte,' p. 175, and pl. xvii.
[3] Second series, vol. xviii, pl. xi, fig. 8, and at p. 684.
[4] January, 1863, and 'Pal. Mem.,' vol. ii, p. 250.

The last milk molar of *E. primigenius* is ordinarily shorter in length and height, and very much broader than that of *E. antiquus*, with closely approximated and uncrimped enamel ridges, without even a tendency to central expansions and angulations of their disks, the formula usually being x 12 x.[1]

The same molar in *E. meridionalis* has a relatively broader crown than even in the Mammoth, with thick plates, generally uncrimped, and a ridge formula averaging only x 8 x.[2]

The Asiatic Elephant has the same high ridge formula as that of the Mammoth, and the crimping is excessive, whilst there is an absence of the mesial expansion and angulation so general in the disk of *E. antiquus*.

In the last milk molar of the African Elephant the low ridge formula x 7 x and the short ridges with the lozenge-shaped disks show peculiarities distinguishable from any of the foregoing.

The third milk molar in the Maltese fossil Elephants holds from 10 to 11 ridges in about three inches in the larger form *E. Mnaidriensis*, and, of course, in a much smaller space in the dwarf *E. Melitensis* and *E. Falconeri*. But, with the exception of these smaller dimensions and less pronounced crimping of the machærides, there is a very close alliance between the last milk molars I have ascribed to *E. Mnaidriensis*[3] and the same teeth in *E. antiquus*.

The closest affinities exist, therefore, between the last milk molar of *E. antiquus*, *E. Namadicus*, and *E. Mnaidriensis*. The thick-plated variety observed in the preceding member of the milk series is again repeated individually in the last of the milk series, showing the disposition to variability, which is a marked feature in the dentition of *Elephas antiquus*, and therefore noteworthy whenever noticeable.

Dr. Falconer after eliminating talons has conceded ordinarily 10 plates as the exponent of the last milk molar of *E. antiquus*.[4]

From the foregoing and other specimens it appears to me that the upper molar usually holds from 9 to 10 plates and 2 talons in a length varying from 4·5 to 5·5 inches; whilst lower teeth usually contain 9 to 11 plates, besides fore and hind talons, in a length varying from 4·5 to 5·8 in. The highest expression of 12 plates and 2 talons is doubtless rare. This tooth shows, I repeat, the tendency to variation, so generally the case with the last milk and first true molar; yet, perhaps, eleven plates and two talons would embrace by far the larger number of, at all events, British molars of *E. antiquus*.

[1] British Museum, several specimens.
[2] 'Pal. Mem.,' vol. ii, pp. 110 and 111; 'F. A. S.,' pl. xiv B, fig. 4.
[3] 'Trans. Zool. Soc. London,' vol. ix, pl. iii, figs. 4 and 5, pp. 21 and 22.
[4] 'Pal Mem.,' vol. ii, p. 176.

3. TRUE MOLARS.

First True Molar.

The first true molar in Elephants is perhaps more subject to variation than any other member of the dental series, and therefore there is a great likelihood of confounding it with the last of the milk series, seeing that their ridge formulæ are ordinarily the same.

A very distinctive instance of this tooth is shown, *natural size*, Pl. III, fig. 2. It is No. 37,241 of the National Collection, and was dredged off HAPPISBOROUGH. Here there are x 10 x in 7 inches, the average thickness per ridge being about 0·5 inch; it maintains the long laminæ with the narrow crown of *E. antiquus* as compared with that of the Mammoth.

This important distinction is always best seen in true molars. The central expansion and angulation are not always very pronounced in maxillary teeth unless the crowns are more than half detrited; whilst in mandibular specimens, from their ridges being more apart, the condition becomes developed soon after the digitations are ground down and the crown has become about one third worn. The anterior fang usually supports the first three ridges, but now and then only the anterior talon. The highest ridge in Fig. 2 is the tenth, which is six inches in height, whilst the maximum breadth of the crown is in front, where in the above it is 2·2 inches. Of course a good deal will depend on the state of attrition as to where the broadest part of the crown will be found, and this is at once obvious when the configuration of upper and lower molars of the various stages of growth are duly considered.

Another upper tooth, also from HAPPISBOROUGH, but in an imperfect state, is represented by the specimen 33,369, B.M., the crown constituents of which are precisely of the same character as in the preceding.

A mandibular example is well shown in the jaw, No. 18,789, B.M., ' F. A. S.,' pl. xiii A, figs. 5 and 5 a. The specimen was presented by the Earl of Aylesford (not Aylesbury, as noted by Falconer[1]). The left tooth is entire, and holds x 11 x in 6·7 inches; the crown is much arcuated, with disks well shown. Posteriorly there are clear evidences of the socket of a much larger molar, which could not have been other than a second true molar.

Either a large last milk or an unusually small first true molar is admirably shown in a mandible from the gravels of WYTHAM, in the Oxford University Museum. The rami contain two fragments of molars with the two succeeding teeth in place; the right is entire, and holds x 11 x in 6·2 inches, thus displaying small proportions for the first

[1] ' Pal. Mem.,' vol. i, p. 440, fig. 5, and vol. ii, p. 182.

true molar, which would be confirmed by the dimensions of the fragments of the third milk in front ; but I am not convinced that they belong to the same jaw, which is broken at the commencement of the diastem, where the fragments of the molars have been glued to the shattered surface. The entire molar has an arcuated crown and the disks are clearly distinctive of the *E. antiquus.*

The lower jaw and molar, 18,967, B. M., is figured in the ' Fauna Antiqua Sivalensis,' Pl. xiv A, figs. 8 and 8 *a*; the latter is stated by Falconer to belong to the first true molar ;[1] it is the same tooth that is shown in Lyell's 'Antiquity of Man' as a second or penultimate true molar.[2] It holds clearly *x* 11 *x* in about 8·3 inches. Here the formula is very small for a second true molar, and, on the other hand, the tooth is long for the first true molar, but, taking everything into consideration, the balance of evidence appears to lean towards Falconer's opinion.

In the Museum of the Geological Society of London there is an entire upper molar from the Norfolk coast deposits, showing an unusual broad crown and an approximation of ridges, with crimping of the machærides, and but for the latter it might have been fairly placed among the first true molars of the Mammoth. It holds *x* 12 *x* in the short space of 6·5 inches. The breadth in front is 2·6 inches, at the middle 3 inches, and behind 2·4 inches ; there is barely what might be called a tendency to central expansion of the disk. This, like the last milk tooth referred to at p. 18, shows the character of the *broad-crowned variety* to be noticed in the sequel. The comparisons between the last upper milk molar, No. 21,301, B. M., Pl. I, fig. 4, and its associated specimens from GRAYS THURROCK, seem to me to receive additional proof of the position assigned to them by a well-worn crown of an upper first true molar in the British Museum from the same locality. The loss by wear in front is indicated, but the original formula was *x* 10 *x*, as may be seen by a careful examination of the surface, where eleven and a half ridges remain in a space of 6 inches. There is not much expansion of the disks ; but, I repeat, this is not always a well-defined character in upper teeth.[3]

There are other characteristic specimens of this stage of growth in the British Museum ; for example, No. 28,512 (2 specimens), from the Dixon Collection, one of which (right upper) holds *x* 11 *x* in 7·8 inches.

A right upper molar in the Norwich Museum, and lately discovered by Mr. Gunn in the FOREST BED, shows only *x* 9 *x* in 6·6 inches. The tooth is apparently too large for a last milk, only seven ridges are invaded ; altogether it is very typical of *E. antiquus.*

A very characteristic example of a lower molar referable to the first true molar is represented by an entire tooth in the same collection and from the POST-GLACIAL BED at MUNDESLEY. It is small for a fourth molar, but the ridges are wide apart, and the formula *x* 11 *x* is contained in 7·5 inches.

[1] 'Pal. Mem.,' vol. i, p. 443.   [2] 'Antiquity of Man,' p. 133, fig. 19.
[3] There is a very striking resemblance in the above and a crown of the second true molar of *Elephas Mnaidriensis* shown in 'Trans. Zool. Soc. London,' vol. ix, pl. iii, fig. 1.

A lower molar from Oundle, Northamptonshire, with nine and a half ridges in a space of 7 inches, with thick plates on an average 0·9 inch per plate, might belong to the above, or else the second true molar.   It is very characteristic of the species, but it is too much mutilated to allow its position in the series to be determined with certainty.

No. 27,906, B. M., from Clacton deposits, is an upper molar, with a highly digitated posterior, and a very fragmentary anterior talon; it holds $x\,11\,x$ in 8 inches.

Other examples are numerous, such as a tooth from the Mendip caves in the Taunton Collection, referred to in Falconer's notes; it holds $x\,12\,x$ in 7·2 inches.   He has also figured a broken tooth, which seems to have held twelve to thirteen ridges in a space of about 7·5 inches.[1]

In the Jermyn Street Museum there is an entire upper first true molar from a cutting of the Great Northern Railway in Huntingdonshire.   The crown, although just invaded and with none of the digitations worn out, is narrow, and altogether typical of the species. It furnishes a formula of $x\,10\,x$ in 7·5 inches.

In the same collection there is an upper molar, with only its first three ridges invaded, from river deposits under St. James's Square, London; it holds $x\,12\,x$ in 7·5 inches. The crown is also narrow.

The portion of a mandible containing a much worn molar discovered on Palling Beach, near Happisborough, and now in the Norwich Museum with the remainder of Mr. Gunn's splendid collection, is one of the two specimens on which Dr. Falconer founded the presence of E. priscus of Goldfuss, in British strata.   The fact that Falconer mistook the characters of these teeth is sufficient to show that they differed very much from the ordinary or typical tooth of E. antiquus, at all events, as then known to him.

In the essay on "British and European Fossil Elephants," as also in the plates in his Memoirs,[2] Dr. Falconer goes into minute details with reference to this mandible and tooth. The specimen he considers to represent a well-worn second true molar; and, seeing that at the time he correlated it with the Loxodontes, the ridge formula could scarcely have admitted a larger figure than eight or nine plates besides talons. The tooth has been recently fixed in its socket so that the fangs cannot now be studied, but the representation in the plate referred to shows an anterior fang supporting two ridges, followed by two other fangs and a large curving posterior root sustaining three plates ; there are clear indications of broken and worn-out ridges in front and deep pressure marks behind.   Considering, therefore, that the anterior fang is now supporting two ridges, I am much inclined to consider this fragmentary tooth to be an antepen- instead of a pen-ultimate true molar, and that it may have lost four and a half of its ridges, there being seven and a half remaining in space of 6·4 inches. Whichever it may be, there can be little doubt as to its claims to a position among the teeth of E. antiquus. Although the plates are thicker antero-posteriorly, especially in the middle, with angular expansions and dilatations, the

1 'F. A. S.,' pl. xiv A, figs. 4 and 4 a.
2 Vol. ii, p. 100. The tooth is shown detached from the jaw in pl. vii, figs. 3 and 4, of the same volume.

enamel is thin and well crimped; in fact, the grinder is nearly worn out, and the plane of detrition passes through the broadest part of the plates, which is ordinarily near the enamel reflections.   The same will be observed in the section of the other molar from GRAYS THURROCK,[1] No. 39,370, B. M., which, with the above, were all the British specimens then known to him in connection with the variety of molar now under consideration. This interesting tooth is designated by Falconer as "a last molar, left side of the lower jaw."[2]   I cannot, however, subscribe to that opinion, inasmuch as a reference to the specimen, or even a glance at the above sections in the 'Memoirs' or in the 'Fauna Antiq. Sival.,' will show a decided pressure mark posteriorly.   Indeed, it may be doubtful if the tooth has claims to be considered other than a first true molar.   Admitting, however, it is the second, we have a crown, nearly worn out, with eight ridges in a space of as many inches.   The disk is wider than in the Norfolk tooth, and evidently the plates were relatively thicker than usually attain in lower jaw teeth; so that the condition is not altogether dependent on the state of wear, but, as will appear in the sequel, on a variety of tooth which I have named the *thick-plated* molar, a character seemingly common to other extinct species, to wit, *Elephas primigenius, Elephas Muaidriensis,* and *E. Falconeri*;[3] and just lately I have been shown by Mr. John Gunn specimens of thick-plated molars of *E. meridionalis,* from the FOREST BED, so that, considered either as a sexual or race character, or even an occasional condition, the thicker plate, like the central portion of the disk of *E. antiquus,* is not confined to one species of Elephant.   No doubt the imperfection of these two specimens misled Falconer a good deal at the time, and it was only after he had examined numerous collections on the Continent that he found in 1863[4] that his so-called *Elephas priscus* was a form of *Elephas antiquus.*   It is also suggestive that on comparing the specimens with the teeth of *E. Africanus* the resemblance was so striking that in his essay he was inclined to consider these molars as representing the teeth of the African Elephant in a fossil state; a sufficient indication of the variability in the crown pattern of the molar of *Elephas antiquus.*

Foreign specimens.—Dr. Falconer describes a portion of a skull, including the last milk, first true molar, and the penultimate in germ behind, from MONTE VERDI at Rome. The first true molar holds *æ* 10 *æ* in 5·5 inches.   He also refers to a well-worn lower molar with ten plates in 5·7 inches from the same locality.[5]   The former is assuredly a small first true molar, and interesting as regards the Maltese pygmies; but, as will be shown presently, such an exception is rare with *Elephas antiquus* as met with in Italian deposits, more especially in connection with the two last members of the dental series.

An injured upper molar, No. 32,589, B. M., from CHAMPAGNE holds ten and a half

---

[1] 'Pal. Mem.,' pl. vii, fig. 2, and 'F. A. S.,' pl. xiv, fig. 7.
[2] 'Pal. Mem.,' ii, p. 96.
[3] Dentition and Osteology of the Maltese fossil Elephants, 'Trans. Zool. Society,' vol. ix, pp. 6 and 35.
[4] 'Pal. Mem.,' vol. ii, p. 251 (footnote).
[5] Ibid., vol. ii, pp. 181 and 183.

ridges in 7·5 inches. There is a clear loss of the first two ridges, and possibly the tooth may belong to the next of the series. It presents, however, distinctive characters of the *E. antiquus*.

I examined in 1863 an entire, and what appeared to me a right lower molar in Baron Anca's collection from the PALERMO CAVES. It contained $x\,12\,x$ in 6 inches. The crown was much arcuated, and presented all the characters of the Elephant in question. It may possibly be a first true molar or else a large last milk; and, if we may judge from the huge last true molars in Italian collections, it is probably a last milk molar of a large individual.

Affinities.—The first true molar of *E. Namadicus*, ' F. A. S.,' pl. xii D, figs. 1 and 2, is in the British Museum. It is very closely allied to that of *E. antiquus*, fig. 4 of the same plate, and contains fourteen ridges or $x\,12\,x$ in 7·3 inches. The intimate resemblances between these teeth at all points are further augmented by a comparison of the mandibles to which each are adhering, as will be pointed out in the sequel. An entire lower-jaw specimen is shown in fig. 3 and 3 *a*, where $x\,12\,x$ are contained in a space of 10·5 inches.

The conditions which render it difficult to determine the last milk and first true molar in *E. antiquus* are just as conflicting in other species. In the Mammoth, from its teeth being short and very broad, together with the constant disposition of the ridges to become crowded, we find that undoubted first true molars often revert to the dimensions of the last milk molar. Ordinarily however there can never be much difficulty in discriminating between teeth of the above forms of Elephants. The intermediate molars, to wit, the last milk and first true molar in the Mammoth, as compared with the above, are much broader teeth, with aggregated plates and absence of pronounced crimping. The latter may be faintly indicated along the margins of the machærides, but never to the extent usually observed in the other. The ridge formula in the first true molar of the Mammoth varies considerably; Falconer establishes an average of twelve plates and two talons, which seems to include the majority of teeth, especially upper molars,[1] but there is much variability in this respect.

The first true molar of *E. meridionalis* is ordinarily large and massive, with a low ridge formula of about $x\,8\,x$ in about 6½ inches, and thick unplaited, although often faintly crimped enamel. The central dilatation and angulation are often pronounced in lower molars, but the smooth polished enamel of the worn disk with the large intervening wedges of cement and less height of the ridges, will, in a majority of instances, determine the specific relations of its molar.[2]

The first true molar of *E. Mnaidriensis*[3] has undoubted close affinities to *E. antiquus*, and holds from ten to eleven ridges in a space varying from 4·3 to 5·2 inches. The

---

[1] 'Pal. Mem.,' vol. ii, pp. 163 and 171 ; ' Ossem. Fossiles,' pl. xii, fig. 3.
[2] ' Pal. Mem.,' vol. ii, pp. 111 and 116; 'F. A. S.,' pl. xiv B, figs. 5 and 6.
[3] ' Trans. Zool. Soc. London,' vol. ix, pl. iii, fig. 3, pl. iv, fig. 4, and pl. viii, fig. 5.

4

crimping is not always so excessive as in *E. antiquus*; at the same time it would be difficult, excepting on the score of dimensions, to make out any decided distinctions.

The ridge formula in the Asiatic Elephant is the same as in the first true molar of the Mammoth, only that the crowns are not so broad and the enamel of the disk is deeply festooned.

The ridge formula in the first true molar of the African equals, according to Falconer and others, that of the last milk tooth, and stands usually at *x* 7 *x*.[1] It is quite possible in the more expanded disk of the *E. priscus* variety of *E. antiquus* to mistake its molars for those of the African; but entire specimens would doubtless clear up any ambiguity created by broken teeth, which cannot be invariably depended on in establishing the dental characters of any one form of Elephant.

In compounding the data evolved from the examination of the foregoing and other specimens of the first true molar of *E. antiquus*, referred to by Falconer in his memoirs and also in collections, it appears that the estimate of the latter authority is below the average deduced from the materials I have been enabled to study. He assigns a ridge formula of ten plates, besides talons, to the first true molar. I find that in upper teeth the ridges vary from eleven to fourteen in a space between 5·5 and 8 inches; whilst thirteen ridges is a very steady number in lower teeth, with a maximum of fourteen ridges, included between 6 and 8·3 inches.

Considering therefore that Dr. Falconer assigns twelve plates and two talons to the *penultimate* true molar of *E. antiquus*, it might be inferred that I may have included teeth in the above list which should have been placed with the second true molar. It will appear, however, that the instance in which the largest number of ridges is shown, to wit, the upper tooth from the Mendip Caves at p. 23, is given on the authority of Dr. Falconer, where *x*12*x* are contained in a space of 7·2 inches, and the upper tooth, p. 22, in the Geological Society's Museum, where the same number of ridges are contained in a space of only 6·5 inches, I admit, however, in this latter instance an abnormal condition of the crown, the other lower molar, p. 25, holding *x* 12 *x* in inches being the one in Baron Anca's possession, is consequently a foreign specimen. Allowing, therefore, that these excessive examples might have a doubtful relationship with the first true molar, we find that, as regards dimensions, they are short compared with instances just adduced of both upper and lower molars with thirteen ridges in a space of 8·3 inches; whilst an analysis of the entire series shows a constant variation in the number of ridges and dimensions, especially in upper molars. Perhaps about *x* 10 *x* to *x* 11 *x* for maxillary, and *x* 11 *x* for mandibular teeth, will fairly represent the ridge formula of the first true molar of *Elephas antiquus*.

[1] 'Pal. Mem.,' vol. ii, p. 89.

Second True Molar.

It will be apparent from the foregoing that long first true molars with the maximum number of ridges (14), more especially mandibular specimens, are apt to be confounded with unusually small second true molars. It is of assistance however to the observer to bear in mind that the graduating height of the ridges posteriorly as characteristic of the last of the series is also pronounced in second molars, especially in the lower jaw, and even in the first true molar; whilst the pressure scar on the heel of such worn teeth precludes the possibility of confounding the penultimate with the ultimate true molar.

The question is frequently suggested during surveys of detached molars of Elephants, When is the pressure scar developed on the disappearing tooth? It seems that certain members of the dental series are pushed forward more rapidly than others. For example, the first or antepenultimate milk tooth is soon shed, and the last milk and first true molars take on the pressure scar and impressions of the advancing septum sooner than the penultimate *milk* and penultimate *true* molars. At all events, the scar and septal pressure hollow or flattening below the posterior talon, and on the posterior fang, in both upper and lower molars become pronounced long before the crown is worn out; whereas in lower molars it is often observed that the last ridges are being ground down before the succeeding molar has made an impression on the heel of its predecessor. There are doubtless individual differences, according to the quickness or otherwise of the growth of the animal, when the teeth advance with greater or less rapidity. Perhaps the greatest strides in the growth of the Elephant take place at the age when the last milk and first true molars are being ground down, the full vigour not being attained until the second true molars come into wear, when the epiphyses of the long bones get consolidated. It may therefore be the case, that the intermediate molars advance with greater rapidity than the succeeding teeth. At the same time I have been informed by a German dealer, who has reared Elephants in the forests of Upper Burmah, that the animal's growth as regards height is pretty steady and about six inches annually.

An upper molar denuded of its external cement and unworn, No. $\frac{23,717}{*}$. B. M., is from fluviatile deposits at SLADE GREEN, ERITH ; a profile view of this tooth, *half natural size*, is shown in Plate II, fig. 1. It displays fifteen ridges, or x 13 x in a space of 10·5 inches. The narrowness of the crown, the height of the collines, the seventh being 6·3 inches, the ribbing and rugæ of the enamel, and thickness of plates, are characteristic of this Elephant. A beautiful plan view (*natural size*) of another second true molar is represented in Plate IV, fig. 2. The tooth is from GRAYS, ESSEX, and is one of two upper molars, right and left, No. 22,017, B. M., of probably the same individual. Like the above, it is typical as regards the long narrow crown, and is somewhat bent. It holds x 12 x in 9 inches. The crown, narrow in front, expands towards the middle, and again narrows posteriorly.

The lower molar, No. 19,844, B. M., from SLADE GREEN, referred to by Falconer,[1] is another excellent example of the usual long tapering and arcuated second true molar. It has lost, however, possibly a ridge posteriorly, leaving 13 or x 12 in 8·6 inches, the injury having taken place since it was examined by Dr. Falconer, as he gives twelve plates and a heel in 10 inches, or else his description refers to another tooth, as the illustrations agree with the molar as it stands at present. This tooth might be the opposing molar to the upper molar, Plate II, fig. 1, as far as state of wear, condition of ridges, general characters, and locality extend.

A fine specimen of an upper second true molar, commencing wear and showing the pronounced characters of the teeth of this Elephant, is represented by No. 22,017, B. M., from GRAYS. Here in 8·2 inches a small figmentary anterior talon and a well-marked digitated posterior talon embrace twelve plates between them.

No. 580 of the Museum, Royal College of Surgeons, is a penultimate upper molar with an injury to the anterior ridge, but the original length of the tooth is preserved. It is a good specimen of the *narrow crown* from GRAYS, and holds seventeen ridges in 9 inches.

The difficulty in determining which is a plate or a talon is well shown in another and similar upper molar, No. 22,017, B. M., from GRAYS. Here the last two ridges do not arise from the common base, just as occasionally a semilunar plate in front takes the place of an anterior talon. The tooth, moreover, shows posteriorly the narrow crown of the second as compared with the breadth of the same part in the first true molar. There are fourteen ridges altogether in 7·7 inches.

A comparison between the last and two perfect lower molars in the Jermyn Street Museum, also from GRAYS, shows no less than fifteen ridges or x 13 x in 10 inches in the latter. They are contained in a jaw with clear traces of the ultimate tooth behind, whilst another specimen of a penultimate lower tooth in the same collection from British strata contains x 12 x in 9 inches. These are again exceeded by the remarkable specimen referred to by Falconer as having been dredged up at HARWICH,[2] where a lower molar, "probably the penultimate," holds x 12 x in 10·8 inches, and an "extremely characteristic" second lower true molar holding x 14 x in 10·1 inches. It would even seem that undoubted penultimate true molars, especially in the lower jaw, have sometimes fifteen plates besides talons.

The enamel, which becomes thicker in last true molars than in any of the preceding, shows a tendency towards this condition in many specimens of the penultimate tooth. An instance in point is shown in No. 21,318, B. M., from GRAYS, ESSEX.

Another illustration is presented by specimen No. 27,916, B. M., dredged off Norwich. This *thick-plated* tooth is entire and of the lower jaw. It holds x 12 x in 8·7 inches.

[1] 'Pal. Mem.,' vol. ii, p. 184, and 'F. A. S.,' pl. xiv A, fig. 10.
[2] Ibid., vol. ii, pp. 183 and 184.

A mandible, No. 28,114, B. M., from BRACKLESHAM BAY, has a molar *in situ*. It contains x 13 x in 8 inches. Here we have a good illustration of the circumstance just noticed in connection with the pressure marks of advancing teeth ; although all excepting the last ridge are invaded, only an insignificant portion of cement has been displaced on the heel ; in fact, there is no deep pressure scar, although the ultimate molar must have been on the point of cutting the gum, as its empty socket testifies. Moreover, the crown of the molar, being protected by a fragment of the first true molar, has preserved its natural round front, which contrasts with the tapering hinder portion. The former condition is worthy of note, inasmuch as a molar unprotected by a fragment of the preceding tooth is, as elsewhere observed, liable to have its anterior portion ground down laterally as well as horizontally, and will therefore give a different aspect to the crown view.

The left tooth in the lower jaw, No. 33,366, B. M., dredged up at HAPPISBOROUGH, exactly proves the truth of this view as regards the two varieties of outline of the crowns of worn teeth. Here there is no trace of a preceding tooth, so that the front of the penultimate is ground down not only horizontally but laterally, and is therefore narrow in front. It holds x 12 x in 8 inches. There are other specimens illustrative of this condition in the National Collection.

A left upper molar, No. 33,330, B. M., dredged off HAPPISBOROUGH, is entire, with two anterior fangs and a general coalescence of the base posteriorly. The crown is just commencing wear, there being seven ridges invaded, with none of their digitations worn out. The specimen, evidently entire, holds fifteen ridges, or x 13 x in 9 inches. There is faint crimping of the enamel of the disk, but otherwise it has more the aspect of a crown surface of a last molar of *E. meridionalis*. This is one of the doubtful molars which, on account of not being sufficiently advanced in wear, presents no characteristic features whereby it can be placed with members of the penultimate true molar; indeed, the specific distinctions are by no means pronounced.

A broken left lower molar, No. 20,809, B. M., from ILFORD, has its anterior ridges just invaded. It has thick plates, and is clearly a true molar of *E. antiquus.* There are ten ridges in 6 inches.

A molar of the lower jaw much arcuated with the loss of posterior ridges, and numbered 599 in the Museum of the Royal College of Surgeons, is probably of this stage of growth. It is from the "Parkinson Collection," and from the "DRIFT or PLEISTOCENE BEDS OF STAFFORDSHIRE." The crown is little more than invaded in front, and holds fourteen ridges in 8 inches.

Foreign specimens.—Distinctive mandibular specimens are cited by Dr. Falconer from the Quaternary deposits of Monte Verdi, where teeth of thirteen ridges are contained each in 9·1 inches. They are said to show very typical disks of *E. antiquus* ;[1] a fragment in a ramus showing the thick plates, from Rome, will be noticed presently when this

[1] 'Pal. Mem.,' vol. ii, p. 184.

variety of last true molar comes to be considered.   I recognised in 1863, in Baron Anca's collection from the Palermo caves, an undoubted second true molar of the lower jaw, containing x 12 x in 8 inches.   Mr. Busk and Dr. Falconer identified an upper penultimate true molar from Europa Point, Gibraltar.[1]

Affinities.—A comparison between the first true molar of *E. antiquus* and *E. Namadicus* is illustrated by the beautiful specimen in B. M. of the second molar, shown in figs. 3 and 3 *a*, plate xii D, of the 'Fauna Sivalensis.'   Here, in a left ramus, x 12 x is contained in 13·6 inches.   The crown, like the other teeth, unprotected by a preceding molar, is excessively narrow, just like the equally characteristic lower first true molar of *E. antiquus*, fig. 4, of the same plate, to which reference has already been made, and also to the last upper molar, fig. 5, to which I shall allude in the sequel.   All the above molars of *E. Namadicus*, as far as characters extend, are simply indistinguishable from accepted teeth of *E. antiquus*, the only exception being the unusually large size of fig. 3 as compared with a second true molar of *E. antiquus*.

The *Elephas Muaidriensis* presents in the second as in the preceding molars all the characters of the *Elephas antiquus* in a much smaller animal, the number of ridges, twelve or x 10 x, being held in an estimated space of 6·5 inches, but, unfortunately, my determinations are computed from specimens not altogether entire ;[2] however, they clearly show by comparison with ultimate molars to have been of the maximum length just stated, but with a ridge formula equal to the first true molar of *E. antiquus*.

The Asiatic Elephant, excepting in the excessive crimping and less lateral dimensions, holds relatively the same formula as the Mammoth.

In the African Elephant the low ridge formula, according to Falconer (x 8—9 x)[3] with the rhomb-shaped pattern of the disk and its short ridges will ordinarily distinguish second true molars from the vast majority of those of *E. antiquus*, excepting, perhaps, the so-called *E. priscus* variety, with which crowns of the former might be easily confounded.

The second true molar in the Mammoth is a broad-crowned tooth, with short and closely approximated ridges, in the great majority of specimens seldom averaging less than x 16 x in its ridge formula.   The enamel is thin, and when at all, only faintly crimped at the outer and inner margins of the enamel.[4]   Sometimes a thicker-plated example may be found, and a broad-crowned variety of the *E. antiquus* may make the diagnosis difficult, especially if the plan of the crown is not fully shown, but the exceptions will be few where the practised observer will fail to distinguish between the respective molars of the above species.

In *Elephas meridionalis* the ridges are nearly as broad as they are long, and never so numerous as in the foregoing, whilst the thick plates and grosser masses of intervening

[1] 'Jour. Geol. Soc. London,' vol. xxi, p. 366.
[2] 'Trans. Zool. Soc. London,' vol. ix, pl. iii ; pl. viii, figs. 2 and 4, p. 27.
[3] 'Pal. Mem.,' vol. ii, p. 90, and 'F. A. S.,' pl. xiv, fig. 5.
[4] Ibid., vol. ii, p. 166.   Numerous suggestive specimens in the British and Norwich Museums.

cement, with the usual uncrimped machærides, and ridge formula rarely above x 10 x, are good exponents of the second true molar of this form of Elephant, as usually noticed in the specimens from the Preglacial deposits of the Norfolk Coast and in Italian Collections.[1]

The ridge formula of the second true molar in *E. antiquus* may be stated to vary in upper teeth, between x 12 x and x 13 x in a space of from 8 to 10·5 inches, whilst the same number of ridges in the lower jaw are included within from 8 to 10·8 inches, with rare instances of as many as sixteen and seventeen ridges. Generally I would concede twelve to thirteen plates, besides talons, to this member of the series, the former probably being the most common number.

Third or Last True Molar.

The last of the dental series is obviously the best for the determination of specific characters. This tooth, from the absence of pressure posteriorly, preserves its integrity better, and the contour of the crown is generally characteristic.

The last molar of *Elephas antiquus* presents the same variability in the proportion of its crown constituents pointed out in the preceding molars; and representing, as it does, the aged condition of the animal, whatever tendencies in these respects are observable in the milk and other true molars, become finally confirmed in the ultimate.

From a large experience in the examination of the teeth referable to this form of Elephant, I find that although the following varieties of crown admit of being joined together by intermediate varieties, still, taking the pointed instances of each, it appears to me that they may be arranged as follows :

A.—A massive broad crown, with the ridges closely approximated.

B.—A long, narrow, and often much arcuated crown, generally typical of the British specimens.

C.—A thick-plated tooth with the dental elements in excess, and with generally a pronounced mesial expansion of the disk. This is the variety ascribed by Dr. Falconer, in the first instance, to the *Elephas priscus* of Goldfuss, and subsequently to *E. antiquus*.[2]

A well-characterised instance of any one of these types shows a crown dissimilar in many respects from the others; hence the importance of an examination of all available materials ascribed in any way to the form of elephant under consideration.

The members of *A* and *C* varieties are often colossal teeth as compared with the long, narrow crown of *B* variety. Moreover, in instances where bones have been found in conjunction with them, the same is observable, showing either that the larger molars belonged to either unusually large individual Elephants, or were peculiarities in the denti-

---

[1] 'Pal. Mem.,' vol. ii, p. 117, and 'F. A. S.,' pl. xiv b, fig. 7, and British Museum, also Norwich Museum.

[2] 'Jour. Geological Soc. London,' vol. xxi, p. 269, and 'Natural History Review,' 1863.

tion of the particular form, branching off towards allied forms, to wit, *E. Namadicus,
E. meridionalis, E. primigenius, E. Africanus, E. Asiaticus, E. Mnaidriensis,* with more
than one of which the *E. antiquus,* as has been shown, is very closely allied.

A. Variety.—The teeth referable to this variety of crown have the ridges packed close
together. The disks have often little mesial expansion, so that they are relatively of a
more uniform thickness from side to side. The angulation is often very faint or
wanting.[1]

A very characteristic example is furnished by No. 16,229, B. M., from the FOREST
BED, OSTEND, NORFOLK. A capital crown and profile view of this upper tooth is shown
in the 'F. A. S.,' pl. xiv A, figs. 5 and 5 a. There is a loss of a few anterior ridges,
leaving sixteen and a half in a space of 9 inches, with a maximum breadth of the crown
of three inches. The crimping of the machærides is the only pronounced character of
the disks.

Another upper tooth, No. 27,007, B. M., Plate V, fig. 1, from CLACTON FRESHWATER
DEPOSITS, has lost about two and a half of the anterior ridges, leaving fifteen and a half
in a space of 10 inches. The crown is very broad, being 3 inches in front, 3·5 inches in the
middle, and 2 inches posteriorly. All the disks are developed excepting the last four,
the digitations of which are not worn out. Each ridge is about 0·7 inch in thickness.

The ridges are crowded and the disks are little expanded in the middle, and, therefore, almost parallel. There are angulations however. This is a very typical instance
of the broad-crowned variety.

A superb specimen of this description of molar is instanced by No. 46 of Miss
Gurney's Collection in the Norwich Museum. It is a right upper molar from CROMER.
Here the ridges are much aggregated with thin sheaths of enamel, which, however, are well
crimped without angulations as in the last. All excepting the two last ridges are in wear.
The formula is *x* 18 *x* in 11 inches, the maximum breadth of the crown being four inches.

A left lower molar, No. 601 (Hunterian Collection), Museum Royal College of
Surgeons of England, from GRAYS, ESSEX, represents a broad crown, with only fifteen
and a half ridges preserved, which are contained in 10·5 inches.

A characteristic fragment of a left lower molar of this variety is shown in the
'F. A. S.,' pl. xiv A, figs. 12 and 12 a. Dr. Falconer states it is from Happisborough,[2] but
the old British Museum Catalogue records it from Siberia. It has certainly more of the

[1] There are numerous fragments and almost worn-out crowns in the Norwich Museum so alike in many
respects to plates of this variety on the one hand, and to the massive molars of *E. meridionalis* on the other,
that in their broken and incomplete state it is impossible to come to a decided conclusion as to their specific
identities. Thus, the enormously broad fragment from Happisborough, described in the 'Palæont.
Mem.,' vol. i, p. 447, 'F. A. S.,' pl. 14 D, figs. 15 and 15 a, seems to me to be the shed portion of a tooth of
the broad-crowned variety of *E. antiquus* rather than that of *E. meridionalis,* to which Falconer refers it.
It is impossible, however, to arrive at certain conclusions with such imperfect material.

[2] 'Pal. Mem.,' vol. i, p. 443.

characters of a dredged tooth, although clearly belonging to *E. antiquus*, the probability is that, like all the early specimens of proboscidian teeth, it was supposed to have come from Siberia.

B Variety.—The long, narrow crown generally much arcuated in lower molars is the most common description met with in British strata.[1] An excellent example is furnished by No. 28,118, B. M., from GRAYS, ESSEX, and is represented in plan, *half natural size*, Plate II, fig. 2. It holds *x* 16 *x* in 11·3 inches. Each plate is about an inch in thickness, and the height of the longest colline is 6·3 inches. The disks are well developed, displaying the central expansions, angulations, and crimping of the enamel. Like ultimate molars, the crown tapers towards the heel, with the ridges not nearly so approximated, nor is the crown by any means so broad as in members of A series.

A lower-jaw specimen, No. 27,907, B. M., is shown *half natural size* in Pl. IV, figs. 1 and 1 *a*. It is from the freshwater deposits at CLACTON, and has a very hook-shaped anterior fang supporting the three first ridges, followed by six pairs of roots, and the usual coalescence posteriorly, invariably the case in teeth not far advanced in wear. There are twenty ridges, or *x* 18 *x*, in 13 inches. The first sixteen are invaded.

Here we have an excellent example of the usual description of lower molars as met with in England. The outline of the crown is spindle-shaped. It is matched by another splendid specimen, No. 3946, B. M., of a lower molar from SAFFRON WALDEN, referred to by Falconer,[2] and figured in the ' F. A. S.,' pl. xiv A, figs. 11 and 11 *a*. It holds seventeen ridges, with a loss of one or two in front, in a space of 12·3 inches. In this tooth the posterior talon rises like the other ridges from the common base. A fragment of the long, narrow crown is seen in No. 42,349, B. M., from the THAMES VALLEY deposits.

C Variety.—The thick-plated variety is typically represented by a tooth from the VALLEY OF THE THAMES, and referred to by the late Professor Phillips.[3]

It is from the low-level gravels at CULHAM, near Oxford, and is preserved in the University Museum. This superb specimen holds seventeen ridges, besides a small vermiform talon on the inside of the last plate. The ridge formula is *x* 16 *x* in 12·8 inches. The eight anterior ridges are invaded, showing large expanded disks with well-defined angulations, central expansions, and pronounced crimping of the machærides. The height of the ridges is enormous, that of the ninth being 9·5 inches, whilst the maximum breadth of the crown is 4 inches. The average of each plate is an inch. I examined, moreover, in the Oxford University Museum, two fragments of a last molar

[1] Professor Boyd Dawkins proposes ('Jour. Geol. Soc. London,' vol. xxviii, p. 413) to name *E. antiquus* the " narrow-toothed elephant," which would restrict the distinction entirely to the members of this series, to the disregarding of the broad-crowned and the thick-plated varieties.

[2] 'Pal. Mem.,' vol. i, p. 443 ; vol. ii, pl. ix, figs. 3 and 4, and p. 184.

[3] 'Geology of Oxford,' p. 465. I regret to have been unable to obtain a drawing of this remarkable molar, which ought to be figured.

5

holding two plates each. Both were also remarkable for the thickness of the enamel and dentine, so characteristic of this type of molar. The specimens were found in BALLARAT PIT, near Oxford.

There have been four late additions to the splendid collection of proboscidian remains in the British Museum, from CROMER FOREST BED and the PLEISTOCENE DEPOSITS near PETERBOROUGH. The latter represent a right and left upper molar, apparently from the same individual; neither is quite entire. The right, No. 47,121, B. M., I have selected as an excellent illustration of this variety; it is shown, *half natural size*, in the crown and plan views, Plate II, figs. 3 and 3 *a*. There is a loss of ridges posteriorly in the above, leaving fifteen ridges in 10 inches. The left tooth, No. 47,120, has fifteen ridges in 9·6 inches, the greatest breadth of crown being 3 inches respectively. The maximum height of the tenth ridge is 7·6 inches. The crowns are worn obliquely, and on that account they have the appearance of the crown of *E. Asiaticus.* The excess in the intervening cement, the thickness of the enamel, excessive crimping, with angulations and expansions here and there, are very pronounced and diagnostic of the variety of molar in question. It is clear, moreover, that if the above teeth were ground down nearly to the enamel reflections there would be a much greater expansion of the disk, approaching the rhomb-shaped dilatation of the so-called *E. priscus.* In fig. 3 *a* there is an intercalation of finger-like ridglets on the sides of the tooth, such as are often noticed in ultimate molars of other species;[1] moreover, with the exception of the central expansions and angulations, the fluted enamel gives the crown quite the aspect of that of the Asiatic Elephant.

The CROMER specimens, No. 47,119, are right and left lower; the latter is shown crown and profile, *half natural size*, in Pl. III, figs. 1 and 1 *a*. They have lost one or two of the ultimate ridges, retaining *x* 17 in 12·5 inches.

The first eleven ridges are invaded, showing large mesial expansions, crimpings, and the angulations, which, however, do not touch each other or overlap as often obtains in *E. Africanus.*

The teeth are much arcuated and narrow, with a maximum breadth of crown of 2·7 inches. The eleventh ridge, the digitations of which are just invaded, is 7·5 inches in height. The large, round, and curved anterior fang is well preserved on the left molar, fig. 1 *a*, and supports three ridges, succeeded by a coalescence of the remaining ridges. Here, again, the plates are colossal, each averaging one inch in breadth, with well-defined transverse rugæ on the enamel.

There is a fragment of the crown of what had been evidently a left upper molar in Mr. Gunn's collection, and from the NORWICH CRAG at HORSTEAD, where heretofore only remains of *E. meridionalis* and Mastodon are said to have turned up. The morsel is nearly worn down to the enamel reflections and was evidently a tooth on the point of being shed. The

---

[1] See 'British Fossil Mammals,' fig. 90, where an enormous lower molar of *E. Asiaticus* (not *E. primigenius*) has numerous accessory ridges on its sides and posteriorly. I found the same in ultimate teeth of *E. Mnaidriensis.* Dr. Falconer, however, supposes the condition to be a morbid state, and confined to domesticated elephants, 'Pal. Mem.,' vol. ii, p. 281.

plane of attrition passes through the broadest portion of the plate, so that the disk is relatively broader in the antero-posterior direction than would obtain at any other point in a transverse section, and looks precisely as in *E. priscus*, with marked crimping and thickness of the enamel. There are $6\frac{1}{2}$ ridges in 5 inches. Considering, however, the above statement, it would be wrong to place the fragment with *E. antiquus*, seeing that crimping, mesial expansion and angulation of disks are sometimes pronounced in specimens of *E. meridionalis*; it is suggestive, however, with reference to further discoveries in the NORWICH CRAG.

I think fragmentary teeth, especially well-worn crowns of the thick-plated variety, are very liable to become confounded with molars of *E. Africanus*, but no cautious observer should come to a conclusion either way on such evidence, unless the characters are clear beyond doubt.

I can find no record or discover any ultimate molar of *E. Africanus* with a larger ridge formula than $x\,13\,x$; indeed, in far the greatest number of specimens it seldom exceeds $x\,11\,x$.

The evidence of Falconer[1] and Lartet,[2] that fossil molars discovered near Madrid, Syracuse, and Palermo, were determined by them as belonging to *Elephas Africanus*, is of such importance in connection with this *E. priscus* variety of *E. antiquus* as met with in British strata, that some account must be taken here of the instances on which their diagnoses were founded. I am unable to verify from personal examination the teeth discovered in Spain and at Syracuse,[3] but the two almost worn-out morsels[4] of teeth referred to by Falconer and represented by Baron Anca, who found them in the Cave of San Teodoro, as also a crown containing several plates, which the latter assured me was discovered in digging a sewer in one of the chief streets of Palermo, were carefully examined by me during a visit to Sicily in 1864, subsequently to that of Dr. Falconer.

With reference to these Sicilian teeth represented in figs. 5 and 6 of plate xi of the seventeenth volume of the 'Bulletin of the Geological Society of France,' and described at pp. 689 and 694, it appears to me that, as one contains only an entire disk and the other the outer, or else the inner, third of an antero-posterior section of a crown with only portions of three disks, even allowing their wide expansion and general thickness of the enamel, it would be premature, on such slender evidence, to assert their identity with teeth of *E. Africanus*, especially after the data here adduced of the thick-plated teeth of *E. antiquus*. Moreover, the planes of detrition in these two fragments pass exactly, as before stated, through the lower and thickest portion of the crown.

A more suggestive instance is represented by the other specimen, which I

[1] 'Pal. Mem.,' vol. ii, p. 283.

[2] 'Comptes Rendus,' 22 Fév., 1858, tom. xlvi.

[3] The latter is described by Canon Alessi in vol. vii of the 'Atti dell' Acead. di Scienz. Nat.,' and is quoted by Falconer.

[4] Plate xi, figs. 5 and 6, p. 684, vol. xvii, 'Bullet. Soc. Geol. de France' (2e série); vol. xviii, p. 90, in a letter to M. Lartet.

examined also on the occasion alluded to: and Baron Anca presented me with
a lithographic plate containing a representation of the above, and also of molars of
E. antiquus discovered by him in the caverns of Palermo. The right lower molar in
question is contained in a portion of a ramus, but is much fractured both anteriorly and
posteriorly. There are seven plates, the disks of five being entire, in a length of 5 inches,
which allows about 0·7 inch for the thickness of each plate.

The central expansions are rhomb-shaped, but not nearly to the extent usually
observed in molars of the African Elephant, with angulations which almost touch, but do
not, as in the latter, *overlap* or *meet*. There is crimping of the enamel; and, altogether from
these and other considerations in connection with left ramus containing the entire third
milk molar (fig. 8 of the same plate) discovered also in the Cave of San Teodoro in the
same deposits, and referred to by me at page 19, and from the fact that the evidence of
the thick-plated molar of *E. antiquus* has been much augmented by later discoveries, I am
bound to acknowledge that the opinion I entertained in common with these two
distinguished anatomists, as to the proofs of the African Elephant having been found in
a fossil state, has, at all events as regards the Cave of San Teodoro, been altogether
shaken by more recent discoveries. It would be premature at present to speculate on the
value of the other two instances; but whether or not *E. antiquus* was the ancestor from
whence *E. Africanus* has been derived, there is no positive evidence furnished by the
above materials from Sicilian deposits to show that they belong to the latter species.

I have digressed somewhat from the strict rule in connection with the description
here of only British fossils, but it will be apparent that determinations so important with
reference to the discovery of the recent species of Elephants in a fossil state have an intimate
connection with extinct forms. I have therefore recorded these instances for the purpose
of confirming the results obtained from studies of the thick-plated tooth of *E. antiquus*
found in British strata.

The question suggested by a study of the thick-plated variety of molar is whether or
not it has been discovered in connection with the other teeth of *E. antiquus*, or under
conditions likely to give rise to a race or permanent variety of the species. The fact of
its discovery in the fluviatile deposits throughout the VALLEY OF THE THAMES, in
connection with the foregoing specimens, shows that the various forms of molars belonged
in all likelihood to contemporaneous individuals, and, as before indicated in the case of
the grinders of the Mammoth and Maltese Elephants, to which further reference will be
made in the sequel, there were thick- and thin-plated varieties, possibly occasional or
sexual conditions. Moreover, the three varieties have been met with in the PRE- and
INTER-GLACIAL DEPOSITS of the NORFOLK COAST, where, however, vast epochs of time
may be represented; but, indeed, there are few well-established evidences of the exact stratigraphical arrangement of the specimens from this coast either as regards the National
Museum, or the valuable relics brought together by Miss Gurney, Mr. Gunn, Mr. Fitch,
and others.

The intermediate varieties of molars which link together the *broad*, the *narrow*, and the *thick-plated* crowns are numerous, and establish such a gradation from the broad to the narrow tooth that a series can be arranged with these extremes at either end. This is not at present so clear in the case of the thick-plated variety, which, however, shows a disposition to pass into the characters of the narrow crown as seen in Plate III, fig. 1. It will appear, from the instances already furnished in relation to the first and second true molars, that the variability so apparent in the last of the dental series is not confined to it; even in milk teeth there are thick plates and broad and narrow crowns, which are evidently youthful conditions of similar appearances in the full-grown Elephants.

The following molars in the National Collection and elsewhere are worthy of being recorded as illustrative of the foregoing, and also of the intermediate conditions which bridge over the extremes.

Two upper teeth, Nos. 37,285 and $\frac{40.9}{47.967}$ B. M., show abnormalities, possibly deformed conditions of their crowns. The former from CLACTON displays a remarkable compression of the ridges on the outer and posterior part of the crown. The tooth is very small, but unquestionably a last true molar. All excepting the two last are in wear, and give a formula of 14 x in 9 inches, there being a loss of plates and the fore talon. This is an instance of a modification of A Variety. The other tooth is of the left or opposite side. It is abnormally flattened on the outside of the crown. The anterior fang supports the two anterior ridges, followed by digitations in pairs, and a contracting hollow shell posteriorly. There are no less than 20 ridges, or x 18 x, in 9·5 inches. The enamel is very thin but well crimped, and the first twelve ridges are invaded, whilst the disks which are packed close together show also central expansions with angulations. This tooth in consequence, probably, of the deformity of its sides has the aspect of a short broad crown of some varieties of the Mammoth's tooth in which there is faint crimping, but the height of the ridges seems to place it with ultimate broad-crowned molars of *E. antiquus*; it is also from CLACTON.

A dredged specimen, No. 33,327 B. M., of a lower molar from HAPPISBOROUGH, is entire excepting a portion of the posterior talon, and holds x 16 x in 11·5 inches. Like the foregoing, its ridges are high, the longest (12th) being 7·5 inches. The ridges are aggregated, and more or less parallel without curving of the horns of the disks. The machærides are much crimped, with thicker enamel than in the last. It shows more pronounced characters of the broad crown, although not to the extent of the more typical members of A Variety.

An injured upper molar, No. 37,271, B. M., in the Brown Collection, is from the brick earths of WALTON, ESSEX. There are posterior ridges wanting, leaving 14 in a space of 8 inches. The tooth has only the first five ridges invaded. The crown is intermediate between the narrow and broad tooth.

Another broad crown is instanced by the upper molar, No. 40,385, B. M., from OUNDLE, NORTHAMPTONSHIRE. The cement has been much denuded. There is a loss of ridges in front, leaving 12 x in 8·5 inches. This tooth is very characteristic of the parallel aggregated disks with little central expansion or angulation; the crown is broad.

An upper molar, No. 27,515, B. M., from WALTON, in ESSEX, is more than half worn, with several of the anterior ridges worn away, leaving 14 ridges and a heel, or 13 x, in 8·5 inches.

The disks here are remarkably parallel and closely packed together; the enamel is thin, and the crimping is not by any means so pronounced as usual; with central angulations, altogether there is a pronounced similarity between the above and varieties of the tooth of the Mammoth. In that respect the broad-crowned variety has assuredly resemblances to the molar of the latter. The above is matched by a lower molar, No. 39,463, B. M., from SOUTHWOLD.

A fine specimen of a modification of the broad-crowned variety was discovered in fluviatile deposits in 1854, in digging the foundation of the JUNIOR UNITED SERVICE CLUB, CHARLES STREET, ST. JAMES'S, associated with remains of *Hippopotamus major*, *Bos primigenius*, and *Cervus*. This upper tooth, nearly entire, is preserved in the drawing-room of the Club. About two ridges have been broken off in front, leaving 15½ in a space of 9 inches, with a maximum breadth of crown of 3·2 inches. Each ridge is on an average 0·7 inch in thickness. The crown pattern and other characters are typical of the species of Elephant in question.

Two mutilated but very suggestive examples of the ultimate molar, marked No. 8 and 9, are preserved in the Museum of the Geological Society, and labelled *E. primigenius*. The locality is unknown. The loss of posterior ridges in both instances prevents an exact estimate being made. It would appear that only two have disappeared ; at all events, the teeth present all the characters of the broad-crowned variety of *E. antiquus*, which was formerly readily confounded with the molar of the Mammoth.

A good instance of a broad upper crown is preserved in the Oxford University Museum. It is from HURLEY BOTTOM, and is entire, with a ridge formula of x 16 x in 9·5 inches. The lower molar of the broad-crowned variety is admirably seen in the rami from BARROW-ON-SOAR, No. 33,796, B. M. I will refer again to the jaw. The molars are not quite entire, several ridges in front having been worn out by use, leaving 12 ridges and a heel in 8·3 inches. The crowns give a maximum breadth of 3·5 inches at their middle, and taper like all ultimate molars towards the posterior talon.

A mandible containing two superb molars, No. 27,908, B. M., is from ST. MARY'S STOKE, near Ipswich. The jaw is that of an aged individual, as there are several of the anterior dental ridges worn out. The teeth are suggestive instances of the broad crown.

An upper molar of the latter description marked BARROW-ON-SOAR ? is preserved in the Museum of the Royal Dublin Society. It has lost the hind talon, and the ridges in front are injured, but there is evidence of a ridge formula of x 17 x in a space of 10·5 inches. An intermediate variety of crown between the broad and narrow molars is further illustrated by a broken tooth, No. 33,337, B. M., in left ramus, dredged up off

HAPPISBOROUGH. All excepting the posterior talon ridge are worn, showing that it belonged to an aged individual. The number of ridges seem to have not exceeded 18, or x 16 x, in a little less than 10 inches.

The entire upper molar just commencing wear, shown in the 'F. A. S.,' pl. xiv B, fig. 16, is in the Norwich Museum. It represents the broad crown just commencing wear, there being only three ridges invaded. This molar was supposed by Falconer at first to belong to $E.$ meridionalis, but the height of the ridges and their mode of arrangement are antagonistic to this belief. It holds x 18 x in 11 inches.[1]

A palate specimen in the British Museum, No. 38,491 contains portions of the last molars in situ. The jaw is from PECKHAM in Surrey, and affords evidence of the preceding molar having been in wear at the same time. The above contains 15 ridges in 8·5 inches. The breadth across the jaws in front of the molars is 7·4 inches. The space between the molars in front is 2·2 inches, at the middle 2·8 inches, and posteriorly 3·2 inches.

In Mr. Gunn's collection at Norwich there is a highly suggestive example of the two entire upper molars in situ, No. 218. They are referred to by Falconer in his notes.[2] The specimen is from the FOREST BED and has pebbles still adhering to the sides of the teeth, which are intermediate between the broad and the narrow crown. Each molar holds apparently x 17 to x 18 x in 9·3 inches, with a maximum breadth of 2·7 inches. The pits of a fragment of the second molar are in front on the right side. The teeth are broad in front, tapering steadily towards the posterior talon. There are twelve of the anterior ridges in wear, and the front of the teeth converge, with an interspace of four inches, and at the posterior talon, five and a half inches. The ridges are, as usual, high, the fourteenth being seven and a half inches in height.

In the same museum, from OVERSTRAND, near CROMER, No. 306 of Mr. Gunn's collection, is a left lower molar, holding 17 x. There is a loss of plates in front. It is very characteristic of the members of A Variety. Here there is well-marked mesial expansion, crimping, and aggregation of ridges.

The molars in the mandible presented to the Norwich Museum by Mr. Windham are referred to by Falconer.[3] The jaw was found near the jetty of CROMER. There is a loss of a ridge or two in front, but 12 x remain in a space of 11 inches. The breadth of the crown at the middle is 3·4 inches. The teeth in this jaw furnish good examples of the crowded ridges and broad crown of A Variety. I shall refer again to this jaw when I come to consider the Mandible.

No. 361 is in a left lower ramus, and belongs to the Gunn collection; it is from the upper portion of the FOREST BED. The pits of the penultimate tooth are in front. The ultimate tooth is hidden in the jaw posteriorly, but its ridge formula can be made out to be x 19 or else x 20 x.

The above is a splendid example of the gigantic tooth of A Variety, and is about 11

[1] 'Pal. Mem.,' vol. i, p. 447; vol. ii, pp. 138 and 182.   [2] Ibid., ii, p. 182.   [3] Ibid., vol. ii, p. 188.

inches in length.[1] It contrasts with another in the Norwich Museum, showing the long, narrow crown of B Variety, from the " Post-Glacial Lacustrine bed at MUNDESLEY." This molar is not entire, and furnishes 16 x, or 17½ ridges, in 10·2 inches.

A magnificent specimen of a mandible, containing five plates of the penultimate and two entire ultimate teeth, is preserved in the Museum of the Geological Society of London. The characters of the jaw are very suggestive of the species, and will be described in the sequel. The last molars have lost the posterior talon only, but its impression is quite evident on the wall of the alveolus, so that the teeth yield x 19 x in 12·6 inches. The worn crowns are broad, and display well-marked characters of the *E. antiquus.* They give a maximum breadth of 3 inches. Unfortunately, the locality from whence the specimen was derived is unknown, but no doubt British. It is referred to and figured by Dr. Falconer.[2]

An intermediate condition of crown between the " broad" and "narrow" tooth is well seen in No. $\frac{1.5}{1.5}$, B. M., from OSTEND, NORFOLK coast. It is of the upper jaw, and remarkable for the excessive ridge formula as compared with the members of A Variety generally. The tooth is almost perfect, and although ground down to the base in front, gives satisfactory indications of having originally held 20 ridges, or x 18 x, in 12 inches. The plates are relatively thicker than in the broad-crowned type, being on an average 0·8 inches in thickness.

The crown and profile view, pl. xii D, figs. 5 and 5 a, ' Fauna A. Sivalensis,' shows a variety of upper molar very like the preceding. Here there are clear indications of an original ridge formula of x 17 x in a space of 11·5 inches. The specimen is in the British Museum and numbered 40,989, " from CANTERBURY Museum." A similar description of upper crown, from GRAYS, ESSEX, with thick plates, is seen in No. 602 of the Museum of the Royal College of Surgeons. These correlate A and B Varieties.

The long, narrow crown is always best observed in lower molars, of which there are abundant examples in public and private collections.

In the British Museum the following may be indicated in addition to the specimens already described.

No. 33,367, B. M., in a lower ramus, is from HAPPISBOROUGH. Here, evidently, there were 20 ridges in 13 inches. Another ramus, No. 40,840, B. M., dredged also on the EAST COAST, off NORFOLK, holds a molar of this type, and evidently x 17 x in a little over 11 inches.

---

[1] Since my attention was drawn to the broad-crowned variety, I am gratified to find that Mr. Gunn has been familiar for the last twenty years with specimens of this description of molar, which in his MS. Catalogue in the Norwich Museum he names the *Leptodon giganteus*; and it may have been such-like worn crowns that led Falconer to surmise what he designates "the pre-glacial variety of the *Elephas primigenius* from the Norwich coast" ('Pal. Mem.,' vol. ii, p. 170). Of the characters of this tooth he (Falconer) observes that they "diverge widely from the ordinary form of *E. primigenius* in the direction of the Indian Elephant, but still maintain all the distinctive marks of true *E. primigenius.*"

[2] 'Pal. Mem.,' vol. ii, p. 185; and 'F. A. S.,' pl. xiii A, fig. 4.

Two very characteristic instances are seen in lower molars " 589" and " 589 A" in the Museum of the Royal College of Surgeons of England. The localities are unknown, but their light colour is indicative of Grays Thurrock specimens. The former is entire, and holds x 15 x in 11 inches. This tooth, unquestionably the last of the series, would indicate the minimum number of ridges, as far as I have been enabled to discover. No. 589 A has lost its first ridge, but contains 18 x in 12·4 inches. In the same collection there is a crown sawn horizontally through the middle into two portions, Nos. 569 and 570. There is here a loss of ridges, leaving 16 in 10·5 inches. It is recorded from " BRENTFORD."

Another instance of the long, bent, and narrow crown, from CLACTON, is in the possession of Dr. Bree, of Colchester, who has kindly allowed me to examine his collection of dredged specimens from the Norfolk coast. Dr. Bree has been at some trouble in ascertaining the exact positions where his specimens of teeth and bones of mammals were picked up by the oyster-dredgers and other persons. The specimen referred to holds x 19 x in 13·5 inches. In this superb specimen is seen all the characters of the tooth of *E. antiquus* of the type of B Variety.

The late Mr. T. Wickham Flower showed me a suggestive example of this long, narrow, bow-shaped lower tooth from GRAYS. It held x 18 x in 13·5 inches.

The foregoing may be accepted as instances of the three varieties of molar crown, and the intermediate conditions which unite the extremes. Thus the broad, narrow, and thick-plated crowns present well-marked differences, which, in the absence of specimens lying between these extremes, might fairly be accepted as belonging to three distinct species ; indeed, the differences are nearly quite as pronounced as between the two living species, so that looking to allied forms, the broad crown assimilates to that of the Mammoth, whilst the thick-plated and expanded disk is barely distinguishable from teeth of the African Elephant. Whatever may be the connection between *Elephas antiquus* and other forms accepted at present as distinct species, it can scarcely, I think, be denied that, as far as their dentitions are concerned, close alliances are traceable. Moreover, looking to the home of the present species in Asia, and the fossil exuviæ from the Mid-tertiary formations of India, it does seem that the genesis of living and extinct Elephants is to be formulated in that region, and that one form, at all events, *Elephas Namadicus*, is seemingly the representative there of the so-called *Elephas antiquus*, as will be further shown in the sequel.

Foreign specimens.—There is an interesting fragment of a large molar, figured and described by Belgrand,[1] in conjunction with a gigantic humerus, from MONTREUIL, near Paris ; the latter bone will be noticed in the sequel. The crown of the tooth is clearly referable to *E. antiquus*, and from its dimensions is suggestive of the broad crown, with the closely packed ridges of the members of A Variety, but whether a penultimate or ultimate does not appear in its fragmentary state.

A detailed account of a mandible containing molars of the thick-plated variety is given

[1] ' Basin de Paris,' pl. xvi, p. 175.

6

by Falconer, who examined the specimen in the Museum at Rome.[1] It was found in "Volcanic Sands," in a railway-cutting between the latter city and Civita Vecchia.

An instance of the "broad crown with the aggregated ridges" of A Variety is also recorded by him. It is of the usual massive dimensions of the British specimens and *E. Namadicus*, with a length of nearly 14 and a maximum breadth of crown of 4·5 inches! It holds the exceptional ridge formula of 24 plates, with a loss of the anterior portion of the crown. The above and other fragments from the same locality, " St. Paulo," he states, " present the marked characters of the species."[2]

There is a suggestive fragment of a right lower ramus in the British Museum, from Rome. The same is figured and described by Falconer.[3] It holds portions of the penultimate tooth, and is confirmatory of the thick-plated variety.

Another remarkable and interesting tooth of the thick-plated variety is, according to Falconer, " a last molar of the lower jaw, left side, nearly entire, the only deficiency being in the anterior talon and part of the first ridge borne upon the large anterior fang."[4] It is preserved in the Natural History Museum of Milan, and is from near Verona. This tooth shows, apparently, evidence of x 12 x in a space of about 12 inches. Now, such a formula applied to the ultimate molar of *Elephas antiquus*, in particular a lower jaw specimen, is perfectly at variance with every other evidence, as far as I know, of the number of ridges in that tooth. It is to be understood, however, that when Falconer wrote his description of *E. priscus* he had a strong impression as to its specific characters and alliance with *E. Africanus* rather than *E. antiquus*, although at the same time impressed by the resemblances between the two latter in certain respects. It is just possible that he may have been mistaken as to the number of lost ridges, or the tooth may be a penultimate true molar ; or else the thick-plated variety often furnished a minimum number of twelve plates besides talons, even in the mandible, which, if that be the case, gives a wide range to the ridge formula in the ultimate true molar of the thick-plated variety, thereby showing a pliability which must interfere materially with other deductions.

There is a tooth, No. 44,132, B. M., of precisely the same type as the broad-crowned tooth, No. 40,385, B. M., referred to at p. 37. It is from the VIA APPIA, ROME, and is unfortunately imperfect. There are several pebbles adhering to its sides. It holds four ridges in 6·2 inches, and gives evidence posteriorly of at least two more ridges, so that the tooth must have been either a penultimate or ultimate, possibly the latter.

A very characteristic specimen, No. 8, B. M., of the narrow crown of B variety, also from VIA APPIA, ROME, is shown in figs. 13 and 13 *a* of plate xiv A, ' F. A. S.' It is a

---

[1] ' Pal. Mem.,' vol. ii, p. 185.
[2] Dr. F. likens this tooth to the Canterbury specimen described at p. 402, and shown in the ' F. A. S.,' pl. xii D, figs. 5 and 5 *a*.
[3] Ibid., vol. i, p. 443, and vol. ii, p. 185 ; ' F. A. S.,' pl. xiv A, figs. 9 and 9 *a*.
[4] Ibid., vol. ii, pp. 101 and 103.

left lower molar, and has lost ridges in front and the posterior talon, leaving 14 in a space of 11 inches. The disk is large and like that of the thick-plated variety, but otherwise it is intermediate between B and C Varieties. The ridges are thick, being on an average as much as one inch. Such a tooth as the above contrasts with the long, narrow crown, and bridges over the differences between it and the typical specimens of the thick-plated molars.

Another reference is made by Falconer to an enormous tooth found near Turin, which clearly from subsequent studies he found to belong to the so-called *E. Armeniacus*.[1] Here it is that confusion creeps in to obscure the Italian history of *Elephas antiquus*, and in the absence of data I do not feel that I can at present clear up the numerous conflicting statements as to the Elephantine molars in collections at Rome, Pisa, Leghorn, &c. Whether the specimens represent the large tooth of A Variety or C Variety, or belong to a distinct species, remains to be worked out. Indeed, the *E. Armeniacus* seemed to Falconer to be very closely allied to the existing Indian species.[2] All these and many more points in relation to the southern distribution of *Elephas antiquus* are worthy of the attention of palæontologists; indeed, no one was more sensible of the want of conclusive evidence as regards the Italian specimens than Dr. Falconer.

Affinities.—It is worthy of record that a superb specimen of the palate region, holding two ultimate molars and portions of the alveoli of the incisors, is preserved in the Museum of the Royal College of Surgeons of England. Unfortunately there is no note of how the collection became possessed of this highly suggestive relic, but the associated crania render the likelihood of its Indian origin probable, whilst the matrix is seemingly of the character generally noticed on fossils from Central India,[3] therefore it may in all likelihood be a portion of the cranium of *E. Namadicus*.

The molars represent the broad-crowned variety of *E. antiquus*, modified to such an extent that they might almost represent huge grinders of the Asiatic. The anterior parts of the crowns are worn to the common base, with indications of the lost ridges, showing a formula of either $x\,16\,x$ or $x\,17\,x$ in a length of 12·5 inches. The crowns have a maximum breadth respectively of 3·5 inches, the average per ridge being about 0·6 inch. All the ridges excepting the last four are in wear. The disks are nearly parallel, with no angulations and little mesial expansion, but pronounced crimping of the machærides.

[1] 'Pal. Mem.,' vol. ii, p. 249.
[2] Idem., pp. 250 and 251, note 1.
[3] Considering the interest Dr. Falconer entertained in connection with all discoveries of Tertiary fossil remains from India, it is remarkable that he has not noted, if at all aware of the above, his impressions on this jaw, supposing the cranium in question is from the East Indies; and this is the more strange from the circumstance that he seems to have examined the other skulls, to wit, the cranium of *E. Cliftii*, in the same gallery: see 'Pal. Mem.,' vol. ii, p. 461, note 2.

There are other highly suggestive instances of the ultimate molar of *E. Namadicus* in the British Museum. For example:

The two upper last molars contained in a skull is represented in ' F. A. S.,' pl. xii B, figs. 2 and 3. Only 11 plates remain in a space of 8·1 inches. The crown shows the closely packed ridges of A Variety of *E. antiquus*.

Another huge cranium contains ultimate molars holding as many as 22 plates in a space of 13 inches.[1]

A magnificent right lower ramus, containing an entire tooth, is well shown in the ' F. A. S.,' pl. xii c, figs. 4 and 5. It is an ultimate molar, and holds x 19 x in 14·7 inches. Another mutilated mandible containing similar teeth is shown in figs. 5 and 5a of the same plate.

Both of these specimens are in the British Museum, as also another ultimate lower tooth, *in sitú*. Dr. Falconer refers to the "crimped characters of *Elephas antiquus*" in connection with the teeth of *E. Namadicus* in several places.[3] These molars seem to me inseparable from varieties of *E. antiquus*, in particular the long, narrow, and the broad crown with its closely packed ridges.

The last true molar of the Mammoth differs generally from that of *E. antiquus* both in contour and number of ridges. There are exceptional instances, however, in well-worn teeth of the latter, such as the specimens from Walton and Southwold described at p. 38, where a broad crown, with closely approximated ridges and faint crimping, becomes scarcely distinguishable, if at all, from an ordinary or aberrant pattern of crown of *E. primigenius*.[3] But considering the vast numbers of the molars of both species in public and private collections in Great Britain and on the Continent, and the pronounced specific dental characters of the two, it seems to me that, as far as odontography extends, nothing can be more distinct than the ordinary molars of these Elephants, and, I repeat, the only wonder is that they should have been so long confounded.

This applies with equal, if not more, force in the case of *Elephas meridionalis*, whose ultimate, like the preceding, molars are easily distinguishable from those of either of the preceding by the massiveness of the tooth, thickness of enamel and plates, with scarcely plaited macherides, the great breadth to height, and low ridge formula, which rarely, if ever, exceeds that of the second true molar of *E. antiquus*.[4]

Another doubtful example is seen in the mandible, No. 32,496, B. M., containing the last true molar in full wear on either side. Each tooth holds 19 x, and clearly did not exceed x 19—20 x, like the Ilford teeth of the Mammoth. It was dredged off Harwich. The ridges are closely approximated as in the members of A Variety, with the macherides

---

[1] ' Pal. Mem.,' vol. i, p. 435.
[2] Idem, vol. i, pp. 116, 437, note 1.
[3] ' Osseous Fossiles,' pl. xii, fig. 5, British Museum, &c.
[4] ' Pal. Mem.,' vol. ii, pp. 112 and 116 ; and ' F. A. S.,' pl. xiv B, fig. 14 ; and British and Norwich Museums.

here and there faintly crimped, although not generally; there is also central expansion of the disk. The jaw, however, has more the characters of the Mammoth than of *E. antiquus*.

With the last true molar of either of the living species that of *E. antiquus* has ordinarily no very close alliance, further than what has been pointed out with reference to the worn disk of the thick-plated variety. The crimping of the machærides, moreover, is very often present in the latter, and generally absent in the teeth of the African Elephant, in which the angulations of the disks *meet* and often *overlap*, which has not, seemingly, been hitherto noticed in the thick-plated variety of *E. antiquus*. Again, the rhomb is more crescentic in the latter, and its anterior border is concave, and the posterior border convex, with the cornua or lateral horn of the crescent bent forwards. The crimping so pronounced in the Asiatic is especially marked in its last molars, the ridge formula of which varies from $x\,24\,x$ to $x\,27\,x$, whilst that of the African Elephant seldom exceeds 13 ridges, and never goes beyond 15 ridges.

The same variability as regards the crown constituents prevail in the Maltese Elephants as in *E. antiquus*. In their teeth there are also clear evidences of, 1st, a broad crown with packed ridges;[1] 2nd, a long, narrow crown;[2] 3rd, a thick-plated crown[3] in penultimate and ultimate milk and all the true molars.

The ultimate molar in the larger form, *E. Mnaidriensis*, usually holds $x\,12\,x$ in 7 inches, and rarely $x\,13\,x$ in 7·5 inches, scarcely equalling in these respects the dimensions of the second true molar of *E. antiquus*; whilst that of the smaller or pigmy forms is of course far more diminutive. It is suggestive, however, that the Maltese Elephants should preserve the tendency to variability in the same directions, although differing in dimensions from one another and from *Elephas antiquus*.[4]

The ultimate molar of the *Elephas meridionalis* is generally distinct from that of *Elephas antiquus*. It holds the same ridge formula as that of the Maltese Elephants,

[1] 'Pal. Mem.,' vol. ii, pl. xi, figs. 1 and 2; and 'Trans. Zool. Soc. London,' vol. ix, pl. ii, fig. 7.

[2] Idem, pl. viii, fig. 8.

[3] Idem, vol. ix, pl. iii, fig. 2; vii, fig. 1; viii, fig. 7; ix, fig. 1; and 'Pal. Mem.,' vol. ii, pl. xii, fig. 4.

[4] It will appear from a comparison of the dentitions of *Elephas antiquus* and *Elephas Mnaidriensis* that, with the exception of dimensions and the ridge formula of the ultimate molars, the teeth of the two, considered as exponents of their affinities, might belong to one species. Therefore it is clear that, if the latter was a variety of the former, it differed much from the ordinary individuals of *E. antiquus* in size, and to a certain extent in the numerical estimate of its ridge formula. As regards the former a significant observation has been made by Dr. Livingstone in his 'Last Journals' at p. 29, vol. ii, where he states having seen in Central Africa a small variety of Elephant averaging 5 feet 8 inches in height with a tusk 6 feet in length. The great traveller, it is presumed, was perfectly conversant with the African Elephant and its growth, which he demonstrates by stating that this dwarf individual had a tusk of the dimensions of the adult. It remains to be ascertained whether or not the above is either an occasional small individual or else a race of the African Elephant or a distinct species. It may be observed that the stature of the *Elephas melitensis* of Falconer has been estimated by Busk at between 4 feet 2 inches and 4 feet 7 inches, whilst I found that, as compared with recent species, the *E. Mnaidriensis* may have stood from 6 to 6½ or 7 feet at the withers (see 'Trans. Zool. Soc. London,' vol. vi, p. 307, and vol. ix, p. 116).

with occasionally an additional ridge or two. The crown is relatively much broader than in *E. antiquus*, and the massive wedges of intervening cement between the plates, with the smooth and usually uncrimped enamel, and the low height of the ridges, distinguish it generally from the same tooth in every other known species of European fossil Elephants.

It will be seen from the foregoing that the last true molar in *E. antiquus*, like its predecessors, is subject to great variations in size and number of ridges, so much so that it seems impossible to establish anything like constancy in the formula. Dr. Falconer puts the dental formula at 16 plates exclusive of talons.[1] An analysis of the British data here given shows, as regards upper molars, that in individual teeth there is a range of between 16 and 20 plates, exclusive of talons, in specimens varying between 9·5 to 12·8 inches ; whilst in lower jaws as few as 15 plates and 2 talons are contained in a space of 11 inches, and ordinarily in the specimens the formula varies from the latter number of ridges to 19 (probably 20) plates, besides talons, in between 9·3 and 13 inches. It may be an approximation to the truth in estimating the ridge formula of upper teeth at 16 to 18 plates, besides talons, and of lower at 18 plates and 2 talons. No doubt larger specimens might be adduced than any entire teeth here recorded ; indeed, several of the injured specimens not included in the estimate evidently attained to greater dimensions than the above ; but, as far as British instances extend, I have seen no case of such a high expression of the ridge formula as is ordinarily attained in the *E. Asiaticus* and Mammoth, although it must be acknowledged that ultimate molars of the latter from Ilford show in the number of their laminæ an agreement, as will be stated presently, to the highest range in the *E. antiquus* ; and, notwithstanding that the tooth of the Mammoth usually shows a considerably higher formula, it will be admitted that these instances of varintion are of the utmost value in the correlation of their dentitions.

The dental formula of *Elephas antiquus* given by Falconer, exclusive of talons, is as follows :

Milk Molars.	*True Molars.*
3 + 6 + 10	10 + 12 + 16.
3 + 6 + 10	10 + 12 + 16.

The elimination of talons in computing the number of enamelled ridges of a proboscidian tooth must be often a questionable proceeding, inasmuch as it may happen that the anterior or posterior ridge is in no way distinct from the succeeding plates, whilst many instances occur of modifications of two terminal ridges, indistinguishable from the ordinary splint or rudimentary ridge, which, again, may be dwarfed to a mere appendage to the last or to the first plate. It would appear that Dr. Falconer applied a too rigorous criticism in regard to what he considered a plate, and such ridges as should be admitted only as talon appendages ; and nowhere is this more evident than in his estimate of the ridge formula of *Elephas antiquus*.

[1] 'Pal. Mem.,' vol. ii, p. 176.

It can never in the future be the interest of the philosophical naturalist to create new species from a few minor characters. It seems to me, therefore, in order to realise the varying features in dental elements of Proboscidians, that strict cognizance should be taken of talons and the like in computing the ridge formula, which varies in every member of the series, not only in the recent, but in all known fossil Elephants; at all events, wherever sufficient materials have been obtained. It need scarcely be observed that the following ridge formulæ are provisional and liable to extension in accordance with future discoveries.

1. From the foregoing details it seems to me that the ridge formula of *Elephas antiquus*, as far as British specimens in particular demonstrate, is, talons included, in upper and lower jaws, as follows :

	Milk Molars.			True Molars.	
I.	II.	III.	IV.	V.	VI.
$x\,2\,x - x\,3\,x$	$x\,5\,x - x\,7\,x$	$x\,9\,x - x\,10\,x$	$x\,9\,x - x\,12\,x$	$x\,12\,x - x\,13\,x$	$x\,15\,x - x\,20\,x.$
$x\,3\,x - ?$	$x\,6\,x - x\,8\,x$	$x\,9\,x - x\,11\,x$	$x\,11\,x - x\,12\,x$	$x\,12\,x - x\,13\,x$	$x\,16\,x - x\,19\,x.$

2. The ridge formulæ of the Mammoth and Asiatic Elephant according to Falconer are the same ;[1] if anything, there is also a greater range in the former than in *E. antiquus*, the ultimate molar varying in number from $x\,19\,x$ to $x\,27\,x$. The lowest number of ridges in the last molar of the Mammoth, according to Falconer, is stated to be $x\,24\,x$, but Mr. Davies in the describing and naming of the valuable materials collected by Sir Antonio Brady, F.G.S., in the Ilford deposits, records entire ultimate molars of the Mammoth containing *nineteen plates* and *two talons* ;[2] consequently, if the extremes in the *Elephas antiquus* and *E. primigenius* meet, with the limitation in the lowest number of ridges of the last true molar as just indicated, the ridge formula of the Mammoth as given by Falconer will stand as follows :

	Milk Molars.			True Molars.	
I.	II.	III.	IV.	V.	VI.
$x\,4\,x - ?$	$x\,8\,x - ?$	$x\,12\,x - ?$	$x\,12\,x - x\,14\,x$	$x\,16\,x - x\,18\,x$	$x\,19\,x - x\,21\,x.$
$x\,4\,x - ?$	$x\,8\,x - ?$	$x\,12\,x - ?$	$x\,12\,x - x\,14\,x$	$x\,16\,x - x\,18\,x$	$x\,19\,x - x\,28\,x.$

3. The dental formula in the African Elephant appears to vary much, but it seemingly never attains to the number of ridges in true molars that is seen in any of the three preceding species. According to Blainville, Owen, and Falconer, none of whom give exactly the same formula, supposing they have not represented more than the exact number of ridges, including talons, it stands thus :

---

[1] 'Pal. Mem.,' vol. ii, p. 157, and footnote, p. 236.
[2] 'Catalogue of Vertebrata for Ilford,' p. 3.

Milk Molars.			True Molars.		
I.	II.	III.[1]	IV.	V.	VI.
$x2x — x3x$	$x5x — x6x$	$x4x — x7x$	$x7x —$?	$x8x —$?	$x10x —$?
$2x — x3x$	$x5x — x6x$	$x4x — x7x$	$x7x —$?	$x8x — x9x$	$x10x — x12x$.

4. The dentition in the Maltese fossil Elephants, as shown by Dr. Falconer,[2] and from materials collected by me in the Island of Malta,[3] furnishes a ridge formula in the *Elephas Mnaidriensis* as follows:

Milk Molars.			True Molars.		
I.	II.	III.	IV.	V.	VI.
$x2x — x3x$	$x4x — x6x$	$x8x — x9x$	$x8x — x$ $9x$	$x10x —$?	$x12x — x13x —$
$x2x — x3x$	$x5x — x6x$	$x8x — x9x$	$x8x — x10x$	$x10x —$?	$x12x — x13x —$

5. It is to be regretted that the dental series of *Elephas Namadicus* is not fully ascertained, seeing the extremely close morphological resemblances between it and the *Elephas antiquus*. As far as the few instances of lower teeth afford materials for comparison, we have :

Milk Molars.	True Molars.		
III.	IV.	V.	VI.
$? — ?$	$? — ?$	$? — ?$	$? — 22.$
$x9x —$?	$x12x —$?	$x12 —$?	$? — x19x.$

6. An analysis of molars of *E. meridionalis* described by Falconer[4] furnishes the following :

Milk Molars.			True Molars.		
I.	II.	III.	IV.	V.	VI.
$x3x —$?	$x5x — x6x$	$x8x —$?	$x8x — x9x$	$x9x — x10x$	$x13x —$?
$x3x —$?	$x6x —$?	$x8x —$?	$x8x —$?	$x9x —$?	$x11x — x15x.$

From which he formulates the series thus :

Milk Molars.	True Molars.
$\dfrac{3 + 6 + 8}{3 + 6 + 8}$	$\dfrac{8 + (8 - 9) + 13}{8 + (8 - 9) \times 13 - 15.}$

It will be observed that the highest expression of the ultimate molar of *E. Meri-*

---

[1] Blainville, as pointed out by Falconer, makes the second milk bold seven, and the third milk molar six ridges, which is at variance with the rules which have hitherto regulated the dental succession in the genus, 'Pal. Mem.,' vol. ii, p. 89. The dentition of *E. Africanus* is still far from being accurately determined.

[2] 'Pal. Mem.,' vol. ii, p. 298.

[3] 'Trans. Zool. Soc. London,' vol. ix, p. 36.

[4] 'Pal. Mem.,' vol. ii, p. 118.

dionalis equals the lowest expression of the last molar in *E. antiquus*, so that as far as the numbers of ridges are concerned we find *Elephas primigenius*, *Elephas antiquus*, *Elephas meridionalis*, and *Elephas Namadicus*, meeting at their extremes, and showing thereby that to sharply define their ridge formulæ, by striking an average in each case, is no exponent of the actual range of variation to which every member of the dental series is more or less subject.

The above suffices to show how much the molars of Proboscidia vary in the number of their ridges, and how arbitrary it would be to formulate an average in the case of any one species or even any one member of a dental series. The stress laid by Dr. Falconer on the dental formulæ as diagnostic of species of Mastodon and Elephant is evident when the fossil materials come to be differentiated. But it is also clear that in correlating members of the genus Elephas any formula professing to furnish an average number of plates per molar must of necessity be subject to exceptionable conditions. The data by which fossil species are determined are too few at present to admit of casting a mean, whilst the desirability of tracing evolutionary characters between them is more or less thwarted by setting up a definite formulary in each case, more especially where two or more forms of Elephants assimilate closely. The very fact that the dental elements of any one species are subject to variation as regards numbers, and that one or more particular member of the series presents exceptional conditions, is of the utmost importance in estimating the character and affinities of the species in question when taken in connection with the sculpturing of the crowns of worn disks.

I have correlated in the foregoing comparisons the dentitions, as far as I have been enabled to make out, of the seven best known species of Elephants including the recent and fossil. It is apparent, however, that there are aberrant forms, such as the *Elephas Columbi* (Falconer) and the *Elephas Armeniacus* (Falconer),[1] with which comparisons should be made ; but I have not ventured on this undertaking, inasmuch as, in order to do justice to even the Elephant here described, it is necessary to compare also the entire Elephantine remains from the Sewalik Ranges of the Himalayan Mountains, the affinities of which with European or North American species are worthy of far more attention than has been bestowed on that subject.

Summary.—It will be apparent from the data furnished in the previous pages that the molars of *E. antiquus* differ considerably individually as regards dimensions and number of ridges in both the upper and lower jaws ; thus in the upper jaw the differences between the extremes in the various members of the series may be instanced as follows :

The difference between the maximum and minimum length in the upper jaw of I^1 (milk molar) is 0·1, of II^3 1·2, of III^4 1·0, of IV^8 2·5, of V^8 2·5, of VI^7 3·3 inches.

In the mandible the differences of length are : for I^8 ?, for II^9 0·5, for III^{10} 1·3, for IV^{11} 2·3, for V^{12} 2·8, for VI^{13} 3·7.

[1] 'Pal. Mem.,' vol. ii, pp. 212 and 247. [2] See page 11, *ante*. [3] p. 16. [4] p. 20. [5] p. 26. [6] p. 31. [7] p. 46. [8] p. 11. [9] p. 16. [10] p. 20. [11] p. 26. [12] p. 31. [13] p. 46.

The maximum and minimum number of ridges (including talons) individually are as follow in upper teeth: I, 4–5; II, 7–8; III, 11–12; IV, 11–14; V, 14–15; VI, 17–22. In the mandible: I, 5; II, 8–10; III, 11–13; IV, 13–14; V, 14–15; VI, 17–22.

The foreign data are not here included, and only such as I have been enabled to confirm by personal examination. Neither are the above advanced as the ultimate possible limits of variation, but only with the view of showing to what extent mutability extends as far as I have been able to find out. As regards the true molars, in particular the ultimate member of the series, it is highly probable that its limits with reference to dimensions and number of laminæ might be increased, especially in specimens from Southern Europe and Eastwards.

The molars of *Elephas antiquus* taken as exponents of the probable variability in the dimensions of the animal show a pliability in this respect far greater than seems to obtain in either of the living species. With reference to the latter, however, it must be borne in mind that they are restricted to smaller areas, and consequently are less exposed to influencing agencies than was the case with their extinct predecessors.

The modifications in the molars ascribed to the *Elephas antiquus* looked on either as sexual, race, or occasional conditions, are sufficiently pronounced to invite the attention of geologists as to their stratigraphical relations.

As regards the Pre-glacial Deposits of the Eastern Coast, it would seem that the large broad crown has been more commonly discovered there than in other situations, but at the same time both the typical and thick-plated molar has also been obtained to all appearances from the above-named situation.

In the lower gravels and brickearths of the Thames, all the varieties have been met with, so that, although the evidence is not altogether irrefutable, still it seems likely that the three varieties were contemporaneous. This, however, is a matter for further investigation.

Looking at the extremes of variation in the molars of *E. antiquus*, it will be observed that the *broad crown* is of the type of that of *E. Namadicus*, an Eastern form, and that this modification also approaches *E. meridionalis* on the one hand and *E. primigenius* on the other. Again, the divergence from the *narrow* or what might be named the typical crown, as far as British specimens are concerned, to the *thick-plated*, is seen to culminate in the disk allied to but distinguishable from that of the existing African Elephant, whilst certain crowns in the crimping of their machærides greatly resemble those of *E. Asiaticus* and *E. Armeniacus*. As to the relations to *Elephas antiquus* borne by the Maltese forms, the main difficulty is in relative dimensions, and if these be admitted as the result of modifying influences or belonging to a variable species restricted to narrow limits, such as we see to some extent in the continental and insular varieties of the Asiatic Elephant, then the Maltese might be accepted as offshoots or diminutive forms of *Elephas antiquus*.

III. OSTEOLOGY.

In attempting the determination of species from fossil Elephantine remains there is considerable difficulty in arriving at a certain diagnosis, partly on account of the fragmentary state and general similarities of specimens, chiefly of the long bones, whilst the minuter points at all likely to be subservient towards distinguishing the species are too often lost, or occupy a debatable position as to constancy. It is only, as elsewhere observed, when the exact distinctions between the osteologics of the living species have been ascertained from the comparison of abundant materials of *wild* individuals, that anatomists will be in a position to speak with confidence of the endoskeletons of the extinct forms. The following determinations, therefore, more especially in connection with the elements of the vertebral column and several long bones, must be considered provisional.

The circumstance of the finding of teeth and bones of the *Elephas antiquus* and *E. meridionalis* together, and of the former and *E. primigenius*, make it difficult to correlate their dental and osseous structures.

The vast number of undoubted bones of the Mammoth from Arctic and other regions seem to point to a general slender frame in this species, as compared with the colossal bones of *E. meridionalis* authenticated from Italian deposits. Again, for example, in the brickearths of the Thames Valley, and in dredging on the east coast (in the latter case, however, *E. meridionalis* is also found), humeri, femora, pelves, and vertebræ are discovered stouter in proportion, and preserving characters different from the same parts in numerous authenticated instances of the Mammoth's remains, even from the same localities. Partly on that account and partly from their larger size many of these have been considered to have belonged to *E. antiquus*, which seems to have varied much in dimensions, if we may judge by the molars alone. But specific characters established on slender and squat or large and small bones must, at the best, be considered uncertain means of diagnosis, inasmuch as these conditions are noticeable in varieties of the Asiatic [1] and likely also of the African Elephant as mentioned at p. 45. Perhaps, however, where variability at present is the exception, it was the rule before and during the later Tertiary periods.

1. CRANIUM.

I have been unable to find references to an instance of an entire skull of *E. antiquus* having been discovered in British strata. It is important, however, in comparing the dental characters of *E. Namadicus*, that the bonnet-shaped vault of the calvarium, as

[1] Falconer, ' Pal. Mem.,' vol. ii, p. 257.

shown in two skulls in the British Museum, and described and figured by Falconer,[1] if
absolutely a natural character, must be considered as eminently characteristic and distinctive of, at all events, the Indian specimens; at the same time, whilst admitting the
singular depression of the frontal in the situation above stated, it is probable, as in the huge
cranium of *Elephas insignis*[2] also in the Sewalik Collection, British Museum, that the same
agency may have distorted the calvarium in question, and thus exaggerated the frontal
hollow, which, judging however from another and smaller cranium, was more pronounced
than in the Asiatic species. In the absence of similar data in *E. antiquus*, I can only merely
refer to the above and the palate specimen of *E. Namadicus* in the College of Surgeons,
already noticed at p. 43.   It may be stated, however, as regards relative dimensions, that
these two crania differ in the latter being larger, whilst the British Museum specimen
from the smaller tusks may, as suggested by Falconer, have probably belonged to a
female.

A cranium and mandible, with other bones of *E. antiquus*, are in the Museum at
Rome.[3]   A few palate specimens of youthful individuals, with teeth *in situ*, are not
uncommon in British collections.

The upper jaw, containing the ultimate milk molars, described at p. 17, and shown in
Plate I, fig. 4, furnishes no specific characters as regards the region represented.   When
compared with a palatal aspect of an Indian Elephant, No. 2666, in the Royal College
of Surgeons of England, where the third milk molar is in full wear and fourteen
inches of tusk protruding beyond the alveolus, the two are found to agree nearly in
the distance between the molars in front, at the middle, and behind, the fossil only
exceeding the recent species to a small extent, which would agree with still more advanced
stage of wear of the teeth of the latter, so that individually the maxillæ of the *E. antiquus*
and the Asiatic, as far as the above stage of growth extends, presented about the same
dimensions.   Another palate specimen of the Indian Elephant in the same collection,
with the last milk molar not so far advanced, gives nearly the same admeasurements.

2. MANDIBLE.

The various stages of growth are represented in several rami.   The jaw, Plate V,
fig. 2, containing the penultimate or second milk molar, No. 21,310, B. M., described at
p. 15, when compared with the ramus, No. 2668, of an Asiatic Elephant, in the
Museum of the Royal College of Surgeons of England, presents no appreciable differences as regards dimensions, the two jaws holding teeth of the same stage of growth and
about the same condition of wear.   The fossil is a left ramus, with the penultimate milk
molar entire, the two fang sockets of the antepenultimate in front and a fragment of the

¹ 'Pal. Mem.,' vol i, pp. 115 and 435 and 436; 'F. A. S.,' xii a and xii b, and pl. xxiv a, fig. 4.
² Ibidem, 'F. A. S.,'pl. xvii, fig. 3.
³ Falconer, 'Pal. Mem.,' vol. ii, p. 187.

empty alveolus of the third milk molar behind. The diasteme is not so erect as in the adult, nor so reclinate as in a ramus of the *E. meridionalis* in the British Museum, and in the African Elephant, and is more in keeping with that of the Asiatic; whilst its mentary foramina are close to the margin. The beak is blunt, and the horizontal ramus produced; the latter resembles that of the African Elephant. These two latter characters, however, do not seem invariable in any one species, and are not to be relied on.

The mandible, No. $\frac{1879}{7}$, B. M., described and figured by Falconer,[1] the molars of which have been already referred to at p. 21, represents the adolescent stage of growth where the first true molar is nearly in full wear. The mentary foramina are irregular in their positions—a condition more or less common to all known species of the genus, although in the African they are usually not so close to the free margin of the diasteme as in the Asiatic, Mammoth, and other species. Their numbers also vary. A large anterior dental foramen is very generally placed about two inches below the alveolus in front, with smaller openings along the side of the diasteme. The latter foramina are often irregular as regards size and numbers, even on opposite sides of the same mandible. In the above jaw the horizontal ramus is prolonged, the diasteme is erect, and the rostrum was apparently short. In all these characters it agrees with the Asiatic and the Maltese pigmy form named *E. Melitensis*.[2] A jaw of the Asiatic Elephant, with apparently the same tooth in full wear, No. 2672, of the Osteological Collection, Royal College of Surgeons of England, is not so large. This, however, may be a small individual; at all events, the discrepancies with reference to dimensions are not such as would accord a great disproportion in the sizes, at the adolescent age, of the two elephants.

The lower jaw containing the second true molar, 28,114, B. M., already noticed at p. 20, is suggestive:—1st. It shows that the beak was not so prolonged as often obtains in the African Elephant. 2nd. That the diasteme was nearly erect, as in *E. Namadicus, E. Asiaticus, E. primigenius*, and the Maltese Elephants. The other left ramus with the second molar, 33,366 B. M., described at p. 29, confirms the character of the last as regards the direction of the diasteme; the rostrum is lost. Here the two mentary foramina are placed within one and two inches of the free margin of the diasteme.

In the Jermyn Street Museum there is a lower jaw containing the second molars described at p. 28, but it is too much injured in front to admit of comparisons. Another lower jaw in the same collection has portions of the fifth and last molars *in situ*. The gutter is entire and displays a well-developed rostrum, but not so prolonged as in the African, yet fully as large as in many of the Asiatic species. The diasteme was evidently nearly vertical. These two jaws are from GRAYS THURROCK, and also belonged to full-grown Elephants.

A lower jaw containing the last true molars, No. 33,796, B. M., from BARROW-ON-SOAR,

[1] 'Pal. Mem.,' vol. ii, p. 183; 'F. A. S.,' pl. xiii A, fig. 5.

[2] 'Trans. Zool. Soc. London,' vol. ix, p. 42, pl. vi, fig. 1 to 4.

referred to at p. 38, is extremely suggestive. It has lost all the hind portions of both rami posterior to the teeth, and the rostrum is injured and its dimensions indeterminable; but the horizontal portion of the ramus is perfect, and presents the following characters: —The diasteme is nearly vertical. The two mentary foramina are situated about midway on the side of the diasteme. The upper aperture is distant about two inches from the margin. The lower is on a line with the floor of the gutter, and about an inch from the border. From the alveolar border in front of the teeth to the middle of the gutter is 5 inches. Breadth of the latter at the middle is 3 inches. Length of gutter is 4·5 inches. Height of the ramus in front of the molar and at the middle is 7 inches.

There is a ramus of the right side containing portions of the penultimate and last true molars in the collection made by Miss Gurney and presented to the Norwich Museum. The teeth are very characteristic of the broad crown with aggregated ridges. Here the large foramen is about 2¼ inches below the alveolar margin, and the mental holes are within an inch of the free margin of the diasteme.

Another lower jaw, No. 33,337, B. M., containing the last molars, already described at p. 38, although not perfect, affords the following data :—A nearly perpendicular diasteme. A small rostrum. An unusually large upper mental foramen, just below the front of the tooth, and about 2·5 inches from the margin. A small foramen close to the free border and about the middle of the diasteme. The latter is 5 inches in length. The height of the jaw in front of the tooth is 7 inches ; at its middle 7·5 inches. The length of the gutter is 5 inches.

A very perfect lower jaw, displaying all the characters just noticed and further data, is seen in the specimen, in the Museum of the Geological Society, already noticed in connection with its molars at p. 40. It contains a portion of the fifth, and almost the entire sixth or ultimate true molar. The condyle, rostrum, and a portion of the lower and inner wall of the alveoli are lost. The jaw is represented in pl. xiii a, fig. 4, of the 'Fauna Antiqua Sivalensis,' and its dimensions are given by Falconer,[1] so I shall only refer to the most characteristic features of the specimen.

The diasteme and rostrum are precisely as in the last. There are two mentary openings and one anterior dental foramen. The latter is large, but not so capacious as in several of the foregoing. It is 4·5 inches from the free margin of the diasteme, and 3 inches below the alveolus. There is a small opening about half way up the diasteme and about 1·5 inch from its border, and a third of large size near the rostrum, and about 2 inches under the symphysial canal.

The dental canal is more gaping than in either the Asiatic or the African Elephant, but the posterior border of the ascending ramus narrows towards the condyle as in the African, whereas it is usually broad and rounded in the Asiatic and Mammoth.

The bulging or greatest breadth of the ascending ramus near the base of the coronoid process is common to the Asiatic and Mammoth. The same part in *E. antiquus*,

[1] 'Pal. Mem.,' vol. i, p. 440.

E. Africanus, E. Namadicus, and the Maltese forms, instead of being circular in contour, is more parabolic, and widens upwards towards the neck of the condyle.

The gutter in the above specimen is not so open as in the Mammoth nor so narrow as in *E. meridionalis* and the African, and is more like the symphysial canal of the Asiatic.

In the ramus, 40,840, B. M., containing an ultimate molar, described at p. 40, the diasteme is also nearly vertical, with the mentary foramina at a distance from its free border. The large opening is as usual just under the anterior fang. The symphysial canal is 5·3 inches in length, and the jaw is 7 inches in height at the base of the coronoid process.

The mandible containing the ultimate molars, referred to at p. 39, from Cromer Jetty, shows a large foramen four inches below the crown in front. The diasteme is erect, with a small scar of the rostrum which is wanting. The mental foramina are within 1½ inches of the free margin.

Another, No. 361, of Mr. Gunn's collection shows the above-mentioned foramen in the same position. The diasteme is injured, but indications of the mentary foramina are seen within a distance of about 1¼ inches of the free margin. The contour of the ascending ramus is decidedly African. These represent aged individuals.

A ramus of the lower jaw of *Elephas Namadicus* in the British Museum is figured in the 'Fauna Antiqua Sivalensis,' plate xii c, fig. 4; it contains the entire last molar already noticed at p. 44; and presents all the characters of the foregoing rami. The diasteme is also nearly vertical. Dr. Falconer states that the coronoid portion of the ramus shelves out more, and the mentary foramina are placed higher than in *E. antiquus.*[1] As regards these distinctions between the specimen, also fig. 5 of the same plate, and mandibles of *E. antiquus,* I fail to discover any marked differences whatever. The uncertainty as to numbers and exact position of the mentary foramina have been demonstrated by the preceding specimens, whilst a comparison between them and the jaws in question, together with the ramus of *E. antiquus,* plate xiii B, fig. 4, gives no appreciable differences.

As regards relative dimensions, although generally the mandible of *E. antiquus* containing the last true molar is relatively larger than the usual specimens of recent species, still there are lower jaws of the latter as large as many of the foregoing; so that the *Elephas antiquus* sometimes maintained the mandibular, and, as will also be shown presently, the general osteological proportions, met with in individuals of the living species.

With reference to the characters of the lower jaw in living and extinct species, I find in comparing the varied materials in the different museums, that as regards, 1, the contour of the chin, 2, direction of the diasteme, 3, general contour of the horizontal ramus, 4, contour of the ascending ramus posteriorly, 5, relative aspects of the symphysial canal, 6, position of the mentary foramina, there is a close relationship between the jaws of *Elephas antiquus, E. Namadicus,* and the Maltese fossil forms. On

[1] 'Pal. Mem.,' i, p. 437.

the other hand, whilst *E. primigenius* differs from all other species in having a very broad and rounded chin, and usually an open expansive gutter, the small rostrum and nearly vertical diasteme are in keeping with the foregoing and *E. Asiaticus*. Again, as in the latter, the contour of the border of the ascending ramus behind is circular and does not display the parabolic curve observed in the others and also in *E. Africanus* and in *E. meridionalis*, and apparently in *E. Hysudricus*. The beak is well developed in *E. Asiaticus*, and very pronounced in the *E. Africanus*, *E. meridionalis*, and *E. Hysudricus*.

Thus *E. antiquus* with *E. Namadicus* and to somewhat less extent the Maltese Elephants present similar characters in the lower jaws ; the Mammoth and Asiatic assimilate to each other also in some important characters, whilst a clear relationship is maintained between the same parts in the *E. Africanus*, *E. meridionalis*, and *E. Hysudricus*. The extent of the alveolar margin from the anterior aspect of the ascending ramus to the diasteme, both relatively and absolutely, in comparison with the breadth of the ascending ramus, is apparently greater in *E. antiquus*, *E. meridionalis*, *E. Africanus*, and the Maltese forms than in *E. primigenius* and *E. Asiaticus*. The deep-rounded chin so marked in the Mammoth is less apparent in *E. antiquus*; and, whilst the small rostrum in both assimilate, we have it produced in the *E. meridionalis* and *E. Africanus*, and sometimes with a downward course. The rostrum varies in size, however, in specimens of the recent Elephants, and may therefore be omitted as characteristic of any one species ; but I repeat, as regards the configuration generally of the mandible of *E. antiquus*, *E. Namadicus*, and the *E. Mnaidriensis*, it seems to me that there is a very close relationship between the three.

3. ATLAS.

On comparing this bone in the recent and the following extinct Elephants, there does not appear much to note of a persistent character in any one species. The contours of the neural and odontoid canals present no invariable distinctions ; but the foramen for the first cervical nerve is seemingly peculiar in certain fossil atlases from ILFORD and SLADE GREEN, as compared with many specimens from the former situation, and referable to *E. primigenius*. In those exceptional atlases the foramen for the above-named nerve opens directly on the side of the arch internally, so that it is invisible on looking down upon the neural canal, and this is apparent also in an atlas of the African Elephant, and also in the one I have referred to the *Elephas Melitensis*.[1] In two typical specimens of atlases of the Mammoth in the Beechy Collection, British Museum, from the Arctic regions, as also in several from Ilford, and many in the Norwich Museum, the foramen is quite visible when the bone is placed in the above position, and the same is seemingly the case in the Asiatic Elephant.

---

[1] 'Trans. Zool. Soc. London,' vol. ix, pl. xiii, fig. 1 a.

The above character, taken in connection with a rather stouter bone than that of the typical atlas of the Mammoth, might, as Mr. Davies has supposed, place the atlas and axis referred to by him in the Brady Catalogue with the remains of *E. antiquus.*[1] It is also worthy of note that this foramen is uncovered in a huge atlas, No. 36,436, B.M., dredged up on the Norfolk coast, and which from its dimensions is comparable with the colossal bones ascribed to *Elephas meridionalis*, although no doubt individuals of *E. antiquus* often attained to as great dimensions.

Dr. Falconer[2] records a scapula three feet three inches in length, along with other bones, obtained from Bracklesham Bay. There are several fragments of large shoulder-blades in both the British Museum and Norwich Museum. This bone, however, does not appear to vary much, if at all, in the recent and extinct species, excepting, perhaps, in the relative length of the glenoid fossa and position of the recurved process of the acromion. The former is relatively broader in the larger of these fossil scapulæ as compared with undoubted specimens of *E. primigenius* and *E. Asiaticus*, and consequently assimilate to the African Elephant. I have not seen a specimen sufficiently entire to admit of determination of the position of the spinal process with exactness, the latter distinction being seldom preserved in the fossil state.

4. HUMERUS.

Whatever may have been the maximum height and general dimensions of *E. antiquus*—and individuals, judging from teeth alone, must have attained to enormous proportions—we find, as Falconer has pointed out, data establishing the belief that relatively this Elephant, as compared with the Mammoth, was altogether a stouter animal. This is well shown from undoubted specimens generally of the long bones of the *E. primigenius*, in particular the humerus and femur. The differences were evidently much the same as prevail between the two recent Elephants, so that the Asiatic Elephant and Mammoth would go together, whilst the *E. antiquus* and the African might be considered relatively broader and stouter animals. It would seem, however, if the bones referred to here belong to *E. antiquus*, that it was often bulkier than any of the foregoing, and approached *E. meridionalis*, which was the largest of the three British extinct forms.

Several undoubted specimens of the humerus of *E. primigenius* in the British Museum show all the characters of the Asiatic Elephant, and are generally in proportion more slender than that of the African, and than fossil humeri obtained from Grays and other deposits where teeth of *E. antiquus* are met with. They contrast, moreover, with huge specimens from the Forest Bed and other situations where teeth of *E. meridionalis* are found.

[1] See 'Catalogue of Mammalian Remains from Ilford,' p. 28, Nos. 9 and 10 D, or Nos. 45,200 and 45,201, B.M.
[2] 'Pal. Mem.,' ii, p. 188.

A humerus, No. 23,151 in the British Museum, purchased from the late Mr. Ball, is from GRAYS. The great tuberosity has been somewhat ingeniously replaced by affixing a portion of an inner condyle of another specimen; nevertheless, with the exception of loss of substance at the distal extremity its entire length is seemingly preserved, and is 41 inches. The scapular articulation is 13·5 inches in the antero-posterior diameter by 10·5 inches transversely; the girth mid-shaft is 22·5 inches.

Seeing that E. meridionalis has not been identified from the beds at Grays, where molars of E. antiquus are abundant, and in consideration of this bone being altogether more robust than that of the Mammoth, I am much inclined, with Mr. Davies, who brought the above-named specimen to my notice, to consider it to be the humerus of Elephas antiquus.

The three stupendous arm-bones referred by Falconer to Elephas meridionalis[1] deserve a few remarks; two are from the Pre-glacial Deposits of Norfolk, and the other is in the museum of Florence. I am indebted to Mr. Gunn for the following measurements of the two former, one of which belongs to his own collection, whilst the other, from Cromer, was presented to the Norwich Museum by Miss A. Gurney. Professor Owen refers to the latter,[2] and also other large humeri from the bottom of the German Ocean. The length of the larger of the two from the Mundesley Pre-glacial beds is 51 inches, whilst that from Cromer is an inch less. The middle girth, however, of the shaft in the latter exceeds that of the other by three inches, and there is a difference of as much as four and a half inches at the least circumference or termination of the deltoid ridge in favour of the Cromer humerus, which is altogether stouter in proportion and may have belonged to Elephas antiquus, whilst that from Mundesley may have appertained to the Elephas meridionalis. This, however, is mere conjecture, inasmuch as there appears to be loss of substance of the external layers of the shafts in both cases.

The entire humerus referred to E. Namadicus gives a length of 47 inches.[3] The proximal fragment, No. 36,700, B. M., shows an open bicipital grove which is 3 inches in breadth. The scapular head is 15 × 9 inches, and the entire girth of the proximal extremity is 45 inches.[4]

An enormous left humerus was discovered in 1866 in a gravel pit at Montreuil, near Paris.[5] The supinator ridge and portion of the proximal extremity are wanting, but the length is preserved and gives the enormous dimension of 1·35 m., or about 53 inches! A cast of this arm-bone is in the Museum of the Royal College of Surgeons of England.

I will refer to the third metacarpal found in the same situation with the above. The humerus in question exceeds any of the foregoing, and, considering that molars of E. antiquus were found in the same pit, the probability is that it belonged to this species.

1 'Pal. Mem.,' vol. ii, p. 143.
2 'British Fossil Mammals,' p. 251.
3 'Pal. Mem.,' vol. i, pp. 480 and 496.
4 'F. A. S.,' pl. xlviii, fig. 1.
5 Belgrand, 'Basin de Paris,' p. 176, pl. xiv.

One of the largest humeri of recent species I have seen is represented by two specimens, right and left, No. 2744 *E*, of the Indian Elephant in the Royal College of Surgeons. Here the length is 36·5 inches; girth of the proximal extremity 33·5 inches; of the shaft (minimum) 16·5 inches; the distal extremity being 27 inches in circumference.

5. RADIUS.

There are two radii, Nos. $\frac{D}{13}$ and $\frac{C}{165}$, B. M., in the Brady Collection, from Ilford,[1] the former has been referred to *E. antiquus* by Mr. Davies; and it appears to me that this decision is well sustained by a comparison with radii of the Mammoth. Although neither of the foregoing belonged to aged individuals, and one was that of a young animal, both preserve stouter proportions than I have seen in radii of *E. primigenius*. There is a flattening of the upper and outer side of the shaft, rather more pronounced in the former than in several specimens of the Mammoth, whilst the inner side of the shaft and its border are quite flat and rounded. These bones seem to carry the radius of the African with them, whilst that of the Asiatic has the slender outline of the Mammoth. The various ridges appear to differ according to age and in individuals, as observed in numerous specimens of this bone belonging to the Mammoth and the Asiatic Elephant.

The larger of the two radii in question is 26 inches in length, and belonged to an adolescent individual, the distal epiphyses being lost. The other, that of a much younger elephant, is 19 inches in length.

I think, as far as the Maltese specimens of the equivalent bone in *E. Mnaidriensis* are concerned, that there is a close resemblance between the latter, *E. antiquus*, and *E. Africanus*, more especially in the general breadth of the shaft at the middle and lower third, whilst the afore-mentioned conditions referable to the upper third of the bone in *E. antiquus* are present in the Maltese, which I have shown elsewhere[2] have the decided aspect of the African as compared with the other living species.

6. ULNA.

Comparing the ulnæ in the Ilford collection, B. M., Nos. D 11 and 12, with similar bones from the same deposits and with Mammoth remains from the Arctic Regions, and likewise with the two recent species, I find the following distinctions:

1. The radial sulcus, round and shallow in the African, is less so in the Asiatic, and much less than either in the above.

2. The pit in front of the inner condyle seen in Asiatic and Mammoth is scarcely noticeable in the African and in the above.

---

[1] 'Cat.' cit., pp. 21 and 29.   [2] 'Zool. Trans.,' vol. ix, p. 54.

3. The head of the olecranon arches more inwards in the African and in the bones in question than in *E. Asiaticus* and Mammoth.

The distal extremities of the specimens D 11 and 12, and also of a detached left ulna in the Museum, locality unknown, are wanting. These bones in proportion are stouter than ulnæ of the same length in the Mammoth.

There are several ulnæ in the Norwich Museum, and apparently as far as the foregoing indications are admissible it would seem that they bear out the characters assigned to the above and *E. primigenius*, by means of several examples in Mr. Gunn's and Miss Gurney's collections; it is still an open question, however, how far the larger specimens and the ulna of *E. meridionalis* differ. As regards the connection of the largest with either of the two stupendous humeri in the same Museum, and which Falconer has connected with the latter species, there can be no doubt that individually all belonged to elephants differing much in size.

Anchylosis of the forearm bones would seem to be not uncommon. I have seen the radius united at its proximal extremity in the larger Maltese form, and the specimen of, perhaps, a Mammoth's ulna and radius completely interossified throughout is preserved in the Gunn collection, showing the restricted functions of the radius in Elephants.

7. PORTION OF A FOREFOOT.

The only portion of the foot of the Mammoth referred to by Professor Owen in the ' British Fossil Mammals '[1] is a fragment[2] from GRAYS, ESSEX, of an enormous right foot comprising the cuneiform, which has lost its apex, together with the magnum, unciforme, second and third metacarpals. The combined breadth of the proximal aspects of the magnum and unciforme are 12·6 inches. The following are the dimensions of the bones :—Cuneiforme—height 4·8 inches ; maximum breadth 5·8 inches :—Unciforme— height 6 inches ; transverse diameter 7·9 inches ; antero-posterior diameter 6·8 inches ; the cuneiform surface is 5·3 inches by 4·8 inches ; third metacarpal facet is 3 by 1 inch, whilst that of the fourth and fifth are 4 inches antero-posteriorly by 7 inches trans-versely :—Magnum—height 5·5 inches ; maximum breadth 6 inches ; the lunare surface is 6 inches in breadth by 5·6 inches in the antero-posterior diameter.

The second metacarpal has lost its distal epiphysis, leaving about 7 inches, with the proximal articulation intact excepting a portion of the inner facet. The magnal facet is 4 inches in antero-posterior diameter by 1·9 inch in breadth ; girth, mid-shaft 10·8 inches.

These carpal and metacarpal bones when compared with authenticated remains of the Mammoth and the two recent species do not appear to differ excepting in their

¹ Page 249.   ² In the British Museum.

longer and broader measurements. A third metacarpal from Eschscholtz Bay of undoubtedly a full-grown Mammoth, when compared with the same bone in the foot here referred to, furnishes the following:—The length in the former is 8 inches, whereas in the latter it is 10 inches, whilst the maximum girth at the middle of the shaft is 10 to 10·4 inches. The marginal facet is 4·8 × 2 to 5 × 3 inches. The distal articular aspect is antero-posteriorly by tape 5·6 to 6·2 inches, and 3 to 3·4 inches in breadth.

Many fore-feet bones of different dimensions from the Norfolk Beds are to be seen in the Norwich Museum; it is at present, however, impossible to arrive at just conclusions from these remains until the characters of the skeleton of E. primigenius have been accurately determined.

The third metacarpal, found at Montreuil, near Paris,[1] in the same deposits with the gigantic humerus and molars already referred to at pp. 58, 41, and 19, measures 26 centimètres in length and 28 centimètres in circumference at the middle of the shaft.

A magnum of smaller proportions than the Grays specimen is also figured and described by Belgrand;[2] it is from the sand pits of Chevaleret, and has a maximum length of 0·146 m., and breadth of 0·117 m.

I mention these instances of the remains from the Paris basin, as they agree very well with the bones from the Thames Valley, both of which exuviæ evidently belonged to enormous elephants, and in all probability to large individuals of Elephas antiquus.

8. PELVIS.

I have seen no authenticated pelvis of the Elephas antiquus. There is the huge Os innominatum, described by Falconer,[3] in Mr. Gunn's Collection from the FOREST BED, and another of the right side of E. primigenius dredged off YARMOUTH.

The differences in these two as regards dimensions are sufficient of themselves to indicate two distinct forms of Elephants. Mr. Busk has pointed out[4] that the foramen ovale is narrowest above in the E. Asiaticus, and the reverse in the E. Africanus; and I find from data in the British Museum, and the portion of the pelvis above referred to from Yarmouth, that the Mammoth assimilates to the Asiatic species, whilst it will be seen that E. Namadicus[5] comes closer to the African, to which possibly the E. antiquus also appertains, as it does in the character of many of the bones of the extremities.

Unfortunately the foramen ovale is not entire in the large pelvis from the FOREST BED; the height of the opening, however, is no less than 10·5 inches, whereas in the smaller pelvis from YARMOUTH it is only 7 inches. Again, the breadth of the upper portion of the oval opening is 7 inches in the former and only 3 inches in the latter, whilst the breadth

[1] Belgrand, 'Basin de Paris,' pl. xiii.   [2] Op. cit., pl. liii.   [3] 'Pal. Mem.,' vol. ii, p. 142.
[4] 'Trans. Zool. Soc. London,' vol. vi, p. 242.   [5] 'F. A. S.,' pl. lvi, fig. 8.

62   BRITISH FOSSIL ELEPHANTS.

at its lower part is 4 inches; unfortunately this measurement is not attainable in the
gigantic pelvis which Dr. Falconer considered might have belonged to the colossal *E.
meridionalis*. The Yarmouth specimen therefore being the more slender bone and
preserving the constricted upper portion of the foramen ovale of the Mammoth and
Asiatic Elephant belongs no doubt to the former.

9. FEMUR.

It is extremely probable that no long bone of *Elephas antiquus* would display more distinctive characters than its femur. Although fragments of both the shaft and extremities of
thigh bones of large Elephants are contained in the Norwich Museum, it does not appear
to me possible at present to differentiate their characters with certainty. A huge femur
in the Gunn Collection, referred by Falconer [1] to the *Elephas meridionalis*, is from the
FOREST BED. Both the extremities are wanting. The shaft does not seem to have lost
much of its external layers, and gives a girth of 20 inches at the middle. The entire
length of the specimen is about 47 inches. In the latter respect it far eclipses any
femur of the Mammoth I have seen; at the same time, in thickness it is assuredly not
in proportion to the usual robustness of the long bones inferred to belong to *Elephas
antiquus*.

Two distal epiphyses of femora from WALTON in ESSEX are preserved in the Museum
of the Geological Society of London. One of them is recorded by Falconer as belonging
to the *Elephas antiquus*.[2]

It seems, as far as I have been enabled to determine from materials, that the
condyles do not converge closely in the African Elephant *E. Alnaidriensis*,[3] and in the
femora from Walton; and it will be seen by comparing the figures or specimens of the
same bone of *E. Namadicus*[4] that in all there is a pronounced resemblance, whilst in
the Mammoth and *E. Asiaticus* the condyles are more apart.

With reference to the Walton epiphysis, which like its fellow is that of a young or
adolescent Elephant, the internal articular surface is 17 inches in the antero-posterior by
5 inches in the transverse diameter; the external condyle being 14·7 inches by
4·6 inches. The former measurements, of course, include the patellar aspect as well as
the tibial. The greatest length of the Nerbudda Valley femur of *E. Namadicus*,
according to Mr. Prinsep, was no less than 5 feet 3 inches, with a girth at the head
of 2 feet 3 inches, and a breadth across the lower condyles of 11 inches, the latter
measurement being 1·4 inch greater than that of the Walton condyles.

[1] 'Pal. Mem.,' vol. ii, p. 144.
[2] Ibid., vol. i, p. 490; and 'F. A. S.,' pl. liii, fig. 13.
[3] 'Trans. Zool. Soc. London,' vol. ix, pl. xiv, fig. 2 *a*, and p. 60.
[4] 'F. A. S.,' pl. lvi, figs. 1, 5, and 6; and 'Pal. Mem.,' vol. i, pp. 495, 496.

The important distinctions between the proximal extremities in the thigh-bones of the recent species naturally suggest inquiries with reference to the same characters in the extinct forms. In the shorter neck and more shallow digital pit I find an accordance in the femora of *E. Africanus*, *E. Mnaidriensis*, and *E. Namadicus*, whilst the longer neck and deep pit are observable in *E. Asiaticus* and *E. primigenius*. There are no materials, however, available by which these characters can be ascertained in the *E. antiquus* and *E. meridionalis*.

10. PATELLA.

There is a large patella from GRAYS, ESSEX, in the British Museum assigned by Falconer to the *E. antiquus*,[1] and, judging from its massive proportions, it is unlike the bone of the Mammoth; whilst the abundance of teeth of *Elephas antiquus* from that situation render it highly probable that the above belongs to this species.

11. TIBIA.

A huge left tibia, 48,134, B. M., from CAMBERWELL, SURREY, is 26 inches in length. Compared with a left leg bone of Mammoth, 24,581, B. M., from ESCHSCHOLTZ BAY, it is relatively stouter, but seemingly does not present any other distinctive character. The concavities posteriorly for the muscles of the ham are pronounced with sharp outer and inner ridges in the Mammoth, whilst in the above specimens it is shallow, and these ridges are not so angular and do not run down the bones with the distinctness seen in several tibiæ of the Mammoth, but perhaps a series would show this character to be variable. The more slender proportions of the Mammoth's tibia seem to me the only points by which the two species can at present be safely differentiated. As to other species, the tibia of *E. Mnaidriensis* is inferred to have been stout in proportion,[2] and, again, it shows an affinity with the above. These characters I found substantiated in tibiæ of Elephants from the Norfolk Forest Bed in the Norwich Museum. As to *E. meridionalis*, there are fragments of huge tibiæ in the Norwich Museum, and which might be referred to that species, and no doubt comparisons might be instituted between the recorded tibiæ[3] of *E. Namadicus* in the British Museum. The latter, however, are not at present available for study.

[1] 'Pal. Mem.,' vol. i, p. 494; and 'F. A. S.,' pl. lv, fig. 4.
[2] 'Trans. Zool. Soc. London,' vol. ix, p. 62.
[3] 'Pal. Mem.,' vol. i, p. 496; and 'F. A. S.,' pl. lvi, fig. 2.

12. CALCANEUM.

In pl. lv, fig. 2, 'F. A. S.,' Dr. Falconer represents what he supposed to be a left heel bone of *E. antiquus*, from GRAYS, ESSEX. It is No. 21,322, B. M., and differs from several calcanea of the Mammoth and of the Asiatic in having its sides equally compressed, with the peroneal facet *large* and *more protuberant*, in which peculiarities it agrees with the entire calcaneum of *E. Melitensis*.[1] This character is not so pronounced in the African, whereas in the Mammoth and *E. Asiaticus* the hollowing out is greater on the inside than the outside of the heel; and whilst the dorsal aspect is narrow in the Grays specimen and the Maltese heel bone, it is more rounded in the others. The interosseous pit is narrow in the Grays specimen as compared with many examples of the Mammoth, where it is usually triangular.

Two enormous calcanea, Nos. 33,420 and 33,419, B. M., from the Norfolk Coast have more the characters of the Asiatic and Mammoth as regards the projection of the peroneal facet. In the Museum at Norwich there are many heel bones in Mr. Gunn's collection; none, however, are sufficiently entire to show the hollow on either side.

IV. GENERAL SUMMARY AND CONCLUSION.

In summing up the foregoing details relating to the dental and osseous characters whereby we are enabled to differentiate three species of extinct British Elephants, it may be asked whether or not the materials admit of being accepted as the variable elements of one species subject to a range of mutability beyond any precedent in the morphologies of living or extinct members of the genus *Elephas*. When the dental materials are arranged with the view of testing their taxonomic values they will be found to admit of a classification into three very distinct series, which as far as is yet known seem to indicate both in their characters and distribution as many distinct forms of Elephants. This is apparent when their typical last true molars are placed side by side. Thus, the teeth from which the names of *Elephas primigenius*, *E. antiquus*, and *E. meridionalis* have been derived, represent such pronounced differences, that, with the knowledge of the well-known specific characters which distinguish the dental materials of the two living species, there can be no possible reason in not accepting their very divergent aspects as true morphological differences. Again, passing to a consideration of the skeletons in general, whilst we find very close affinities, still there are points

[1] 'Trans. Zool. Soc. London,' vol. ix, pl. xvi, fig. 5.

apparently distinctive of the three forms, and doubtless more extended means of comparison will afford conclusive evidences on that head.

The geological and geographical distributions of these forms as far as known are suggestive, and may admit of greater extension. At present the *Elephas meridionalis* has not been identified in British deposits more recent than the Pre-glacial beds of the Norfolk Coast, where it is associated with the *E. antiquus*, whilst the latter is also found in more recent deposits of Pleistocene age in conjunction with the remains of the *Elephas primigenius*, which has been asserted by several authorities, including the late Dr. Falconer, to be also of Pre-glacial origin.[1] This statement, however, is not clearly proven as far as England is concerned, whereas in Scotland, and probably in one instance in Cavan, Ireland, teeth of the Mammoth are said to have been found below the Boulder Clay.[2] No doubt the future will clear up a great deal of obscurity with reference to the distribution of these forms in space and in time. Suffice it for the present that, whether they merge into one another or into other forms, it is evident that individually these so-called species are subject to considerable variation in the characters of their dental elements, and in particular the form I have attempted to describe in the foregoing pages, the distinguishing features of whose dentition and osteology I shall now finally proceed to recapitulate briefly.

The general features of the incisor teeth have yet to be defined, whether they were straight as has been alleged, or much curved like the more arcuated defensors of the Mammoth, or, as in the Meridional and recent Elephants, they preserved a gentler curve; moreover, the enamel covering of the deciduous incisor of the African and Maltese Elephants has not apparently been observed on the milk-tusk of any other species.

The molars referred to *Elephas antiquus* are, as a rule, both narrower and higher than obtain in the two other British fossil species, whilst the conditions of the worn disk, to wit, the crimping of the machærides, and central expansions and angulations, maintain features broadly distinctive as compared with them. The number of ridges are also characteristic both individually as regards the successional teeth and in the aggregate of the entire laminæ of the dental series. Such are the main points of difference in the dentition, modifications of which lead towards the *Elephas meridionalis* on the one hand, and *E. primigenius* by the broad crown, which in a more pointed degree assimilates to the typical molar of *Elephas Namadicus* of India.

The ante-penultimate, or what is usually named the first, milk molar shows generally a lower ridge formula than that of the Mammoth and Asiatic Elephant, but agrees in this respect with the same tooth in the Meridional and Maltese Elephants; in its general characters we find it comes close to the Maltese forms; whilst that of *E. Namadicus* is unknown.

The second milk molar agrees in outline and characters with the Maltese, only it is

[1] 'Pal. Mem.,' vol. ii, pp. 240 and 586.
[2] Bald, 'Mem. Wernerian Soc.,' vol. iv, pp. 64 and 58.

9

larger, and is usually broadly distinctive as compared with the recent species. Unfortunately I have been unable to compare it with the same tooth of *E. Namadicus*. It is sufficiently variable, and shows considerable diversity both in the ridge formula and sculpturing of the disk.

The last of the milk series being usually subject to considerable discrepancies in all known recent and extinct species of Elephants seems equally if not more various in its ridge formula and dimensions in *Elephas antiquus* than in any other form. Compared with the same tooth in the larger Maltese form and *E. Namadicus*, there is the closest affinities, and the thick-plated, narrow, and broad crowns which characterise the varieties of the molars of *E. antiquus* generally are pronounced in specimens of the ultimate milk tooth.

The first true molar is equally if not more variable than the last, and it is seemingly subject to unusual discrepancies in *Elephas antiquus* both as regards dimensions and the number of ridges. Like the ultimate milk, it has its closest ally in the same tooth of the *E. Namadicus* and *Elephas Mnaidriensis*; the latter, however, is considerably smaller.

The second true molar generally maintains a more equable ridge formula and more constant dimensions than any of the other members of the series, and this is the case to a certain extent in *Elephas antiquus*.

In all respects it is indistinguishable from the same tooth in *E. Namadicus*, and agrees in general features with the second true molar of the *E. Mnaidriensis*, which has a smaller ridge formula, as far as I have been enabled to determine, and is, of course, relatively a much smaller tooth; but the crown patterns of the two are indistinguishable, and it may be likely that second molars of *E. Mnaidriensis* will be found with a numerical expression of the colliculi equal to *E. antiquus*, although I have not met with an instance.

The last true molar, of all others, establishes the dental characteristics of the form of Elephant under consideration far better than any other member of its series. The long narrow crown tapering to a narrow heel posteriorly, with the unusual great height and the well-known worn disk, has been the general accepted molar of *E. antiquus*, and, as far as these peculiarities extend, they are very characteristic; but on viewing a vast number of teeth, and on becoming habituated to a manipulation of them, one will soon perceive the divergencies before referred to, which are traceable in every member of the dental series. Confining my observations to collections from the Norfolk Forest Bed and the fluviatile deposits of the Thames Valley between Grays Thurrock and Oxford, I find a broad crown with closely packed ridges, faintly crimped, and not displaying the central expansion and angulation to the extent observed in the long narrow crown. This type represents the usual molar of *E. Namadicus*, and is seen in the Maltese forms, which, strange to say, present the same three varieties of crown in very much smaller teeth. The broad-crowned variety can be traced gradually merging into either a thick-plated or a narrow crown, which again as gradually assumes the character of the open disk of the African Elephant. I again refer to the probability that these different varieties of crown may be sexual or individual characters, inasmuch as they have been found in the same deposits and often associated. At the same time the possibility of local varieties is quite admissible, and the divergence of the broad crown into the tooth of the *Elephas primigenius*, on the one hand, and the thick rhomb-like disk into that of the molar of *E. Africanus*, is also a possible contingency, neither of which, however, can be safely accepted as evidences of the genesis of either species, at all events, without a more extended comparison with the other extinct forms.

As to *Elephas Namadicus*, it seems to me, as far as its dentition extends, to be indistinguishable from *Elephas antiquus*; indeed, Dr. Falconer appears to have been constantly impressed with the relationship, and had he lived to carry out the brilliant researches with which his name is so intimately associated, it appears to me that, with all his bias in favour of the immutability of species, the conclusion I have come to must at length have been forced upon him.

The last true molar of the largest Maltese form is a miniature of the same tooth in the *Elephas antiquus*, with a ridge formula only equal to the second true molar of the latter; so that whilst the two go hand in hand in respect to ridge formula and crown pattern from the first milk to the first true molar, they seemingly differ in regard to the two remaining members of the series. These differences, however, may not be constant, although I found them general in a number of specimens of the ultimate molar of *Elephas Mnaidriensis*. No doubt, however, future researches in Southern Europe and eastwards will develop many seemingly discordant points in connection with *Elephas antiquus* and allied forms.

The uncertainty in regard to the bones ascribed to *Elephas antiquus* render the foregoing observations on its osteology of little value. As regards the relative dimensions of maxillæ and mandibles, it would seem that ordinarily they do not differ materially, especially in young and adolescent individuals, from those found with similar stages of growth in the Asiatic and African Elephants; and, whilst aged individuals attained to colossal proportions, the usual adult may have not averaged over 11 feet in height, or, perhaps, a little over the larger individuals of the African Elephants, which rarely exceeds 12 feet at the shoulder. The mandible, being the only available portion of the skull of *Elephas antiquus* in any way entire, presents the general characters of the African, as far as the contour of the horizontal and ascending rami are concerned, whilst the diasteme is more erect and the chin somewhat rounded, but not to the same extent observed in the Mammoth, which again bears a close resemblance in its mandible to the Asiatic Elephant, as it does generally in the other bones of the skeleton.

The general resemblances between the mandibles of *Elephas antiquus, E. Namadicus*, and *E. Mnaidriensis* are pronounced, whilst *E. meridionalis* has more in common with *E. Africanus*.

As regards the long bones, it would seem that as compared with the Mammoth the humerus and femur are stouter in *E. antiquus*; and this stoutness was, doubtless, the main feature in its general outline. At the same time the *E. meridionalis* was not only of colossal dimensions, but, judging from the relative thickness of its bones, presented a like proportional stoutness, so that it is impossible at present to say to which form the Elephantine bones from the Forest Bed belong, as teeth of the two species are often found together. Indeed, the relative connections between varieties of the broad crown of the molar of *E. antiquus*, and certain teeth ascribed to *E. meridionalis*, are striking and cannot be determined with certainty until the dentition and osteology of the latter have been carefully worked out.

It seems apparent from the data here advanced that the Proboscidian, to which the name *Elephas antiquus* has been given, lived in Britain before the Glacial epoch along with an allied form, *E. meridionalis*, and that both, judging from the quantities of their remains met with in Southern Europe, were southern and probably eastern forms with pedigrees extending backwards into Miocene times, as shadowed forth by their congeners from the deposits of Northern India.

It is further established that the *Elephas antiquus* survived the Ice Age, and flourished subsequently along with the Mammoth on British soil. Unlike the latter, it has not hitherto been traced to the Arctic regions nor to North America; perhaps it was not suited for boreal regions, and may have only so journeyed in England after the cold period had passed away. That it was a distinct species or form from the Mammoth cannot, I think, be doubted; at all events, the dental and apparently the osteological characters are as broadly distinctive as those which obtain between the two species now living in Asia and Africa.

PLATE I.

Figs. 1 and 1 *a*.   Crown and profile of No. 21,654, British Museum, a right upper ante-penultimate milk molar, from Grays Thurrock, Essex.   (Natural size.)

Figs. 2 and 2 *a*.   Crown and profile of a left lower ante-penultimate milk molar, from Victoria Cave, Settle, Yorkshire.   (Natural size.)

Fig. 3.   Crown of a right lower penultimate milk molar, No. 18,810, British Museum, from Grays Thurrock, Essex.   (Natural size.)

Fig. 4.   Palate, with crown views of third milk molar, No. 21,301, British Museum, from Grays Thurrock, Essex.   (Natural size).

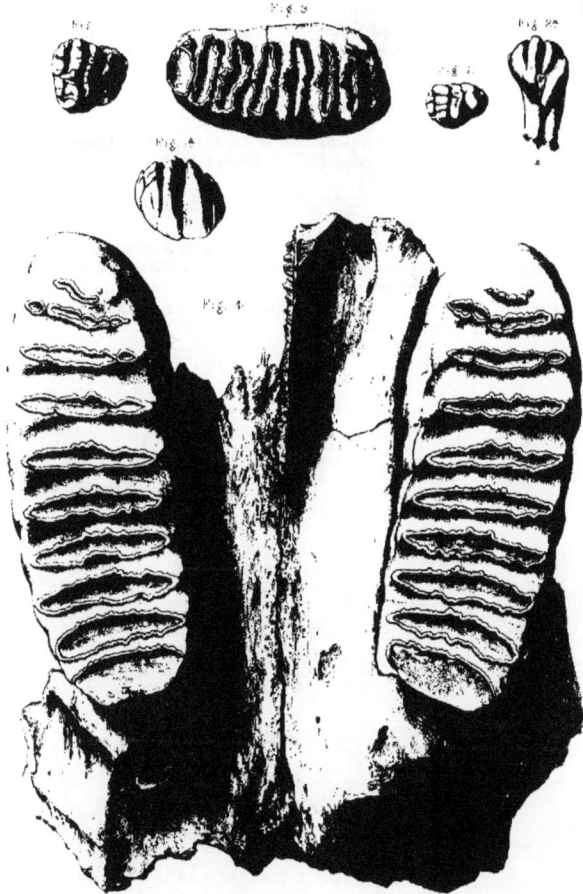

PLATE II.

Fig. 1. Profile of a right upper second true molar, No. $\frac{23,717}{}$, British Museum, from Slade Green, Erith, Essex. (Half natural size.)

Fig. 2. Crown view of a left upper last true molar, No. 28,118, British Museum, from Grays Thurrock, Essex. (Half natural size.)

Figs. 3 and 3 *a*. Crown and profile views of No. 47,121, British Museum, a right upper last true molar, from Peterborough. (Half natural size.)

I have just been shown (January, 1877), but too late for description in the text, a very characteristic left upper molar, almost entire, by Professor Ramsay, F.R.S., Director-General of the Geological Survey, who lately discovered it in a marine deposit near the sea-gate of Tangier. It is of the narrow-crowned variety, like the tooth from Gibraltar, which was also found in a marine deposit.

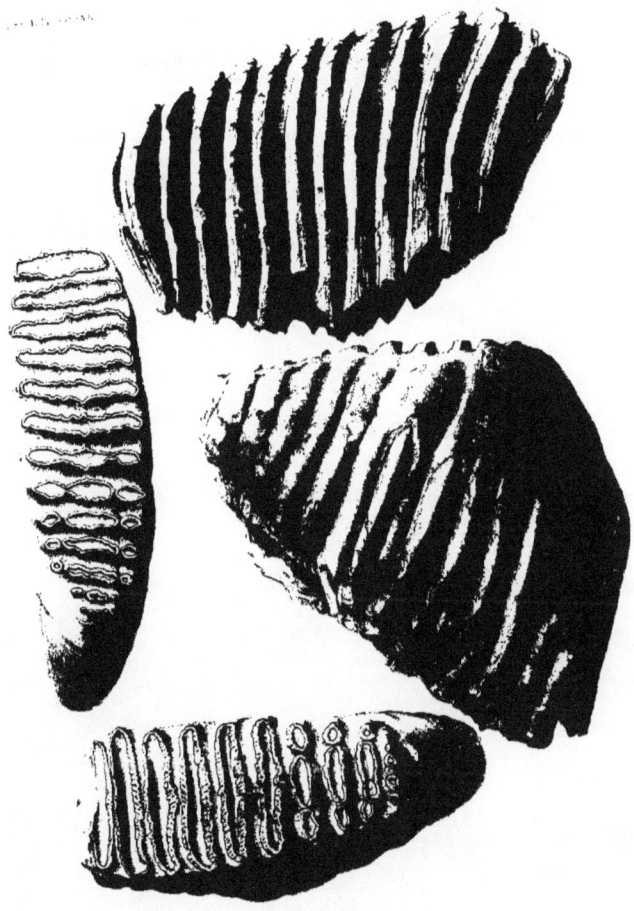

Figs. 1 and 1 *a*. Crown and profile of No. 47,119, British Museum, a left lower last true molar, from Cromer, Norfolk. (Half natural size.)

Fig. 2. Crown of No. 37,241, British Museum, a right upper first true molar, dredged from the bed of the German Ocean, Happisborough, Norfolk. (Natural size.)

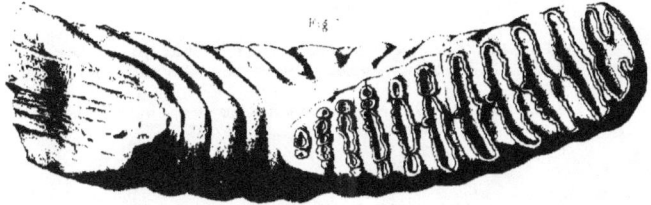

Fig. 7

b nat size   Fig. 8

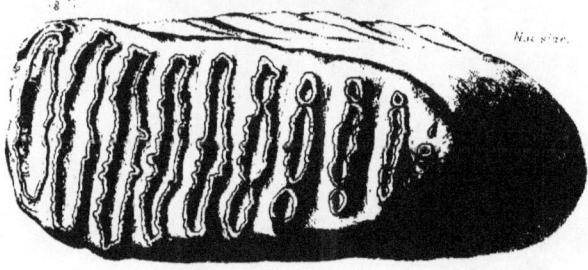

Fig. 9   Nat size.

PLATE IV.

Figs. 1 and 1 a. Crown and profile of No. 27,907, British Museum, a right lower last true molar, from the freshwater deposits at Clacton, Essex. (Half natural size.)

Fig. 2. Crown of 22,017, British Museum, a right upper second true molar, from Grays Thurrock, Essex. (Natural size.)

Fig. 9

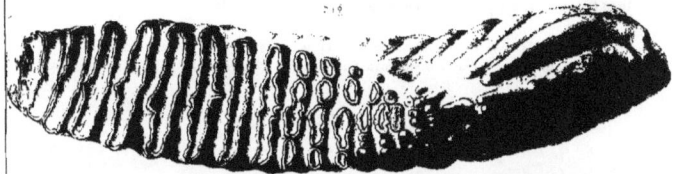

Fig. 8

Fig. 10

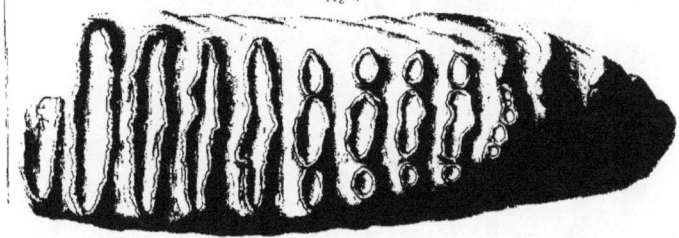

PLATE V.

Fig. 1. Crown view of No. 27,907, British Museum, a right upper last true molar, from the freshwater deposits, Clacton, Essex. (Natural size.)

Fig. 2. Portion of the left ramus of a lower jaw, No. 21,310, British Museum, from Ilford, Essex, containing a penultimate milk molar. (Natural size.)

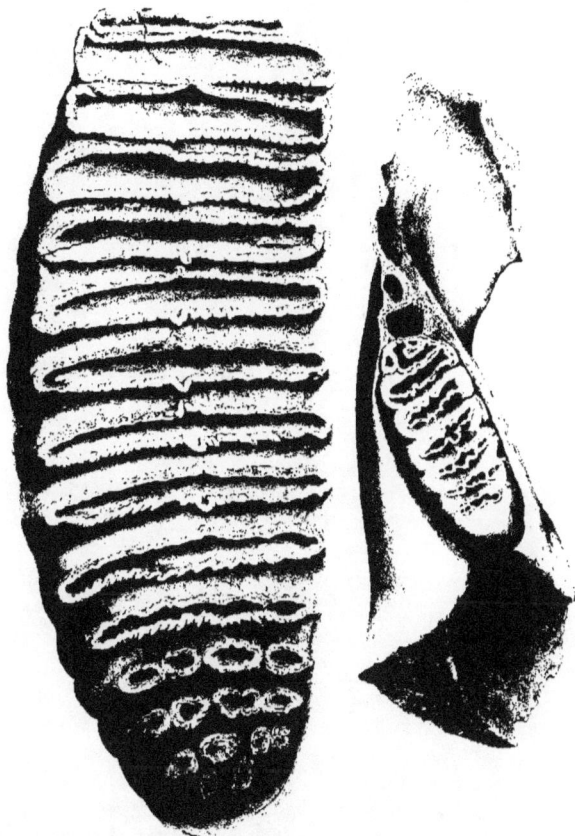

THE

PALÆONTOGRAPHICAL SOCIETY.

INSTITUTED MDCCCXLVII.

VOLUME FOR 1879.

LONDON:
MDCCCLXXIX.

MONOGRAPH

ON THE

BRITISH FOSSIL

ELEPHANTS.

BY

A. LEITH ADAMS, M.A., M.B., F.R.S., F.G.S.,

PROFESSOR OF NATURAL HISTORY IN THE QUEEN'S COLLEGE, CORK.

PART II.

DENTITION AND OSTEOLOGY OF ELEPHAS PRIMIGENIUS
(*Blumenbach*).

Pages 69—146; Plates VI—XV.

LONDON:

PRINTED FOR THE PALÆONTOGRAPHICAL SOCIETY.

1879.

MONOGRAPH

ON THE

BRITISH FOSSIL ELEPHANTS.

ELEPHAS PRIMIGENIUS.

I.—INTRODUCTORY.

THE vast quantities of remains of the Mammoth, *Elephas primigenius* (Blumenbach), discovered of late years in and around the British Islands represent almost every element of the skeleton, and therefore afford sufficient materials for the descriptive osteology of the species. On that account I propose in the following Monograph to describe, first, the Axial, and, secondly, the Appendicular Skeleton.

The early history of the discovery of Elephantine remains in the British Islands and elsewhere is fully recorded in the works of Cuvier, De Blainville, Bronn, Owen, and Falconer. The confusion and uncertainty, however, arising from the belief in the unity of the species which, with the exception of Falconer, was maintained more or less by these and other comparative anatomists, make many of the records so far valueless, inasmuch as wherever the data do not clearly indicate the characters of specimens it must remain doubtful whether they refer to *Elephas primigenius E. antiquus*, or *Elephas meridionalis*.

II.—DISTRIBUTION.

Remains of *Elephas primigenius* have turned up in many localities in England, and have been found so frequently associated with *E. antiquus*, that in the absence of proper confirmation I will only enumerate the instances known either to myself or to geologists and palæontologists experienced in manipulating molars of fossil Elephants.

10

I have availed myself largely of Professor Boyd Dawkins' List,[1] and he has kindly revised my notes on the Distribution, and has added some localities previously unknown to me.

The foreign distribution might doubtless be very greatly extended if all the localities of specimens in European Museums were recorded. Indeed, the following is by no means advanced as a complete list, but I believe it will be found accurate as far as it extends. I have made distinctions between (1) remains from RIVER, VALLEY, and ALLUVIAL DEPOSITS, (2) remains from CAVERNS, and (3) DREDGED specimens.

1. *Remains from River, Valley, and Alluvial Deposits.*

Neither CORNWALL nor DEVON, as far as known to me, have produced any remains of the Mammoth from their river, gravel, and surface deposits.

In SOMERSETSHIRE, remains have been met with at HINTON (Mus. Roy. Coll. Surg. of England), LARKHALL and HARTLIP (Mus. Geol. Surv.),[2] LOXBROOK, ST. AUDRIES, WESTON-SUPER-MARE, CHEDZOY, FRESHFORD (Dawkins).

In GLOUCESTER, at Gloucester (Dawkins), BARNWOOD (Dawkins), BECKFORD (Dawkins), STROUD (Dawkins), TEWKESBURY (Owen).

In DORSETSHIRE, at BRIDPORT (Mus. Geol. Surv.), PORTLAND FISSURE (Busk, Mus. Geol. Soc. London).

In HANTS, in GALE BAY[3] (B. M.), NEWTON (Woodwardian Mus. and Mus. Geol. Surv.).

In WILTS, at CHRISTIAN MALFORD (Oxon. Mus.), FISHERTON (Blackmore and Sanford), MILFORD HILL, near SALISBURY (Blackmore).

In BERKS, at MAIDENHEAD and TAPLOW (Wood. Mus.), READING, HURLEY BOTTOM (Oxon. Mus.).

In OXFORDSHIRE, at YARNTON, "in gravel," BED of CHERWELL, City of OXFORD, "in gravel," WYTHAM and CULHAM, "in gravel" (Oxon. Mus.).

In ESSEX, at LEXDEN (B. M., Wood. Mus., Mus. Geol. Surv.), ORFORD, HEDDINGHAM, LAMARSH, "railway cutting," ISLE OF DOGS (B. M.), WALTON-ON-THE-NAZE (Wood. Mus.), ILFORD (B. M., and Mus. Geol. Surv.), WENDEN (Mus. Geol. Surv.), HARWICH (B. M.), COLCHESTER (Dawkins), BALLINGDON (B. M.), WALTHAMSTOW (B. M.).

In HERTS, at CAMP'S HILL (Dawkins).

In SUSSEX, at BRACKLESHAM BAY, "raised bench" (B. M.), BRIGHTON, "gravel

[1] " British Post-Glacial Mammals," ' Quart. Journ. Geol. Soc.,' vol. xxv, p. 196.

[2] The Museum of the Geological Survey being incorporated with that of Practical Geology the two terms when used here must be considered synonymous.

[3] I cannot find out whether this specimen was dredged or found on dry land.

and raised beach " (B. M. and Mus. Geol. Surv.), LEWES, VALLEY OF ARUN, PAGHAM (Dawkins).

In SUFFOLK, at IPSWICH "railway cutting " (B. M.), HOXNE (Dawkins).

In NORFOLK, at BACTON, CROMER (B. M.), YARMOUTH (Owen).

In CAMBRIDGE, at BARRINGTON, "gravel," BARNWELL, CHESTERTON, GREAT SHELFORD, BARTON, WESTWICK, HALL (Wood. Mus.).

In HUNTINGDONSHIRE, at HUNTINGDON, "railway cutting" (B. M.), ST. NEOT's, (Wood. Mus.).

In BEDFORDSHIRE, at LEIGHTON BUZZARD (Oxon. Mus.).

In MIDDLESEX, at LONDON, under various streets, &c., to wit, ST. JAMES's SQUARE, PALL MALL, KENSINGTON, BATTERSEA, HAMMERSMITH, &c., "in river gravel" (B. M. and Mus. Geol. Surv.), TURNHAM GREEN (Busk), Bed of Thames at MILLBANK, BRENT-FORD, KEW, ACTON, CLAPTON, &c. (B. M.), THAMES, near LONDON (Owen), KINGSLAND (Owen).

In SURREY, at WALLINGTON, TOOTING (B. M.), PECKHAM (B. M.), DORKING, PEASEMARSH, near GUILDFORD (Prestwich).

In KENT, at CRAYFORD, ERITH (B. M. and Mus. Geol. Surv.), DARTFORD, AYLESFORD, HARTLIP, OTTERHAM (Mus. Geol. Surv. and B. M.), ISLE OF SHEPPEY, BROUGHTON FISSURE, MEDWAY (B. M.), SITTINGBOURNE (Mus. Geol. Surv.), NEWINGTON, GREEN STREET GREEN, BROMLEY (Dawkins), WHITSTABLE (Dawkins).

In BUCKS, at FENNY STRATFORD (B.M.).

In NORTHAMPTONSHIRE, at OUNDLE, KETTERING, NORTHAMPTON (B. M.).

In WARWICKSHIRE, at RUGBY, WELLESBOURNE, LAWFORD (B. M.), BROMWICH HILL, HALSTON (Dawkins), NEWNAN (Buckland).

In WORCESTERSHIRE, in STOUR VALLEY (B. M.), DROITWICH, BANKS OF AVON, FLADBURY, MALVERN (Dawkins).

In LEICESTERSHIRE, at KIRBY PARK "gravel" (Wood. Mus.).

In STAFFORDSHIRE, at COPEN HALL (Dawkins), TRENTHAM (Buckland).

In CHESHIRE, at NORTHWICH ["pre-glacial," Dawkins).

In LINCOLNSHIRE, at SPALDING (B. M.).

In YORKSHIRE, at WHITBY, ALDBOROUGH, GRISTHORPE BAY[1] (Wood. Mus.), HARS-WELL, Leeds (Dawkins), BIELBECKS (Phillips), BRANDSBURTON (Dawkins), MIDDLETON, OVERTON, ALWICK, HORNSEA (Owen).

In HEREFORDSHIRE, at KINOSLAND (Falconer).

The remains of Mammoth from glacial and other deposits in Scotland are as follows :

1. In AYRSHIRE, at KILMAURS "peaty clay," "pre-glacial " (Bryce), "Inter-glacial " (Geikie).

2. Between EDINBURGH and FALKIRK.

3. CHAPEL HALL in LANARKSHIRE, and BISHOPBRIGGS.

[1] Not stated whether dredged or from dry land.

4. At CLIFTON HALL.

In IRELAND, remains of the Mammoth have been found in lacustrine deposits at BELTURBET in CAVAN.

In ANTRIM, at CORNCASTLE, "marine deposit."[1]

In WATERFORD, near WHITECHURCH (somewhat doubtful).[2]

2. *Caverns.*

The following caverns have produced remains of the Mammoth.

DEVONSHIRE, KENT'S CAVERN (B. M., and Mus. Torquay), ORESTON (B. M.), BEACH CAVE (Sanford), BRIXHAM (Busk).

SOMERSET, in HUTTON CAVE and a CAVERN, near WELLS (B. M.), WOOKEY HOLE (B. M.), BLEADON CAVE (Falconer), BOX HILL, near BATH (Dawkins), DURDHAM DOWN (Falconer), SANDFORD HILL (Dawkins).

KENT, in BOUGHTON CAVE near MAIDSTONE (B. M., and Mus. Geol. Soc.).

NOTTS, in CHURCH HOLE (Dawkins).

DERBYSHIRE, in CRESWELL CRAGS (Dawkins, Busk), ROBIN HOOD CAVE (Dawkins), CHURCH HOLE (Dawkins).

GLAMORGAN, in LONG HOLE, SPRITSAIL TOR, PAVILAND (Falconer).

CARMARTHEN, in COYGAN CAVE (Dawkins).

WATERFORD, in SHANDON CAVE (Carte, Mus. Science and Art, Dublin).

3. *Submarine and Littoral Deposits.*

The coast-line and bed of the German Ocean, extending along the shores of Norfolk and Suffolk, and especially the well-known locality where the so-called "Forest Bed" is traced, presents remarkably interesting features with reference to the range of the Mammoth in Time.

This subject has been discussed by Falconer and Dawkins ; the latter, in an exhaustive memoir,[3] shows that the teeth and bones said to have been derived from the Forest Bed had never been found *in sitû*, and this view is still maintained by the Rev. J. Gunn, F.G.S., who has informed me that his latest experiences give him no cause to alter his views on that head. Molars of the Mammoth have been found on the Norfolk coast, either at low water, or dredged, either alone or with teeth of *E. antiquus* and *E. meridionalis.* However, all the three have been discovered encrusted with the same description of matrix which forms a component of the Forest Bed. At the same time, as pointed out by Gunn, Dawkins, Clement Reid, and others, precisely the same mineral characters prevail in beds which overlie glacial deposits in the above situation ; therefore the evidence of the

[1] Adams, 'Proc. Roy. Irish Acad.,' vol. iii (2nd series), p. 93.

[2] Harkness, 'Geol. Mag.,' vol. vii, p. 2.   [3] 'Geol. Mag.,' vol. v, p. 316.

Mammoth having lived during pre-glacial periods has not been established by the specimens from the coast of Norfolk, at all events as far as the instances hitherto recorded are concerned.

Professor Boyd Dawkins, in a communication made to the Geological Society, as late as November, 1878, recants his former opinions and returns to the belief that the Mammoth was *pre*-glacial. This view he maintains on the above-mentioned evidences from the Forest Bed and other bygone and hitherto disputed statements, supported by a discovery lately made [1] in making a boring at Northwich, in Cheshire. This latter piece of evidence is, however, like the others, faulty, from the absence of direct proofs as to, 1st. The exact stratigraphical horizon; 2ndly. The age of the deposits; and 3rdly, the mode by which the information was obtained.

Admitting, indeed, that I feel almost assured the Mammoth preceded the Ice Age, yet in all justice to facts it appears to me that this verdict stands at present " not proven." I am not aware of marine or littoral discoveries north of the DOGGER BANK, which, however, has yielded to the dredge enormous quantities of bones and teeth in conjunction with relics of other Pleistocene Mammals. A large collection, made by Mr. Owles from the above situation, has been just lately acquired for the British Museum.[2] It represents almost every stage of growth from the adolescent to the aged; and the grinders, as will be noticed in the sequel, are interesting, as they accord closer with the characters of ARCTIC and the so-called Mammoth molars from the UNITED STATES, rather than with the thick-plated tooth from the fluviatile deposits of ILFORD, in the Thames Valley.

It would be tedious and unnecessary to enumerate the various points on the East Coast where remains of the Mammoth have turned up, more especially in the case of the majority of Forest Bed fossils, which are " waifs and strays," cast up and rolled about by the waves. Numbers of teeth and tusks have been dredged as far eastwards as trawlers and oyster-dredgers proceed off YARMOUTH, HARWICH, &c.[3] The channel of BRIGHTLINGSEA has been also prolific of specimens. My distinguished friend Dr. Bree, of Colchester, has a collection made, from ten miles off DUNKIRK, where, he informs me, the sea-bottom is so full of Mammalian fossils that sailors call it the " Burying Ground." The discoveries along the English Channel have not been so numerous, but teeth have been dredged on

[1] ' Geol. Soc. Abstracts and Proc.,' No. 357, p. 2.

[2] Davies, ' Geol. Mag.,' vol. v, p. 77. The National Collection now contains, perhaps, the most extensive assortment of extinct proboscidean remains ever brought together under the same roof. This I feel amply justified in stating, from personal observation, has been owing in no small degree to the discernment of my friend Mr. W. Davies, F.G.S., whose intimate knowledge of fossil zoology is always at the service of whomsoever seeks for information in the galleries under his immediate supervision. I, therefore, who have oftentimes been benefited by his accurate and painstaking discriminations, take this opportunity of recording the valuable assistance I have received from Mr. Davies in the working up of the materials for this Memoir and my previous Monograph on the *Elephas antiquus*.

[3] ' Brit. Fossil Mammals,' p. 246, *et seq.*

a submerged forest as far west as Torquay,[1] in Devonshire. A mandible with molars is in the British Museum, from the Harbour of Holyhead;[2] and I lately was shown by Mr. Davies a humerus obtained by the Earl of Enniskillen from the Bay of Galway, which is the most western point in the European distribution of the species.

FOREIGN DISTRIBUTION.

The Mammoth has left its remains in the valley gravels and many caverns throughout France,[3] and has been traced to Northern Spain.[4]

Dr. Falconer identified molars from the neighbourhood of Rome and northwards towards the Alps. Its remains have turned up in Switzerland, Austro-Hungary, Germany, the Netherlands, Holland, and Central and Northern Russia,[5] but not, as far as I am aware, in Denmark, Norway, nor Sweden. The identity of the species whose remains have been discovered in the Crimea, Odessa, Black Sea, and Bosphorus, together with the so-called *E. Armeniacus*, from Turkey in Asia, requires further investigation.[6] The close affinities of molars of the latter with those of *E. Asiaticus*, on the one hand, and *E. Columbi* on the other, require more extended comparisons.

The South-European extension of the Mammoth is far greater than its cuticular covering has led naturalists to suppose. Falconer has confirmed its presence from deposits around Rome, and I have examined molars from near Santander in Spain; but, excepting the somewhat doubtful molar referred to in the sequel, from the Black Sea, I know of no instance from the lands or islands of the Mediterranean area, and its eastward extension.

The continual discoveries of remains along the shores and river-valleys of Siberia, Behrings Straits, and Alaska, are too well known to need me to make special records of these localities. Until just lately European palæontologists, reasoning from the following data, believed that the Mammoth had been traced as far south as Texas. But Professor Marsh, who informs me that his authority for the following statement is Dr. Leidy, states that "this species does not appear to have extended east of the Rocky Mountains, or south of the Columbia River, but was replaced there by the American Elephant, which preferred a milder climate. Remains of the latter have been met with in Canada, throughout the United Sates, and in Mexico."[7] Notwithstanding this

1 Lyell's ' Principles of Geology,' vol. i, p. 514.
2 Ib., vol. i, p. 545.
3 Cuvier, De Blainville, Lartet, Lortet, Chantre, &c.
4 Adams, ' Journ. Geol. Soc. Lond.,' vol xxiii, p. 537.
5 See Falconer's essay " On Range of Time and Earliest Headquarters of the Mammoth," ' Pal. Mem.,' ii, 239, &c.; ' Geology of Russia,' vol. i, p. 492.
6 Demidoff, ' Voy. dans la Russie Méridionale,' vol. ii ; Falconer, *op. cit.*
7 " Introduction and Succession of Vertebrate Life in America. An address delivered before the

statement, Orton refers to Mastodon and Mammoth remains having been found associated in an old forest-bed, some twenty to forty feet below the present level of the Ohio.[1] This opinion resolves itself into a matter of careful observation, so that unless critical attention had been paid to the study of Elephantine remains, associated with much practical experience in the manipulation of specimens, the molars of *E. primigenius* might have been mistaken for those of its ally, the American Elephant.

The question as to the North-American distribution of the Mammoth would, therefore, appear at present not to be precisely determined; it seems necessary, therefore, to refer more fully to the materials on which European palæontologists have based their conclusions. Cuvier, Owen, De Blainville, and Falconer confirm each other's diagnosis from the specimens in the INSTITUTE OF FRANCE, BRITISH MUSEUM, MUSEUM OF THE ROYAL COLLEGE OF SURGEONS OF ENGLAND, and WOODWARDIAN MUSEUM, CAMBRIDGE, and I have carefully, with the exception of the French, examined all the specimens. They are said to be from various parts of the UNITED STATES, to wit, OHIO (BIG BONE LICK), KENTUCKY, MISSOURI, CAROLINA, and TEXAS.

All show precisely the same mineral characters, being black and deeply stained like the remains of Mastodon from Ohio, just as if they had lain long in peat. The dental characters are precisely similar to, and indistinguishable from crowns of Arctic molars, that is, they display the very *thin* enamel and *crowded* discs which, with few exceptions, characterise the molars from Northern Asia and Arctic America.

Now, if a fraud had been practised, it must have been extensive, from the great numbers of specimens in the English and French museums. Moreover, the donations to the French Institute, we are told by Cuvier, were made by the President of the United States,[2] but the English specimens seemed to have been acquired by purchase.[3]

The discovery, in 1863, in " sand and gravel " at HAMILTON, on the banks of LAKE ONTARIO, of molars and mandibles of Elephants has been referred to by Mr. Billings and by Falconer.[4] The former arrived at an opinion that the species was distinct from

American Association for the Advancement of Science, 1877." Dana is of opinion that the Canadian Elephant was the Mammoth—' Manual of Geology,' p. 563.

[1] 'Report on the Geol. Survey of Ohio,' vol. i, p. 428. It is possible, however, that this Elephant may have been *E. Columbi*.

[2] 'Ossemens Fossiles,' vol. ii, p. 148, pl. xv, figs. 9 and 11.

[3] I am indebted to my friend Professor Flower, LL.D., for the following record relating to the purchase of the specimens for the Museum of the Royal College of Surgeons of England. A printed list is preserved in the Library of the College of the sale, which took place at Stevens's Auction Rooms in the year 1835. Referring to the Elephant's teeth and bones it is stated that the "bones were said to be found twenty-two feet below the surface at Big Bone Lick, in Boone County, State of Kentucky, in the autumn of 1830, dug up by B. Finnel and others. Big Bone Lick lies back from the Ohio River about ten or twelve miles, and about sixty miles below Cincinnati. Brought from North America by Mr. Ingham, of Kentucky."

[4] 'Geological Survey of Canada,' p. 914, figs. 495 to 498 ; Falconer, 'Pal. Mem.,' vol. ii, 239.

the Mammoth on account of the chin being narrower, whilst the teeth resembled the
crown of the latter.

As far as the indifferent representations of these teeth will permit me to judge, the
molars and mandibles seem indistinguishable from the same parts of the Mammoth, the
symphysial junction of whose rami, as will appear in the subsequent woodcuts, is not always
of the truncated and rounded character usually distinctive of the typical lower jaw. The
thin parallel plates also consort with crowns of that species. The same might be said of
three rudely executed representations of mandibles and molars under the name of
E. Jacksoni.[1]

The distribution, therefore, of the Mammoth in North America, as defined by Marsh
and Leidy, is quite opposed to that indicated by the reputed remains from the United
States in European collections, and I must admit, without prejudice to either view, that
although the specimens I have examined bear striking resemblances in external colora-
tion to Mastodon remains from the swamps of Ohio, they likewise resemble, in that
respect, specimens from the frozen soil of the Arctic regions, and still more so in their
closely packed and attenuated ridges. I must leave the subject, therefore, of the North
American distribution of the Mammoth for further confirmation. A Monograph on the
fossil Elephants of North America, compiled from specimens in museums and private
collections, is, indeed, a desideratum which, it is hoped, the able and indefatigable
palæontologists of the New World will not defer much longer.

Associated Mammals.

Reference has been made in my Monograph on *E. antiquus* to the British localities where
remains of the Mammoth have been associated with the latter species;[2] the only difficulty
at present is the contemporaneity of the Mammoth with *E. meridionalis*. I am not aware
of one instance of the relics of these two Elephants having been found together on the
Continent of Europe or elsewhere, whilst their so-called contemporaneity, as far as the
British Islands are concerned, requires apparently further confirmation. The Mammoth
has been found associated with nearly all the British Post-tertiary and many of the
Recent Mammals.[3] It survived up to the Stone Age in England and on the Continent
of Europe.[4]

[1] Silliman's 'American Journal,' vol. xxxiv, p. 363.
[2] Page 6.
[3] Dawkins, 'Quart. Journ. Geol. Soc. London,' vol. xxv, p. 194.
[4] Dawkins, 'Quart. Journ. Geol. Soc.,' vol. xxxiii, p. 590. The famous etching on the fragment of a
tusk in the cave of La Madelaine in the Dordogne (see *Reliquiæ Aquitanicæ*, also British Bone Caverns, &c.).

III.—DENTITION.

The differentiation of three species of Elephants from remains found in the fossil state in Great Britain was not fully admitted until the labours of the late Dr. Falconer, F.R.S., became generally known. Professor Owen, whilst impressed with the remarkable differences in the dental characters of remains referable to the *Elephas primigenius*, was not then (1846) prepared to consider them as indicative of more than one species.[1] The precise descriptions and beautiful illustrations of the varieties of molar teeth represented in the work of that illustrious comparative anatomist could not otherwise than arrest the attention of palæontologists, and of all others the distinguished naturalist above mentioned, whose famous discoveries in the Sewalik Hills had made him familiar with the dentition of extinct Proboscidea.

The remarkable essay published by Dr. Falconer on the SPECIES OF MASTODON and ELEPHANT occurring in the FOSSIL STATE in GREAT BRITAIN was commenced in 1857,[2] but he did not live to complete the latter part, referring to *Elephas primigenius*, and the entire description of *Elephas antiquus* is wanting.[3]

Every student of extinct forms of animal life is familiar with Falconer's classification of the Proboscidea, based on the characters of their molar teeth, and of his methods of constructing the ridge-formulæ characteristic of the various sub-genera and species. The terms "isomerous," "anisomerous," and "hypisomerous," used by him to distinguish the specific characters, although not advanced as mathematically exact in every case, being, as the author states, "liable to vary within certain limits dependent on the race, sex, and size of the individual, but it may safely be asserted that the numbers are never transposed or reversed, *i. e.* the younger tooth among the 'intermediate molars' never normally exhibit in the same individual a higher number than the older."[4] As an example, in the members of the sub-genus *Euelephas*, and notably the *Elephas primigenius* and *Elephas Asiaticus*, the ciphers of whose molars, he states, are precisely alike in number, he formulates their ridges in upper and lower teeth thus :— 4+8+12 :: 12+16+24, showing that, with the exception of the first and ultimate true molars, the others increase by increments of 4, or, as he terms it, by an "anisomerous mode of progression." But, as will appear in the sequel, it is by no means easy to determine what ciphers should even fairly represent the average number of ridges in certain

[1] 'British Fossil Mammals,' p. 243.
[2] 'Quart. Journ. Geol. Soc. of London,' vols. xiii, xiv, and xxi.
[3] In the 'Palæontological Memoirs' of the late Dr. Falconer the editor has appended certain "note-book entries" to the end of the essay on *Elephas primigenius.*—' Pal. Mem.,' vol. ii, p. 172.
[4] 'Pal. Mem.,' vol. ii, p. 10.

11

members of the dental series, the range of variability being often so great that the average of a given number of specimens is no reliable exponent of the numbers and variations to which the tooth is subject.

A similar conclusion was come to by me with reference to the dental series of *E. antiquus*; and therefore, as in the latter case, I am compelled to believe that the only true method of expressing the ridge-formula of elephantine molars is by giving the minimum, mean, and maximum number of ridges of each member of the dental series.

Therefore, Dr. Falconer's method of demonstrating the ridge-formulæ of his sub-genus *Euelephas* by progressive increments of 4, or anisomerous ciphers, seems to me both arbitrary and dogmatical. It is, in fact, too absolute a method, and is at variance with the laws of mutability of species, which advancing knowledge shows is far greater than has been supposed.

In the Synoptical Table of the Species of Mastodon and Elephant Dr. Falconer distinguishes the worn crowns of molars of *E. primigenius* from the teeth of all other known living or extinct species thus:—" Colliculi confertissimi, adamante valde attenuato, machæridibus vix undulatis."[1]

Cuvier had previously established broad marks of distinction between the molar of the Mammoth and that of the Asiatic Elephant, with whose skeleton generally he had noted certain well-marked affinities. But although more experienced than, perhaps, any of his contemporaries and predecessors, as far as the manipulation of remains of extinct Elephants was concerned, he applied the specific name of *Elephas primigenius* to all the fossil Elephant remains discovered in his time, and previously, in Europe, Arctic Asia, and North America. It is but justice, however, to his great name, and also to the credit of several of his successors, to remember that the light which shone dimly on them by reason of scanty data shines now brightly on account of the enormous amount of materials accumulated even since the publication of the ' British Fossil Mammals.'

The molar crown of the Mammoth is distinguishable from that of other and allied species by the—1, great breadth of the crown as compared with the length; 2, the narrowness of the ridges; 3, the crowding or close approximation of the ridges; 4, the tenuity of the enamel; 5, the absence of crimping.[2]

These characters combined suffice to distinguish the grinder from that of its near allies, such as of the *E. Asiaticus*, *E. antiquus*, and *E. meridionalis*.

With reference to (1) the great breadth of the crown. This character, although also present in *E. meridionalis*, is distinctive of the Mammoth as compared with the other two species, to which may be added the *Elephas Columbi*, with whose remains it is said to

[1] ' Quart. Journ. Geol. Soc. Lond.,' vol. xiii, p. 319; also ' Pal. Mem.,' vol. ii, p. 14. As in the case of *Elephas antiquus*, I shall refer to these essays in his Memoirs, for the reason that they are published together, and are, therefore, more convenient for reference.
[2] I have adopted the same terms used in my Monograph on *Elephas antiquus*. All enamelled laminæ, whether plates or talons, are indiscriminately named *ridges*. A colliculus is an *unworn ridge*. The letter *x* stands for *talon* as opposed to *plate*.

have been found associated in North America, and also with *Elephas Armeniacus*, which is closely allied, if not identical in its dental characters, with *E. Columbi* and *E. Asiaticus*. The affinity between the Mammoth and certain Miocene (?) Sewalik species will be referred to in the sequel. According to Falconer, it belonged to the " EURYCORONINE " series of his sub-genus EUELEPHAS.

(2.) The narrow ridges of the Mammoth's molar are peculiar as compared with its allies, and are usually parallel, more or less, although they may be sometimes rather bent, as seen in Plate XI, fig. 2, but rarely to the extent observed in *E. antiquus*.[1] The above character is best seen on the worn crown. The disc has not the central dilatation and angulation of that of the latter species, and its outline is more even than in either the Asiatic or Meridional Elephant. Falconer truly observes that the enamel plates " in *E. primigenius* are only half as thick as in *E. meridionalis*, and thinner than in the Indian Elephant or in *E. antiquus*."[2]

(3.) The close approximation of the ridges is a marked feature of the Mammoth's tooth. The cement wedges without are smaller, just as is the dentine within the ridges. The above point of distinction is ordinarily characteristic *per se*. The digitations of the unworn ridge or *colliculus* are numerous, but never so large and massive as in *E. antiquus* and *E. meridionalis*. They are greatly lengthened sometimes, as seen in the worn crown (Pl. VIII, fig. 2).

(4.) The enamel of the molar of the Mammoth is relatively thinner than in any other known species, but there is considerable variability, as will appear in the sequel. It is remarkably attenuated in teeth from the Arctic regions, and the so-called Mammoth teeth from the United States, also in molars from certain districts in the British Islands and Continent of Europe, to be noted presently, whilst the reverse obtains from remains discovered at Ilford, in the Thames Valley, and elsewhere, as first pointed out by Davies;[3] but these extremes may be found in teeth from the same localities, and even the same deposits. The enamel has a tendency apparently to become thick in the penultimate and ultimate true molars, and apparently so in individuals and in small teeth containing the lowest ridge-formula of the individual member of the series, whatever it may be. Consequently age, and perhaps sex, besides individual peculiarities, may have a good deal to do with either extreme. The terms, therefore, THICK- and THIN-plated so characteristic of the teeth of *E. antiquus* and the Maltese fossil Elephants,[4] indeed, as will appear hereafter, also in *E. meridionalis*, although not so pronounced as in the two former, are present also in *Elephas primigenius*. The advantages of narrow bands of enamel to the Arctic individual, as compared with the broader ridges of the crowns of teeth from the Thames valley deposits, might furnish matters for speculation in connection

[1] Pl. I, fig. 4, Monograph.
[2] 'Pal. Mem.,' vol. ii, 146.
[3] 'Trans. Zool. Soc. Lond.,' vol. ix, p. 7 ; 'Cat. Brady Collection,' p. 4.
[4] Op. cit.

with the probable food of the denizens of the two regions, and the results of natural
selection. How far a race character can be determined on one or other conditions I am
not at present prepared to say, but with the view of arriving at some conclusion on this
head I have carefully attempted to determine the relative thickness of the ridges in a
large number of molars from British and foreign localities with the following results :[1]

All the teeth from KENT's CAVERN, Devonshire, show the Arctic type, and have
thin enamel. In two molars from BRIGHTON, in the British Museum, one from " gravel "
is *thin*-plated, whilst another from a " raised bench " (?), and in Mantell's Collection, is *thick*-plated. It might be asked were these two deposits contemporaneous ? In
the National Collection the following localities have produced Mammoth molars with *thin*-
plates :—No. 27,903, railway-cutting IPSWICH ; No. 47,122 KETTERING, Northamptonshire; No. 41,081, ISLE OF DOGS, "in peat ;" and FENNY STRATFORD, in Bucks ; also
LEXDEN, in Bucks, "in peat ;" at LAMARSH, a railway-cutting in the Stour Valley,
furnished three molars, and which are now in the British Museum. One tooth has *thick*
enamel, and in two it is *thin*. With one exception, and that is in the mandible referred
to at p. 108, all the DOGGER BANK molars are *thin*-plated. So numerous are Mr.
Owles' gatherings in the British Museum that no less than twenty-four ultimate true
molars of the Mammoth are represented.

A tooth from a " raised beach," Pl. XI, figs. 1 and 1c, in BRACKLESHAM BAY, is very
thin-plated.

Falconer refers to a *thin*-plated molar from the MENDIP CAVES ;[2] there is a
similar tooth from a cavern near WELLS, Somersetshire, in the British Museum, and
another from HINTON, in the same county, in the Museum of the Royal College of Surgeons ;
a tooth in the National Collection, from WOOKEY HOLE, is also decidedly *thin*-plated, as
seen in Pl. X, figs. 3 and 3a. It is, however, only a penultimate milk-molar, and may
be considered as scarcely characteristic.

The molars dredged up on the EAST COAST of NORFOLK are, for the most part, *thin*-
plated, but specimens from HARWICH and CROMER, in the British Museum, have *thick*
enamel. Their exact stratigraphical positions, however, are uncertain. The teeth from
ILFORD, as shown by Davies, not only represent a small form or race, but are unexcep-
tionally *thick*-plated, whilst those from CRAYFORD and ERITH, on the opposite side of the
river, are *thin*-plated ; and whilst a *thick*-plated tooth is represented by a molar from the
river deposits of the Thames under PALL MALL, in London, the other extreme is well
shown by Pl. XIV, fig. 1, from MILLBANK, higher up, and others from Thames river
deposit at BATTERSEA, CLAPTON, and from OXFORD gravels ; the last named are

---

[1] It is of importance in calculating the actual thickness of the plates and space occupied by each to
take the measurement at the enamel reflections, as the ridges have a tendency to bend towards one
another about the middle of the molar. The enamel, on the other hand, is generally thickest about the
middle of the plate.

[2] 'Pal. Mem.,' vol. ii, p. 172.

represented by numerous instances in the Museum of the University. The smallest ultimate molar of the Mammoth I have seen is *thick*-plated. It is that shown in Pl. XIII, figs. 1 and 1*a*, from KIRBY, in Leicester.   Several molars from DUNKIRK, Northern and Central FRANCE, GERMANY, AUSTRIA, and the DANUBE, in the British Museum and Woodwardian Museum, Cambridge, are decidedly *thin*-plated, whilst one from Moscow, in the former, has *thick* enamel.

Now, although apparently not much reliance can be placed on the state of the enamel as characteristic of race, at the same time the Arctic or typical crown represented by the North-Asiatic and North-American specimens, on the one hand, and Kent's Cavern on the other, presents a decided contrast to the molars from Ilford on the Thames, where not only is the enamel thicker, but the teeth themselves are all much smaller. The same character, as will be shown in the sequel, obtained in other parts of the skeleton, so that we are, at all events, fairly justified in concluding that many small-sized individuals sojourned in the Valley of the Thames during the deposition of its sands, clays, and gravels, whilst the Leicester molars represent what must have been a *dwarf Elephant* scarcely larger than the *Elephas Mnaidriensis* of Malta.   Altogether these facts prove much variability in dimensions of full-grown individuals.

(5.) The external or outer surface of the flattened enamel of the plate of the Mammoth grinder may be either smooth or rough, to the extent that the plane of detrition presents an even edge or slightly crimped border, the latter character being generally pronounced towards the middle of the plate.   Indeed, the *rugæ* on the outer surface may be scarcely defined, or so prominent that a transverse section presents the above character.   These variations may be noticed in individual discs of the same molar and are well represented in the Plates.   The outline of the enamel disc is usually even, but occasionally undulating, and the inner surface of the plate is smooth.   As to the degree of crimping of the unchœrides, in comparison with allied forms, it is not nearly so pronounced as in the *Elephas antiquus*, in which the crimping or festooning involves the entire thickness : this is not generally the case in the former, the roughening being generally confined to the outer edge of the enamel. The excessive crimping in the Asiatic Elephant is a marked character of its molar, and although there may be no such appearance of the enamel in the tooth of *E. meridionalis*, it is readily distinguished from the Mammoth's, by the thickness of the enamel, excess of intervening cement, and other well-developed points, which will be fully noted hereafter.

With reference to the other crown constituents, to wit, the dentine and cement :—An excess or a diminution of the former does not present a remarkable feature in the molar of the Mammoth.   As usual in all species, the dentine of the base and the cement increase in quantity with the age of the tooth ; that is, the common base is augmented as the ridges are being ground completely down, and attains to considerable thickness in ultimate molars, as in examples which will be referred to.   The cement also increases in quantity in much-worn last true molars, occupying often, as in the mandible (Pl. VIII, fig. 3), a considerable space between the enamelled ridges and socket, so as to keep the tooth steady, as it has no successor and must carry on the mastication to the death of the animal.

1. INCISORS.

There is no record, as far as I know, of the discovery of the MILK INCISOR of the Mammoth. It may, as occasionally obtains in the recent species, have been diminutive and often deformed, and was shed very early to make room for the ponderous permanent tusk.

The slight divergence in the alveoli, from the root to the margins of the pre-maxillary, will be noticed with the cranium.

The direction of the tusk on leaving the jaw is, as in the Asiatic and African Elephants, downwards, outwards, and finally upwards, with the tips directed *inwards*, presenting a strange contrast to that of *E. ganesa*, where the tusks may be said to converge in their sockets, then become *parallel* to near the tips which curve *outwards*.[1] The tips, therefore, of the tusks of the Mammoth curve inwards like in the recent species, as demonstrated by Mr. Davies, in the Ilford cranium, Plate VI, fig. 1a; indeed, to his careful manipulation at the exhumation is owing the preservation of this precious relic, which is the only cranium of the Mammoth anyways entire, hitherto recovered from the Pleistocene deposits of the British Isles.[2]

The direction of the tusk, although generally spiral, especially in old males, appears to have constantly assumed various degrees of curvature, from almost a perfect straight defensor to nearly a complete circle. Sometimes it was remarkably slender. It was doubtless present in both sexes, the smaller and more attenuated being likely that of the female.

The contrast between the incisor and the cranium, as represented in Pl. VI, fig. 1 a, is remarkable, and shows their disproportionate dimensions. Although the generality of tusks from the ARCTIC REGIONS exceed in size the majority met with in the British Isles and Europe, at the same time, comparisons between the former and the latter, as presented by the collection in the British Museum and elsewhere, show instances from British strata of the tusk attaining to as large a size as any from Siberia, or Boreal North America. This is well shown by a colossal specimen in the last-named collection, found with the huge last molar, Pl. IX, fig. 2, at Fenny Stratford near SPALDING in Lincolnshire, and which will be referred to in the sequel.

The measurements of tusks are unimportant; besides, few specimens are perfectly entire. The disposition towards a spiral direction is decidedly more evident in the

[1] See 'Fauna Antiqua Sivalensis,' pl. xxiii. This magnificent specimen is placed behind the Ilford cranium of the Mammoth in the British Museum to show their cranial contrasts.

[2] 'Geol. Mag.,' vol. ii, p. 239, and Mr. Woodward's description, vol. i, p. 244, and vol. v, p. 540.

incisor of the Mammoth than that of any other known species, and seemingly on that account there is reason to admit the peculiarity as a character of the species. The tusks of *E. meridionalis*, and as far as is known of *E. antiquus*, do not appear to have exceeded the gentle curve of the recent Elephants. I repeat, however, a statement made previously, that, considering the vast quantities of teeth of *E. antiquus* discovered in British strata, no entire tusk different in curvature from that of the Mammoth has, as far as I know, turned up.

Exceptions occasionally occur at Ilford and elsewhere of nearly straight tusks; in proportion, however, to the numbers of molars of *E. antiquus* there are not only few remains of tusks, but these when at all entire show the arcuation of that of the Mammoth; the only instance I know of to the contrary is that referred to by Falconer, from Bracklesham Bay.[1] There is also a probability that the defensor may not have been developed to the same extent in the latter species, just as in the Cingalese as compared with Continental varieties of *E. Asiaticus*.

2. MILK MOLARS.

The Pre-ante-penultimate or First Milk Molar (?).

The existence rarely of a tooth so named in the mandible of the African Elephant rests, as far as known to me, on one instance. The specimen is No. 708[b] of the Osteological Collection, British Museum; it comprehends an entire skull, which is stated to have been taken from a skin procured in Paris. The skin has been stuffed, and is placed in the Zoological Gallery along with other Mammals. I have before alluded to the tooth in question,[2] and both De Blainville and Dr. Falconer[3] have given illustrations of the mandible, and Mr. Busk has also noticed it.[4] It is much to be regretted that neither De Blainville nor Falconer, who had opportunities of examining the mandible soon after its extraction from the skull, have furnished precise details beyond figures. As the specimen now stands it is extremely difficult to understand how the three teeth fitted into the space they now occupy in the left ramus. A large portion of the inner wall of the horizontal ramus has been cut away, and the septum between the penultimate and ante-penultimate has been also removed, whilst the first and second molars are jammed so close together that absolutely their fangs cross one another, so as to make it clear that

[1] See my 'Monograph on *E. antiquus*.'

[2] " Dentition of *E. antiquus*," 'Monograph,' p. 11, and "Dentition of the Maltese Elephants," 'Trans. Zool. Soc. Lond.,' vol. ix, p. 10.

[3] 'Ostéographie,' pl. xiv, fig. 4; 'Faun. Antiqua Sival.,' pl. xiv, fig. 4; and 'Pal. Mem.' (Falconer), vol. ii, pp. 89 and 441, and *Corrigenda.*

[4] 'Trans. Zool. Soc. Lond.,' vol. vi, p. 287.

they could not have had separate alveoli. Again, neither in extent nor in direction of wear do the planes of detrition of the upper and lower jaws, left side, agree. The extent of worn surface of the two teeth on either side of the maxilla is 46 millimètres, but it is 60 millimètres on the left lower jaw and 40 on the right, so that the *pre*-ante-penultimate tooth does not seem to have had an opposing grinder, although its crown, as may be seen in De Blainville's plate iv, fig. 1, is more than half detrited. Further, the tips of the collines of the penultimate of the left lower ramus should present fewer abrasions than those of the right side from the additional tooth in front; but this is not so, the two being equally detrited. De Blainville's figure shows three well-marked septa between the teeth of the left ramus, none of which, however, remain in the specimen, excepting a remnant of the one in front of the penultimate; besides, the ante-penultimate tooth of the right lower ramus is now wanting. Altogether, the specimen is at present hopelessly useless as an exponent, *per se*, of this so-called abnormality—a conclusion I have arrived at after a careful re-examination of the specimen in consort with my friend, Mr. W. Davies, F.G.S. It is to be desired, therefore, that all like abnormalities should be carefully described, in order to farther establish the existence of this so-called First milk-molar.

Among the varied and interesting Mammalian remains discovered in Kent's Cavern, Devonshire, is the remarkably diminutive milk-molar, No. 5774 (Pl. IX, fig. 4).[1]

In a memorandum kindly furnished me by Mr. Pengelly, F.R.S., he states that the tooth was found "on the 2nd of December, 1871, in the Cave of Rodentia, in the four-foot level of cave-earth, with one tooth of Hyæna, and bones and bone fragments." It is described by Mr. Busk, F.R.S., with his usual care and precision; and he surmises, I think justly, that it may be the *pre*-ante-penultimate milk-molar of the Mammoth.[2] It was originally entire, but a fragment of the crown has been recently lost. In dimensions this tooth is one of the smallest milk-molars of any Elephant with which I am acquainted, and is even more diminutive than the first milk-teeth of the Maltese Pigmy Elephants. It is 0.4×0.3 inch in breadth, the smallest from the Maltese Elephants being 0.4×0.32, whilst the *pre*-ante-penultimate of the African Elephant is 0.65×0.4.

The crown-formula of fig. 4*a*, Pl. IX, is *x* 2 *x*. The tips of one of the digitations show signs of detrition, and the well-formed and consolidated fangs give evidence, at all events, that the animal did not die in the womb. The probability is, therefore, that this very small tooth may be a rare instance of the *pre*-ante-penultimate appearing in the lower jaw of the Mammoth, its long divergent fangs leading to the belief that it belonged to the mandible.

[1] For permission to figure this interesting object and other Mammoth remains from the above-named rock cavity I am under obligations to the Kent's Cavern Committee of the British Association, and to that laborious and painstaking cave-digger, Mr. Pengelly, whose troglodytic researches have done much to advance our knowledge of the Pleistocene fauna of Great Britain, and to systematize cave-explorations in general.

[2] 'Report Brit. Association,' 1872, p. 37.

The remarkable specimen from a cavern near Zwickau, in Saxony, described and figured by Kaup as the *Cymatotherium antiquum*,[1] is referred to by Falconer, who believes it is the *ante*-penultimate milk-molar of the Mammoth.[2] This tooth differs from the last in resembling certain molars of *E. antiquus* and the Maltese Pigmy Elephants[3] by possessing a single, connate, compressed fang, with a groove down the sides, indicating the line of partition between the fangs. It holds two plates besides an anterior and posterior talon in a length of 9 millimètres (about 0·35 of an inch), which make it even more diminutive than the Kent's Cavern specimen. The empty socket behind it, as represented in the figure referred to, indicates the position of, possibly, the ante- as well as the penultimate. This, however, is not determined. The slightly worn tips of the molars and the consolidated fang also show that it did not belong to a uterine individual. Whichever tooth it may be, it is, at all events, the most diminutive Elephant's molar with which I am acquainted.

The low ridge-formula is not a character, seeing that instances of *x* 2 *x* are not rare in other extinct, and also in the ante-penultimate milk-teeth of the recent species. But the above and the Kent's Hole tooth are so excessively small in comparison with the next molars described here, that, unless the ante-penultimate is subject to great discrepancy in that respect, and I see no reason why such should not be the case, as it prevails in the other members of the dental series, it may just be likely that they belong to the anomalous condition represented by the African mandible referred to. At all events, the single compressed and grooved fang which is sometimes present, as I have shown in the case of *E. antiquus* and the Maltese fossil Elephant,[4] occurs also in *E. primigenius*. I have seen no such instances, however, from jaws of the recent species. The above may be suggestive of possible reappearances of ancestral homologies.

Ante-penultimate or Second Milk Molar.

An excellent representative of this member of the dental series is presented by No. 1063 of the Kent's Cavern Collection, shown in Plate IX, fig. 3. It is of the upper jaw and probably of the right side. The fangs are wanting, but, as demonstrated by fig. 3, they are bifurcated, the larger (fig. 3 *c*), as usual, being the posterior. The tips of the digitations of the four anterior plates (fig. 3*a*) being slightly detrited show the owner to have been, at all events, not a uterine individual. According to Mr. Pengelly's memorandum, "it was found, 21st December, 1865, in the Great Chamber in the four-foot level of cave earth." The ridge-formula is *x* 4 *x* in 0·8 × 0·6, showing dimensions equal to the

[1] 'Akten der Urwelt,' tab. iv, p. 11, and De Blainville's 'Ostéographie,' pl. x.

[2] 'Pal. Mem.,' vol. ii, p. 161.

[3] 'Monograph,' Pl. I, fig. 2 ; 'Trans. Zool. Soc. Lond.,' vol. ix, pl. i, fig. 6.

[4] 'Monograph on *E. antiquus*,' p. 10, Pl. I, figs. 2, 2 *a*, and 'Trans. Zool. Soc. Lond.,' vol. ix, p. 10, pl. i, figs. 3—6.

largest of any equivalent milk-molar of the Asiatic Elephant which has come under my notice; indeed, the breadth somewhat exceeds that of the largest I have examined, and is, therefore, in keeping with the relatively greater breadth of the Mammoth tooth. The plates are *thin* as compared with those of the upper ante-penultimate of *E. antiquus* (Pl. XII, fig. 3 *a*), but are indistinguishable in that respect from specimens of *E. Asiaticus.*

The same tooth in *E. Africanus*, although generally as large, and frequently even larger, is, like that of *E. meridionalis*, easily distinguished from the Mammoth's by the thick massive plates. The ridge-formula, however, of *x* 4 *x*, as I have shown at p. 11 of my Monograph on *E. antiquus*, is found not unfrequently in upper and lower molars of the African.

With reference to the *ante*-penultimate milk-molar in *E. antiquus*, the above is a very suggestive specimen, and is now in the Museum of Practical Geology, Jermyn Street. It was presented to the Collection by the late Dr. Cotton, and is shown in Pl. XII, fig. 3, for the purpose of still further elucidating the dental succession of this species. The frag- ment belongs to a maxilla, and is from ILFORD; it shows the ante-penultimate and penultimate milk-molars of *E. antiquus*. The former (fig. 3 *a*) contains *x* 2 *x* in a space of 0·9 × 0·7 inch, while the latter (fig. 3) holds *x* 5 *x* in 2·5 inches. The thick- ness of the plates and crimping of the machærides of the disks are sufficiently charac- teristic of *E. antiquus*, which was contemporary with the small variety of the Mammoth during the period of the deposition of the brick-earths of Ilford; and, although all the numerous evidences from this locality show that the latter greatly predominated, it is clear that *E. antiquus* was also not uncommon, and, as regards size, was decidedly the larger and stouter of the two species.

A fragment of the left ramus of a mandible from ILFORD is represented by specimen No. 21,311 in the British Museum, and is shown half natural size, Pl. X, fig. 2. It displays the double fang-pits of an ante-penultimate milk-molar, with a large socket posteriorly for the successional tooth. This fragment, when compared with that of *E. antiquus*, Pl. V, fig. 2, of my Monograph, shows a relatively broader ramus, and a wider and shorter socket for the penultimate. On these grounds it seems to me, taking into consideration that both fragments represent the same stage of growth, that Pl. X, fig. 2, belongs to the Mammoth.

Dr. Falconer refers to the fragment of a mandible, No. 33,403, in the Layton Collec- tion in the British Museum, containing "the sockets of the two anterior milk-molars."[1] It is clearly a dredged specimen from the NORFOLK COAST, and appears to me to represent a more advanced stage of growth than the preceding, the sockets referred to being of the last and penultimate milk-teeth. This specimen is not, to my mind, diagnostic of any one species in particular, in consequence of being a mere fragment.

A suggestive mandible, No. 37, of the ILFORD Catalogue, is shown in Plate X,

[1] 'Pal. Mem.,' vol. ii, p. 161.

figs. 1 and 1 *a*. Mr. Davies has recorded its chief admeasurements. I may observe, however, that there is only one *fang-pit* for the *ante*-penultimate milk-tooth. It might be inferred that the posterior was obliterated by the advancing penultimate molar, but this is rendered unlikely by the circumstance that the tips of the anterior ridges only are worn down. There is a greater likelihood, therefore, that the ante-penultimate tooth had one connate fang, like the Saxon specimen and those already referred to. Thus, I repeat, they confirm the condition as of occasional occurrence also in *E. primigenius*.

This mandible shows a produced chin (fig. 1 *a*) and low inclination of the diasteme (fig. 1 *a*), which descends nearly perpendicularly at first, but soon declines and becomes nearly horizontal before it reaches the rostrum, which is rudimentary, thus displaying a feature of the jaw of the adult Mastodon, and repeating a character common also to the young stages of growth in *E. antiquus*, *E. meridionalis*, and the two recent species.

I am indebted to my friend, Professor Dawkins, F.R.S., for permission to figure (and print his notes on) the following specimens of *ante*-penultimate milk-molars discovered by him in the Caverns of Somersetshire and Yorkshire.

Notes on the First Functional Milk Molar of *Elephas primigenius*. By Professor
BOYD DAWKINS, F.R.S.

" The specimens of the very rare teeth which form the subject of these remarks were discovered in the WOOKEY HOLE HYÆNA-DEN in 1864, and in the ROBIN HOOD and CHURCH HOLE CAVES, CRESWELL CRAGS, YORKSHIRE, in 1876, in both cases in cave-earth along with[1] the remains of Hyænas, Lions, Woolly Rhinoceroses, Reindeer, Bisons, Horses, and other animals usually found in Hyæna-dens north of the Alps and Pyrenees as far as the latitude of Kirkdale in Yorkshire. They consist of four teeth:

" 1. (Pl. VIII, fig. 5) right lower milk molar (DM. 2), from Church Hole Cave.

" 2. (Pl. VIII, fig. 6) right lower milk molar (DM. 2), from Wookey Hole Cave.

" 3. (Pl. VIII, fig. 7) right upper milk molar (DM. 2), from Robin Hood Cave.

" 4. (Pl. VIII, fig. 4) right upper milk molar (DM. 2), from Wookey Hole Cave.

" *Measurements.*—Their size, as compared with the corresponding teeth of other individuals and species, may be gathered from the following table, in which, also, is placed the ridge-formula.

[1] Boyd Dawkins, 'Cave Hunting,' p. 295 ; 'Quart. Geol. Journ. Lond.,' August, 1877, p. 590, *et seq.*

"*Comparative Measurements of Milk Molars* (2) *in the Fossil Elephants.*"

	Ridge formula. Talons x.	Length (inches).	Breadth.	Circumference of crown.	Circumference of neck.
First Lower Milk Molars (DM.2).					
Elephas primigenius.					
No. 1. Plate viii, fig. 5......................	x, 3, x	0·5	0·45	1·6	1·3
No. 2. Plate viii, fig. 6......................	x, 3, x	0·025	0·5	1·95	1·5
E. antiquus.					
Leith Adams, Foss. Eleph. Pal. Soc., pt. i, p. 11	x, 3, x	0·7	0·4		
E. meridionalis.					
Falconer, Pal. Mem., ii, p. 114	x, 3, x	0·7			
E. Meaidriensis.					
Leith Adams, loc. cit.	x, 3, x	0·6	0·4		
—	x, 3, x	0·55	0·3		
First Upper Milk Molars (DM. 2).					
E. primigenius.					
No. 3. Plate viii, fig. 7	x, 4, x	0·75	0·6	2·2	
No. 4. Plate viii, fig. 4	x, 4, x	0·78	0·63	2·2	2·0
Busk, Trans. Zool. Soc., vi, p. 307......	4, x	0·8	0·7		
E. antiquus.					
Leith Adams, loc. cit.	x, 3, x	0·95	0·75		
Leith Adams, loc. cit.	x, 2, x	0·8	0·7		
—	x, 3, x	0·9	0·7		
E. meridionalis.					
Falconer, Pal. Mem., ii, 110	x, 3, x	0·95	0·75		
E. Mnaidriensis.					
Leith Adams, op. cit.	x, 2, x	0·5	0·4		
—	3, x	0·4	0·32		

"*Description of* DM. 2.—The two specimens of the lower first functional milk-molar of the Mammoth consist of a crown just coming into wear (Pl. VIII, fig. 5) and a tooth with the crown worn and the fangs well preserved (figs. 6, 6 a). In both the crown is composed of three ridges (figs. 5 a, 6 a) and two talons. In fig. 5 the ridges are connected together by a longitudinal secondary ridge on the inner, while they are perfectly free down to their confluent bases on the outer side. The inner side of the crown presents an arc in longitudinal section, while the outer is nearly flat, the widest portion being behind (fig. 5 b) and the narrowest in front. In fig. 5 c the fangs are undeveloped. In fig. 6 a the crown is so embedded in enamel that its structure is only suspected by a minute comparison with the preceding tooth. It is supported on a stout bony pedestal composed of two connate fangs, which branch off at a distance of 0·95 inch from the top of the crown at acute angles to each other, the front being the smaller, as in the case of the corresponding tooth in the closely allied Asiatic Elephant. I do not, however, attach any great importance to this character, since I find the variations in the development of fangs in living and extinct Mammalia very great, and especially in the milk-molars. The total length of fig. 6, from the posterior fang-tip (broken) to crown, is 1·7 inch. As may be expected, the ridges are smaller and the enamel thinner than in the corresponding teeth of E. antiquus.

"The first upper functional milk-molar is proved by these two specimens (figs. 7 and 4) to have been composed of four ridges and two talons. They are both unworn, and are supported upon a base of connate fangs, proved, by the constriction shown in 3 A, to have been two in number and the front being the smaller, as in the lower jaw. The ridges are not so coarse as in E. antiquus, and are four in number, as compared with the three of the latter species.

"These specimens fill a blank in the history of the dentition of the Mammoth, defined by Dr. Falconer. The rest of the milk-teeth, of which some hundreds have passed through my hands, offer no characters of sufficient importance to be described.

"August 25th, 1878."

A comparison between the dimensions of the foregoing molars and Pl. IX, fig. 3, from Kent's Cavern, attests the varieties in size to which these small teeth were subject in the Mammoth; whilst, on the other hand, their general agreement in possessing narrow plates, as compared with similar teeth of E. antiquus, E. meridionalis, and E. Africanus, and their affinities to the crown of the E. Asiaticus, from which they differ again in greater breadth, fully support characters distinctive of molars of E. primigenius.

Prof. Boyd Dawkins's specimens represent four individuals; and whilst in Pl. VIII, figs. 5, 4, 7 belonged to newly born Elephants, as indicated by unworn ridges and undeveloped fangs, fig. 6, by its well-worn crown embedded in cement and fully developed roots, shows that the owner had been browsing, and the pressure scar (fig. 6 b) on the heel proves that the penultimate milk-tooth was in part invaded. Although the fangs are absent, or rather undeveloped, in the others, it will be observed, at all events in figs. 7 c and 4 c, that they were divergent, the same being not so apparent in fig. 5 c, which from its smaller size may have had a single fang only.

All these molars are extremely interesting, seeing that they complete the entire molar series of the Mammoth, and must, in consequence, be considered a valuable addition to Proboscidean odontology.

Affinities.—The *ante*-penultimate milk-molar in *E. Asiaticus* varies in the number of its ridges, but in no instance of many I have seen was the ridge-formula under x 3 x; it is not unfrequently x 4 x in either jaw. The plates are attenuated, like those of the Mammoth, but the enamel is deeply crimped. Its dimensions are not smaller, as compared with those of other species,[1] whilst it agrees in ridge-formula with that of the Mammoth.

From *E. antiquus* (Pl. XII, figs. 3 and 3 *a*) the upper-jaw teeth will, I apprehend, distinguish themselves always by a higher ridge-formula and less thickening of plates—characters which are still more apparent in the teeth of *E. meridionalis* and *E. Africanus.*

The Third or Penultimate Milk Molar.

This tooth is plentiful in cavern and river deposits, but its small size prevents it being dredged with the larger members of the dental series. There is great sameness in dimensions of upper third milk-teeth of *E. primigenius* especially, more so perhaps than in any other species whose molars have been collected in equal numbers. The penultimate may be often mistaken for that of *E. antiquus*, more especially mandibular specimens. The ridges vary considerably in number. Falconer[2] sets down the formula at x 7 x to x 8 x, and Owen makes a similar statement,[3] but does not indicate whether or not the talons are included. A large proportion of British and foreign specimens examined by me point to a belief that the majority of upper teeth hold x 6 x, and lower x 7 x; but the extremes mark a considerable range, as will appear from the following.

The largest specimen I have seen, doubtfully stated as being from the brick-earth of ILFORD, is No. 582F, of the Collection in the Museum of the Royal College of Surgeons of England. It is an upper tooth, and holds x 9 x in 3·3 × 1·4 inches in width.

No. 4642, B. M. (Pl. X, figs. 3 and 3 *a*), from WOOKEY HOLE in the Mendip Hills, displays the broad crowns with *thin* enamel, somewhat crimpled towards the middle, but there is no *central expansion* or *angulation* of the disk as in *E. antiquus*. The oblique anterior, double middle, and large single posterior fang (fig. 3*a*), are represented fractured ;

[1] 'Monograph on *E. antiquus*,' p. 12.

[2] 'Pal. Mem.,' vol. ii, p. 159 to 163.

[3] 'Brit. Foss. Mam.,' p. 223. The Kirkdale specimen here referred to, fig. 87, was afterwards shown by Falconer, 'Pal. Mem.,' vol. ii, p. 179, to belong to *E. antiquus*.

they always indicate a well-worn crown whose plane of detrition shows in the above six disks, with the anterior and posterior talons nearly obliterated.

The fangs in some upper teeth present considerably larger dimensions. A specimen lately obtained in the river-gravels during excavations in Oxford, connected with the main drainage works, shows a ridge-formula of x 6 x in $2\frac{1}{4} \times 1\cdot 1$ inch. It has a broad anterior fang of $\frac{3}{4}$ of an inch in width, followed by a long narrow root, which rises from the middle and inner side of the crown, and a posterior fang of about the same size as the anterior.

A good illustration of this tooth is seen in No. 44,734, B. M. (Pl. VI, figs. 2 and 2 a). It is a lower molar from HUTTON CAVE, and, as far as the stage of dentition is of value in determining the thickness or otherwise of the enamel, it is decidedly *thick*-plated. It holds x 7 x in $2\cdot 6 \times 1\cdot 3$ inch, and is equalled by another specimen of the upper jaw from the same locality, which contains x 6 x in $2\cdot 5 \times 1\cdot 4$. In both eight ridges are contained in a space of about two inches.

In the collection of milk-molars belonging to the KENT'S CAVERN Museum there are ten penultimate deciduous teeth, four of which belong to the upper jaw. The upper molars are noted as follows :—" No. $\frac{11}{377}$ was found on the 8th of September, 1870, in 'Smerdon's Passage,' in the one-foot level of cave-earth, with two teeth of Hyæna, three of Horse, two of Rhinoceros and one of Deer, three of Badger, besides bones and fine fragments." It is a crown with the six anterior ridges invaded, and holds x 6 x in $2\cdot 2 \times 1\cdot 3$.

Another crown, more than half worn, No. 315, was found 23rd June, 1865, in the Great Chamber, in the four-foot level of cave-earth. It holds x 6 x in about the same dimensions. The enamel is rather thicker in this specimen than in the generality of Kent's Cavern molars, but milk-teeth vary in these respects, and are not of diagnostic importance in respect to thickness or thinness of the enamel. The same formula and dimensions are presented by the still more detrited crown No. $\frac{11}{1617}$, from the same depth, in the "North Sally Port, with five teeth of Hyæna, five of Horse, two of Rhinoceros, and one of Lion." The fourth example, No. 5968, is from the "Long Arcade, in the three-foot level of cave-earth, with five teeth of Bear."[1]

The lower-jaw specimens from KENT'S CAVERN represent various stages of growth, and differ considerably in dimensions and numbers of ridges, as will appear from the following table (see next page) :

[1] See 'Report Brit. Assoc.,' 1872, p. 46. The stratigraphical positions of the others are copied from an extract sent along with the original specimens.

Number.	Ridge-formula.	Dimensions.	Disks in wear.	Thickness of plates.	Remarks.
1218	$x\,6\,x$	$1\cdot9 \times 0\cdot85$	6	0·16	Great Chamber, 4-foot level, 10th February, 1866.
1059	$x\,6$	$1\cdot5 \times 09\cdot5$	6	0·2	Ditto ditto 20th December, 1865. The cement is denuded from the sides of both of these molars, and also portions of the enamels.
2 3489	$x\,8\,x$	$2\cdot5 \times 1\cdot4$	0	0·3	Smerdon's Passage, 4-foot level, with teeth of Hyæna, Horse, Irish Elk, and Rhinoceros, October 5th, 1870.
6066	$x\,8\,x$	$2\cdot3 \times 1\cdot25$	5	0·2	Long Arcade, 2-foot level, 16th January, 1873.
2677	$x\,7\,x$	$2\cdot1 \times 1\cdot3$	2 to 3?	0·26	Great Chamber, 2-foot level, 4th July, 1867.
2135	$x\,7\,x$	$1\cdot9 \times 1\cdot27$	9	?	Vestibule, 4-foot level, 13th February, 1867.

The molar, Plate XIII, fig. 2, shown in profile, also from KENT'S CAVERN, is now in the British Museum. Here $x\,6\,x$ in a lower-jaw tooth is contained in $2 \times 1\cdot2$ inch, the average thickness of each plate being 0·3 inch. The crown is not invaded.

The teeth in mandible No. 44,967, No. 37, Brady Collection, B. M. (Plate X, figs. 1 and 1 a), display crowns just invaded, and holding six plates besides two talons in $2 \times 1\cdot1$ inch.

This mandible is very characteristic of the above stage of dentition of the species. The open gutter, thick horizontal ramus, low diasteme, and rather pointed chin are present, with the empty socket of the ante-penultimate in front; whilst the scarcely detrited crowns of the penultimate show that the individual was very young.

An occasional tooth may present unusual breadth of crown. Thus, I was shown by Mr. Fitch, F.G.S., of Norwich, a second penultimate milk-molar from the Norwich Coast holding $x\,6\,x$ in a space of $2\cdot7 \times 2\cdot2$ inches in width. The enamel was very thin.

All the penultimates, like the succeeding molars from ILFORD, present thicker enamel than typical crowns of the species, but they also belonged to relatively smaller individuals than represented by equivalent teeth from the Arctic regions, and by specimens from certain British localities, to which reference has been made in connection with the former condition, as I shall have frequent occasion to point out in the sequel.

From the foregoing and numerous other specimens I find the penultimate milk-molar of the Mammoth varies constantly from $x\,6\,x$ to $x\,9\,x$ in variable dimensions, not, however, always dependent on the number of ridges.

Affinities.—Of the affinities between this member of the dental series and that of *E. antiquus* and *E. meridionalis* there is little to add to what I have already stated in connection with *E. antiquus* at page 15 of my Monograph on that Elephant. As regards breadth of crown, there is a similarity between that of the Mammoth and *E. meridionalis*, but the latter shows invariably a larger quantity of intervening cement, and presents a less variability in its ridge formula, which does not appear to exceed x 6 x in either jaw. The tooth altogether, like the succeeding, is relatively more massive and the enamel thicker, and more wavey in outline than is ever seen in the Mammoth.

The close affinities between the skull of the Asiatic Elephant and the Mammoth extends also to the molars. In the latter this is apparent as regards the ridge formula, which is precisely the same in both, as also the attenuation of the plates to some extent.[1] When the molar crown of *E. antiquus* and *E. meridionalis* were confounded with that of the Mammoth, one was apt, from fragmentary specimens of the former resembling *E. Asiaticus*, to correlate the two more closely in their dentition, and even weather-stained molars of the latter were not unfrequently mistaken for Mammoths' teeth.[2]

I am not aware that the teeth, or any portion of the skeleton of the youthful stages of growth above described, have been found in either Scotland or Ireland. The penultimate milk tooth is common in collections from the brick-earths of Ilford and neighbouring localities, also in gravels and river deposits about Oxford. It has been found, as just indicated, in the caverns of Devonshire and Mendip Hills, Somersetshire, where, doubtless, as in similar situations, it represents the *rejectamenta* of numerous victims of the great Carnivores. As to the specimens from the Norfolk Coast, the same uncertainty as to their stratigraphical relations obtains as with other portions of the skeleton of the Mammoth asserted to have been found in the Forest Bed.

The Fourth or Ultimate Milk Molar.

The last of the milk series is plentiful in collections. It invariably marks a rapid increase in the growth of an Elephant, as revealed by the much larger sizes of the incisors and molars in comparison with penultimate milk teeth.

---

[1] Falconer, in summing up the data regarding the ridge formula of the milk series in comparison with the same teeth in the Indian Elephant, observes that the former is "liable to the same variation as regards the *ante*-penultimate (the italics are mine) upper and lower as is met with in that species, namely, the ridges varying from seven to eight," 'Pal. Mem.,' vol. ii, p. 163 ; see also 'Quart. Journ. Geol. Soc.,' vol. xxi, p. 327. Clearly this "slip of the pen" refers to the third or penultimate, and not the second or ante-penultimate. The mistake is apt, however, to mislead, and seems to me worth indicating.

[2] Among the very varied and very imperfectly named and classified proboscidean remains of the 'Fauna Antiqua Sivalensis' there are several figures referred by Dr. Falconer to *E. planifrons* and *E. Hysudricus*, which might be most advantageously compared with the remains of the European and living Elephants, but as this would imply a detailed acquaintance with all the vast and heterogenous materials collected by Falconer, Cautly, and others, in the British Museum and elsewhere, an undertaking the first, with his profound knowledge of the subject, seems to have shrunk from entering upon. I can, therefore, only indicate here a few of the more suggestive teeth and bones with which the same parts of the Mammoth might be compared ; for example, the first and second milk molars of *E. planifrons*, erroneously named *E. Hysudricus* (see 'Pal. Mem.,' vol. i, p. 442, footnote ; pl. xiv, fig. 10 ; and pl. vii, figs. 5 and 6), representing the same dental conditions in *E. Hysudricus*.

13

Upper molars.—A suggestive example is furnished by the incisive alveolus with the two tusks *in situ* (woodcut, fig. 1, p. 130), and a detached upper and two lower molars of the same individual from the brick-earths of ILFORD in the Museum of Practical Geology. Unfortunately the remainder of the skull is wanting, but the gradual divergence of the incisors from the roots to the points of exit is well shown. The intermediate distance between them at the former is $5\frac{1}{2}$ inches, and at the latter 9 inches; the maximum breadth of the alveolus at its free border being 12 inches.

The tusks diverge and protrude a distance of 16 inches beyond the incisive sheaths, and are blunt-pointed, and curve outwards, with a maximum girth of $7\frac{1}{2}$ inches. These defensors far exceed the dimensions of the tusks of either of the recent species at a corresponding age.

The upper molar in the above is just commencing wear, the last two or three ridges not having been invaded. It shows, as well as the lower teeth, the *thick* enamel of the ILFORD molar as compared with teeth from CRAYFORD on the opposite side of the Thames. The ridge formula in the upper tooth is x 11 x in $4\frac{3}{4} \times 2$ inches, whilst the lower hold each x 12 x in $5\frac{1}{2} \times 2$ inches.

A palate specimen, No. 19, Brady Collection, B. M., and also from ILFORD, contains two molars *in situ*, showing the same characters and dimensions of the upper tooth just referred to; it is a good illustration of the palatal region of this stage of growth or that of adolescence.

A very characteristic specimen of a well-worn upper molar is shown by No. 5489 (Pl. XII, fig. 2), from " the Sloping Chamber, KENT's CAVERN," where it was found in " the fourth-foot level of cave-earth, 24th June, 1871, along with a tooth of Hyæna." This tooth is a further illustration of the *thin*-plated or typical crowns of the Mammoth as distinguishable from the *thicker* enamel of such as the molars found at ILFORD. The fore part of the crown in fig. 2 has been ground away, leaving ten disks in wear, and traces of an original ridge formula of x 10—11 x. It is entire as to length and breadth, and has a fragment of the alveolus attached. The two other crowns, from KENT's CAVERN, of upper molars, Nos. $\frac{13}{3139}$ and 2002, fully support the characters of the above.

I have been thus desirous to refer at some length to the deciduous molars from KENT's CAVERN, not only on account of the typical character of the worn crown, but as exponents of the exhaustive method pursued by Mr. Pengelly in chronicling the records of the famous Cavern of Torquay—a mode of procedure deserving of imitation in the working of future bone caves.

Another palate specimen in the British Museum is from HUTTON CAVE, in the MENDIP HILLS. The right tooth is in place, but instead of x 12 x shows a ridge formula of x 11 x in $4\frac{1}{2} \times 1\frac{1}{4}$ inches.

The enamel and dentine are *thick*, so that eight ridges are contained in $3\frac{1}{4}$ inches. The molars of the Elephant found in 1715 at BELTURBET, in Cavan, and figured by

Molyneux in Vol. xxix of the ' Philosophical Transactions' (fig. 2 of Plate to No. 346), represented an upper ultimate milk tooth holding x 11 x in $5\frac{3}{4} \times 1\frac{3}{4}$. In the late acquisition made by the authorities of the British Museum of the collection of Pleistocene Mammals collected by Mr. Owles from dredgings on the DOGGER BANK, off the Yorkshire Coast,[1] is a palate containing two ultimate milk molars, each of which has a ridge formula of x 12 x in $5\cdot2 \times 2\cdot4$ inches. The crowns converge in front where the intervening space is $1\cdot0$ inches. At the middle it is $2\cdot9$ inches, and posteriorly at the talons $3\cdot6$ inches. The machærides of the enamel are slightly crimped near the middle of the disk.

Through the kindness of my friend Professor McKenny Hughes, I have been enabled to examine the fine collection of Proboscidean remains contained in the Woodwardian Museum, Cambridge. Among the treasures from British strata is a series of Mammoth molars from KIRBY, MELTON MOWBRAY, in Leicestershire, amounting to some twenty specimens, which were presented by the late Professor Phillips. The remarkable feature relating to these teeth is, as before stated, their small size, as compared with the ordinary grinders of the species, and their consequent resemblance in that respect to the Ilford molars. A third upper milk molar (No 42) holds x 12 x in $4\frac{1}{4} \times 1\frac{3}{4}$, and eight ridges in a space of $2\frac{1}{4}$ inches. This tooth, when compared with No. 39 of the above collection, is relatively smaller, and would indicate that the latter belonged to the next in succession, with which I have no hesitation in placing it.

The crown elements here indicate a *thin* plate, but not so pronounced as in many other teeth from British localities.

Another (No. 22) in the same collection, from gravel at BARTON, near Cambridge, holds x 12 x in $4 \times 2\frac{1}{2}$. Here the crown is unusually broad, and the tooth short and stumpy. The plates are *thin*, and eight ridges are contained in $2\frac{1}{2}$ inches.

The BRADY COLLECTION (No. 20, B. M.) contains two upper ultimate milk molars, with as low a ridge formula as x 10 x in $5 \times 2\cdot4$. Each contains eight ridges in $2\frac{3}{4}$ inches, and I have seen another molar of the upper jaw, also from Ilford, with x 10 x in only $3\cdot8 \times 1\cdot6$ inches. There were eight ridges to $2\frac{1}{4}$ inches. These small teeth and low formulæ in Mammoth molars from ILFORD will be seen to agree with the disposition to similar characters in their true molars, especially the last of the series, and, as has just been stated, in connection with the penultimate milk molar.

The lowest ridge formula I have seen in this member of the milk series, repeating in fact the maximum number in the penultimate, is displayed by a specimen in the British Museum from Epplesheim, in Germany. It holds x 9 x in $4\frac{1}{2} \times 1\frac{1}{2}$ inches, and eight ridges in a space of 3 inches. The enamel is *thin*, with rather an unusual excess of the other dental elements. It is interesting to compare the above with the penultimate milk tooth from ILFORD, described at p. 90, as it shows Falconer's rule, that " the members are

---

[1] Mr. Davies, F.G.S., has lately contributed a paper to the Geological Magazine, vol. v, 1878, on the Animal Remains from this situation.

never transposed or reversed,"[1] does not invariably hold good by any means. To suppose that the specimen, p. 90, is also a last milk molar would make the owner a dwarf.

Of fourteen entire last *upper* milk molars, nearly all of which were from British strata, I found *one* with a ridge formula of x 9 x, *two* holding x 10 x, *six* with x 11 x, and *six* with x 12 x. It would seem, therefore, that the plates vary from 11 to 12 in upper-jaw molars.

Lower molars.—Mandibular last milk molars are equally plentiful, and they are oftener seen *in sitû* than the opposing tooth. Great variation in size obtains as usual in jaws of the same age, at all events containing teeth similarly worn, and is, no doubt, a consequence of sex, individual peculiarities, and, as before stated, perhaps local varieties.

Several molars showing various stages in the detrition of this member of the milk dentition from WALTON-ON-THE-NAZE, Essex, are contained in the Woodwardian Collection. Among them is a left ramus of a mandible (No. 26), with the third milk tooth in full wear and the fourth appearing above the alveolus, the heel of the former being in a line with the anterior border of the coronoid. The tooth holds x 10 x in $4 \times 1\frac{3}{4}$ inches. The height of the jaw in front of the milk molar is 4·5 inches, and maximum thickness of the ramus is 3·6 inches. There is no internal foramen in the spout, which is an abnormality in the Mammoth. This ordinarily would be considered a small last milk molar, and is out of proportion to ultimate true molars from the same locality, to be described in the sequel.

A mandible in the Museum of Practical Geology, Jermyn Street, from the brick-earths of OTTERHAM, shows the crowns of two last milk molars with a morsel of the penultimate milk tooth in front of them, and the loose collines of the first true molar in their capsules behind.[2] The stage of growth is that, when the penultimate milk tooth is on the point of disappearing and the last is just coming into use, there being only six of its disks invaded : there is a loss of the condyles and the coronoid, and the left ramus is broken across through the middle of its diasteme. Each milk molar holds x 10 x in $4\frac{1}{2} \times 1\frac{1}{2}$ inches, the enamel of which is *thin*. The height in front of the fragment of the second tooth is 4·2 inches, and the maximum thickness of the jaw at the base of the coronoid is $3\frac{1}{4}$ inches.

The diasteme is nearly vertical, with a large nutrient foramen at the anterior root of the second milk molar, besides two smaller openings within half an inch of the free margin, and one within the spout.

Another portion of a lower jaw in the same Museum, and from CRAYFORD, in the Thames Valley east of London, presents precisely the same dental conditions as the last, only the ultimate milk molars hold x 11 x in $4 \cdot 4 \times 1\frac{1}{2}$ inches, the height in front of the penultimate milk is $4\frac{3}{4}$ inches, and the thickness at the base of the coronoid is 3 inches, and there are two external and one internal mental foramina on either side.

[1] Op. cit., vol. ii, p. 10.
[2] The mandible, fig. 86 of the ' British Fossil Mammals, seems to represent this stage of growth.

Three fragments of mandibles from ILFORD in the Brady Collection exhibit teeth holding eleven to twelve plates besides talons. One, No. 41, Pl. VIII, fig. 1, is more entire than the others, and has the last milk molar in full wear; and although the first true molar is wanting, no doubt a few of its more anterior ridges had also been invaded.[1] The height of this jaw at the commencement of the diasteme is 4·3 inches, and the maximum thickness of the ramus is 2·5 inches. The diasteme is nearly vertical, and measures 3½ inches from the summit to the floor of the gutter, which has the usual open contour of the Mammoth. It is 4 inches in the antero-posterior diameter. The chin, as usual, is rounded, and the mental foramina amount to two outer and one inner in either ramus. Although the rostrum is lost, like the others, it was evidently small.

The occasional crimping of the machærides of the enamel of the disk is well shown in a much worn lower last milk tooth in the ramus No. 39 of the same collection. This jaw has three outer and one inner mentary openings.

There is a cast of a mandible presented by M. Lartet to the British Museum from LYONS. It shows a last milk tooth holding x 12 x in 3⅝ inches. The maximum thickness of the ramus at the base of the coronoid is 3¼ inches. The latter is quite erect, but the diasteme is not so perpendicular as in the foregoing. Here there are three mentary foramina on one side and only two on the other.

One of a pair of very typical lower last milk molars, No. 39,041, B. M., from a "Raised Beach" at BRACKLESHAM BAY, is shown, crown and profile, in Plate XI, figs. 1 and 1 a. It holds x 12 x. The enamel is very thin, and almost cordate, without the faintest indication of crimping. The crown is quite concave with an anterior curved fang and coalescence of the posterior into a shell, showing that the tooth is not half worn down, and in just that state of detrition which best displays the specific characters of a molar.

No. 16 of the Woodwardian Museum, Cambridge, is a fragment of mandible containing a milk molar from gravel at CHESTERTON, in the neighbourhood. Here the plates are thick, but the grossness arises from an increase of all the elements, more especially the cement and dentine. It holds x 12 x in 4½ × 1¼, and 8 ridges in 4·1 inches.

The lower molar, No. 21,315, B. M., from ILFORD, and cited by Falconer as a good illustration of the last milk tooth,[2] shows a remarkably narrow crown for that of the Mammoth, but on close inspection of the specimen I find the seven posterior ridges do not belong to the same tooth, and have been cemented to the anterior portion, from which it is clear that the specimen was made up, probably by the late Mr. Ball, who seems to have displayed much ingenuity in patching up broken fossils.

The same average of plates appears to obtain in ultimate lower milk molars as in the upper jaw; possibly an occasional extra ridge may occur in the former.

[1] Pl. ii, fig. 5, of the 'Ossemens Fossiles,' exhibits, perhaps, this stage and state of wear, or nearly so; also De Blainville, pl. x, fig. 3.
[2] 'Pal. Mem.,' vol. ii, p. 162.

The dimension of this tooth varies considerably.   In upper molars the antero-posterior measurement is as low as $3\frac{1}{2}$ inches and the maximum $5\frac{1}{2}$ inches, whilst the breadth varies from 1·4 to 2·5 inches.

The lower molar does not appear to exceed the maximum length of the upper, but I have not seen one of the former so low as 3·9 inches in length. Its width is seemingly the same as in the upper. Sometimes molars of this, as in succeeding teeth, show, especially in the mandible, a tendency to arcuation, which, however, as a rule, is not general in the Mammoth.

Affinities.—The ridge formula of this member of the series in *E. primigenius* and *E. Asiaticus* are precisely alike, ranging from nine to twelve plates besides talons. In *E. antiquus* and *E. Namadicus* the numbers extend from nine to eleven plates, whilst in *E. meridionalis* it seldom exceeds eight plates; the same, seemingly, and even a lower number, obtaining in *E. Africanus, E. Hysudricus* (?), and *E. bombifrons.*

The only species with which the ultimate milk molar of the Mammoth is likely to be confounded is that of the *E. antiquus.* Ordinarily, the higher expression of the ridge formula and disks will distinguish the former when the crown is well worn; but sometimes, should the wearing down be not pronounced and the number of plates come within the range of that of the Mammoth, the diagnosis might be uncertain. As to the differentiations from the last milk molars of other species, I need not repeat what are detailed at length in my Monograph on *E. antiquus,* p. 20.

Like its predecessor, the last of the milk molars is plentiful in collections from the brickfields east of LONDON, and, whether through accident, disease, or attacks of enemies, the Mammoth did not attain to old age without running many risks, and this is further shown by the undiminished numbers of last milk teeth from bone caverns throughout England.   It has also been recovered from the bed of the German Ocean, and represents the most youthful examples of its owner hitherto recorded from Ireland.

3. TRUE MOLARS.

The Ante-penultimate or First True Molar.

A small first true molar may be easily mistaken for a large ultimate milk molar, and the latter for a small first; indeed, the chances of such deceptions are the lot of the most experienced manipulators of Proboscidean teeth. The only certainty occurs either when the molar is found in the jaw or when the larger size indicates dimensions beyond what usually obtains in last milk teeth.

The rapid growth of the living species of Asia, whose life-history is best known, makes greatest progress between the decadence of the penultimate milk and the commencement of the detrition of the penultimate true molar,[1] and, judging from the sizes of jaws, molars, and tusks, and as far as is known of the long bones, the same obtained in the Mammoth. The first true molar ushers in the adolescent stage, when the animal is said to attain sexual maturity.

Upper Molars.—The molar, No. 46,211, B. M., from the DOGGER BANK, shown Pl. XI, fig. 2, presents the very unusual anomaly of containing only nine plates and two talons, and comparable in that respect with the penultimate and ultimate milk-molars referred to at pp. 90 and 95. The double falcated anterior fang supports the first two ridges, and the posterior talon is intact, so that there can be no question whatever of the ridge formula. The crown is $6 \times 2\frac{3}{4}$ inches, and contains the very unusual proportion of not less than eight ridges in a space of $4\frac{1}{2}$ inches, there being nearly 0·8 inch to each plate. This arises entirely from an excessive quantity of cement, which appears to take up the space occupied in other teeth by plates.

A comparison between this anomalous crown and that of a first true molar of *E. antiquus* (Monograph, Pl. III, fig. 2) shows striking likenesses, only that the latter holds x 10 x in 7 inches, and its crown is not nearly so broad.

Upper-jaw teeth, *in sitú*, are not nearly so plentiful as lower. The Brady Collection from ILFORD, No. c 1, contains a mutilated palate holding two well-worn crowns, but the right is imperfect, and therefore affords little information of the relative dimensions of the palate region. The remains of large incisive sheaths show that the tusk was fully developed. The left molar appears to me to furnish evidence of a ridge formula of x 12 x in $5·5 \times 3$ inches, and to contain eight ridges in $3\frac{1}{2}$ inches.

The Woodwardian Museum possesses a molar from GRISTHORPE BAY, Yorkshire. It contains x 12 x in $5 \times 2\frac{1}{2}$, and holds eight ridges in 2·7 inches, and might be fairly placed with the *thin*-plated teeth.

There are two detached upper molars, Nos. 15 and 23, in the same collection from the CAMBRIDGE gravels, presenting a ridge formula of x 12 x; the former is $5·5 \times 2·8$ inches, the latter is $5·5 \times 2·5$ inches, but whilst the former holds eight ridges in 3 inches, the latter shows the same number in a length of $3\frac{1}{2}$ inches. A molar from a cave in the north of Spain, holding x 12 x in $5 \times 2·3$ inches, is recorded by me elsewhere.[2] The enamel is *thick*, like that of Ilford molars, and there is faint crimping of the borders of the ridges.

Another upper tooth from Cambridge, No. 14, with x 12 x in 7×3 inches, holds eight ridges in $3\frac{3}{4}$ inches.

Another from Langford, near Rugby, in the Oxford University Museum, with the same ridge formula in 5×3 inches, has eight in $3\frac{1}{4}$ inches, and shows unusual *thickness* of the enamel or dentine, in other words " thick plates."

A tooth found in fluviatile deposits of the Thames Valley at BATTERSEA, London, holds

[1] This is well seen at present in the young Indian Elephants lately presented to the Zoological Society of London by H.R.H. The Prince of Wales.

[2] 'Journ. Geol. Soc. Lond.,' vol. xxxiii, p. 537.

x 13 x in 6 × 2·7 inches, and eight ridges in $3\frac{1}{4}$ inches. The enamel in this specimen is conspicuously *thin* as compared with that usually seen in true molars from Ilford in the neighbourhood. This specimen is in the British Museum.

The fluviatile gravels in and around BARNWELL, Cambridgeshire, have been prolific in remains of the Mammoth. There is a series in the Woodwardian Museum of associated grinders of this species from one situation, comprising two upper well-worn ultimate milk teeth, and two upper first true molars, evidently of the same individual, besides two lower penultimate true molars, and fragments of other permanent teeth, representing, at least, two individuals.

The upper tooth, No. 57, holds x 13 x in $6\frac{3}{4} \times 2\frac{1}{2}$, and contains eight ridges in $3\frac{1}{2}$ inches. The enamel is *thick*—a character which runs through the set.

The tooth (No. 42) from KIRBY, Leicestershire, referred to the last of the milk series (p. 95), is rivalled by another and larger molar in the same collection (No. 39). It holds x 13 x in $4\frac{3}{4} \times 2\frac{1}{2}$, and eight ridges in $2\frac{1}{2}$ inches. According to the ordinary size of the last milk, this specimen would be considered by no means a large one ; but it contains a ridge over the usual number in a proportionately small species, and is a quarter of an inch longer than the tooth No. 42. These facts, taken into account in relation to the diminutive ultimate molars from the same locality, described at p. 111, one of which is shown in Plate XIII, figs. 1 and 1 *a*, seem to associate all with a small form or race, or else dwarfed individuals. I have therefore placed the above molar among the first true, rather than the last milk teeth. The characters of the crown constituent are as in the other tooth at p. 95, the plates being rather thin and crowded

A still higher expression of the ridge formula in upper molars of this stage of growth is well shown in a tooth in the University Museum, Oxford, from the OXFORD gravel under the city. It holds x 14 x in $5\frac{1}{2} \times 2\cdot8$ inches and eight in $2\frac{1}{2}$ inches, showing the differences in dimensions as compared with the number of ridges and the *thinness* of the plates as compared with the ordinary Mammoth's molars met with in the lower parts of the river below London. The latter is well shown in an ILFORD molar, in which x 14 x are contained in $6\frac{1}{4} \times 2\frac{1}{2}$ inches and it holds eight in $3\frac{1}{2}$.

A molar (No. 25) found in gravel at WESTWICK HALL, near Cambridge, and now in the Woodwardian collection, contains x 14 x in $7 \times 2\frac{1}{4}$ inches and eight ridges in $3\frac{3}{4}$. The enamel is rather thick and there is slight crimping of the machærides of the disks.

The highest expression of the ridge formula in a tooth referable to this stage of the dentition is represented by two very entire and beautifully preserved molars (Nos. 11 and 12) in the Woodwardian museum from ST. NEOT's, Huntingdonshire. Each tooth holds x 15 x in $5\frac{1}{2} \times 2$, and has eight ridges in 2.6 inches. The enamel is *thin*. These teeth were accompanied by a long and slender tusk which measures 52 inches in length.

Lower molars.—The same Museum contains two lower molars from LEXDEN, near Colchester, Essex (Fisher Collection). Each tooth holds x 13 x in 6 × 2$\frac{1}{4}$ inches, and contains eight ridges in $4\frac{1}{4}$ inches.

The plates are rather *thick*, but mostly with reference to the cement and dentine; indeed, all Lexden specimens I have seen vary considerably in the thickness of their plates.[1]

Foreign specimens.—The Museum of the Royal College of Surgeons of England contains several admirable illustrations of lower as well as upper-first true molars, said to have been obtained from Ohio, N. America. They are described with Dr. Falconer's usual fidelity, and need no further reference here, excepting as regards their ridge formulæ, which do not exceed *x* 12 *x*, and the *very attenuated enamel* pointed out by Owen and Falconer.[2] I have already referred to these teeth in connection with the American distribution of the species.

An upper molar, No. 37,293, B. M., from " gravel pits " near Moscow, holds *x* 12 *x* in 5¾ × 2·7 inches with 8 ridges in a space of 3½ inches. The enamel is crimped somewhat near the middle of the disk and is *thick*.

Several suggestive specimens of this tooth are contained in mandibles.

A lower jaw figured and described by Falconer[3] displays the first true molar fully worn, and the empty socket of a fragment of the last milk in front with the tips of the collines of the penultimate true molar just appearing.

In the Brady Collection a further stage in the detrition of the molar in question is well represented in the mandibles, Nos. 43 *c* and 44 *c*. The former is shown (Plate VIII, fig. 2). A crown very slightly more worn, with the second true molar just above the gum and one of its ridges attrited, is represented by No. 47 and No. 45 of the same collection, where several of the anterior plates of the first molar are worn away and two of the anterior of the second in use, whilst No. 46 shows only half of the ante-penultimate remaining and five plates of the penultimate invaded.

All these mandibles present considerable discrepancies in size, irrespective of the state of wear of the first true molar and its predecessor and successor as they happen to be in use or not, and no doubt refer to sexual and perhaps also individual peculiarities; thus the maximum length, thickness, and divergence of the rami, in the order of advancement of detrition of the crown just given, are as follows :

	Length of mandible.	Thickness of ramus.	Maximum divergence of ramus.
F. A. S., pl. xiii, fig. 2.— B.M.	16·8 inches	4·8 inches	16 inches.
No. 43, Brady Collection	19 „	4·3 „	16·5 „
No. 44 ditto	21 „	5 „	20·5 „
No. 45 ditto	23 „	5·5 „	22 „
No. 46 ditto	22 „	5 „	19 „
No. 47 ditto	20 „	4·8 „	21·5 „

[1] Refer to pp. 80 and 110.

[2] 'Brit. Foss. Mammals,' p. 258 ; 'Pal. Mem.,' II, 247, and pp. 164 and 171.

[3] 'Fauna Antiqua Sival,' pl. 13 A and B, and figs. 2 and 2 *a*, 'Pal. Mem.,' vol. i, p. 439. This specimen from Germany is preserved in the British Museum.

14

When compared with two jaws of the Asiatic Elephant presenting precisely the same states of wear, the differences in these and other characters already noted become at once apparent. In all of the following jaws the ridge formula of x 12 x is present. The ante-penultimates show well-worn crowns, with the anterior ridges nearly ground down to the common base. The penultimates are in germ with the tips of their collines appearing. They furnish the following metrical data.

	E. Asiaticus, No. 1445 a, Osteological Catalogue, B.M.	E. Asiaticus, No. 2674, Cat. Mus. Roy. Coll. Surg. Eng.	E. primigenius, No. 47 Brady. Collection, B.M. Ilford.	E. primigenius, Epplesheim, B.M. (F. A. Siv., pl. 13 A, B, fig. 2).
	Inches.	Inches.	Inches.	Inches.
Extreme length of the mandible	22½	25	21	16·8
Greatest thickness in front of ascending ramus..	5¾	5½	5	4·8
Height in front of the molar	8	6	6	4·7
Greatest expansion of rami (from their outer borders)	18	15¾	20½	16
Length of the molar	6¼	6	5·9	5·4
Width at sixth ridge	2¼	2	2·2	2·2
Space between the molars (in front)	3·3	3½	3·4	2·4
Ditto ditto (behind)	5½	3	6	4·8
Space occupied by eight plates	4¼	4	3½	
Tip of rostrum to posterior border of the gutter...	6¼	5½	5½	
Antero-posterior length of symphysis below	3¾	3½	3½	
Width of the gutter at its middle	2	2¼	3	

Mandible No. $\frac{6}{6}$ of the Brady Catalogue and Collection just referred to, as figured in Plate VIII, fig. 2, is somewhat remarkable for the number and length of its digitations, showing thirteen disks in wear and only five with their digitations worn out. The molars contain respectively x 12 x in 5·2 × 2·2 inches.

These jaws are fully described by Davies, and present the best series of mandibles of the adolescent stage of growth in the Mammoth that have come under my notice.

The jaw No. $\frac{6}{6}$ presents the remarkably long rostrum shown in Woodcuts, figs. 11 and 25 (p. 139), fully 4½ inches in length; but it descends, and is therefore not in the way of the pre-maxillaries. The well-worn crowns of the molars in the jaw show considerable crimping of the machærides near the middle of the disk. The condyles are entire in this specimen, the distance between them being 13 inches, and each is 3 inches in the antero-posterior, by 3½ inches in the transverse diameter.

No. $\frac{6}{6}$ (Woodcuts, figs. 12 and 26, p. 139), B. M., presents a similar long beak, grooved and continuous with the spout. The mental foramina are irregular as to position. The crowns of the molars show thicker plates than usual in crowns from Ilford; indeed, in all or nearly all of the first true molars from ILFORD examined by me there are about eight plates in a space of 4 inches, and in the mandible, No. 47, already cited, that number is included in the space of 4½ inches. There is an abnormal character worth noting in the jaw No. $\frac{c}{c}$ (Woodcuts, figs. 12 and 26). The dental canal, which as a rule opens, as has been stated, directly upwards in the Asiatic Elephant and in the Mammoth, faces directly backwards in the above, thereby presenting an exception to a very general rule as far as the Mammoth is concerned; the jaw, moreover, shows an anomaly as regards the corresponding levels of the mentary foramina; the beak is also more horizontal than usual (Woodcut, fig. 26, p. 130).

Although the ILFORD mandibles of the Mammoth above described belong to smaller Elephants than equivalent remains from several other parts of England and elsewhere, and in length and thickness of the jaw, height of the horizontal ramus, and length of the molars, are conspicuously smaller than in the two mandibles of the recent species, it will be observed that the rami diverge much more, the gutter is wider, and the distance between the heels of the teeth greater in the Mammoth. With reference to the distinguishing characters of the mental region, horizontal and ascending rami, direction of the diasteme, and other points to be again referred to when describing the mandible, although the distinctions are well marked, I find that, as compared with the same parts in the jaws of all other known species of the genus, the mandible of the Asiatic Elephant is more closely related to the Mammoth than to any of them.

To sum up the materials, it would appear that out of twenty upper and lower anterior ante-penultimate molars one holds a formula of $x\ 9\ x$, twelve of $x\ 12\ x$, three of $x\ 13\ x$, three of $x\ 14\ x$, and one of $x\ 15\ x$.

Affinities.—The points of difference between the first true molar of the Mammoth and *E. antiquus* are usually well marked. The enamel, whether thick or thin, is never so much crimped, and the absence of the central angulation and expansion, together with the relative greater width to length, can scarcely fail in experienced hands to distinguish a true molar from that of *E. antiquus* and *E. Namadicus.* As to *E. meridionalis*, its massive size, excessive development of cement, thicker enamel, and low ridge formula, will suffice to establish a diagnosis. The Asiatic Elephant, with its narrower crown and densely crimped enamel, make distinctive characters, which are common also to *E. Armeniacus*, *E. Columbi*,[1] and *E. Hysudricus*,[2] with which it deserves to be compared most carefully.

The Penultimate or Second True Molar.

The penultimate true molar, as with its predecessors, shows a progressive increase in the number of its ridges, from the maximum ridge formula of the ante-penultimate to the minimum number in the ultimate true molar; consequently nearly the same uncertainty

[1] Falconer, 'Pal. Mem.,' vol. ii, p. 220 and 247, pl. x.
[2] 'F. A. Sival.,' pl. vii, figs. 2 and 10. *E. Hysudricus* holds $x\ 12\ x$ in its first true molar.

attaches itself to this tooth, as has been pointed out in connection with its predecessors in the dental series.

Until Falconer's differentiations established a ridge formula of x 16 x for the second true molar of the Mammoth, none of his contemporaries or predecessors had estimated the number very definitely.[1] But the average number assigned by him is subject to numerous exceptions, and is apparently, as far as I have been enabled to observe, too high an expression. Falconer states, "I have seen no authentic specimen of an upper penultimate of the Mammoth presenting more than sixteen or seventeen ridges. That exceptional cases do occur in which as many as eighteen may be seen is not improbable, but, I believe, that as holds in the existing Indian species the prevailing and normal number is sixteen."[2] He also refers to the tooth described by De Blainville,[3] in which fourteen collines exist, and doubts if the molar belongs to the Mammoth. That a penultimate true molar of the Mammoth may contain this ridge formula is proven, it appears to me, by the following instances.

Upper molars.—In the rich collection of molars belonging to the Mammoth lately obtained from the OXFORD gravel, and now in the University Museum, is an upper and lower penultimate true molar, each containing x 14 x. The upper is 6·7 × 2·8 inches, and contains eight ridges in 3¼. The other will be referred to presently.

Another and smaller upper tooth, holding the same x 14 x ridge formula in 5 × 3 inches, and eight ridges in 3½, is preserved in the Museum of Practical Geology, Jermyn Street. It is from the lower brick-earths of CRAYFORD on the Thames, and is interesting also on account of the *thin* enamel of the crown, as compared with that of the Ilford specimens, as will be referred to again presently.

The two molars, No. 23,115, evidently of the same individual, from MAIDSTONE, KENT, in the National Collection, show the ridge formula of x 14 x in 7 × 2½, and eight ridges are contained in 3·9 inches. That these teeth are penultimate true molars is at once apparent from their size and the characteristic declination of the posterior ridges, and the flat pressure mark on the last ridge and fang. The disks present the usual parallel, narrow, and uncrimped characters of the Mammoth. The enamel is *thick*, and the plates much digitated, as often prevails. It is noteworthy that several of the posterior plates present roughenings and irregularities, as if several additional ridges had been suppressed during development, and might, if unsupported by further data, be considered deformed teeth, but the other instances and examples in lower teeth, to be referred to immediately, appear to me sufficient to establish the not uncommon ridge formula of x 14 x in second true molars.

[1] Owen states it "may have from sixteen to twenty-four plates." De Blainville mentions molars with fourteen, eighteen, and nineteen plates or collines. ' Brit. Foss. Mam.,' ' Odontography,' p. 666, and ' Ostéographie des Éléphants,' pp. 195, 337.

[2] Op. cit., vol. ii, p. 168.

[3] 'Ostéog. des Éléphants,' p. 195.

There is an upper molar in the Oxford University Museum from CHRISTIAN MALFORD, in Wilts, which was found "in stiff clay." It holds x 15 x in $6\frac{1}{2}\times3$ inches, and eight ridges in 3 inches. This tooth is assuredly a second true molar, and the plates are *thick*, whilst the crown is diagnostic of the Mammoth.

A tooth in the Museum of Practical Geology, from MAIDSTONE, has x 15 x in $7\times2\frac{3}{4}$ inches. Its enamel is rather *thick*.

A tooth, No. 46,147 (Pl. IX, figs. 1 and 1 a, half natural size), from the DOGGER BANK, in Mr. Owles's Collection, B. M., shows x 15 x in $8\times2\cdot6$ inches, and eight ridges in $3\cdot2$ inches. It displays a very broad heel and posterior talon. The crown is typical of the Mammoth, and is *thin*-plated.

A fine specimen, supposed to be from the ARCTIC REGIONS, is in the collection of the British Museum. It holds distinctly x 15 x in $7\frac{1}{4}\times3$ inches. The sculpturing of the worn disk is typical of the Mammoth; and the size and contour of the tooth assuredly represent the penultimate.

The upper molar, No. 21,272, B. M., from EPPLESHEIM, shows a ridge formula of x 15 x in $6\frac{1}{2}\times2\frac{1}{2}$ inches, and eight in $3\frac{1}{4}$ inches. There is no crimping, and the tooth is very typical, having *thin* enamel.

The addition of another ridge to form the formula x 16 x, asserted by Falconer as distinctive of the second true molar of the Mammoth,[1] although present in a few lower teeth, has not come under my notice in a perfectly entire upper-jaw specimen. There are a few penultimate upper molars holding sixteen ridges in the British Museum and in other museums, but none are so entire as to show the sixteen plates, with an anterior as well as a posterior talon. I make no doubt, however, that numerous instances could be added to those given by Falconer; and even another ridge is most probably often present, although I have not hitherto seen an upper tooth with such a high ridge formula. Indeed, looking to the data furnished by the specimens of upper molars which have come under my notice, I find out of seven entire and, to all appearances, undoubted instances of this tooth from various British and foreign localities, three exhibited a ridge formula of x 14 x and four of x 15 x.

Lower molars.—The lower penultimate true molar fully sustains the variability of the formula represented by its upper tooth.

No. 40,790, B. M., from the THAMES VALLEY " brick-earths " (?), exhibits x 14 x in $8\times2\frac{1}{2}$, and holds eight ridges in $4\frac{1}{2}$ inches. Here the plates are *thick*; there is little cement, but thick enamel, with the crown well arcuated.

The same number of ridges is contained in a tooth from the OXFORD gravels in Oxford University Museum. It is $6\frac{1}{2}\times2\frac{1}{2}$ inches, and holds eight ridges in $3\cdot8$ inches.

Two molars, evidently of the same individual, each holding x 15 x in $8\times2\cdot8$ inches, and eight ridges in $3\frac{1}{2}$ inches, are preserved in the Museum of Science and Art, Dublin.

---

[1] Op. cit., vol. ii, p. 166.

They were found in SHANDON CAVE, along with other remains of the Mammoth, including two upper penultimate molars, possibly of the same individual, but the last-named teeth have been ground down to their common base in front, consequently cannot be placed in their position in the dental series with the same certainty, although I doubt not they were the opposing teeth of the two in question. Judging from the small size of the tusks which accompanied them, the probability is that they belonged to a female. The enamel is *thick*, and the cement is in excess, whilst the crowns of the upper molars are unusually convex, and those of the lower preternaturally concave.

A superb specimen of a lower second true molar, Plate XII, fig. 1, from CRAYFORD, Thames Valley, holds x 15 or else 16 x in $8\frac{1}{2} \times 3\frac{1}{4}$ inches. The anterior portion of the crown is worn to the common base, so that the number of ridges is not quite clearly defined; however, the tooth is perfect with that exception, and the loss cannot exceed a ridge at the most. It was obtained from the "lower brick-earth," and is in the Museum of Practical Geology, Jermyn Street. Like other molars from the above locality, it presents a *thin* enamel as compared with the *thick* of the Ilford specimens.

Two molars (Nos. 54 and 55) in the Woodwardian Museum, from gravel at BARNWELL, near Cambridge, hold x 16 in $7 \times 2\frac{1}{2}$ and eight ridges in $3\frac{1}{4}$. Neither is quite entire, but No. 54 does not seem to have lost more than its posterior talon. I have referred before[1] to this tooth as one of a series from the above locality. The specimens indicate rather small individuals, which contrast with the stupendous femur in the Museum of Zoology, Cambridge, from the same locality, the length of this thigh bone being 50 inches.

Two somewhat arcuated molars, each showing x 16 x in $8\frac{1}{4} \times 2\cdot8$ inches, and containing eight ridges in $3\frac{1}{4}$ inches, are present in a mandible lately discovered during the OXFORD main drainage works. The specimen is in the University Museum. The mandible, like the teeth, presents all the characters of the Mammoth. The height of the jaw in front of the molars is $6\frac{1}{2}$ inches, and breadth of the spout in front between the crest diastemes is $2\frac{1}{4}$ inches. The posterior portion of the jaw is wanting.

There are several fragments, and nearly entire true molars, from HEDDINGHAM, Essex, in the British Museum. Among them is a nearly entire penultimate lower molar, holding x 15 in $8\frac{1}{4} \times 2\frac{3}{4}$ and eight in $4\frac{3}{4}$ inches. The remarkable peculiarities of these teeth are that this penultimate and another fragment show unusual *thickness* of enamel and cement, whilst another displays the *very reverse*. In consequence of these discrepancies in teeth from the same locality and evidently similar deposits, it seems to me that all attempts to correlate thick and thin plated varieties of the crowns of molars in connection with localities receives a marked exception in this instance and in other cases, as will be shown in the sequel.

A ridge formula of x 17 x in $7\frac{1}{4} \times 2\cdot7$ inches, and containing eight in $3\cdot3$ inches, is well shown in another mandible in the Oxford University Museum, from deposits underlying OXFORD.

[1] Page 100.

A crown, No. 614, Museum Royal College of Surgeons of England, supposed to be of Arctic origin, and likely so, as the tooth is withered and dark-coloured like Siberian teeth, holds distinctly x 17 x in. 8 × 3·8 inches, and eight ridges in 2·8 inches. The enamel is very *thin* and uncrimped.

In the Woodwardian Museum there is a lower molar, No. 300, which holds x 18 x in 7 × 2$\frac{3}{4}$, and contains eight ridges in 4·2. The locality unfortunately is unknown : that it is a second or penultimate true molar is at once demonstrated by the flattening on the heel, and pressure scar of the ultimate in that situation.

Another in the same collection from St. Neots, Huntingdonshire, has the crown much bent, and holds 18 x in 8$\frac{1}{4}$ × 2$\frac{3}{4}$, with the loss of the anterior talon only. Here the narrow crown is like that of the Mammoth, with which, however, it has no other common characters. These two teeth bring the extremes of the second true molar up to the minimum expression in the ultimate, as will appear presently.

Mandibles representing various states of wear of the penultimate molar are not uncommon in collections. They exhibit similar individual discrepancies in relative dimensions as mark the jaws of the preceding member of the dental series, and are suggestive of the characters of the mandible of the Mammoth.

A typical instance is shown in a mandible from Erith, Kent, in the British Museum, where three collines of the last tooth are seen emerging above the gum, but are 1$\frac{1}{2}$ inches below the level of the crown, whilst the second true molar, with fourteen plates and a posterior talon, is more than half ground down. Perhaps the anterior talon and first plate are worn out, as the heel of the tooth is 1$\frac{1}{4}$ inch in front of the anterior border of the coronoid. The diastema has been restored with plaster, but the height of the jaw in front of the tooth is 5$\frac{1}{2}$ inches. The enamel, as in the Crayford molars, is *thin*. The length of the crown is 6$\frac{1}{2}$, and breadth 2·9 inches.

The jaw, No. 48 C., Brady Catalogue, is another good illustration. It is broken across behind the penultimate molars, and the preceding teeth have lost a ridge or two, leaving 15 x in 7·7 × 3·3 inches.

Here the enamel is *thick* and crimped, a character oftener seen in Ilford molars than in the majority of teeth from British strata, the abnormal crimping and expansion of the disks of this specimen are, as suggested by Davies, doubtless owing to the obliquity of wear of the crowns.

The rostrum in Woodcuts, figs. 10 and 24 (p. 139), shows a shallow groove down the middle, and the mentary foramina are irregular, there being three on the right and only two on the left.

A mandible, No. 38,567, B.M., with the second true molar much detrited, and the last coming into wear, there being only five of the anterior ridges just invaded, is represented by a specimen "from Peat," in the harbour of Holyhead, got during excavations in connection with its docks.[1] (See Woodcuts, figs. 6 and 20, p. 138). The jaw has lost its

[1] Lyell, 'Principles of Geology,' vol. i, p. 545.

posterior portion behind the third molars, which are also incomplete, there being only eighteen anterior plates remaining. The second is more than two thirds worn, with only nine plates remaining, and its heel is three inches in advance of the anterior border of the coronoid.

The disks are narrow, free from crimping; the enamel is *thin*, with rather an excess of cement.

The diastemes (fig. 20) are erect, and contract the interspace in front (fig. 6), considerably more so than usual, their borders being only two inches apart, and one of the mental foramina passes directly through the jaw into the gutter close to the internal nutritive canal of that channel. The upper and outer opening is just under the fang of the anterior tooth.

In the *thinness* of the enamel, narrow disks, and rather thick intervening cement, the above and some molars said to have been found in the Forest-bed present agreements.

The superb mandible, No. 49,196, dredged off the DOGGER BANK, is figured and described by Falconer,[1] who, however, does not appear to have been aware of its origin. It represents the transition stage when the second true molar is two thirds worn and about one third of the ultimate tooth is invaded. The heel of the penultimate is three and a half inches in front of the anterior border.

The above is an interesting specimen in two ways. The *thick* enamel is exceptional in Dogger Bank specimens; secondly, it is rather a famous jaw, having been the one represented on the front covers of the ' London Geological Journal ' during its able editorship by Mr. Charlesworth, F.G.S.[2]

About as large a number of lower teeth as is exhibited by the ridge formula of $x\,14\,x$, but imperfect specimens, holding as many as sixteen plates and a talon, might be also adduced, but their imperfection makes the diagnosis uncertain. On the whole it seems to me that the majority of penultimate upper molars of the Mammoth will be found to contain a formula of $x\,15\,x$.

The entire or nearly perfect skull in the Royal Museum of Brussels from Belgian deposits —a cast of which is in the Museum of the Royal College of Surgeons—displays well-worn crowns of the second true molar. The skull is described at page 128. The mandible holds two teeth, which seem to contain a ridge formula of $x\,16\,x$ each. The disks of the latter are very narrow, without any crimping of their machærides; but on comparing the crowns of the upper and lower molars, it seems to me, unless the specimens represent a rare abnormality or deformity in the upper molars, that the maxillary teeth, as will be observed in the sequel, do not belong to the jaws, indeed, it may be questionable if the mandible is that of the same individual as the owner of the cranium.[3]

[1] ' F. A. Sival.,' pl. xiii A, fig. 3 ; 'Pal. Mem.,' vol. i, p. 439.
[2] Davies' supplementary note to " Pleistocene Mammals dredged off the Eastern Coast," ' Geol. Mag.,' vol. v (1878), p. 443.
[3] I may observe that this cranium was presented to the College as being the skull of *E. antiquus*, which it certainly is not.

By compounding the foregoing and other data it seems to me that the ridge-formula of the second true molar of the Mammoth exhibits a formula ranging from x 14 x to x 16 x (rarely), and in the lower jaw from x 14 x to x 18 x. Moreover, that the most usual formula in upper molars would seem to be x 15 x, and in lower x 16—17 x. The ratios in the latter being, out of twelve entire molars, as follows :—Two had a formula of x 14 x, two of x 15 x, three of x 16 x, two of x 17 x, and two of x 18 x.

The range in equivalent teeth of *E. Asiaticus* is not, as far as I have been able to make out from many specimens, so great as in the Mammoth, and although as low a figure as fifteen plates, and even seventeen plates, with talons, may occur occasionally, the normal and very steady number of sixteen, besides accessory ridges, seems to prevail in that species.

The *E. Hysudricus*, whose dental characters present several interesting comparisons with both of the preceding, shows in the approximation of its ridge-formula, as well as the disk patterns, certain affinities with them, but more especially with the Asiatic Elephant.[1]

In comparing the tooth of *E. antiquus* with that of the Mammoth, I have stated elsewhere[2] that the ridge-formula of the latter seldom averages less than x 16 x, being then unaware of the instances I have just pointed out, and resting on the data furnished by Falconer. I believe this number is not nearly so frequent, at all events in teeth from British strata, as the formulæ x 14 x and x 15 x, which seem to me about equally common to the second true molar in either jaw. Moreover, it appears to me extremely unlikely that any practised observer would confound entire specimens of the Mammoth's second true molar with that of any of its congeners. Fragmentary specimens will always be puzzling, but a well-worn crown, with its high ridge-formula and characteristic sculpturing of the worn surface, can scarcely be mistaken for that of any species hitherto described.

The Ultimate or Third True Molar.

The ridge-formula of the last of the dental series in the Mammoth ranges from x 18 x to x 27 x, and probably individuals may be met with presenting a still higher number of plates.

The characters of the last tooth are too patent to lead to mistakes in practised hands, admitting, as in all cases of other members of the series, it is perfectly entire and the crown sculpturing pronounced.

Upper Molars.—The lowest expression of ridges which has come under my notice is shown in No. 47,122, B. M., in a tooth from "river gravel at KETTERING, Northampton." This upper molar holds x 18 x in 10 × 4½ inches, and eight ridges are contained in 4¾ inches. The plates are *thin* and there is faint crimping of the machærides.

[1] Compare pl. vii, fig. 3, 'F. A. Sival.,' with fig. 4 of the same plate, erroneously stated as being the tooth of *E. Hysudricus*, whereas it belongs to *E. Asiaticus*, 'Pal. Mem.,' i, p. 428.

[2] 'Monograph,' p. 30.

There is an ultimate upper molar in the Woodwardian Museum, possibly that referred to by Falconer as bearing "all the marks of having come out of the licks of America or a peat-bog in England." If this be the one in question he overlooked the low ridge-formula of x 18 x, which is contained in 9 × 3 inches.

Another in the same collection from "NEWTON, Isle of Wight," holds x 18 x in 9 × 3 inches, and contains eight ridges in 4 inches. The enamel is *thin*, but the dentine, and especially the cement, is somewhat in excess.

Mr. Davies appears to have been the first to indicate so low a ridge-formula as x 19 x in the Mammoth[1], inasmuch as Dr. Falconer had fixed the range between x 22 x to x 26 x, the prevailing number being about twenty-four plates.[2]

The remarkable smallness of the teeth in the ILFORD collections, as compared with molars from the opposite bank of the Thames and its upper portion, is well seen in this member of the series. That the Mammoth which frequented the valley of the river at and below London during the period of the deposition of the Pleistocene brick-earths and gravels should have differed from others in the immediate neighbourhood is scarcely likely, supposing all were living in the district at the same time; but indeed it would be difficult to prove that they were denizens of the exact localities where their remains are now found.

There are several remarkably small molars described by Davies, in which only nineteen plates and two talons exist. One is No. 3 of the Brady Catalogue, showing x 19 x in the small antero-posterior measurement of *eight* inches; the maximum breadth of the crown is 3·2 inches

The cranium (Pls. VI and VII, figs 1, 1 a) from the same locality represents an aged Mammoth with an ultimate molar, containing the ridge formula of x 19 x. The posterior portions are partly hidden in the alveoli, but the breadth of the crown is 2·8 inches, and maximum girth of the tusks 24½ inches. The specimen is suggestive, even with reference to the recent species, by showing that, as in them, the largest Elephants do not necessarily present the largest tusks.[3] The dimensions of this skull will be referred to presently.

Several remarkable specimens of true molars were discovered in a peaty deposit at LEXDEN, near Colchester, and are now preserved in the British Museum.[4] Of these, No. 36,426 is a right and left upper ultimate molar, probably of the same individual. Each holds x 19 x in 9·4 × 2·8. The former is shown in Pl. XIV, fig. 2.

In all the teeth from the above situation the enamel is *very thin*, but the cement and dentine are in excess, so that eight ridges are contained in a space of 3½ inches. The disks are more or less crimped, and the specimens are light and present the black

[1] Brady, 'Catalogue,' p. 3.

[2] 'Pal. Mem.,' vol. ii, p. 168.

[3] 'Livingstone's Travels in South Africa,' p. 562 ; Tennent's 'Ceylon,' vol. iv, p. 291 ; Baker, 'Nile Tributaries of Abyssinia,' p. 533 ; 'Albert Nyanza,' vol. i, p. 275.

[4] A full description of this discovery is given by the Rev. O. Fisher, F.G.S., in the 'Quart. Journ. Geol. Soc.,' vol. xix, p. 393.

colour and friable consistence characteristic of remains from peat. They are recorded
to have been found in conjunction with remains of *Rhinoceros leptorhinus*. The crown
constituents of all these Lexden molars—and they represent, at all events, two individuals
—present the same relative proportions as the Mammoths' molars from the Dogger Bank ;
there are, moreover, a last upper and a fragment of another true molar from the same
locality in the Museum of Practical Geology. Both present similar features, and hold
eight ridges in $3\frac{1}{2}$ inches.

The British Museum has acquired lately an upper molar from AYLESFORD in
Kent, the ridge-formula of which is x 19 x in $10 \times 2\frac{1}{2}$ inches. It is stated to have been
from " gravel."

The molar figured in the ' Fauna Antiqua Sivalensis,' pl. 1, fig. 1, and sawn up the
middle, is in the British Museum. It is labelled from BACTON, Norfolk, and appears to
me to show a ridge-formula of x 19 x in 11×3 inches. Falconer states that it holds
twenty-one plates, with the supposition that it is not quite entire, but I think a careful
inspection of the tooth will show that it is entire, and has two accessory ridges or
talons. The plates are rather thick, the excess being about equally divided in the
three elements. As many as 4 inches are included in an antero-posterior measurement
of eight plates.

The progressive increase of plates is well illustrated by numerous British and foreign
specimens in various collections.

During the formation of the Stowe Valley Railway, in a cutting near LAMARSH,
several molars of the Mammoth were discovered, which are now in the National Collection.
Among others is an upper ultimate, containing x 20 x in 9×3 inches, and eight ridges
in $3\frac{1}{4}$ inches.

In the Oxford University Museum there is an ultimate molar, containing x 20 x in
$10 \times 3\frac{1}{2}$, and eight ridges in $3\frac{1}{2}$ inches. It was obtained from LEIGHTON BUZZARD,
Bedfordshire.

In the Woodwardian Museum, Cambridge, there is a molar, No. 7, from CRAYFORD,
which contains x 20 x in $10\frac{1}{2} \times 3\frac{1}{4}$, and holds eight ridges in 4 inches. The machærides
of the disks are slightly crimped in the usual position, viz. along the central portion of the
anterior border, and the enamel is *thin.*

In the Phillips collection of teeth, from KIRBY, in the Woodwardian Museum, already
referred to at p. 95, are several ultimate molars, two of which are among the smallest
upper last molars of the Mammoth that I have examined.

No. 35, represented in Pl. XIII, fig. 1 and 1 a, has the following inscription
indistinctly written on the cement of the left side of the tooth :—" From Kirby Park, 12
feet beneath the surface, 1821. For this and other specimens I am indebted to the liberality
of Mr. (name effaced), Melton Mowbry." Indeed, as regards dimensions, this tooth is
not larger than the equivalent molar of the largest of the Pigmy Maltese Elephants,

E. Mnaidriensis.[1] There may be a loss of possibly a ridge or two in front, as the crown is detrited to the common base, to about an inch at its anterior extremity, but the scar of the anterior fang, recently broken, is seen on the lower surface, showing that the specimen is almost entire.

It holds x 20 x in $8\frac{1}{4} \times 2\frac{2}{3}$, and contains eight ridges in 2·8 inches. The enamel is slightly in excess, as compared with Pl. XIV, fig. 1, from Millbank, on the Thames. The cement having been much denuded from the grinding surface and sides, the crimpings of the anterior machærides of the disks come out in bold relief. There are fifteen ridges in wear, and the seven posterior have their digitations still visible. The crown is rather arcuated. Such, like very small grinders, are extremely suggestive, as showing, in comparison with the colossal teeth described at p. 114 and elsewhere, how very much the Mammoth varied in size; as I have stated was the case also with *E. antiquus* and the Maltese dwarf species. Two other ultimate molars from the above locality (Kirby) are of the same small dimensions, to wit, Nos. 30 and 40. The former is of the left side, and is also an upper tooth. It is less perfect than fig. 1, but it holds 20 x in only $6\frac{3}{4} \times 2\frac{2}{3}$ inches, and contains eight ridges in $2\frac{1}{2}$ inches. This tooth is clearly much smaller than the foregoing, and from the void in front appears to have held more than one plate; so that, supposing it had contained two or three additional ridges, it would have scarcely been as large as the last molar of the dwarf *Elephas Mnaidriensis*, shown in pl. xii, fig. 1, vol. ix, of the 'Transactions of the Zoological Society of London.' Indeed, it may be well said that "there were dwarf Mammoths as well as dwarf Maltese Elephants." At the same time, that larger individuals sojourned in the same locality with the above is shown by the other molars referred to already, and ultimate molars to be noticed presently.

The same collection contains three molars from WALTON-ON-THE-NAZE, Essex. No. 64 *bis* holds x 19—20 x in $11\frac{1}{2} \times 3$ inches, and is quite a typical crown; the other, No. 104, is much bent and very narrow, like that of *E. antiquus;* it holds x 20 x in 12×3. The enamel here is *thin* and the cement is much in excess, and the machærides are very little crimped. The crown contains eight ridges in 5 inches.

An upper tooth of large size from EPPELSHEIM, and holding x 20 x in $12 \times 3\frac{1}{2}$ inches, is in the National Collection. The plates are not thick for the dimensions of the molar, eight being contained in 4 inches. Another, but fragmentary, specimen of a true molar from the same locality presents *thin* enamel, with little intervening cement, and holds eight ridges in a space of 3 inches.

The addition of an extra ridge, or a formula of x 21 x, in upper last molars is represented by numerous specimens from British and foreign localities.

---

[1] "Dentition and Osteology of the Maltese Fossil Elephants," 'Trans. Zool. Soc. Lond.,' vol. ix, p. 36. I apprehend that last true molars of the largest of the Maltese Elephants attained a length of eight inches. Dr. Falconer refers to "a dwarf-sized molar of *E. primigenius* in the possession of Mr. Prestwich from a railway-cutting at Bedford, 'Pal. Mem,' vol. ii, p. 169.

A very large molar, dredged up from the bed of the German Ocean off WALTON, on the Essex coast, and now in the British Museum, holds x 21 x in $11\frac{1}{2} \times 3\frac{1}{2}$ inches. There is faint crimping of the crown-disk, but none of the constituents are in excess.

Another in the same collection, with thick edges of cement and *thin* enamel, from a railway-cutting near IPSWICH, Suffolk, contains x 21 x in $9\frac{2}{3} \times 3\frac{1}{4}$ inches, and eight plates in a space of 4·2 inches. A fragment of a third milk-molar was also discovered in the same situation. It holds eight ridges in 3 inches, and indicates a similar character.

No. 37,248, B. M., a superb and typical crown (Pl. XIV, fig. 1), dredged up from the THAMES near MILLBANK, holds x 21 x in $9 \times 3\cdot 2$ inches, and eight ridges in 3·2 inches. The enamel is *thin*, but there is no excess of cement nor of dentine, nor any indication of crimping.

A tooth from BROUGHTON FISSURE, near Maidstone, holding x 21 x in 9 inches, and eight plates in $3\frac{1}{2}$ inches, is preserved in the University Museum, Oxford.

In the collection in the British Museum from the DOGGER BANK, already referred to at p. 73, are numerous, entire, ultimate molars, with ridge-formulæ varying between twenty-one to twenty-six plates, besides talons. They show the great discrepancies in dimensions between molars with the same ridge-formula. One, a superb specimen, carries x 21 x in $12 \times 3\frac{1}{2}$ inches, and eight ridges in 3·2 inches; whilst another holds x 21 x in $8\cdot6 \times 3$, and eight ridges in 3 inches.

In the Cotton Collection of the Museum of Practical Geology, there is an ILFORD ultimate upper molar holding x 21 x in $8\frac{4}{5} \times 3$ inches, and eight ridges in a space of $3\frac{1}{2}$ inches.

In Dr. Bree's collection, dredged on the EAST COAST and ENGLISH CHANNEL, I examined a large last molar holding either twenty-two or twenty-three plates, besides talons, in $10 \times 3\cdot 2$ inches.

In the collection of dwarf Elephants' teeth from KIRBY, in the Cambridge Museum, is the small, imperfect, upper molar (No. 29), holding 21 x in $9 \times 2\frac{3}{4}$ inches, and eight in 3 inches. It contrasts with Nos. 30 and 35 already noticed, in not only holding a larger formula, which possibly exceeded the above, but it is also a longer tooth. The plates are *thin*, but the cement is rather in excess ; the characters, however, are the same as the other dwarfed molars from the above-named locality.

There are several well authenticated cases of molars holding x 22 x.

A tooth from a cavern near WELLS, in Somersetshire, in the British Museum shows a ridge-formula of x 22 x in 9×3, and contains eight ridges in a space of 3 inches. It is decidedly *thin*-plated.

A molar recovered from the OXFORD gravels during the main drainage operations of 1877, and now in the University Museum, contains x 22 x in 10×3 inches, and contains eight plates in 3 inches.

There is a tooth, supposed to have been dredged in the Medway, in the British Museum with *very thin* enamel, sparse dentine, and rather an excess of cement. It holds x 22 x in $10 \times 3\frac{1}{4}$ inches, and contains eight plates in $2\frac{3}{4}$ inches.

The following are the only two instances of a last upper molar holding $x\,23\,x$ that have come under my notice.

A last true molar and an enormous spirally curved tusk were dug up within ten miles of SPALDING, in Lincolnshire, and are now in the National Collection. The former, No. 39,695, Plate IX, fig. 2 (half natural size), is truly a superb specimen, and contains a ridge-formula of $x\,23\,x$ in $13\frac{1}{2} \times 3$ inches. The plates are rather thick, but not from any marked excess of any of the elements in particular. It contains eight plates in $4\frac{3}{4}$ inches. The tusk has been already referred to at page 82.

A DOGGER-BANK specimen holds $x\,23\,x$ in $10\frac{1}{2} \times 3\frac{1}{2}$, and eight plates in 3·2 inches. Like all the ultimate molars from this shoal in Mr. Owles's collection, B. M., the enamel is *thin*. The abnormality in the configuration of the disks whereby they are united near their middle by reflections of the enamel as shown on the crown, fig. 94 of the British Fossil Mammals, is further represented on that of an enormous last upper molar, No. D, 11, 33 a, of the Woodwardian Museum. Unfortunately the locality of this specimen is unknown. The above irregularity is confined also to the anterior disks, which are more or less detrited, to near the common base, and to the extent that only half a disk is preserved on one side, showing that the plates were incomplete near the enamel reflections as well as united for some distance along the middle of the plate. The character is unimportant as a distinction and deserves little attention, but for the circumstance that the somewhat similar condition was advanced by Parkinson as a specific character, apart from that of the usual crown of the Mammoth as then known to palæontologists.[1]

The tooth in question holds $x\,23\,x$ in $12 \times 3\frac{1}{2}$ inches and contains eight ridges in $4\frac{1}{2}$ inches.

The ridge-formula of $x\,24\,x$ is common in upper molars.

A molar from the DOGGER BANK showing the attenuated enamel, holds a ridge formula of $x\,24\,x$ in $11\frac{1}{2} \times 4$, or eight ridges in 3·7 inches, without a trace of crimping on the enamel of the disks.

Another dredged specimen from BRIGHTLINGSEA, Essex coast, in Dr. Bree's collection, has $x\,24\,x$ in 9 inches. Like the Dogger-Bank teeth it is remarkable for its *thin* enamel.

There is a very typical specimen of an ultimate upper molar from OHIO among the collection in the Museum of the Royal College of Surgeons, and purchased on the occasion referred to at page 75. It is numbered 615 of the Catalogue and is described by Falconer.[2] Here, there are clear indications of twenty-four ridges, and the tooth is seemingly entire. The maximum antero-posterior measurement of the crown is $12\frac{1}{4}$ and the greatest width $3\frac{3}{4}$ inches. It holds eight ridges in $4\frac{1}{2}$ inches. Cement here is in excess, but the enamel and dentine are sparse as usual in the Ohio teeth.

The *thin-plated crown* appears to characterise also the teeth of Mammoths from CENTRAL FRANCE, as is well shown by M. Logard in the plates of the 'Archives du Mus.

[1] 'Organic Remains,' pl. xx, figs. 5 and 7, reproduced in British Fossil Mammals, as above stated.
[2] 'Pal. Mem.,' ii, p. 169.

d'Hist. Naturelle de Lyon.' Teeth holding apparently x 24 x in about $10\frac{1}{2} \times 3\frac{1}{2}$ inches are represented in vol. i, plate xi, figs. 1 to 5. The ridge-formula in one specimen, apparently not entire, amounts to twenty-nine plates (see plate xiii, fig. 1). Here the ridges are crowded together and the crowns have all the appearance of Arctic specimens.

A mandible, with the two last molars, in the British Museum, from BERGSTRASSE, near Heidelberg, has the hinder parts of the teeth hidden, so that the ridge-formula cannot be ascertained with certainty. There are twenty-one plates besides the anterior talons exposed in a space of 9×3 inches. Here the enamel and the other constituents are in moderate quantities, showing a typical crown.

A dark-coloured specimen, said to have been from the THAMES VALLEY, has *thin* plates. The anterior ridge is broken off, leaving 24 x in 9 inches. It contains eight in $2\frac{3}{4}$ inches. This tooth, No. 612 of the Catalogue of the Museum of the Royal College of Surgeons, like 600 of the same collection, being imperfect, is not reliable as regards the formula. The latter is the very characteristic ultimate tooth figured by Parkinson and Owen, and referred by the latter to be a second true molar.' It is from WELSBOURNE, in Warwickshire, and is remarkable for the *thinness* of its enamel, with faint crimping of the machærides of the worn disk, which are well shown in Professor Owen's figure. Only twenty-one or twenty-two plates besides the posterior talon remain, the tooth being much worn; its contour, however, and the unusual ridge-formula for a second true molar, place it unquestionably, as indicated by Falconer, among the ultimate upper true molars of the Mammoth.[2]

There is a huge upper molar, No. 50, in the Woodwardian Museum, holding twenty-four to twenty-five plates besides talons in 12×4 inches. The crown is much arcuated. The locality is unknown, but it is possibly of British origin.

A superb specimen in the DOGGER-BANK Collection, British Museum, holds x 26 x in 13×5 inches, and contains eight ridges in 4 inches. The inordinate width in this specimen arises from the obliquity of the plane of detrition, which is at an angle of 45°. This condition is not unfrequent in domesticated Elephants fed on dry food, but is rarely seen among wild animals, at all events to the extent shown in the above specimen.

There is in the Beechey Collection from ESCHSCHOLTZ BAY, in the British Museum, a palate specimen holding a fragment of the penultimate and entire last true molars on either side. The latter contain x 26 x in 9×3 inches, and hold eight plates in $2\frac{1}{2}$ inches. Here, as usual, the enamel is *very thin*, and the ridges are packed closely with little intervening cement.

The only instance of an ultimate molar containing x 27 x that has come under my notice is represented by a specimen from the "bed of the CHERWELL," in the Museum of Oxford University. The tooth is $10\frac{1}{2} \times 3$ inches, and contains eight ridges in a space of $3\frac{1}{4}$ inches. The enamel is *thin*, and the disk free from crimping.

1 "Organic Remains;" 'Brit. Fossil Mammals,' p. 238, figs. 91 and 92.
2 'Pal. Mem.,' vol. ii, p. 168.

Several typical *thin*-plated crowns of Mammoth molars, including the last of the series, with from twenty-five to twenty-six plates, are well shown in pls. xi, xii, xvi, and xvii of the 'Archives du Museum d'Histoire Naturelle de Lyon,' by Dr. Lortet and M. Chantre. The specimens were obtained from the valley gravels of the Soane and Loire.[1]

Lower Molars.—I have not seen a lower last molar with so low a ridge-formula as $x\,18\,x$, but doubtless examples might be adduced.

A tooth in the British Museum, from ILFORD brickfields, holds $x\,19\,x$ in $9\frac{1}{4} \times 2\frac{3}{4}$. The crown shows slight crimping of the enamel, which is *thin*.

A dredged specimen in the collection of Dr. Broe, from the NORTH SEA, holds $x\,19\,x$ in 11 inches. The plates are *very thick*.

No. 127 of the Woodwardian Museum (locality unknown) is possibly the tooth referred to by Falconer,[2] and if so it is surprising that he overlooked the formula, seeing that it clearly holds $x\,19\,x$, being at least three ridges below what he believed obtained in the ultimate molar of the Mammoth. It is $10\frac{1}{2} \times 3\frac{1}{4}$, and contains eight ridges in 5 inches, all the elements being in excess.

The formula of $x\,20\,x$ is exhibited in the following :

A mandible, No. 624 A in the Museum of the Royal College of Surgeons of England, from the brick-earths (?) of GRANTHAM, near Crayford, below London, is nearly entire, and besides the ultimate there had been a fragment of the second molar also in use, but it is lost. The former holds $x\,20\,x$ in $12 \times 2\frac{3}{4}$ inches. The jaw is characteristic of the species, with a high diastema. The height at the summit of the latter is $7\frac{1}{2}$ inches, and the width of the guttar in front is $2\frac{3}{4}$ inches. The mental foramina maintain their general positions, being near the margin with the larger one, close to the anterior fang of the second tooth.

A mandible with the ultimate molars in place from ERITH, Kent, is in the British Museum. Each tooth holds $x\,20\,x$ in $9\frac{1}{2} \times 3$ inches. The enamel is *thick*.

No. 582, Mus. Roy. College of Surgeons, is a right ramus with a third molar and fragment of a second in front. The locality is unknown, and the tooth represents a cluster of digitations on the posterior ridge, as in a major degree marks occasional deformities, where the ultimate portion is often doubled up upon the side of the crown. The tooth is much arcuated and thick-plated, and shows a formula of $x\,20\,x$ in $12 \times 2\frac{1}{2}$ inches, with eight ridges in as much as $4\frac{1}{2}$ inches.

I am indebted to my friend Mr. Davies, F.G.S., for drawing my attention to a very interesting collection of Pleistocene remains in the British Museum, from PORCUPINE RIVER, on the eastern frontier of Alaska. The collection comprehends two molars and an astragal of the Mammoth, besides remains of the bison, musk-ox, and horse, all of

---

[1] These authors also figure pls. xix and xx, large massive crowns, which they refer to *E. meridionalis*, from Central and Southern France. These teeth, however, appear to me to belong to *E. antiquus*, and represent the broad and thick-plated crowns described in my ' Monograph,' p. 31.

[2] 'Pal. Mem.,' vol. ii, 174.

which are said to have been discovered in the same deposits by the Rev. R. Macdonald. An entire lower last molar of the left ramus, No. 44,060, holds x 20 x in 9 × 3¼, and eight ridges in a space of 5 inches. The tooth, as usual in Arctic specimens, has very *thin* enamel, but the cement is in great excess. There is very faint crimping of the thread-like machærides of the former. A fragment of a nearly worn-out crown of a true molar of another individual shows a similar condition of its constituents, whilst the astragal has the projecting posterior and inner angle of the species, and represents a rather small individual. Some of the bones appear to have been gnawed. Mr. Davies had carefully compared the remains of the Bison with the European fossil species, and was unable to make out differences. Similar remains of the latter species are contained in Kellet's collections, in the British Museum, from Kotzebue Sound, and also from Eschscholtz Bay, where Mammoth remains are plentiful.

The presence of x 21 x in lower ultimate molars is demonstrated by a rolled specimen from SIBERIA, in the British Museum. It is 11 × 2 inches in width and is somewhat arcuated. The enamel is *thin*, with slight crimping and rather an excess of cement, eight ridges being contained in 3¼ inches. This tooth, although much attrited by rolling possibly in the bed of some mountain torrent, is altogether remarkably narrow for that of a Mammoth.

Dr. Bree's collection contains a dredged specimen, from the EAST COAST, of an ultimate molar, which holds x 22 x in 9½ × 2½ inches.

No. 40,699, B. M., a crown view of which is shown in Plate XIV, fig. 3, is one of the " waifs and strays " either cast ashore by the waves or fished up by the troll net. It is remarkable for its rather thick enamel, and the plates are much digitated, and the crown considerably arcuated. It holds x 22 x in 11½ × 2·8 inches, and contains eight ridges in 4¼ inches. It is recorded in the Catalogue as having been " dredged off CROMER FOREST BED."

A tooth from the DOGGER BANK holds x 22 x in 8½ × 2·6 inches and contains eight in 3·1 inches. It is remarkable for its small size, and is therefore exceptional as compared with the other ultimate molars from the above-mentioned shoal; even a molar which has evidently lost only its anterior talon holds 22 x in 11¼ × 3¼ inches, and contains eight in 3·6 inches. In both the enamel is *thin*.

The DOGGER BANK Collection furnishes two specimens of lower molars with a ridge formula of x 23 x each. One is 13 × 3 inches and contains eight in 4·4 inches. The plates are rather thick for the size of the tooth, which is 4½ inches longer than the first mentioned. There is, as usual in Dogger-Bank teeth, no crimping of the machærides. The crown is arcuated. The other tooth is 11¾ × 3 inches and contains 8 ridges in 3·9 inches. Here the enamel is *thin*, as usual in its companion molars from the above situation. The crown is much arcuated.

In the collection of Dr. Bree, I noticed a molar holding x 23 x, recorded to have been dredged off DUNKIRK. It was 9 inches in length and " *thin*-plated."

16

The formula of x 24 x in lower last molars is well seen in a superb specimen in the Museum of Zoology, Cambridge University, in which the above is contained in a space of 12 × 3 inches, and eight ridges are held in a space of 4¼ inches. The crown is considerably arcuated, and the specimen shows every indication of having been dredged.

Broken molars.—The largest molar of the Mammoth I have seen from British soil is a fragment of an upper tooth, No. 33,328, B.M., in the Layton Collection, which was made on the NORFOLK COAST. This molar when entire must have been of gigantic proportions. There are sixteen plates in 9¾ × 4½ inches, the half of which are contained in a space of 5 inches. The enamel is not particularly thick for the size of the tooth, but the ridges are very high for a molar of the Mammoth, the eighth ridge being 8 inches in height. The disk presents all the features of the crown of the species in question as distinguishable from *E. meridionalis* or *E. antiquus.* Although no history is attached to the specimen it was evidently either dredged up or found on the shore.

Another broken tooth, but evidently of enormous size, is represented by a fragment in the British Museum, from FENNY STRATFORD, Essex. It holds x 12 in 7 × 4½. Here the enamel is *thin* and the cement scant, but the dentine is in excess, causing unusual width of the plate. There is likewise a large tusk in the Museum, from the same locality, to which I have already referred to at p. 52.

In Mantell's Collection, British Museum, there are several true molars, none of which are entire, from a raised beach at BRIGHTON, Sussex. All are deeply impregnated with chalk. They evidently belonged to *thick-plated* teeth of very large dimensions. But a fragment of a true molar from "gravel (?) BRIGHTON," in the Museum of Practical Geology, has *thin* enamel with rather an excess of cement, and holds eight in 3¼ inches.

A very large molar is instanced by the fragment of an upper molar from OUNDLE, Northamptonshire, in the British Museum. It has none of its collines invaded, and holds x 19 in 11 × 4½ inches. The plates are *very thick* with excess of cement.

Another broken tooth in the same Museum, from Northampton, has x 19 in 10 × 2 inches, and holds eight in 4 inches. Like the preceding it is characterised by its *thick* plates and abundance of cement. The crown is arcuated a good deal, and the tooth may have belonged to the mandible of the foregoing.

I examined very carefully the imperfect ultimate upper molar in the Woodwardian Museum, stated by Falconer to belong to "the *pre-glacial* variety of *Elephas primigenius* from the NORWICH COAST."[1] Assuredly, the matrix with which it is intimately encrusted is indistinguishable from that on the crowns and palate of a superb specimen of the ultimate molars of *E. meridionalis* and other teeth of the latter "from the Forest Bed," in the Woodwardian Collection.[2] Whether or not certain *post-glacial* beds, as I believe

---

[1] 'Pal. Mem.,' vol. ii, p. 170. Falconer further substantiates his belief in the Mammoth having been *Pre-glacial* by statements elsewhere (see 'Pal. Mem.,' vol. ii, p. 240).

[2] Professor Boyd Dawkins points out instances similar to the above from the Forest Bed at Bacton,

has been suggested, were derived from the "Forest Bed," there can be no question whatever as to the correctness of Falconer's diagnosis of the above molar. It has clearly the typical crown of the Mammoth, with rather *thin* enamel, according to my experience, whilst Falconer says "slightly thick." He observes, moreover, that the plates are "perfectly free from crimping." This is not apparently quite the case, as there is a little crimping towards the middle of the mineral machærides.

The tooth is about 11½ inches in length by about 4 inches in width, and contains eighteen ridges, and eight ridges in 4 inches. It represents that of an aged individual, and only wants the assurance of its reputed origin to establish the existence of *E. primigenius* in *pre-glacial* times.

A *thick-plated* tooth in a fragmentary condition from "blue clay at Lawford, near RUGBY," is in the University Museum, Oxford. It holds 19 *x*, and contains eight ridges in 4 inches. The thickness of the plates here appear dependent on a general increase of the crown constituents, and not of one element in particular.

In the Museum of Science and Art, Dublin, there is a mutilated molar of the upper jaw of the Mammoth, received from the "BLACK SEA." Unfortunately there is no further history attached to it, but my friend Dr. Carte, M.R.I.A., Conservator of the Museum, is of opinion that it was presented to the collection by an officer during the Crimean War. It has evidently been dredged, as it contains shells of *Cirripedia* and cells of *Flustra* on its outer surface. There is a loss of plates behind as well as in front, so that its exact position in the series cannot be accurately defined. It holds thirteen plates in 4½ inches. The enamel is very *thin* and altogether similar to the very *thin*-plated Arctic molars.

There is a fragment (No. 10) of a last molar, containing about twelve plates, in the Woodwardian Museum, from the "Valley of the DANUBE." Its enamel is somewhat *thick*.

Two lower teeth, No. 572 of the Museum of the Royal College of Surgeons, from BRIDPORT, Dorsetshire, are remarkable for their narrow crowns and *thick* plates, and contain 19 *x* in 11 × 3 inches. There are eight ridges in 4·2 inches.

A fragment from the "ISLE OF DOGS," near mouth of the Thames, is in the British Museum. It is stated to have been procured from a peaty deposit. The enamel is *thin*, and eight ridges are contained in 3 inches.

Another broken tooth, showing very closely packed plates and *thin* enamel, is in the same collection. There are nineteen ridges; and eight ridges in only 2½ inches. The specimen is evidently that of an ultimate molar, and was found in gravel at BALLINGDON, in Hertfordshire.

Norfolk Coast, 'Quart. Journ. Geol. Soc.,' vol. xxviii, p. 418. I must here correct a surmise made by me with reference to the above molar in supposing that the specimen was probably the broad-crowned variety of *E. antiquus* ('Monograph on *E. antiquus*,' note 1, p. 40). This supposition, after having examined the specimen, which I had not seen at the time, I now fully admit was wrong.

Another lower ultimate tooth in the British Museum, from WALTHAMSTOW, Essex, holds twenty-two plates in $10\frac{1}{2} \times 3$ inches and eight in $4\frac{1}{2}$ inches. This a *thick-plated molar*, but the cement is also in excess.

A lower ultimate in the British Museum, from the Thames near BRENTFORD, Middlesex, has twenty-one of the anterior ridges remaining in $11 \times 2\frac{1}{2}$ inches, and contains eight in 5 inches. The plates are *very thick*, with much cement. The crown is narrow and much arcuated.

A mutilated lower ultimate molar, holding *æ* 18, from the "post-pliocene," DARTFORD, Kent, is in the Museum of Practical Geology. It is noteworthy for its very thick plates and crimped enamel; the latter, however, is not abnormal as regards thickness, but the dentine and, chiefly, cement are in excess.

An imperfect crown from gravel at CHESTERTON, Cambridgeshire, in the Woodwardian Museum, presents *thin* enamel, which is crimped. There are from twenty to twenty-one plates, besides a posterior talon, in $8\frac{1}{2} \times 3$ inches, and eight ridges are contained in a space of 2·8 inches. There is also a fragment of a tusk from the same locality. The molar contrasts, as regards the thickness of its plates, with a milk molar from the same situation, described at p. 97, whose plates are decidedly *thick*, whilst both indicate small individuals of their respective ages as is seen in the Ilford molars.

The Museum of Zoology, Cambridge, contains a fragment of an ultimate molar holding fourteen collines in 7×3 inches. It is interesting as being from WHITBY, in Yorkshire. The crown is *typical*.

The same collection contains a fragment of a true molar from WENDEN, in Essex, with a *typical* crown pattern, and another fragment from "valley gravel," BOCKING, Essex, with rather *thick* enamel; also a piece of a last molar from BUXTON, Derbyshire, and also a broken tooth from gravel at KENSINGTON, London, containing eight ridges in $3\frac{1}{2}$ inches. The plates in the last-named tooth are rather *thick*, with the enamel like that in Ilford molars, whilst two other specimens from the "brick-earths" at SITTINGBOURNE, Kent, are *thin*-plated, both the enamel and cement being thin.

An incomplete true molar, possibly an ultimate, recorded from "COMPTON BAY, Isle of Wight (Forest Bed)," is in the Jermyn Street Collection. It is *thick*-plated at the expense of the enamel, which is inordinately *thick*. There is also a germ of either an ultimate or penultimate in the same collection from "Freshwater Gravel, CHALE BAY, Isle of Wight." The characters of this tooth are not determinable with certainty.

A fragment of one or other of the last of the series from KENT'S CAVERN is in the British Museum. It shows, as has been already noted, *thin* enamel (p. 94) with faint crimping of the disks.

There is an imperfect right lower last true molar from BARRINGTON, in the Woodwardian Museum, Cambridge, containing 17 *æ* in $11 \times 2\frac{3}{4}$ inches. All the elements of the crown are in excess, the cement in particular, and the disks present crimping with central dilatation, like as in *E. antiquus*, but not to the extent at all likely to lead to a doubt as to the species to which the molar belonged.

Among the foreign molars in the British Museum is a fragment of a last lower molar from SIBERIA, in the Sloane Collection. It is noteworthy for the *thick* enamel and cement in an Arctic specimen, there being eight ridges in 4¾ inches.

A good instance of the deformities to which ultimate molars of Elephants are subject is represented by a remarkable abnormality in a molar in the British Museum, from ESCHSCHOLTZ BAY, the plates being rolled up like a " roly-poly " pudding.[1]

In the Woodwardian Museum there is a very large ultimate upper molar containing about twenty-four ridges, with the hinder ones also doubled on the side of the heel, as in the foregoing specimen. This is the tooth referred to in Dr. Falconer's ' Palæontological Memoirs,' from some entry in a note-book, wherein he is stated to have written that the above-mentioned molar "bears all the marks of having died in captivity in the service of man of the flint-knife period."[2] This would, of course, imply that Falconer held a belief that the man of the Stone Age had probably reclaimed the Mammoth, but a subsequent explanation (pp. 281 and 285 of his paper " On the food of Elephants ") shows clearly that the deformity in question is ascribable to causes not necessarily dependent on captivity, as might be readily supposed. The tooth is otherwise typical of the Mammoth; its locality however, is unknown. I fail, therefore, to notice any further character which could in any way account for the above statement, which, after all, was merely the jottings-down of a memorandum book, and might have been judiciously omitted in transcribing his notes.

A curious and interesting specimen of an excessively worn ultimate molar of the Mammoth was brought to my notice by Professor McKenny Hughes in the Woodwardian Museum. The ridges were nearly ground to their enamel reflections, the plates being nearly all converted into insular-shaped loops on the surface of dentine, whilst the fangs had become consolidated into a ridge running along the base of the crown like the keel of a vessel. It is a lower tooth of the right side. It moreover serves well as an illustration of the state of knowledge of proboscidean anatomy one hundred and fifty-three years ago, as may be inferred from the following entry in ' A Catalogue of the Foreign Fossils in the Collection of J. Woodward, M.D.,' part 2, p. 23, July, 1725, London, in which the above is described, p. 40, " as a very large grinder of some cetaceous fish, weighing . . perfect, and entire; dug up in the DUCHY of WIRTEMBERG."

Mr. Davies showed me a drawing of a lower last true molar, in the possession of Mr. Dawson, of Beccles, Suffolk, in which only three small rounded islands of enamel remain in a mass of dentine 7¾ × 2 inches in breadth. The height of the ivory base is

---

[1] The very fine specimen of the lower ultimate molar of the Asiatic Elephant, ' Brit. Fossil Mammals,' fig. 90, shows a similar deformity, which is repeated in various teeth of recent and fossil species, such as those shown in pl. vii, fig. 6, and pl. ix, fig. 6, of De Blainville's ' Ostéographie.'

[2] Vol. ii, p. 169.

4½ inches, and indicates that the latter had been increased when the ridges were being worn out. The interesting fragment from Parkinson's Collection in the Museum of the Royal College of Surgeons, and figured by him and Professor Owen, is equalled by nearly a precisely similar fragment, No. 3448 of the KENT's CAVERN Collection, lately sent to me for examination by Mr. Pengelly. These teeth attest the extreme age attained by the animal.[1]

The two North-American molars, figured and described by Cuvier,[2] one from near the mouth of the " MISSISSIPPI," the other from " BIGBONE LICK," Kentucky, show, as in the lower molar from Siberia, described at p. 117, very evident traces of having been much rolled. Neither specimen was seemingly entire. One of these contains twenty-two ridges, and presents precisely the same *thin*-plated characters of the foregoing and the molars from BEHRING STRAIT and the Arctic Circle generally.

There are two fragments of true molars, possibly ultimate teeth, in the Woodwardian Museum, from "BIGBONE LICK, Kentucky," bearing the peculiarly Arctic aspect of the above, in the enamel being *very thin*. Like the Ohio molars the specimens are blackened, as obtains also in Mastodon remains from the latter State, as if all had come out of peat. A fragment from the same locality is in the British Museum, and as far as appearances go is indistinguishable from the foregoing.

Mandibles with teeth in situ.—There are two mandibles in the British Museum of very old Elephants, in the Owles Collection, from the DOGGER BANK. One is No. 46,197, and shows (as in Plate VIII, fig. 3, from Ilford) the usual characters of ultimate teeth in containing more cement externally than in the preceding teeth, for the reason that this material is needed to fill up the space between the tooth and the jaws. In the former the round heel is nearly level with the border of the coronoid, and, although the jaw is broken across immediately behind, a considerable fragment of the cancellated plug remains where, in the case of a second or any other member of the dental series, the crown of a successor would have appeared. The crowns of the molars are detrited to the common base in front, and only twelve plates and posterior talon remain. The rostrum in this specimen is conspicuously long (Woodcut, fig. 23, p. 139), being over 3 inches in length, and the antero-posterior diameter, including the spout, is 1J inches. The mental foramina (Woodcut, fig. 9, p. 135) are further apart from the free margin of the diastema than usually obtains in the species. The jaws are thick, being about 6·2 inches at the base of the coronoid, and the height of the symphysis is 4·2 inches. The teeth converge a good deal, being 4 inches apart in front, 5 at the middle, and 8 behind.

The other mandible, No. 46,215, B. M., shows molars with *very thick* enamel and much cement as compared with the usual crown from the DOGGER BANK. Here the mental foramina are also unusually irregular, there being four on the right and three on the left, at irregular distances relatively to the border of the diastema. The tooth is

[1] 'Organic Remains,' pl. xx, fig. 7 : 'Brit. Fossil Mammals,' fig. 95.
[2] 'Ossemens Fossiles,' vol. ii, p. 181, and pl. xv, figs. 9 and 11.

more detrited than the preceding, having lost a few more plates, and the heel is level with the anterior border.   There is no rostrum, only a slight beak, with the borders of the diastema running down to a point in front of the chin, to meet and form the chevron-shaped front shown in the Woodcut, fig. 7 (p. 135).

The molars from the Arctic regions, although very characteristic on account of the extreme tenuity of their enamel, exhibit exceptional instances, which, with similar cases from British and European localities, seem to me to point to the *thick-* and *thin-*plated teeth as being often casual differences and individual peculiarities.   A mandible in the British Museum, from Eschscholtz Bay, a front and profile view of which are shown in Woodcut, fig. 5 (p. 135), is referred to by Buckland in the Appendix to Beechy's ' Voyage of the Blossom.'   It has lost a portion of the right ramus, and both of the coronoid processes, otherwise the jaw is entire.   This mandible is typical of the Arctic specimens.   The dental canal is large, gaping, and opens directly upwards, with a small projecting spine on its anterior border.   The condyle and its neck viewed from behind show a pronounced concavity on the inner border of the latter, but it is not so deep as in the Asiatic, yet it has the prominent crotchet which seems very general in the Asiatic as pointed out by Busk, and considered by him to be characteristic of that species.[1]   The height in front of the molar is 6¼ inches, and maximum width of the ascending ramus at the base of the coronoid is 6½ inches.   The front portions of the teeth are ground down, leaving thirteen plates with a projecting heel in 8½ × 3¼ inches, whilst eight plates occupy a space of 4½ inches.   The plates here are *thick*, and the machærides *crimped*, such as are not common in Siberian and North-American molars.   The breadth in front between the teeth is 2¼ inches, at the middle 5 inches, and posteriorly 7½ inches.   The elevated and rounded heel is just half an inch behind the anterior border of the coronoid, yet the part of the ascending ramus behind is made up of spongy and cancellated bone without any appearance of plates.   This must have been a very old Elephant.

There is another mandible of Siberian origin in the British Museum, holding two well-worn ultimate true molars; the rounded heel, however, is 3 inches behind the anterior border of the coronoid, and quite flattened, as in the preceding, with a space[2] of 7 inches between it and the entrance to the dental canal.   Mr. Davies caused, as in the preceding, an incision to be made in the back portion of the ascending ramus, but without meeting with a trace of a colline, and only the spongy septum present, made up

[1] 'Trans. Zool. Soc. London,' vol. vi, p. 237.
[2] The position of the heel of the molar in wear with reference to the anterior border of the coronoid will readily indicate to the student the state of advancement he may expect of the successional tooth, as shown by numerous beautiful examples in the rich and instructive collection of the Royal College of Surgeons. In a nearly similar instance to the above in the Asiatic Elephant the second true molar has thirteen of its anterior ridges invaded, and heel two inches behind the anterior border of the coronoid, whilst the vault of the third molar is just broken through, and the collines are lying loose in their capsule. See also the mandible of the Mammoth with the first true molar in full wear in the 'F. A. Siv.,' pl. xiii A, fig. 2, and that of *E. Hysudricus*, fig. 7.

of spiculated particles of cancellated bone, and earthy material.[1] There is a loss by dentrition of the fore part of each molar, which holds 13 *r* in 9 × 3¾. The enamel is *thick*, with much cement and some crimping of the machærides ; indeed, eight ridges are contained in 4¾ inches, which show the great thickness of the plates as compared with the usual crowns from the Arctic regions.

The molars converge considerably, being 2·9 inches apart in front, 3¾ at their middle, and 3¾ posteriorly. The ramus is 7 inches in thickness at the base of the coronoid. The jaw has all the characters of that of the Mammoth already noticed.[2]

Another nearly entire mandible in the British Museum, dredged off Harwich, presents some rather remarkable peculiarities. The two molars are in full wear, with a loss of some ridges in front by detrition, without a trace of a third tooth in the cavity posteriorly, as proved by inspection, although the round prominent heels are elevated, and 2½ inches behind the anterior border of the coronoid.[3] Each molar holds seventeen plates in 10½ × 3½ inches, and is considerably arcuated and converges ; the distance between them in front is 3 inches, at the middle 3½, and behind 7¼ inches. The maximum length of the jaw from the posterior border of the ascending ramus 20 inches. Height in front of the molar 8½ inches. Maximum thickness of the ramus 6¾ inches. Maximum expanse of the jaw at the middle of the ascending ramus 20 inches. The diasteme is perpendicular.

The numerous molars of the Mammoth derived from peat at Lexden, near Colchester, Essex,[4] several of which have been already noticed, point to the fact that the *thickness* or *thinness* of the enamel cannot always be depended upon as characteristic of races or local varieties, although, as has been shown, it is peculiarly *thin* in Arctic and the so-called Ohio and North-American molars, as well as in many teeth from British strata.

The mandible (No. 95, Fisher Collection) in the Woodwardian Museum contains two ultimate molars from Lexden. The teeth are very much detrited, indeed, they are nearly worn out, seeing that the heel is only an inch behind the anterior border of the coronoid. The rami are lost just behind the teeth, but a fragment of the plug remains in the space which a succeeding molar would have occupied. Only eleven to twelve

[1] In the mandibles (2674 and 2664) of Asiatic Elephants in the Museum of the Royal College of Surgeons of England, the heels of the first true molars, which are in full wear, are almost in line with the anterior border of the coronoid, whilst the second has four collines appearing above the gum, and six visible, but none are nearly on a level with the grinding surface of the tooth in use.

[2] The portion of a mandible with two molars holding thirteen worn plates is well shown in the 'Fauna Antiqua Sivalensis,' pl. xiii A. The teeth are of such gigantic dimensions that I cannot help assigning their age to be exactly as represented by the Siberian jaw just noticed, *i. e.* an ultimate molar more than half detrited. Falconer had not evidently made up his mind on that subject, 'Pal. Mem.,' vol. i, p. 439.

[3] The mandible 2675 (Asiatic Elephant), Royal College of Surgeons Museum, has the second true molar with twelve to thirteen ridges invaded, and the heel two inches behind the anterior border of the diasteme. The vault of the third molar is broken through, and the tips of the collines are just visible.

[4] See p. 110.

plates remain in a space of $7 \times 2\frac{1}{2}$ inches. The enamel is *thick*, as is generally the case in the ultimate molars of small individuals as the above must have been. Measured along the surface in wear, eight ridges are contained in $4\frac{3}{4}$ inches. The height in front of the molar is $6\frac{1}{2}$ inches. The greatest expansion of the rami at the angle is $17\frac{1}{2}$ inches, and the maximum thickness of each is $5\frac{3}{4}$ inches. The teeth converge, being 3 inches apart in front, 4 inches at the middle, and $7\frac{1}{2}$ inches behind.

There are fragments of other true molars in the collection from the same locality, showing *thick* and *thin* enamel. One, evidently portion of a lower last tooth, has decidedly *thin* enamel. Associated with the above is a cuboid and a fourth metatarsal; the former is $3\cdot6 \times 3\cdot4$ inches, and the latter is 4 inches in length. Teeth of *Rhinoceros leptorhinus* (Owen ?) are preserved also from the same peaty deposit.

The nearly entire mandible (Pl. VIII, fig. 3) described by Davies[1] shows the last true molar nearly half worn. The ultimate tooth, for its length and number of ridges and the usual tectiform contour of the upper surface, lasts very much longer than any of the preceding molars. At all times it represents senility, the degree of which becomes excessive when the crown is so ground down that its heel, rising above the level of the alveolus, is in front of the anterior border of the coronoid. Then the part of the ascending ramus becomes filled by a plug of cancellated bone, which runs up to the opening of the dental canal.

No member of the dental series varies more in the number of ridges than the ultimate molar of the Mammoth. Dr. Falconer does not seem to have come across a specimen with a lower ridge formula, at all events in the upper jaw, than x 22 x,[2] or a higher than x 26 x, the prevailing number being x 22 x. Taking all the materials which have come under my notice, I find of perfectly entire teeth the following ridge formulæ:

	x 18 x	x 19 x	x 20 x	x 21 x	x 22 x	x 23 x	x 24 x	x 25 x	x 26 x	x 27 x	x 29 x
Upper Molars	4	5	7	8	4	4	5	0	2	1	1 (?)
Lower Molars	1	3	5	1	4	3	1	0[3]	0	0	.

According to the foregoing and numerous other specimens not so entire it appears to me that the ridge formula varies *constantly* between x 19 x and x 24 x, so that it is difficult to say what is the prevailing number. It may vary possibly between twenty-two or twenty-three plates besides talons. Many Arctic molars, like the incisors, attain to very large dimensions, and the thinner the plates the greater the number, and *vice versd*; the rule, however, is not absolute.

[1] 'Cat. Brady Collection,' p. 11, $\frac{x}{39}$. [2] 'Pal. Mem.,' ii, p. 168.

[3] The higher expressions in lower molars requiring a considerable length of crown would be very subject to injury, and this is the case more or less with many of the lower teeth when they attain a length beyond 9 to 12 inches.

17

The last true molar of the Asiatic Elephant attains not unfrequently to the maximum limit of that of the Mammoth, but I have not seen an entire tooth with a lower ridge formula than x 20 x, whilst the average is about x 22 x. Indeed, although the Asiatic Elephant goes hand-in-hand in all its leading characters with the Mammoth, it maintains more regular averages of the various members of the dental series than the latter.

The affinities, therefore, between the ridge formulæ of the Mammoth and the Asiatic Elephant are of the most intimate character, and there seems a close relationship in that respect between the last and E. $Armeniacus$ and E. $Columbi$, which are apparently closely correlated, not only as regards the ridge formulæ, but also the morphological characters of their grinders. Dr. Falconer was impressed with the relationship between the former and the Asiatic Elephant, but considered the latter Elephant to be "between E. $antiquus$ and E. $Indicus$."[1] I must observe, after repeated comparisons of the dental materials of E. $Armeniacus$ and E. $Columbi$, available in the British Museum and Royal College of Surgeons, with those of E. $Asiaticus$, E. $primigenius$, E. $antiquus$, E. $Namadicus$, and E. $Hysudricus$, that I fail to distinguish distinctive characters of any value between the molars of the Asiatic and the so-called Columbian or American and the Armenian Elephants; so that, as far as teeth are concerned, the existing species may be the survivor of an Elephant whose fossil remains have turned up in Italy (?), Turkey in Asia, and throughout the temperate regions of North America.

The last molar of E. $antiquus$, especially the broad-crowned variety, might be mistaken for that of the Mammoth, and the same might be said of the E. $meridionalis$; and although the ridge formulæ might not be of assistance as regards the diagnosis with reference to the two former, still, in entire specimens and in crowns sufficiently detrited to show the pattern, I can scarcely conceive that in practised hands there would be much difficulty with reference to E. $meridionalis$. The lower ridge formula of the latter, apparently rarely rising above seventeen ridges altogether, with the massive proportions of the crown constituents, and its absence, with doubtful exceptions, from the deposits in which Mammoth remains are found, render its molars of easier distinction.

The ridge formula of the Mammoth, according to the latest differentiations made by Falconer, stood thus after eliminating talons :

Milk Molars.				*True Molars.*		
4	8	12		12	16	24

He maintained a theory that these figures were expressive of the usual number of plates in the six molars. Now, were the above in any ways general, their use as exponents of the ridge formula of the species would at all events be of taxonomial value. But from the data here furnished this must appear questionable, and I have no hesitation in stating that, were the collections on the Continent of Europe carefully examined, the range of the ridges in each member of the series might be further extended.

---

[1] Op. cit., vol. ii, pp. 447 and 214.

In my 'Monograph on *E. antiquus*,' I showed a similar variation and inconstancy in the number of ridges in its molars.   I had not then, however, made a close study of the teeth of *E. primigenius*, whose ridge formulæ, according to the results of late researches, appear to me to stand as follows:

(*Elephas primigenius.*)

Milk Molars.

	I.	II.	III.	IV.
Upper Molars	?—?	$x\,3\,x - x\,4\,x$	$x\,6\,x - x\,9\,x$	$x\,9\,x - x\,12\,x$
Lower Molars	$x\,2\,x -$	$x\,3\,x - x\,4\,x$	$x\,6\,x - x\,9\,x$	$x\,9\,x - x\,12\,x$

True Molars.

	V.	VI.	VII.
	$x\,9\,x - x\,13\,x$	$x\,14\,x - x\,16\,x$	$x\,18\,x - x\,27\,x\,(x\,29\,x\,?)$
	$x\,9\,x - x\,15\,x$	$x\,14\,x - x\,16\,x$	$x\,18\,x - x\,27\,x\,(x\,29\,x\,?)$

(*Elephas antiquus.*)

Milk Molars. — *True Molars.*

	II.[1]	III.	IV.[2]	V.	VI.	VII.
Upper Molars	$x\,2\,x - x\,3\,x$	$x\,5\,x - x\,7\,x$	$x\,8\,x - x\,10\,x$	$x\,9\,x - x\,12\,x$	$x\,12\,x - x\,13\,x$	$x\,15\,x - x\,20\,x$
Lower Molars	$x\,3\,x -$	$x\,6\,x - x\,8\,x$	$x\,9\,x - x\,11\,x$	$x\,11\,x - x\,12\,x$	$x\,12\,x - x\,13\,x$	$x\,16\,x - x\,19\,x$

IV. OSTEOLOGY.

I. CRANIUM.

The skull of the Mammoth presents much closer affinities to that of the Asiatic than to the African Elephant, or, indeed, any other proboscidean, as far as is known of their skeletons.   This opinion, enunciated by Cuvier, has received further confirmation since his time.   He characterised the skull of the Mammoth from that of every other species of Elephant then known to him, by the following :—1. A lengthened cranium.   2. Concave forehead.   3. Very long incisive alveoli.   4. Obtuse lower jaw.   5. Large grinders with closely packed and parallel laminæ.

[1] The presumed presence of the pre-ante-penultimate milk molar requires the numbers to be arranged accordingly.   It is here believed that the $x\,2\,x$ in the upper jaw of *E. antiquus* represents the minimum ridge formula in the second or ante-penultimate, whilst the so-called pre-ante-penultimate or first milk molar shown in the ridge formula of the Mammoth has not hitherto been recognised in *E. antiquus*.

[2] Just lately a molar came under my notice in the Museum of Zoology, Cambridge, from the "gravel" in the neighbourhood, with so low a ridge formula as $x\,8\,x$ in 3·9 inches.   I therefore make this alteration in the ridge formula as given at p. 47 of my Monograph.

Cranial contour.—Conjointly these foregoing characters are fairly distinctive of the Mammoth (Pl. VI, figs. 1 and 1 *a*), and broadly so as compared with the short-crowned Elephants, such as the African species, and seemingly *E. meridionalis*, an entire skull of *Elephas antiquus* not being known ; but the crania of certain Sewalik Proboscidea, to wit, *E. planifrons* (African-like ?), *E. insignis*, *E. bombifrons*, as far as their fossil remains permit one to judge, were very different from the long-crowned Mammoth and Asiatic Elephant, to which *E. Hysudricus*, with its distorted (? deformed) forehead, might be added. Consequent on these short and long cranial vaults the length from the vertex to the extremities of the premaxillaries, as compared with the breadth of the forehead at the post-orbital processes, varies considerably. Cuvier estimated the measurements in the two recent species as 5 to 3 in the Asiatic, and 3 to 2 in the African, and these appear to me from various measurements to be pretty general. The skull of the Mammoth agrees with the former, whilst according to Falconer and Nesti, that of *E. meridionalis* seems to come closer to the latter. No skull of *E. antiquus* being, as far as I know, yet described, we can only make comparisons with its very close Eastern representative, *E. Namadicus*. Supposing the extraordinary frontal rim of its calvarium in the British Museum[1] was absolutely of the character and extent shown in the specimen, and not the result of pressure or injuries after death, there never would be much likelihood of confounding it with the above, or in fact any other known proboscidean.

The configuration of the vertex and degrees of depression, flatness, and convexity of the forehead seem to differ widely in different species of Elephant.

The vertex in the Mammoth rises high, like that of the Asiatic Elephant, but it is decidedly narrower, and the pronounced depression in the recent species is not apparently so deep in the Mammoth. This is well seen in Pl. VII, figs. 1 and 1 *a*, and also in a cast of a nearly entire cranium from Brussels, in the Museum of the Royal College of Surgeons, London.[2] In *E. meridionalis*, according to Nesti, and as stated by Falconer, the posterior border of the vertex is transverse, the occipital fossa, of which the depression is the upper termination, being over-reached by a produced fold of the vertex.[3] The so-called " bonnet-shaped summit " of the cranium of *E. Namadicus* just noticed is still more peculiar, whilst the broad circular crown of the African distinguishes it from any of the foregoing, and assimilates its characters rather with *E. planifrons* and *E. bombifrons*.

Frontal depression.—The Mammoth's skull presents a slight depression or concavity of the forehead, with a small prominence above it. This is very evident in the Brussels skull, and although the part is somewhat injured in that from ILFORD (Pl. VII, fig. 1) it

---

[1] ' Fauna Antiqua Sival.,' pls. 12 a and 24 a.

[2] A well-preserved cranium of the Mammoth is very rare considering the enormous quantities of its teeth and bones discovered throughout Europe. Dr. Falconer (1865) knew of only one entire specimen out of Russia. Besides that, two nearly entire skeletons in the Royal Museum of Brussels, a skull of which is here referred to, and the Ilford cranium, pls. VI and VII, are the only instances known to me.

[3] ' Pal. Mem.,' vol. ii, p. 122.

is quite apparent also in the latter.[1] Evidently, as in the Asiatic, where a similar sinking exists, it varies considerably with age, and is deeper in some individuals than in others ; and varies, no doubt, also in the sexes. *E. ganesa* and *E. insignis* show also slight depressions in the same situation. It is more pronounced in drawings of *E. meridionalis* ; whilst the beetling crown of *E. Namadicus* is quite unique ; and the excessive sinking in the forehead, amounting to a cranial deformity in the skull, of *E. Ilysudricus*, in the British Museum, as compared with the perfectly even surface of the part in the adolescent cranium of the same species by its side, suggest the probability that the former may have undergone compression some time after death.[2]

Again, the forehead is flat in the young of *E. Africanus*, becoming slightly convex in the adult and aged. *E. planifrons* and *E. bombifrons* appear to have also flat frontals.

Breadth of forehead.—The breadth of the forehead at its narrowest part between the temporal ridges varies apparently in the insular and Continental varieties of the Asiatic Elephant, but the Mammoth agrees better in the character with the Asiatic than any other species. This part seems broadest in the short-headed Elephants, to wit, *E. Africanus*, and *E. planifrons*, gradually narrowing through the two preceding, and *E. Ilysudricus*, and *E. meridionalis* to *E. bombifrons*, where the forehead is excessively narrow as compared with the crown and occiput.

Nares.—The outline and position of the narial aperture are similar in both the Asiatic Elephant and the Mammoth. It is generally reniform in shape, with the horns directed forwards; the latter character, however, does not seem invariable in the Mammoth, and is reversed in young crania of the recent species, whilst the configurations of the apices of the cornua are more circular in certain individuals than in others. But these characters are not confined to the above species, being more or less observable in *E. Africanus*, *E. meridionalis*, *E. Namadicus*, &c. The aperture, however, is placed at about the same relative distance from the vertex in the Mammoth and Asiatic Elephant, whilst it is nearer to the crown in the African *E. meridionalis*, *E. Namadicus*, and other brachycephalic species. It is a part, however, so liable to injury in the fossil skull that one rarely meets with it in a state of integrity.

Incisive sheaths. — Dr. Falconer states that the incisive alveoli of the Mammoth form an angle with the frontal plane, thereby necessitating the truncation of the mandible at its symphysis.[3] This is somewhat apparent in the Brussels skull, and, although the

---

[1] This hollow is also evident in the Siberian skull shown in pl. xiv, fig. 2, and in the cranium of Adams's skeleton, pl. xvii, of the ' Ossemens Fossiles.' The skull etched on the fragment of ivory from the Cave of La Madelaine, in the Dordogne, is so truthful that, supposing we had never seen a Mammoth's skull, there could be no difficulty whatever in at once differentiating the characters of the profile of the above from that of either of the recent species, at all events from the African Elephants. This essay of an artist belonging to the early stone age of Southern France is assuredly a most laudable performance.

[2] Compare pl. xlv, fig. 20 A, with fig. 20 B of the ' Fauna Antiqua Sivalensis.'

[3] 'Pal. Mem.,' vol. ii, p. 121. The same is stated to obtain in the *E. ganesa*, famous for its enormous incisors.

supports are a good deal in the way of seeing it in the ILFORD specimen, the same appears to me to be slightly indicated in the latter also (Pl. VI).[1] In neither, however, does it appear so pronounced as to produce a decided inflection of the premaxillaries. Nothing, however, of the kind seems present in numerous skulls of the two recent species examined by me. In *E. meridionalis*, Falconer states that the alveoli " are produced in the same plane, or with a little obliquity ;"[2] and *E. Namadicus* maintains to all appearances the same character.

The parallelism of the massive alveoli in the Mammoth is dwelt upon by Falconer as characteristic, in comparison with *E. meridionalis*, where, instead of being parallel, " they diverge from the sub-orbitary foramina on to their extremity, where the divergence becomes sudden and as marked as in the African Elephant."[3] Now, although the divergence of the alveoli is not so pronounced as in either of the two living species, nor apparently as in *E. meridionalis*, it is clear that the alveoli are also not parallel in the Mammoth, but tend in opposite directions gradually from their commencement towards the extremities of the premaxillaries, where they diverge rapidly. This disposition to divergence in the alveoli of the Mammoth is further seen in the accompanying Woodcut, fig. 1 ($\frac{1}{12}$th natural size), from ILFORD. It represents the third milk stage of dentition, as proven by its three molars preserved with the specimen in the Museum of Practical Geology, to which I have referred at page 94.

FIG. 1.

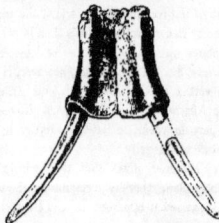

From Ilford : Museum of Practical Geology.

The same is seen in Plates VI and VII of the skull from the same locality. Here the right alveolus has been considerably injured, but has been restored carefully by the artist from the left side, which is entire. The cast of the skull from Brussels, in the Museum

[1] Compare also the Siberian cranium of the Mammoth, ' Ossemens Fossiles,' pl. xiv, fig. 2 *f*, with that of *E. meridionalis*, pl. xv, fig. 1.
[2] Op. cit., vol. ii, 125.
[3] Op. cit., vol. ii, p. 121.

of the Royal College of Surgeons, also repeats the above-mentioned character. The intervening hollow, which, of course, varies with the size of the tooth, becomes broader and shallower towards the alveolar border. The decided parallelism of the tusks of *E. ganesa*, not only in their sockets, but for some distance beyond, is remarkable as compared with other fossil species. No doubt there were individual differences, as obtain in the Asiatic, where the divergence is sometimes more pronounced, in such as the Dauntela Elephant of Corse, in the British Museum, and the celebrated Choone (Asiatic), and an African in the Hunterian Museum, Royal College of Surgeons (Woodcuts, figs. 2 and 3). The alveolar divergence is pronounced also in the skull of *E. Namadicus*.[1]

<table>
<tr><td style="text-align:center">Fig. 2.</td><td style="text-align:center">Fig. 3.</td></tr>
</table>

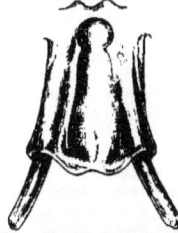

E. Asiaticus, Choone (No. 2654, in Collection of Royal College of Surgeons).	*E. Africanus* (No. 2845, in Collection of Royal College of Surgeons).

Sub-orbital foramen (Pl. VII, fig. 1 *a*) is apparently larger in the Mammoth and Asiatic than in the African. The part is not sufficiently well preserved in other fossil crania to allow of comparison.

The *post-orbital process* (Pl. VI, figs. 1 and 1 *a*) is more lengthened, pointed, and hooked in the Mammoth than in the recent species, but it is more so apparently in the Asiatic than in the African. Falconer states that this process in the *E. meridionalis* is "like that of the Mammoth."[2]

The *lachrymal tubercle*, as pointed out by Cuvier, is more prominent in the Mammoth than in the Asiatic, where it is apparently less projecting than in the African. It is pointed in *E. meridionalis*, according to Falconer.[3]

The *zygoma* in the Mammoth (Pls. VI, VII) and in *E. Asiaticus* is just below the condyles; whilst it is much lower in *E. Africanus*, *E. meridionalis*, *E. Namadicus*, and

---

[1] 'F. A. Sival.,' xxiv A, fig. 4.   [2] 'Pal. Mem.,' vol. ii, p. 123.   [3] Idem, p. 123.

the other short-crowned Elephants. It is, moreover, nearly parallel with the molars in the Mammoth and Asiatic Elephant, whereas, according to Falconer, this arch in *E. meridionalis* inclines to that of the molars, at an angle of about 35°.[1] The enclosure formed by the zygomatic arcade, as viewed from below, is circular in the African and ovoid in the Mammoth (Pl. VII, fig. 1 *a*)[2] and Asiatic.

The outline of the *temporal fossa* of course varies with the height of the dome. The antero-posterior extent, in relation to the vertical height, increasing progressively in different species, as stated by Falconer; in other words, the relative differences between the two measurements become less as the crown decreases. Consequently there must be wide differences in the outline of the temporal fossæ of the Mammoth and *E. meridionalis*. In *E. Namadicus* the contour is like that of the latter, the two measurements being nearly equal, whilst that of the Mammoth is rather peculiar (Pl. VII, fig. 1) as compared with other Elephants, being narrower and converging more to an apex at its upper and posterior angle. This feature is observed in other crania besides the above, but is not quite so pronounced,[3] which inclines me to believe that the compression of the occiput after death has exaggerated the character in the Ilford skull.

The *occipital* of the Mammoth (Pl. VI) is very large, and although the bosses on either side and deep centre for the ligament are not pronounced in the Ilford specimen, owing, doubtless in part, to injury and pressure, both are well shown in the Brussels skull, the hollow forming a pit large enough to hold the clenched fist. No doubt these characters were subject to variations, as observed in crania of the recent species.[4]

The *parallelism of the molars* in either jaw (Pl. VII, fig. 1 *a*), as compared with that in the living Elephants, was considered to be diagnostic of the Mammoth by Cuvier, but as Falconer truly observes, the character is not constant. The latter moreover states that they invariably converge in young and old of *E. meridionalis*:[5] indeed such is the case, more or less, in all members of the genus.

Little appears to be known of the *basal aspect* of the skull of the Mammoth in consequence, most probably, of the imperfect condition of the parts in the majority of specimens. In the Ilford skull the supports are in the way, irrespective of mutilations; the artist, however, has managed to afford a truthful representation of the chief parts in Pl. VII, fig. 1 *a*. As before stated, the alveolus of the right tusk has been restored in the drawing from that of the opposite side, and the left zygoma is also made up from the left, which is entire; there are besides restorations of the vault in places, but taken

[1] Op. cit., p. 125.

[2] This is the only part in my friend Mr. Griesbach's otherwise excellent illustration that is not quite true to nature. The outline of the arcade should have been more oval.

[3] Compare the above with pl. viii, fig. 1, and pl. xiv, fig. 2, of the 'Ossemens Fossiles,' which are indistinguishable in the contour of the temporal fossa from that of the cast in the Museum of the Royal College of Surgeons.

[4] 'Ossemens Fossiles,' pl. viii, fig. 1.

[5] 'Pal. Mem.,' vol. ii, p. 127.

generally, however, the skull is tolerably entire, and is unique as far as the British Islands are concerned.

The following admeasurements of crania of the Mammoth are compared with the recent species. Unfortunately no accurate data of the kind in connection with *E. meridionalis* have been, as far as I know, published, although there are magnificent skulls in the Museum of Florence.

	Ilford Cranium,[1] British Museum, Pl. VI, fig. 1. (E. primigenius).	Borzole Cranium,[2] cast in Mus. Roy. Col. Surg. of Eng. (E. primigenius).	Siberian, Oss. Fossil.,[3] vol. ii, 208, pl. 14, 2 (E. primigenius).	Siberian, Oss. Fossil.,[4] pl. 8, fig. 1, and 'Phil. Trn.', vol. 41, pl. 4 (E. primigenius).	Siberian, Oss. Fossil.,[5] pl. xvii (Adam's skeleton), (E. primigenius).	Volga Cranium,[6] Oss. Fossil., pl. 15, fig. 7 (E. primigenius).	India,[7] British Museum, presented by Corse (E. Asiaticus).	Ceylon,[8] 2855, Mus. Roy. Coll. Surgeons, England (E. Asiaticus).	African,[9] 2845 n, Mus. Roy. Coll. Surgeons, England (E. Africanus).
	Inches.	Inches.	Inches.	Inches.	Inches.	Inches.	Inches.	Inches.	Inches.
From the vertex to the premaxillaries	49½	41	56½	46½	51	47¼	42	44	24½
From the vertex to the nasals	16½	21	23½	...	...	19½	16	23	10
Breadth at the post-orbital processes	25½	28	...	...	...	27¼	27	23	21
Greatest breadth of the cranium	24	24	...	34½	...	...	34	30	22
Space between the glenoid fossæ	16	12½	...	...	...	...	16	13½	10½
From the occipital to the premaxillaries	36	33	37	...	37½	...	34	35	27½
From the occipital condyles to the vertex	19	21	...	26½	30½	...	22	22	16½

It is important, since bones and teeth of *E. meridionalis* and *E. antiquus* were constantly confounded with those of the Mammoth, until Falconer established the presence of three distinct species of Elephants among the materials in British collections,

[1] This cranium represents an aged Elephant with the ultimate true molars nearly one half invaded : from the size of the tusks, which are each 8 feet 8 inches from the alveolar border to the apex, and 26 inches in their greatest girth, it was no doubt a male.

[2] The teeth in wear are the second true molars, which are more than half detrited. The individual was, therefore, full grown, but as the tusks are slender it may possibly have been a female.

[3] The tooth in this jaw has all the appearance, and Cuvier's description points to it, of being the last true molar, well worn. The size of the alveoli of the tusks indicates an old bull Elephant.

[4] Undoubtedly the last molar was in use in this skull.

[5] I am not aware of any record of the exact state of the dentition of this famous specimen, but unquestionably the last of the series must have been in use.

[6] One of the largest specimens of skulls of the Asiatic Elephant, belonging to the long-tusked or Dauntelle variety. It is referred to by Corse, 'Phil. Trans.,' 1798, p. 221, and may be the same cranium shown in pl. 18, fig. 4, of 'Ossemens Fossiles.' The tusk in the above is 46 inches along the convex side, and its maximum girth is 14 inches. The last true molar is in wear.

[7] The second true molar is more than half detrited, and the last is about one third worn. Tusks large.

[8] The first true molar is invaded in this skull. Tusks wanting.

18

to fully realise the differences between them. As regards the skull of *E. meridionalis* generally, he observes " that the cranium differs more from that of the Mammoth than does the latter from the existing Indian Elephant." The Italian form in this respect greatly resembles the cranium of *E. Ilysudricus* from the Sewalik Hills, and is intermediate between it and the African Elephant, although widely different from both.[1] Unfortunately the skull of *E. antiquus* is not sufficiently known to admit of forming a like comparison ; the distinctions, however, as far as they extend, fully substantiate the diagnosis established by Falconer from the molars.

It is therefore in the *narrow summit, narrow temporal fossa*, and *inordinate long incisive sheaths*, that the Mammoth skull is chiefly distinguished from that of other species. The closest ally at present known is unquestionably the Asiatic Elephant.

2. MANDIBLE.

The mandible is usually found in a better state of preservation than any other portion of the skull. It shows much variability in character and dimensions irrespective of age, and bears out the same appearances observable in the teeth and other elements of the skeleton. But the discrepancies in the sizes of individuals and variations in skeletal characters are likely results in an animal which enjoyed such a very extensive distribution in space ; the only wonder is that it maintained its specific distinctions so well. As with the recent species, no doubt certain regions presented more favorable conditions for the growth of the Mammoth, whereby local varieties and races, distinguishable by certain appearances, were developed ; for it is well known to elephant hunters and elephant catchers that a herd is a family.[2]

The *round* and *truncated chin* of the Mammoth has been advanced as a very distinctive character, and in the majority of instances, especially the typical specimens from the boreal regions of Europe, Asia, and America, both points are very apparent. In such jaws the rami meet at the symphysis by more rounded curves than ordinarily obtain in other species, but the rule is by no means invariable, and must not be considered absolutely diagnostic, inasmuch as the jaw in many instances is indistinguishable from that of the Asiatic, especially in mandibles of the latter containing the first and second true molars. In aged Elephants the horizontal rami becomes attenuated by absorption of the walls of the dental cavities. These discrepancies in the contour of the mental region are well shown in the following woodcuts, which represent the mandibles of full-grown Mammoths from various localities.

In *E. antiquus* the rounding was also pronounced, as is well seen in Woodcut, fig. 13, and indeed the same, to a great extent, characterises the chin of *E. Namadicus ;* however, although there are individual instances, such as the superb specimen of the mandible of *E. meridionalis*, in the Woodwardian Museum, Cambridge, from the Forest Bed, where

[1] Op. cit., vii, p. 126.
[2] Sanderson, ' Thirteen Years among the Wild Beasts of India.'

Fig. 4.

Fig. 5.

Fig. 6.

E. primigenius, London. (British
Museum Collection, No. 38,136.)

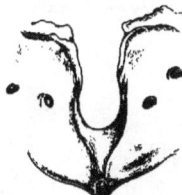

E. primigenius, Arctic America.
(British Museum Collection, No. 61 *a*.)

E. primigenius, Harbour, Holyhead.
(British Museum Collection, No. 38,567.)

Fig. 7.

Fig. 8.

Fig. 9.

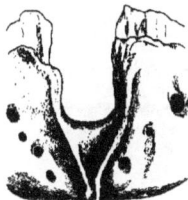

E. primigenius, Dogger Bank.
(British Museum Collection, No. 46,215.)

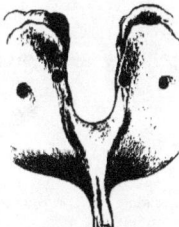

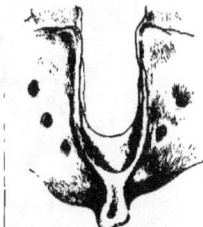

E. primigenius, Ilford. (British
Museum Collection, No. 44,974.)

E. primigenius, Dogger Bank.
(British Museum Collection, No. 46,197.)

Fig. 10.

Fig. 11.

Fig. 12.

E. primigenius, Ilford.
(British Museum Collection, No. $\frac{c}{18}$.)

E. primigenius, Ilford.
(British Museum Collection, No. $\frac{c}{12}$.)

E. primigenius, Ilford.
(British Museum Collection, No. $\frac{c}{16}$.)

the chin is nearly as rounded as in Woodcut, fig. 4, such is by no means the case in the
jaws from the Val d'Arno at Florence and the cast in the British Museum, shown in
Woodcut, fig. 14.

FIG. 13.   FIG. 14.

E. antiquus, British.
(Collection of Geological Society of London.)

E. meridionalis, Val d'Arno.
(British Museum Collection, No. 37,334.)

In the two recent species there are good distinctions to be made on this character,
the chin of the Asiatic Elephant presenting the usual aspect of that of the Mammoth,
subject to the same variations, whereas of several mandibles of the African I have never
seen the broad round chin of Woodcut, fig. 15. The more pointed mental region of the
mandible of the African agrees with that of *E. meridionalis*, to which species there is a
closer relationship in other skeletal elements than with the Mammoth.

FIG. 15.   FIG. 16.

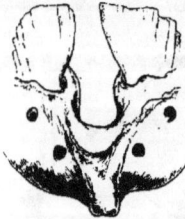

E. Asiaticus. (Collection
of Royal College of Surgeons, No. 2656 a.)

E. Asiaticus. (Collection
of Royal College of Surgeons, No. 2674.)

Fig. 17.   Fig. 18.

E. *Asiaticus*.   (Collection of Royal College of   E. *Africanus*.   Collection of Royal College of
Surgeons, No. 2675.)   Surgeons, No. 2847.)

The so-called truncated chin which Falconer and others have referred to as diagnostic of the Mammoth, will be also seen from the foregoing cuts and those on p. 135 to be by no means regular, there being much variability, from an obsolete rostrum (figs. 4 and 7) to the long beak of Woodcut, fig. 11, which is fully three inches in length, and grooved; indeed, the beak is variable in the recent species likewise; and, like the angle of convergence of the rami at the symphysis, it is not a reliable character in any one of the living or extinct Elephants hitherto described.

Horizontal and ascending ramus.—The relative and absolute lengths of the horizontal and ascending rami furnish some important comparisons in the different species. The Mammoth and Asiatic Elephant display close affinities in these respects; *E. meridionalis* and *E. Africanus* are closely associated; and *E. antiquus* and *E. Namadicus* are, as far as the specimens I have examined extend, also come together, the two latter being nearer to the two former than to the Meridional and African forms, where the disparities in relative lengths between the horizontal and ascending rami are far greater than in the other four. Again, there are less differences between the length of the horizontal ramus and maximum width of the ascending ramus in the Mammoth, and also in the Asiatic (but to a smaller extent in the latter), than in *E. antiquus*, and notably *E. meridionalis* and *E. Africanus*, as will appear presently.

In point of depth of the horizontal ramus and consequent length of diasteme, both attain their maximum in the middle period of life, and decline in very old age, when the teeth grow up and cover a space between them and the alveoli, which become absorbed, so that the mandible is then not nearly so thick and deep as in younger individuals. This is well seen in Pl. VIII, fig. 3, which represents a very old individual, the last true molar being more than half worn away, whilst the surrounding socket as shown, p. 122, seems too large for the tooth.

Symphysial gutter and its foramina.—The wide spout or gutter of the mandible of the Mammoth is, as far as I am aware, unequalled by that of any known species. There are usually two good-sized internal foramina, which, however, may be wanting. These are also present in the Asiatic, but are usually smaller and more numerous, whereas in many mandibles of the African Elephant I have examined not a trace of these canals is seen. They seem to be present in both *E. antiquus* and *E. meridionalis*.

The length of the symphysis being dependent on the prominence or otherwise of the chin, it will usually be longer in the long-beaked species than ordinarily in the Mammoth and Asiatic Elephant. But the great width of the gutter, although very general, is not an invariable character. It is well shown by the Woodcuts at p. 135, an exceptional instance being seen in the jaw (fig. 6) dredged in Holyhead Harbour, as compared with fig. 7 and other mandibles.

The *diasteme* is nearly vertical in the majority of mandibles of the adult Mammoth that have come under my notice, but there is no uniformity in this character, and its height increases from youth to mature age. It is high in *E. antiquus*, *E. Namadicus*, and *E. Asiaticus*, and more depressed in *E. Africanus*, *E. planifrons*, and *E. meridionalis*.[1] In the last named " it slips gradually into the beak, making a longer symphysis and spout."[2] The diasteme appears, therefore, like the rostrum, to be subject to variation in the degree of inclination in the adult Mammoth, but upon the whole it is more erect in it than in either of the recent, and in any jaws of extinct species hitherto recorded. The following woodcuts represent this character in various specimens and species.

FIG. 19.   FIG. 20.   FIG. 21.

E. primigenius, Arctic. (British Museum Collection, No. 61 a.)

E. primigenius, Harbour Holyhead. (British Museum Collection, No. 38,567.)

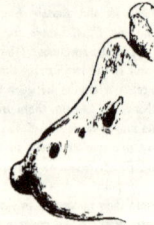

E. primigenius, Dogger Bank. (British Museum Collection, No. 46,215.)

---

[1] The dip of the diasteme in this species, although low as compared with the Mammoth, is not always so, as Woodcut fig. 28 shows, while a still higher angle is displayed in the ramus from the Forest Bed lately mentioned, to which further reference will be made in my Monograph on *E. meridionalis*.

[2] 'Pal. Mem.,' vol. ii, p. 127.

Fig. 22.   Fig. 23.   Fig. 24.

E. primigenius, Ilford. (British
Museum Collection, No. 44,979
and $\frac{6}{74}$.) Brady Cat.

E. primigenius, Dogger Bank.
(British Museum Collection,
No. 46,197.)

E. primigenius, Ilford. (British
Museum Collection, No. $\frac{9}{48}$.)

Fig. 25.   Fig. 26.

E. primigenius, Ilford.
(British Museum Collection, No. $\frac{9}{73}$.)

E. primigenius, Ilford.
(British Museum Collection, No. $\frac{9}{74}$.)

Fig. 27.   Fig. 28.   Fig. 29.

E. antiquus, British.
(Collection of the Geological Society
of London.)

E. meridionalis, Val d'Arno. (British
Museum Collection, No. 37,334.)

E. Asiaticus. (Collection of
Royal College of Surgeons,
No. 2656 a.)

FIG. 30.   FIG. 31.   FIG. 32.

E. Asiaticus. (Collection of Royal College of Surgeons, No. 2673.)   *E. Africanus.* (Collection of Royal College of Surgeons, No. 2817.)   *E. Asiaticus.* (Collection of Royal College of Surgeons, No. 2674.)

Expansion of the mandible.—The mandible of the Mammoth expands more at the angles and between the condyles than in either of the recent species. The ascending rami converge more at their summits in the Asiatic than in the Mammoth and *E. meridionalis.* I have not seen a mandible of *E. antiquus* with the condyles preserved, but otherwise this character is like that of the Mammoth as regards the greater relative breadth of the jaw at the middle and base of the ascending rami. This expansion at all stages of growth is marked in these extinct forms, as compared with the Asiatic Elephant; and shows a relatively broader jaw, at all events as far as the Mammoth is concerned. There is likewise a relatively greater expansion of the mandible of *E. meridionalis* than in the Asiatic, especially about the angle of the ascending rami.

Posterior border.—The posterior border of the ascending ramus of the Mammoth and Asiatic are much alike, being more rounded than in that of the other British fossil Elephants and the African species, demonstrating the contrast just referred to in relation to the length of the horizontal ramus.

The inferior margin of the lower jaw of *E. meridionalis* shows " a well-marked concave arc," which I have not seen in any ramus of the Mammoth.

The dental canal.—In both the Mammoth and Asiatic Elephant the posterior and inner border of the ascending ramus usually descends from the inner side of the condyle, and is lost after passing the rim of the dental canal, whilst it is still traceable in the African to the angle, at all events in many specimens of the latter I have been enabled to follow its course to that point which does not seem possible in the jaws of the other two species.

The canal looks directly upwards in the Mammoth and Asiatic (Woodcuts, figs. 33, 34, 35, and 37). This I have noticed is almost constant; indeed, I have only seen the exception (fig. 35), which is recorded at p. 103, where the opening is low down and directed backwards. In *E. meridionalis, E. Africanus,* and, as far as a single imperfect specimen (Woodcut, fig. 36) extends, in *E. antiquus,* the opening is also directed *inwards.*

The crotchet on the brim, so pronounced in the Asiatic (Woodcut, fig. 37), is by no means as prominent in the Mammoth, *E. antiquus*, and *E. Africanus*; indeed, it is seemingly sometimes scarcely pronounced and almost obsolete in the Mammoth, as shown in figs. 33, 34, and 35, nor is it very prominent in *E. Africanus* (fig. 38).

FIG. 33.   FIG. 34.   FIG. 35.

E. primigenius, Ilford. (British Museum Collection, No. 44979, ⁵⁄₉.)   *E. primigenius,* Ilford. (British Museum Collection, No. ⁵⁄₇.)   *E. primigenius,* Ilford. (British Museum Collection, No. ⁷⁄₈.)

FIG. 36.   FIG. 37.   FIG. 38.

  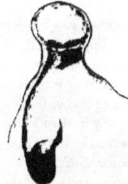

E. antiquus. (Museum of the Geological Society of London.)   *E. Asiaticus.* (Collection of Royal College of Surgeons, No. 2675.)   *E. Africanus.* (Collection of Royal College of Surgeons, No. 2847.)

The contour of the condyle is subject to individual differences even in the same jaw, as shown in Woodcut, fig. 30; but usually the outlines of the head are relatively broader in the Mammoth and Asiatic Elephant than in the African. The affinities between the two former are no doubt close, as appears from Woodcuts, figs. 34 and 37, whilst that of

19

the African (fig. 41) shows a greater disposition to constriction at the middle—a character seemingly present also in *E. meridionalis* (fig. 40). I must admit, however, that the condyle does not seem to me a satisfactory means of diagnosis.

The *posterior aspect of the neck of the mandible* is seemingly alike, with very little variation, in both the Mammoth and the Asiatic Elephant, being relatively narrower than obtains in the Meridional and African species, which again present close affinities. This will be more or less apparent from the following Woodcuts, figs. 39, 40, and 41.

Fig. 39.   Fig. 40.   Fig. 41.

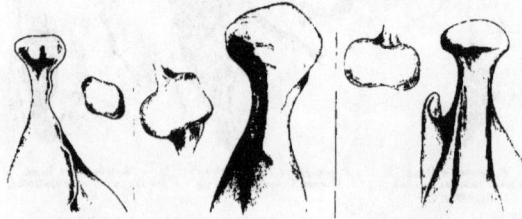

E. primigenius, Ilford.   *E. meridionalis*, Val d'Arno.   (British   *E. Africanus*.   (Collection of Royal
(British Museum Collection,   Museum Collection, No. 37,339.)   College of Surgeons, No. 2816.)
No. $\frac{4}{50}$.)

Coronoid.—The coronoid in the Mammoth does not generally rise within two inches of the upper surface of the condyle. Its anterior border is sometimes straight, sometimes concave, generally slightly concave with thickening of the apex. In the Asiatic it is nearly level with the summit of the condyle, the anterior border presenting a similar variability to that of the Mammoth, whereas it is usually concave in the African, whose condyle is nearly level with the apex of the coronoid. The characters of the anterior border are, however, so subject to variation, that little reliance can be placed on it as distinctive of any one species.

The beetling of the anterior and upper portion of the coronoid has been considered a character of the two recent species; but this is by no means the case, as the contour is constantly varying in specimens, and is very variable also in the jaw of the Mammoth, as also seen in the accompanying Woodcuts, figs. 42, 43, 44, 45, and 46.

Foramina.—The external mental foramina are, as a rule, closer to the free margin of the diasteme in the Asiatic Elephant and Mammoth than in the African, and, perhaps, the *E. meridionalis* and *E. antiquus*; but that there are exceptional instances, and that the condition

[1] Falconer, op. cit., vol. ii, p. 128.

Fɪɢ. 42.   Fɪɢ. 43.   Fɪɢ. 44.

E. primigenius, Ilford. (British Museum Collection, No. $\frac{6}{11}$.)   *E. primigenius*, Ilford. (British Museum Collection, No. $\frac{6}{19}$.)   *E. antiquus*, British. (Collection of Geological Society of London.)

Fɪɢ. 45.   Fɪɢ. 46.

E. Asiaticus. (Collection of Royal College of Surgeons, No. 2664.)   *E. Asiaticus.* (Collection of Royal College of Surgeons, No. 2674.)

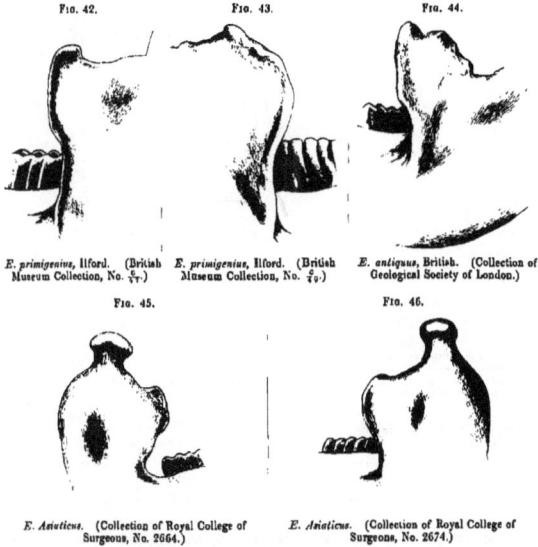

constantly varies, as will at once be very apparent from the woodcuts from p. 135 to p. 140 ; indeed, as a means of diagnosis the numbers and positions of the mental foramina are not reliable in any one species, recent or extinct.

The following table gives the measurements of mandibles of the three extinct British species and the jaw of the Asiatic Elephant, with the view of showing the comparisons of the more important parts in individuals of about the same relative ages.

	No. 5, B. M. Blond. Very old, only 16 ridges of last molar in use, Pl. VIII. fig. 3 (E. primigenius).	No. 61a, B. M.? Eschscholtz Bay, Arctic America. Last molar more than half denuded (E. primigenius). Woodcut, fig. 5.	Gent. Soc. Mus., Darlington River, locality unknown.? Last true molar commencing wear, portion of second in use, Penn. Ant. Simi., p. 23 a and b, fig. 4 (E. antiquus). Woodcut, fig. 13.	Woodwardian Museum, Cambridge. "Forest bed," Norfolk Coast. Last molars in full wear (E. meridionalis).	No. 37,334, B. M., cast, Val D'Arno. Same state of dentition as in mandible of E. antiquus (E. meridionalis). Woodcut, fig. 14.	Mandible of Cuvier's specimen (B. M.) of the erratica, referred to at p. 133, with two last molars in use (Damnichio variety of E. Asiaticus).
Extreme length of the jaw	22	25	20	22	29	29
Maximum thickness at front of the ascending ramus	5·7	6·5	7·	7·5	7·	6·
Height at the summit of the diasteme	5·8	8·	10·	9·	9·	8¼
Greatest expansion of rami at their outer borders	21·	Lost	24·5	23·	22	22
Length and breadth of ultimate molar	8·2×3·2	8·×3·	12·×3·1[3]		8·×3·5[4]	8·×3½
Space between molars in front	3·5	3·5	3·2	...	4·4	3·5
" " middle	4·	...	3·6	...	3·	...
" " behind	10	7·5	...	...	...	8·5
From tip of rostrum to posterior border of symphysial gutter	7·5	5·	5·2	...	7·	8·5[5]
Greatest width of gutter in front	2·5	2·8	3·6	3·5	4·	2·
Height of ascending ramus to summit of condyle	15·2	15·5	16·3[7]	...	17	19
Breadth of ascending ramus	12·	Lost	11·5	...	9·5	11·5
Length of horizontal ramus from diasteme, to anterior border of coranoid	8·	8·	8·8	8·	11·	9·5

The general characters which distinguish the mandible of the Mammoth from that of its extinct co-species may be epitomised as follows :—1. The chin is usually broad. 2. The rostrum poorly developed. 3. The diasteme is nearly erect, very generally high. 4. The symphysial gutter is wide. 5. The posterior border of the ascending ramus is rounded. 6. The sides of the condyle are only slightly compressed. 7. Dental canal opens upwards. 8. There is less difference in length between the horizontal and ascending rami. 9. The posterior surface of the neck of the condyle is narrow.

In all these characters it approaches closer to the Asiatic Elephant than to any other species hitherto recorded. The Asiatic has a relatively less expansion of the rami and a

[1] Referred to p. 123.

[2] Referred to Monograph on *E. antiquus*, p. 54.

[3, 4, 5] Last molars hidden in jaws ; the lengths, therefore, are from the parts exposed.

[6] Rostrum is very long, four inches in length.

[7] The condyles are wanting, therefore the length is from the *neck*.

[6] Condyles and neck lost. I have only given a few measurements of this very interesting mandible, as I propose to describe and figure it in my next Monograph.

more pronounced crotchet or process on the margin of the dental canal, but otherwise the variability to which the jaw of the Mammoth is subject seemingly goes nearly hand in hand with the variations in the mandible of the Asiatic Elephant.

3. SHOULDER GIRDLE.[1]

Scapula.—Cuvier was the first to record the points of resemblance between the scapula of the Mammoth and that of the Asiatic Elephant;[2] and Nesti makes a similar statement with reference to *E. meridionalis*.[3]

Unfortunately the shoulder-blades of *E. antiquus* have not been described, whilst the scapula in the so-called Adams's skeleton in St. Petersburg has been shown by Cuvier to be wrongly put together; indeed, it would appear that this is the case with various other portions of that skeleton, which has been constructed from bones of several individuals. The neck of the scapula in the Mammoth is broader and the glenoid cavity relatively wider than in the recent species, as pointed out by Cuvier.

According to De Blainville the recurved process, or crotchet, is less curved than in the Asiatic, and the acromion is nearer to the articular surface, whilst the suprascapular border is more arched than in the latter species.[4]

With reference to the contour of the glenoid cavity, Busk has observed that it is broad and oblong in the African, whilst there is a constriction of the sides in the Asiatic and Mammoth.[5]

The almost entire, and the only well-preserved specimen of the scapula I have seen from British strata is shown in Pl. XV, fig. 1 *a, b*. I am informed by Mr. Davies that its integrity is owing entirely to the care bestowed, in its removal from the matrix, by the Rev. Nicholas Brady, M.A., son of Sir Antonio Brady, F.G.S., to whom science is indebted for the recovery of numerous other Pleistocene remains from the famous brickfields of Ilford. Only a small portion of the anterior border is wanting in the specimen. The above-mentioned characters are well shown in Pl. XV, fig. 1 *a, b*, whilst the distinctions between the scapulæ of the two recent species and that of the Mammoth will appear from Pl. XV, figs. 2 and 3.

The spine (fig. 1 *a*) rises higher above the plain of the scapula in the Mammoth than is apparently the case in either of the recent species.

---

[1] The vertebral column should properly follow the preceding details, but entire specimens of its elements are not easily procured. I hope, however, to be enabled to obtain sufficient data to enable me to point out their characters in my next memoir. In the meantime I shall proceed to the consideration of the anterior extremity of the Mammoth.

[2] 'Ossem. Foss.,' vol. ii, p. 216.

[3] ' Fossili del Val d'Arno,' fig. 6.

[4] 'Ostéographie des Mamm.,' p. 171.

[5] 'Trans. Zool. Soc. Lond.,' vol. vi, p. 244.

20

In the African (Pl. XV, fig. 3) the anterior border is more rounded than in the Asiatic (fig. 2), and apparently in the Mammoth ; and the crotchet is more bent downwards than in either of them. The antero-posterior length of the neck is relatively smaller in the African, but it is apparently broader in the Mammoth than in the Asiatic Elephant. The position of the crotchet would seem to stand in its relation to the glenoid cavity in the following order :—It is nearest in the African, further up in the Asiatic, and slightly more so in the Mammoth.

The glenoid is clearly, as shown in figs. 2 a and 3 a, broadly distinctive in the African as compared with Asiatic and the Mammoth (fig. 1 a) and even *E. meridionalis.*[1]

The supra-scapular border is seemingly more arched in the Mammoth than in the Asiatic, and is more even in the African than in either of them.

The following are the measurements of the three scapulæ in question :

	Plate XV, Fig. 1. No. $\frac{c}{m}$ Brady Collection, B.M., Ilford.	Plate XV, Fig. 2. E. Asiaticus, 2744b,[2] Mus. Roy. Coll. Surg. Eng.	Plate XV, Fig. 3. E. Africanus, 706b, B.M.[3]
	Inches.	Inches.	Inches.
Extreme length...	32	34	27·5
Extreme breadth	37	30·5	26
Height of the spine	8	8·5	5
Length of the spine	28	31	29·5
From coracoid to the tip of the acromion	6·2	4	4
Coracoid to the tip of the crotchet...................	15	13	10
Acromion to the upper and inner border of the recurved process	15·5	14·5	11·5
Acromion to the tip of the recurved process	11	10	9·5
Length of the anterior border..........................	—	22	22
Length of the posterior border	22	19	13
Length of the supra-scapular border to the commencement of the spine	27·5	32	24
Dimensions of the glenoid cavity	6·8 × 4	7 × 4·2	6·8 × 3·6
Antero-posterior length of the neck	10	10	8

Besides the above there are several other fragments of shoulder-blades from the Ilford brick-earths in the Collection and in the Catalogue. For example, No. $\frac{C}{120}$ has a glenoid cavity of 6·5 × 3·9 inches; No. $\frac{C}{122}$, 6·8 × 3·3 ; No. $\frac{C}{123}$, 6·8 × 3·8. In Mr. Owles's Collection from the Dogger Bank, the glenoid cavity of No. 46,256 is 7·7 × 4·7, and No. 46,257 is 8· × 5· inches.

[1] 'Ossemens Fossiles,' pl. xiii, fig. 5.
[2] This is the largest scapula of the Asiatic Elephant I have seen. The pelvis and humerus of the same individual is preserved in the Museum. I have referred to the latter in my Monograph on *E. antiquus,* p. 59.
[3] The second true molar is in wear in the skull of this individual, showing that it was an old Elephant.

Elephas primigenius.

Fig. 1. Reduced to about ⅛ natural size, and fig. 1 *a* a much reduced drawing of the same cranium from Ilford, Essex, in the British Museum.

Figs. 2 and 2 *a*. Crown and profile of No. 44,734, British Museum, a right lower penultimate milk molar from Hutton Cave, in the Mendip Hills, Somersetshire. (Natural size.)

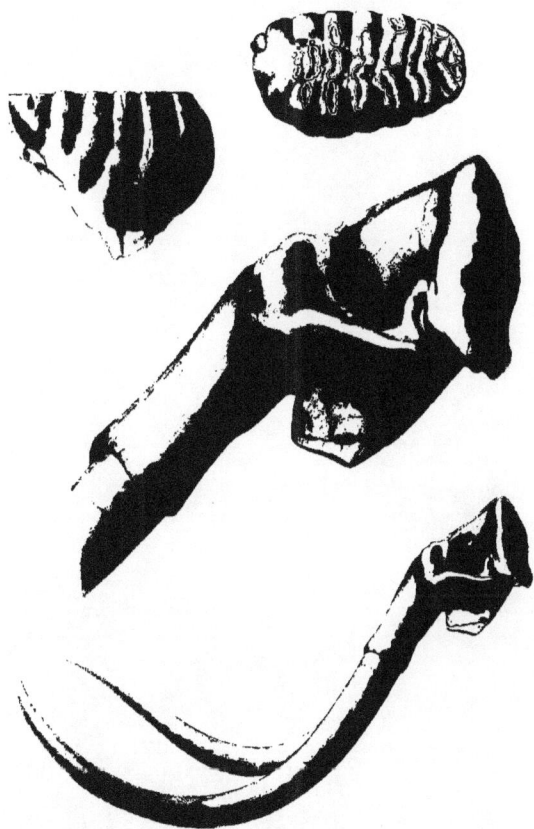

Elephas primigenius.

Figs. 1 and 1 *a*.   Frontal and basal aspects of the Ilford cranium, British Museum. (⅓ natural size.)

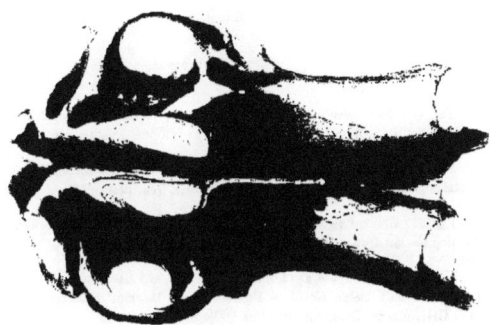

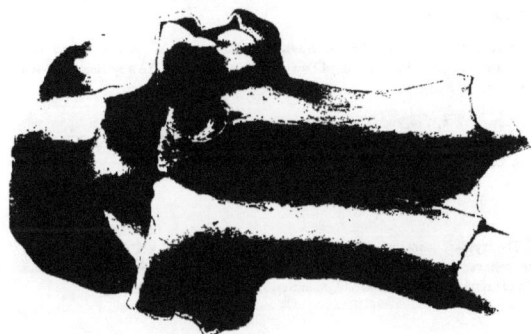

PLATE VIII.

Elephas primigenius.

Fig. 1. Crown view of a mandible, No. c 41, Brady Collection, British Museum, showing the last milk molar, from Ilford, Essex. (About ¼ natural size.)

Fig. 2. Crown view of the mandible, No. c 43, Brady Collection, British Museum, containing the first or ante-penultimate true molars, from Ilford. (About ¼ natural size.)

Fig. 3. Crown view of the mandible, No. c 49, Brady Collection, British Museum, showing the last true molar, from Ilford. (About ¼ natural size.)

Figs. 4, 4 *a*, 4 *b*, and 4 *c*. Profile, crown, back, and basal views of an upper ante-penultimate milk molar, No. 4 of Professor Boyd Dawkins' Collection, from Wookey Hole Cave, Mendip Hills, Somersetshire. (Natural size.)

Figs. 5, 5 *a*, 5 *b*, and 5 *c*. Profile, crown, back, and basal views of lower ante-penultimate milk molar, No. 1 of Professor Boyd Dawkins' Collection, from Church Hole, Notts. (Natural size.)

Figs. 6, 6 *a*, and 6 *b*. Profile, crown, and back views of lower ante-penultimate milk molar, No. 2 of Professor Boyd Dawkins' Collection, from Wookey Hole. (Natural size.)

Figs. 7, 7 *a*, 7 *b*, and 7 *c*. Profile, crown, back, and basal views of upper ante-penultimate milk molar No. 3 of Professor Boyd Dawkins' Collection, from Robin Hood Cave, Creswell Crags, Derbyshire. (Natural size.)

The expenses connected with the lithographing of the Plates VIII, IX, XII, and XV were defrayed by the British Association for the Advancement of Science, in accordance with the resolution of the General Committee, dated September 19th, 1878.

Fig. 3

PLATE IX.

Elephas primigenius.

Figs. 1 and 1 *a*. Profile and crown of No. 46,147, British Museum, an upper penultimate true molar in the Owles's Collection, from the Dogger Bank, German Ocean. (Half natural size.)

Fig. 2. Profile of No. 39,695, British Museum, a left upper last true molar, from Spalding, in Lincolnshire. (Half natural size.)

Figs. 3, 3 *a*, 3 *b*, and 3 *c*. Profile, crown, back, and basal views of the right (?) upper ante-penultimate milk molar, No. 1063 of the Kent's Cavern Collection, Torquay, Devonshire. (Natural size.)

Figs. 4, 4 *a*, and 4 *b*. Profile, crown, and back views of the *pre*-ante-penultimate milk molar (?), No. 5774 of the Kent's Cavern Collection, Torquay. (Natural size.)

PLATE X.

Elephas primigenius.

Figs. 1 and 1 *a*. Upper and profile views of mandible, No. 44,967, Brady Collection, British Museum, containing the penultimate milk molars, from Ilford, Essex. (Natural size.)

Fig. 2. Upper view of a fragment of a left ramus of a mandible, No. 21,311, British Museum, showing the alveoli of the ante- and the penultimate milk molars, from Ilford. (Half natural size.)

Fig. 3 and 3 *a*. Crown and profile views of a left upper penultimate milk molar, No. 46,422, British Museum, from Wookey Hole Cave, Mendip Hills, Somersetshire, (Natural size.)

PLATE XI.

Elephas primigenius.

Fig. 1 and 1 *a*. Profile and crown views of a right lower last milk molar, No. 39,041, British Museum, from Bracklesham Bay, Sussex. (Natural size.)

Fig. 2. Crown view of a right upper first true molar, No. 46,211 of the Owles's Collection, British Museum, from the Dogger Bank, German Ocean. (Natural size.)

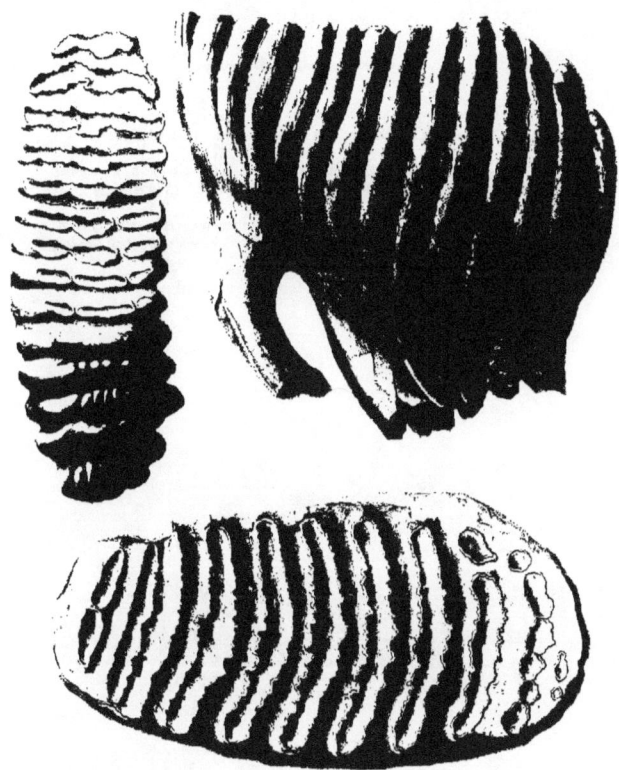

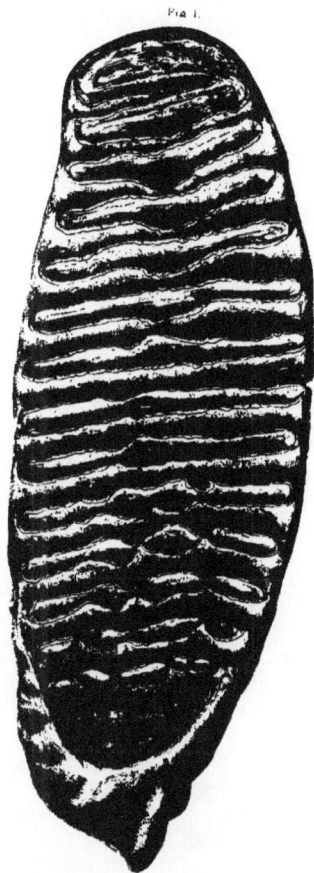

PLATE XIII.

Elephas primigenius.

Figs. 1 and 1 *a*. Profile and crown views of a left upper last true molar, No. 35 of the Woodwardian Museum, Cambridge, from Kirby Park, Melton Mowbray, Leicestershire. (Natural size.)

Fig. 2. Profile view of a lower penultimate milk molar, in the British Museum, from Kent's Cavern, Torquay, Devonshire. (Natural size.)

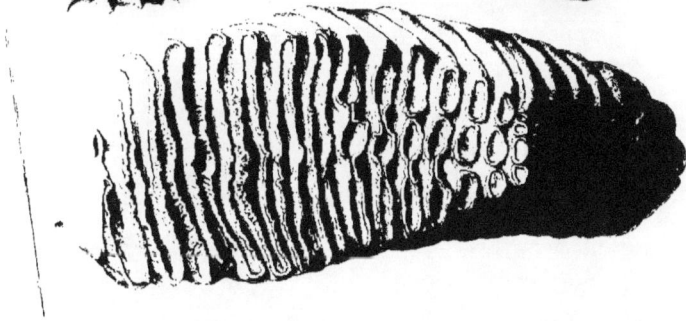

PLATE XIV.

Elephas primigenius.

Fig. 1. Crown view of a right upper last true molar, No. 37,248, British Museum, from Millbank, Thames Valley, Middlesex. (Natural size.)

Fig. 2. Crown view of a right upper last true molar, No. 36,426, British Museum, from Lexden, near Colchester, Essex. (Natural size.)

Fig. 3. Crown view of a portion of a right lower last true molar, No. 40,699, British Museum, "dredged off Cromer Forest Bed," Norfolk coast. (Natural size.)

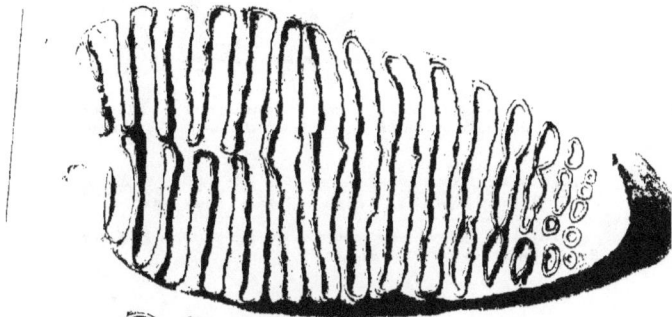

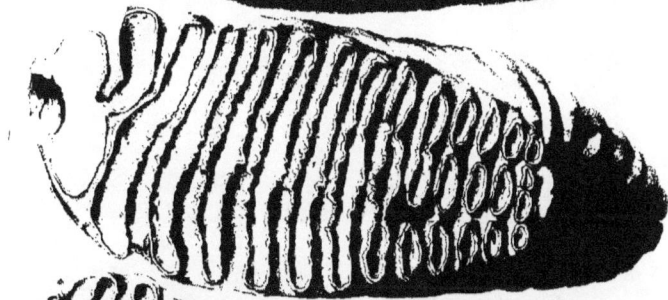

PLATE XV.

Elephas primigenius, E. Asiaticus, and E. Africanus.

Figs. 1, 1 *a*, and 1 *b*. External, anterior, and articular views of a left scapula, No. 119 c, Brady Collection, British Museum, from Ilford, Essex. (One fifth natural size.)

Figs 2 and 2 *a*. External and articular views of a right scapula of *E. Asiaticus*, No. 27,449 Museum Royal College of Surgeons of England. (Much reduced.)

Figs 3 and 3 *a*. External and articular views of a right scapula of *E. Africanus*, No. 708[1], British Museum. (Much reduced.)

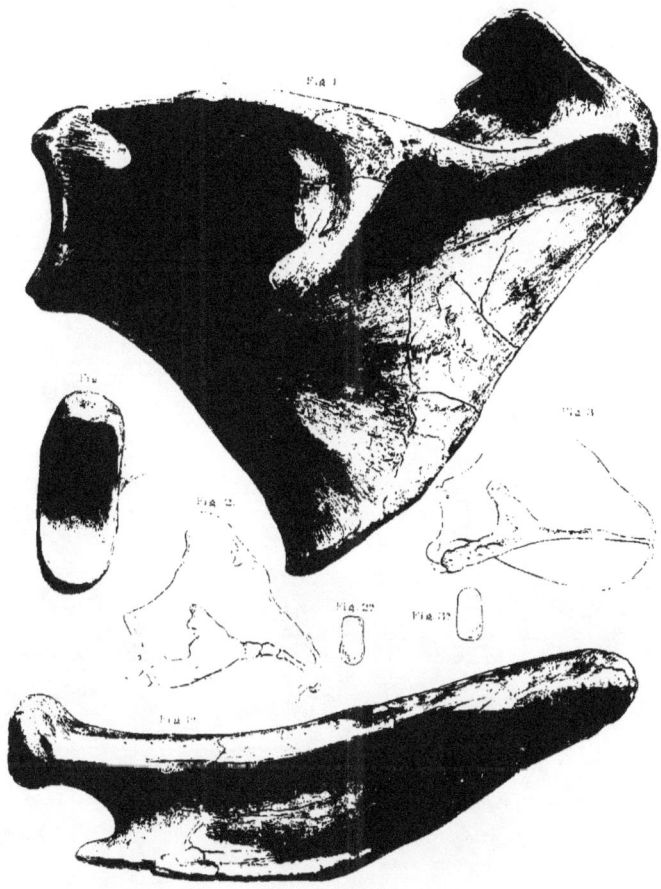

Fig. 1.

MONOGRAPH

ON THE

BRITISH FOSSIL

ELEPHANTS.

BY

A. LEITH ADAMS, M.A., M.B., F.R.S., F.G.S.,

PROFESSOR OF NATURAL HISTORY IN THE QUEEN'S COLLEGE, CORK.

PART III.

OSTEOLOGY OF ELEPHAS PRIMIGENIUS (BLUMENBACH)

AND

DENTITION AND OSTEOLOGY OF ELEPHAS MERIDIONALIS (NESTI).

PAGES 147—265; PLATES XVI—XXVIII.
WITH TITLE-PAGE AND DIRECTIONS FOR BINDING.

LONDON:
PRINTED FOR THE PALÆONTOGRAPHICAL SOCIETY.
1881.

PRINTED BY
E. ADLARD, BARTHOLOMEW CLOSE.

The Ilford scapula, as compared with that of the Asiatic Elephant, although shorter than the latter, is 6½ inches broader.

The acromion is near to the glenoid cavity in the Asiatic, but altogether there is little of much importance to distinguish the scapula of the Mammoth from that of the Asiatic Elephant, thereby adding an additional proof to the close dental and osteological characters of the two species ; and doubtless, were the same parts of other allied species forthcoming, similar interesting data would be furnished.

4. SPINAL AXIS.

The various elements, in particular dorso-lumbar vertebræ of the Mammoth are plentiful in collections, but from their susceptibilities to injury are seldom found entire. The more perfect specimens belong to individuals from the frozen ice cliffs of Arctic lands, or were dredged from the basin of the German Ocean.

Atlas.

This element of the vertebral column of the Mammoth presents characters which, if persistent, would be very valuable in the differentiation of species ; but I find, as recorded at page 56, that there is individual variability both in the living and extinct species. However, the following seem worthy of notice. Referring to the atlases shown in Pl. XVII, of the Mammoth, *E. antiquus*, and *E. meridionalis*, I have observed that the foramina for the first cervical nerve in the majority of first cervicals of the Mammoth open internally on the sides of the body, which are perpendicular, so that the apertures are not visible when viewed from above ; and the same obtains in that of the Asiatic Elephant generally. I have seen several exceptions, however, in bones of both species. In *E. meridionalis*, *E. Africanus*, and *E. antiquus* it is quite visible from above, so that the internal surface of the canal is less perpendicular in them ; but also this character may not be constant. The configuration of the anterior articular surfaces is nearly semilunar, as seen in fig. 1, as compared with that of *E. antiquus* and *E. meridionalis* (figs. 2 and 3). Again, the greater width of the odontoid and vertebral canals in the Mammoth and *E. antiquus* will be seen to contrast with the same in *E. meridionalis*, the height to breadth being not so marked in the two former as in *E. meridionalis*, whilst the flattening of the upper aspect of the arch in them seems distinct from the round surface in the latter. But a series of specimens of the atlases of *E. antiquus* and *E. meridionalis* can only determine these apparent distinctions, which, as regards the Mammoth and Asiatic Elephant, seem disposed to individual variation. The atlas in the Mammoth seldom seems to exceed fifteen to sixteen inches in its greatest breadth, and eight inches in height, both of which measurements fall very short of that of the enormous cervicals of *E. meridionalis*, and often of *E. antiquus*.

21

A good representation of a small atlas of the Mammoth is shown in Pl. XVII, fig. 1. The specimen is from Ilford,[1] No. 45,025, B. M., and has been described by Davies in the Catalogue of the Brady Collection. The dimensions there given are: height 7·4 inches; breadth 13; neural arch 2 × 2·6 inches in width; odontoid fossa 1·7 × 1·9 in width; length of the body inferiorly 2·5 inches.

The above bone goes hand-in-hand with the other portions of the skeleton of the Mammoth from Ilford, and supports the diagnosis deducible from Davies' description of the teeth of this small-sized race or variety.

What may be considered a fair-sized atlas of the Mammoth is shown by No. 26,233, B. M., dredged on the Dogger Bank, German Ocean. Its dimensions are as follows:

Maximum breadth	15·5 inches.
Maximum height .	8·8 „
Breadth of neural canal	3·5 „
Height of „	3 „
Breadth of odontoid canal	2 „
Height of „	1·8 „

Axis.

An axis belonging to the skeleton of a Mammoth found in Shandon Cave, Co. Waterford, Ireland,[2] presents the following dimensions:—Height 8·5; anterior posterior diameter 4·4 inches; vertebral canal 2·4 × 2·3 inches; anterior articular facet 3 × 2·4 inches.

Here, again, the disproportions between the height and breadth of the neural canal in both the Asiatic and Mammoth, and to a less extent in *E. antiquus*, contrast with the same in *E. meridionalis* and *E. Africanus*, which are much alike in these points. As regards the three extinct species, the above characters are shown in Pl. XVII, figs. 6, 5, and 4. The anterior articular surfaces will also be seen to present discrepancies, being ovoid and circular; but, as in the case of the atlas, these may likewise be subject to individual variations; at all events, the distinctions are worthy of notice, and will be reverted to in connection with *E. meridionalis*.

The other cervical vertebræ, of which there are several British and Arctic specimens in the British Museum, do not appear to present any characters at all useful for diagnostic purposes. As regards size, like the other bones, they are small in comparison with the same parts in *E. meridionalis* and *E. antiquus*.

[1] $\frac{c}{77}$, p. 16.

[2] Adams' "Report on the Shandon Caves," 'Trans. Roy. Irish Acad.,' vol. xxvi, p. 214. This specimen, along with the other portions of the skeleton, is preserved in the Museum of Science and Art, Dublin.

Dorso-lumbar Vertebræ.

The first dorsal vertebra (Pl. XVII, fig. 7) was dredged off LOWESTOFT, Suffolk, and is in the possession of J. J. Colman, Esq., M.P., of Corton, who has kindly furnished me with an excellent photograph of this entire specimen. It would be difficult to say with accuracy to which of the three species it belonged; the probability is, however, in favour of its being a first dorsal of the Mammoth, seing that in characters and size it agrees with similar authenticated specimens from British and Arctic deposits. The total height is 20 inches. Height of spine and neural canal 14 inches; spine, from neural canal to apex, 11·5 inches; total breadth 13·5 inches. Height of centrum 6 inches; breadth of centrum 6·5 inches; thickness 3 inches. Neural canal 3 × 4·8 inches in width.

A first dorsal vertebra, presumably belonging to the same individual as the axis just described from SHANDON CAVE, is 13 inches in height by 11·5 in its greatest breadth. The vertebral canal is 2·4 inches in height by 3·5 inches in width. These two specimens pretty well indicate the dimensions of the bone in the Mammoth. As regards the Asiatic and African Elephants, the contour of the neural canal approaches closer to the former. I have no data wherewith to compare the above with the same part in the other two extinct Elephants, seeing that in them the arches are rarely sufficiently preserved to admit of comparison.

A third dorsal vertebra of the Mammoth, in the British Museum, from Admiral Kellet's Collection, made in ESCHSCHOLTZ BAY, Arctic America, is nearly entire, excepting the loss of the neural apophysis, which had not been anchylosed to the spine, and therefore belonged to an adolescent individual.

The height is 20 inches; maximum breadth 10 inches. Centrum, 4·5 × 4·4 inches in the transverse diameter.

The neural canal is similar to that of fig. 7.

A posterior dorsal in the same Museum, from KOTZEBUE SOUND, Arctic America, had belonged to a youthful individual, as the anterior and posterior surfaces of the centrum are without the epiphyses, and the neural spine is wanting.

The entire length is 18 inches; maximum breadth 10 inches. Centrum 4 × 4·4 inches. The canal is 1·9 × 2·4 inches; thickness 2·1 inches.

There are centra and portions of other dorso-lumbar vertebræ in the British Museum and elsewhere, but none seem worthy of particular notice, as they present no diagnostic characters of importance, only that they are small as compared with FOREST-BED specimens referable to *E. meridionalis* and *E. antiquus*, as will appear in the sequel.

The *ribs* and *sternum* are represented by fragments in the British Museum, none of which, however, are sufficiently entire to be useful for diagnostic purposes.

150   BRITISH FOSSIL ELEPHANTS.

5. PELVIC GIRDLE.

The relative dimensions of the pelvic borders do not seem to offer any very reliable data, either in the recent or the extinct species. The following details, however, are worth recording.

1. As indicated by Cuvier, Busk, and myself,[1] the proportion between the length and breadth of the *foramen ovale* is greater in the Mammoth than in either of the recent Elephants. This is well seen in various Arctic examples of the former and specimens of the latter. Moreover, the smaller end of the oval is superior in the Asiatic, Mammoth, and Meridional, and the channel for the nerve more pronounced, indeed, in some it is almost a foramen; whilst the broader end of the oval is superior, and the groove small, in the African. I have not seen a pelvis of the Ancient Elephant.

2. The acetabulum in eight examples of the Mammoth from the Arctic region shows the vertical to be the largest measurement, whereas in the recent species, and also one of *E. meridionalis*, it is shorter than the transverse.

3. As far as detached *ossa innominata* of the Mammoth are concerned, I am unable to show any marked distinctions of the antero-posterior to the lateral diameters as compared with the two recent species, and leastwise in the huge pelvis in the Gunn Collection referred to by Falconer,[2] which I compared carefully with the same bone in recent species.

4. The cotyloid notch in the Asiatic Elephant and the Mammoth opens on a flat surface, which is absent in the African to the extent that the notch opens directly on the upper and outer border of the *foramen ovale*; moreover, it is wider generally in the Mammoth and Asiatic than in the *acetabulum* of the African.

5. I find that the *obturator* border of the *ischium* is narrower and the internal spine of the latter more pronounced in the Mammoth and Asiatic than in the African; moreover, as far as the somewhat injured parts of the huge pelves from the East Coast are concerned, they seem to follow the two former in their characters.

The following data may be cited in connection with the pelvis of the Mammoth. In the Kellet and Beechy Collections there are several portions of the pelvic basin from ESCHSCHOLTZ BAY and other Arctic regions, presenting the following:

Specimen 1 shows the same contour of the *foramen ovale* as in the Asiatic. The *acetabulum* is 6·5 × 6·3 inches in breadth. The width of the neck of the *ilium* is 5 inches.

The gaping cotyloid notch opens on a flattened space.

[1] 'Ossem. Fossil.,' vol. ii, 221, pl. xvi, figs. 1 and 2. Busk, 'Trans. Zool. Soc. London,' vol. ix, p. 49. Adams, p. 61, *antea*.
[2] 'Pal. Mem.,' vol. ii, p. 142, figs. 1 and 2.

Specimen 2. The *acetabulum* is $6 \times 5\frac{1}{2}$ inches; width of the neck of the *ilium* 8 inches.

Specimen 3. Repeats the two former.

Specimen 4. Maximum breadth of *ilium* 33 inches.

　　　Width of neck of　　ditto　7　„

The sciatic notch is here so deep as to form almost a foramen at the upper end of the oval.

The *acetabulum* is $6 \times 5\frac{1}{2}$ inches.

Specimen 5 includes the *sacrum*, with five anchylosed vertebræ; its lumbo-articular surface is $4\frac{3}{4}$ in a. p. diameter, by $6\frac{3}{4}$ inches in the transverse diameter.

In the Owles Collection, B. M., from the DOGGER BANK, there are several fragments. No. 40,268 has an *acetabulum* $7 \times 6\frac{3}{4}$ inches, with a nearly complete sciatic notch. No. 40,267 has the *foramen ovale* $9\frac{3}{4} \times 4$ inches, whilst the *acetabulum* is $7\frac{1}{2} \times 7\frac{1}{4}$. In this bone the *foramen ovale* and cotyloid notch are as in the Asiatic.

The Brady Collection from Ilford furnishes also further data, viz., $\frac{C}{180}$. *Acetabulum* $6 \times 5\cdot6$ inches. *Foramen ovale* 6 (height), $3\frac{1}{4}$ (breadth). No. $\frac{C}{181}$. *Acetabulum* $6 \times 5\cdot6$.

A right *os innominatum* of *E. primigenius*, in the Gunn Collection, Norwich Museum, dredged off Yarmouth, has the *foramen ovale* 7×3 inches.

The pelvis, No. 2744 z, of an enormous Asiatic Elephant in the Museum of the Royal College of Surgeons of England is portion of a skeleton of, perhaps, one of the largest individuals hitherto brought to Europe. The humerus is referred to at pages 59, 153 and 215, and shown in Plate XVI, fig. 4, and the femur at page 164. The perfection of the *ossa innominata*, which are completely anchylosed at the pubic symphysis, offer some excellent measurements in comparison with the pelvic elements of the extinct species, more especially the huge bones of *E. meridionalis*, from the Forest Bed in the Norwich Museum. These are as follows:

1. From the anterior superior spine of *ilium* to the *symphysis pubis* is $24\frac{1}{2}$ (linear), and 27 inches by tape along the margin. In No. 225, *E. meridionalis*, Gunn Collection, Norwich Museum, the former is 34 inches.

2. From anterior superior spine of *ilium* along the upper border to the *sacro-iliac symphysis* is 28 inches (linear), 33 by tape. In No. 225, Gunn Collection, the former is 48, and the latter 67 inches.

3. Height from brim of *acetabulum* to the anterior superior spine of *ilium* 13 (linear), 15 by tape. In No. 225 these two are 18 and 21 inches respectively.

4. Girth of neck of *ilium* $19\frac{1}{4}$ inches. In No. 225 it is $29\frac{3}{4}$ inches.

5. *Pubic symphysis* to *sacrum* 18 linear, round the basin 23 inches. In 225 the former is 20 inches, latter 26 inches.

6. Maximum breadth of *ilium* 16 inches. In 225 it is 25 inches.

7. *Sacro-iliac symphysis* 14×9 inches.

8. Depth of the *pubic symphysis* 18 inches. It is 15 inches in No. 225, therefore less than in the Asiatic.

9. *Acetabulum* $6 \times 6\frac{1}{4}$ (linear), by tape along the floor of the cup $8\frac{1}{2} \times 7\frac{1}{2}$ inches. In 225 it is (linear) 8.5×9. The wide notch and flattened portion in front are pronounced.

10. *Foramen ovale* $6 \times 4\frac{1}{2}$ inches. In 225 it is 10.5×7.

11. Girth of *pubis* midshaft $8\frac{1}{2}$ inches.

12. Girth of *ischium* midshaft 9 inches. In No. 225 it is 12 inches.

6. HUMERUS.

Cuvier states that the humerus of the African is more slender than that of the Asiatic Elephant, whilst De Blainville asserts that the long bones generally are stouter and shorter than in the Elephant of Asia. Moreover, these two authorities further differ in opinion as to the degree of saliency of the supinator ridge, Cuvier stating that it is *less*, and De Blainville *more*, salient in the African as compared with the Asiatic. They agree that the bicipital groove is *narrower* and the deltoid crest not *so low down* in the Asiatic as in the African. The values of these characters seem, however, questionable, owing to the absence of sufficient instances of the skeleton of the latter in collections in comparison with bones of the former. The abundant materials relating to the Asiatic Elephant appear to me to show considerable inconstancy as regards the stoutness of the limb bones, more especially specimens from both Continental India and its islands. The "slender built" Sumatran Elephant contrasts with the "squat built" form of Central India, and are known by distinct designations.[1] The Central Indian Elephant is smaller than Ceylonese and sub-Himalayan. The same is reported of the Burmese and Siamese, which are said to be still smaller and shorter varieties, whilst some are tuskless. According to travellers there is considerable variability in the size of the African Elephant in different districts.[2]

1. As to the deltoid crest, it seems to me often difficult to exactly define its limits excepting on bones of aged wild individuals. (Pl. XVI, figs. 4 and 5.)

2. The head and tuberosity in two specimens of the African Elephant appear more compressed in the African than in any instance of that of the Asiatic examined by me.

3. With reference to the breadth and depth of the bicipital groove. It is shallow and open in the African (70Sn), and also in the humerus of a skeleton in the Royal College of Surgeons of Ireland, whereas it is very generally deep and narrow (almost tubular in certain instances) in the Asiatic, but there are exceptions, of which I have notes of two

[1] Falconer, op. cit., vol. ii, p. 257. Tennent's 'Ceylon,' vol. iv, p. 291.

[2] Livingstone, 'Travels in South Africa,' p. 562, and 'Last Journals,' vol. ii, p. 29, where he alludes to a dwarf race averaging 5 feet 8 inches in height with a tusk 6 feet in length.

instances where the groove was fully as open as in the African.   Looked upon, however, generally, the above is fairly reliable in the diagnosis of the two species.

4. As to degrees of saliency of the supinator ridge; individual instances in the Asiatic appear precisely to accord with 70Sɪɪ of the African. The ridge was less salient in many instances of the former, but here again there seems so much variability that one is not disposed to place much reliance on this character. Compare fig. 4 with 5.

5. The ridge proceeding from the supinator upwards and backwards to the epiphysis, is very often so pronounced in the Asiatic as to form a carina at its upper part, and would be of value if invariably persistent, but it is not so, being sometimes, as in 70Sɪɪ African, lost before it reaches that point. Compare fig. 4 *a* with 5 *a*.

6. As to the position of the nutritive foramen, when *one* is present and of conspicuous size to entitle it to be considered the main opening, there appears considerable inconsistency as to its exact position in the Asiatic Elephant, but when at all pronounced it is usually in a line with the apex of the supinator ridge, whereas in 70Sɪɪ it is in the lower third. In fossil specimens it is so frequently obliterated by mineral infiltrations as to be quite undiscernible; moreover, the multiplicity of these canals on various parts of the shaft, and their agreement in size, make it uncertain which to rely upon as the normal condition.

7. With reference to the configuration of the distal articular surface, the following points are referred to by Busk,[1] which, if persistent in the African, as they are in all adult humeri of the Asiatic I have examined, would be invaluable in establishing specific characters. These refer to the (*a*) contours of the outer condyle; (*b*) the configuration of the arc formed by the lower border of the articular surface; and (*c*) the contour of the trochlear depression posteriorly, as shown in his monograph referred to on the Maltese fossil Elephants.[1]

The above characters are, viz.:

(*a*) A more globose margin and general contour of the external condyle in the African. This is pronounced in 70Sɪɪ, whereas the same parts are less rounded in the Asiatic. Compare fig. 5 *b* with fig. 4 *b*.

(*b*) The arch of the lower border formed when the humerus is placed erect on a level surface is shorter and nearly central in the African, whereas in the Asiatic it commences gradually from the margin and extends from nearly one to the other. Compare fig. 5 *b* with fig. 4 *b*.

(*c*) The trochlear depression below the pit is narrow in the Asiatic, with nearly perpendicular sides, whereas it is shallow in the African, with gently undulating margins, in fact, as in the case of the bicipital groove, the one is deep and narrow, and the other broad and shallow. Compare fig. 4 *b* with 5 *b*.

8. The depth of the olecranon pit and the hollow surface above it are seemingly greater in 70Sɪɪ African than I have seen in the Asiatic. These, however, may be con-

[1] 'Trans. Zool. Soc. London,' vol. vi, p. 257.

sidered of little value, and are apparently subject to variations in connection with individuals, and perhaps age. Compare fig. 5 a with 4 a.

9. The internal condyloid ridge is narrow and prominent in 708u African, whilst, as far as I have observed, in all humeri of the Asiatic it is blunt and rounded. This character, from its apparent constancy in the latter, seems to me trustworthy. Compare fig. 5 a with 4 a.

The magnificent collections of Mammoth remains in the British Museum from British and Arctic localities are rich in specimens of arm-bones, a few of which are entire. The small race which frequented the Thames Valley during and prior to the deposits of the brick-earths of ILFORD, as shown by the teeth, pectoral girdle, and axial elements just described, is maintained by the humerus and other portions of its skeleton ; whilst, on the other hand, even in the same situation and elsewhere in the neighbourhood, and throughout the islands, we find a larger race differing only in minor morphological characters. Reverting to the Mammoth of Ilford, with reference to what has just been enumerated in connection with races of the Asiatic and African species, it is interesting to observe the same tendencies to variability in the case of the species now under consideration, but with this exception apparently—that whilst the characters of the recent race are general to the individuals frequenting a particular district, in the case of the Mammoth, we find at Crayford and in the neighbouring localities around Ilford remains ascribable to the typical skeleton of the species. But this anomaly may be more apparent than real, seeing that the ages of the strata in which they are found cannot be calculated or distinctly correlated with the adjacent fluviatile deposits.

The arm-bone of the Mammoth is represented in the above-mentioned collections in the British Museum by no less than nineteen, specimens, for the most part fragmentary, but all are suggestive as regards the age and dimensions of their owners. The best preserved specimens, No. $\frac{C}{125}$ of the Brady Collection, is stated by Davies to have been "that of a young individual," but after a careful re-examination of the bone he quite agrees with me that from the fact that the epiphyses are firmly united and not a trace of the union is visible either at the proximal or the distal extremities, there can be no doubt but that it belonged to an adult individual. It is rivalled by another, but less perfectly preserved, specimen, No. $\frac{C}{130}$, which is 27 inches in length, the former being 28·7. The chief dimensions of $\frac{C}{125}$ are given in table at page 215.

The following characters of the arm-bone of the Mammoth, as compared with what have been just stated of the humeri of the two recent species, I shall now indicate.

1. The bone (Plate XVI, fig. 1) altogether is more robust than that of either of the living species, and this stoutness relates more particularly to the relatively larger deltoid crest and the antero-posterior diameter of the upper or proximal third, a feature

altogether more pronounced than in the latter, in fact, a larger expanse for muscular insertions. This character, as far as some fifty humeri of the Mammoth extend, seems to be invariable. Even the superb humerus in Plate XVI, fig. 4 and 4 *a*, of the Asiatic Elephant represents a more slender upper third as compared with the shorter bone of the Mammoth, figs. 1 and 1 *a*.

2. The antero-posterior to the transverse diameter of the head (fig. 1) is 170 to 127 millimètres. The deltoid crest is broad (fig. 1 *a*), and bulges conspicuously outwards about its middle, more so a great deal than I have seen in either of the living, even in that huge bone of the Asiatic (fig. 4), which represents an aged individual said to have died in its native haunts.

3. The bicipital groove is deep and narrow, being 1½ inches in its greatest breadth.

4. The supinator ridge (fig. 1) is not so salient as in the African (Plate XVI, fig. 5), and it is altogether shorter.[1]

5. The posterior ridge proceeding from the supinator ridge to the head, as in the African, and not unfrequently in the Asiatic, although not always clearly traceable, is pronounced in fig. 1 *a* to the proximal articular surface, as in the Asiatic humerus (fig. 4 *a*).

6. The contours of the outer condyle, lower border, and trochlear depression of the distal articulation (fig. 1 *b*) are much as in the Asiatic. These characters I have found very general in all undoubted humeri of the Mammoth which have come under my notice. Compare fig. 1 *b*, Mammoth, with fig. 4 *b*, Asiatic, and fig. 5 *b*, African, also with fig. 6 *b*, *E. antiquus*, and fig. 3 *b*, *E. meridionalis*.

7. The internal condyloid ridge (fig. 1 *b*) is relatively broader than that of the Asiatic Elephant (fig. 4 *b*), and therefore widely different in this respect from the African (fig. 5 *b*).

There are other humeri of considerably larger dimensions in the above Collection (Brady), such as $\frac{C}{126}$, the extreme length of which is 32·5 inches, and another, $\frac{C}{127}$, 33· inches.

I have selected the foregoing as a good typical example illustrative of the humerus of the Mammoth. It is No. 30,531, B. M., and is interesting as being the most westerly indication of the Mammoth in Europe, having been dredged in the BAY OF GALWAY. Its history has been verified to me by the Earl of Enniskillen, who came into the possession of the specimen soon after the discovery, and subsequently presented it to the National Collection. The surface is dark-coloured, as if derived from mud, and covered with shells of *Balanus* and *Polyzoans*. There is a loss of portion of the great tuberosity

---

[1] But there are exceptions in individual humeri of the Mammoth both as to the length and inclinations of the supinator ridge. These are well seen in No. 26,259, B. M., Owles' Collection from the DOGGER BANK, where there is a very short supinator ridge, the upper border of which is nearly at right angles to the shaft, whilst another, No. 46,258, in the same collection, and also from the DOGGER BANK, has the supinator ridge much inclined.

and a small piece of the supinator ridge, otherwise it is quite entire. The dimensions are given in the table, page 215. It is seven inches longer than the smallest adult humerus from Ilford in the British Museum, and is six inches shorter than that of the Lena skeleton in St. Petersburgh, which is forty inches long. The nutrient foramen in the former is situated about 15·5 inches from the head.

A summary of the characters appertaining to the humerus of the Mammoth and Asiatic Elephant, in contradistinction to the same bone in the African species, and supported by numerous examples, refers to—

1. Greater depth and narrowness of the bicipital groove.
2. Greater compression of the head and tuberosity,
3. Less saliency of the supinator ridge.
4. Prominence of the deltoid ridge.
5. Greater hollowing out of the shaft at the insertion of the supinator ridge.
6. Narrow and deep trochlea.
7. More defined margins of the cubital articular surfaces.

A few comparisons between the humerus of *E. primigenius* and that of *E. antiquus* and *E. meridionalis* are referred to at p. 57, and will be further noticed in the sequel, page 216, in connection with the latter species.

7. CUBITUS.

Ulna.

1. Cuvier states that the radius crosses the ulna in a more oblique direction in the Asiatic than in the African; and this appears to be the case as regards the forearm of 708 u, B. M., African, as compared with several specimens of that of the Asiatic.

In the Mammoth the bone commences to cross lower down than in either of the above, about the junction of the middle with the lower third, as shown in Plate XVIII, fig. 1.

2. Busk has pointed out[1] that the radial sulcus of the *ulna* is more rounded and shallower in *E. Africanus* than in *E. Asiaticus.*

Several ulnæ of the Mammoth seem to agree with *E. Asiaticus*, as shown in fig. 1 *a*. It will be noticed, however, presently, that there are exceptions to this condition among Arctic specimens in the British Museum.

3. Busk further observes that the inner articular facet is wider at what may be termed the neck in the *E. Africanus* than in *E. Asiaticus.* Here, again, in the Mammoth, as seen in fig. 1 *a*, it presents the character of the latter.

4. The anterior and lower third of the shaft is more flat in the African (708 n) than I have seen it in the Mammoth and Asiatic, which are much alike.

[1] Op. cit., p. 247.

5. The posterior or olecranon ridge is more rounded and blunt in the African ulna than in any of the Mammoth and Asiatic I have examined ; it is also more arcuated in the former.

6. The external border of the shaft is more rounded in the African specimen than obtains in many ulnæ of the Asiatic, whereas in the Mammoth it is scarcely so sharp as in the latter.

7. The distal articular surface varies so much in the convexity and configuration of the cuneiform aspect in the Mammoth and Asiatic as to appear to me of little value as a means of diagnosis.

The above seem to me the only differences in any way persistent, at all events as far as many ulnæ of the Mammoth and Asiatic are concerned. Of course, the data obtained from a single instance of the African Elephant cannot be considered very reliable.

The two elements of the forearm of the Mammoth are well seen in specimens from the Arctic regions in the British Museum. Three ulnæ from Escnscholtz Bay present only one character in any ways different from similar bones from Ilford and other British localities. The exceptional condition is in the radial notch, which is wide, like that of the African, in two ; whilst the third is like that of the Asiatic and all other ulnæ of the Mammoth I have examined.

The Brady Collection, B. M., contains fourteen specimens either entire or fragmentary. The right cubitus from Ilford (Pl. XVIII, figs 1 and 2), although somewhat longer than any of the above, preserves the same characters. Of these forearm bones the ulna (No. 38,101) is 28 inches in length and its radius (38,012) $2\frac{1}{2}$ inches. The width of the proximal articulation is $7\frac{1}{2}$, the cuneiform facet being $2\frac{3}{4}$ inches in the antero-posterior by $3\frac{1}{2}$ inches in the transverse diameter.[1]

The smallest entire ulna, $\frac{C}{146}$, Brady Collection, is 26 inches in length, being quite in proportion to the small humerus, $\frac{C}{128}$. Thus, the arm and forearm of an individual of these dimensions would be about 4 feet 6 inches, and supposing the above and other bones proportionate to those of a recent Elephant they would give a height of about 8 feet at the shoulder, or the ordinary height of an adult of the Central-Indian variety, which, on the whole, furnishes a fair estimate of the size of the Mammoth which frequented South-eastern England and the banks of the Thames during the period of the deposition of the brick-earths of Ilford.

Besides the instance recorded at p. 60, of anchylosis of the radius to the ulna, there is another highly characteristic example of the cubitus of a young Mammoth from ILFORD in the National Collection, showing a complete bony union of the two elements.

[1] I may here observe that the articulating surfaces of the long bones were measured by tape along their surfaces ; the same with the acetabulum and glenoid cavity of the scapula, &c.

As compared with *E. antiquus*; the radial sulcus is deep and narrow in the latter, whilst it is wide and shallow in *E. meridionalis*.

The head of the olecranon seems to tend more inwards in *E. antiquus* than in the Mammoth, and apparently in *E. meridionalis*.

Radius.

Like the fibula, the radius is subject to certain individual differences in the prominence or otherwise of ridges and the degree of flattening, breadth, or rounding of its surfaces. But there are a few characters apparently characteristic of species.

1. The anterior aspect is in general much more rounded in the Asiatic and Mammoth (Plate XVIII, fig. 1) than in the African. In the radii referred to the *E. antiquus*[1] it is apparently broader, and more flattened than in the two former. In the enormous radius of *E. meridionalis*, in the collection of R. Johnson, Esq., from Palling, on the Norwich coast, this aspect is not so pronounced as in the Asiatic; but the narrowness so prominent, amounting to a shin, in the anterior upper third of the African is not observed in any of the British fossil radii nor in *E. Asiaticus*.

2. The upper and outer side of the shaft is more flattened in *E. antiquus*, *E. Africanus*, and in *E. meridionalis*, than in *E. Asiaticus* and *E. primigenius*.

3. The inner aspect of the shaft in the above presents these characters. It is round in *E. primigenius*, flattened in *E. Africanus*, *E. antiquus*, and *E. meridionalis*, whereas it is narrow and sharp in *E. Asiaticus*.

4. A prominent ridge rises close to the inner aspect of the head in the African, and runs obliquely downwards towards the external malleolus, where it joins the anterior ridge or shin.

In the Asiatic and Mammoth this character is not nearly so pronounced, nor is it the case in *E. antiquus* and *E. meridionalis*.

Neither the proximal nor the distal articulations present seemingly distinctive characters of a reliable nature.

5. The radius generally is relatively stouter in the Mammoth and *E. antiquus* than in the two recent Elephants; on the other hand, considering the much greater dimensions of that of *E. meridionalis*, it has a more slender aspect than in the two former.

Owing to the slender form of this bone it is rarely found entire in the fossil state. The Brady Collection contains several specimens, a few of which are nearly entire, but none so perfect as that belonging to the ulna (Plate XVIII, figs. 1, 2) already noticed.

[1] Page 59.

8. MANUS.

The elements of the fore foot of the recent species present a few apparently distinctive characters, but collectively there does not appear much difference in relative size.

Carpus.

Scaphoid.—In my monograph on the 'Maltese Fossil Elephants'[1] I have referred to differences in the configuration and articular surfaces of this bone in the two recent species and the Mammoth, which a more extended field of observation does not seem to controvert. These are, briefly—(*a*) The posterior border is more rounded in the African and Mammoth than in the Asiatic, in which it is more constricted about the middle. (*b*) The radial facet is generally (I have met with one or two exceptions, however) more erect in the Asiatic and Mammoth than in the African. (*c*) The trapezoidal and magnal articular aspects form a triangle in the African, and are slightly concave, whereas in the Asiatic and Mammoth the hollowing out is confined to the magnal surface, and the entire articular aspect is quadrilateral and slightly convex about the middle, and is oval at the summit, where it is rather concave. This surface is more continuous in the African; the facets for the magnum and trapezoid not being so defined as in the Asiatic and Mammoth.

I have not seen a scaphoid referable to *E. antiquus*, but a colossal specimen of that of *E. meridionalis*, No. 150, of the Gunn Collection, Norwich, from the Forest Bed Series, shows a narrow constriction at the middle, as in the Asiatic and Mammoth. The trapezoidal and magnal facets are, however, like the African, the surface for the former being nearly flat and the radial aspect nearly horizontal.

This bone varies in length, being usually between $5\frac{1}{2}$ to $4\frac{1}{2}$ inches in the Mammoth, whereas the colossal bones from the Norfolk coast often exceed that by two inches.

Lunare.—The ulnar facet is more erect in the Asiatic and Mammoth than in the African specimen, 708 II, B. M. In the large lunare, No. 155, Gunn Collection, Norwich, it is intermediate, being not so perpendicular as in the former.

The magnal surface is hollowed out to a greater extent in the Mammoth and Asiatic than in the African, but it is still more so in No. 155 just referred to, in which the anterior aspect is quite flat. The latter, moreover, has no scaphoidal facets, which are, however, sometimes very small, and even wanting in large individuals of the other forms, indeed, in another specimen, No. 151 of the Norwich Collection, from the same locality and of the same size as No. 155, both the scaphoidal facets and the flattening are absent.

The dimensions of the lunare of *E. primigenius* seems seldom to exceed a maximum

---

[1] 'Trans. Zool. Soc. London,' vol. vi, p. 66.

length of 5 inches, whereas the above specimens referred to *E. meridionalis* from the pre-glacial deposits of Norfolk are as much as 10 inches in length.

Cuneiforme.—The ulnar surface of this bone is concave in the Mammoth and Asiatic about the middle, and the same obtains likewise in several colossal specimens referable to *E. meridionalis*, or else large individuals of *E. antiquus* in the Gunn Collection. This central depression is absent in the cuneiforme of 708 u, African, in the British Museum, in which there is a depression at the anterior apex not observable in any of the above.

The bone is relatively thicker at the external margin of the pisiform facet in the Asiatic and Mammoth generally than in the African specimen, and the same is apparent in the enormous bones from the Norfolk coast; the character, however, is not invariably pronounced. The length of the cuneiforme in the Mammoth seldom exceeds 5½ inches, whilst, as will appear in the sequel, the same bone in *E. meridionalis* and in *E. antiquus* attained far greater proportions.

The *pisiforme* is not preserved in any collection of the British fossil Elephants examined by me.

Trapezium.—This element of the carpus, like the trapezoid, if the specimens figured on Pls. XIX and XXI are typical of the species, would seem to present some valuable diagnostic characters. The following are in the British Museum :

1. The specimen (Pl. XIX, fig. 8), No. 36,611, left foot, referred to *E. primigenius*, is from MAIDSTONE, Kent. The length is 2·5, and maximum breadth 2·8 inches, girth 7 inches. In the Asiatic the first two proportions stand as 2·3 to 3 inches. The bone is relatively longer, but the contour is not very different; the same may be said of the African Elephant.

2. No. 20,821 (fig. 9) is a right trapezium of *E. antiquus* from GRAYS, Essex, where remains of this species are plentiful. It is 4 inches in length, with a maximum breadth of 4 inches and girth of 10·4 inches,

3. No. 33,418 (fig. 10), a right trapezium of either *E. meridionalis* or *E. antiquus*, is in the Layton Collection from the EAST COAST. The bone is dark-coloured, and may, on that account, have been derived from the Forest-Bed Series. The length is 3·5 inches breadth 3·8 inches, girth 9·4 inches. The specimen is decidedly small for *E. meridionalis*; but unless the bone is subject to much variability in the configuration as well as dimensions, it seems quite distinct from the other two, which also present individual peculiarities. These discrepancies are well shown in the figures, and refer to the following points :

1. General outline. The contour of the inner border of the bone from MAIDSTONE (fig. 8) rises from the metacarpal surface at an angle of about 45°, and declines suddenly at the summit, whilst its outer border is slightly concave, and its breadth exceeds the length.

The outline of the GRAYS specimen (fig. 9) shows a remarkable concavity of the inner border, and a more horizontal upper surface, whilst its length and breadth are nearly equal. The outer border is somewhat convex.

The inner border of the EAST-COAST specimen (fig. 10) is inclined below, suddenly becoming erect, and gradually declines towards the summit; the outer border is very uneven. It is broader than it is long.

2. The scaphoidal and trapezoidal facets of fig. 8 a, as regards outlines and surfaces, are widely different from figs. 9 a and 10.

3. The metacarpal aspects are also perfectly distinct in figs. 8 b, 9 b, and 10 b.

How far a series of specimens would show these to be only individual and variable characters I cannot say, at all events the above appears to me worthy of illustration.

Trapezoid.—The two bones just described from GUAYS and MAIDSTONE, referable to *E. antiquus* and to *E. primigenius*, present, in their trapezoids, discrepancies equally noteworthy. Possibly the two elements of the foot belonged to the same individual, seeing that the trapezoids are from the same localities.

The trapezoid of the Mammoth (Pl. XXI, fig. 3), 23,119, B. M., from MAIDSTONE, is of the left side, and fits fig. S, Pl. XIX. It is 4·5 inches by 2·5 inches, with a girth of S·5 inches. It is remarkably narrow as compared with the GUAYS specimen of *E. antiquus* (Pl. XXI, fig. 4), which represents a left trapezoid, No. 36,609, B. M.; it is 3·5 by 2·8 inches, the girth is S·4 inches.

The general contours of these two bones, and of their carpal and metacarpal facets, supposing fig. 3 is that of *E. primigenius* and fig. 4 belongs to *E. antiquus*, are certainly very remarkable. These are, however, the only instances known to me of this bone, excepting a much larger example of *E. meridionalis* from the Norfolk coast. The latter partakes more of the characters of *E. antiquus* than of the Mammoth. Here, again, it is desirable to examine several specimens before a definite conclusion can be come to.

In the Asiatic Elephant the bone, as regards relative dimensions and contour, is certainly more closely allied to fig. 4 than fig. 3.

Magnum.—The characters of this bone are much alike in the recent and fossil Elephants. The lunare aspect is generally more concave in the Mammoth and Asiatic than in the African, and this is more or less apparent also in the specimen I have referred to *E. antiquus*.[1] Large magna from the FOREST BED will be referred to in the sequel. Very often the trapezoidal facet is divided in the Asiatic and Mammoth, but it is not so in 70S II, African. This bone seldom exceeds 5 inches in its greatest length in the Mammoth, the generality of specimens being little over 4½ inches, whereas individuals of *E. antiquus* and *E. meridionalis* show a maximum length of 7 inches.

Unciforme.—The facet for the third metacarpal, said to be absent in the Asiatic,[2] is certainly not an invariable condition; indeed, from what I have seen, it is usually present. It was present in the magna of *E. antiquus* and *E. meridionalis*, as recorded at p. 60.

[1] Page 60.
[2] De Blainville, vol. iii, p. 42.

The maximum length in the Mammoth seldom exceeds 3½ inches, whereas in *E. antiquus*[1] it is 6·8 inches; and several still larger specimens are represented in the British Museum, Gunn Collection, and that of A. Savin, Esq., of Cromer, all of which may probably belong to *E. meridionalis* or *E. antiquus*.

Metacarpals.

First digit.—The first metacarpal of the Mammoth does not seem to present any character different from that of the Asiatic, which, however, as far as the afore-noticed single instance of the African is concerned, may be distinguished by the upper and lower surfaces of the shaft in the two former being not so broad and flattened as in the latter. This bone and its homologue of the hind foot are seemingly shorter in the African than in the Mammoth and Asiatic Elephant, and there is apparently a few differences in the contours of the distal articulating surface in the Mammoth and Asiatic as compared with the African species and *E. meridionalis*, which are more alike.

A colossal bone of this member of the manus, 4½ inches in length, found on the beach at *Cromer*, is in the Gunn Collection. This specimen in the concave upper aspect of the distal facet presents a character of the African, but otherwise the general outline and circular contour of the proximal articular surface show no very close affinities with either of the recent Elephants.

Second digit.—Comparisons of these elements of the fore foot of the Mammoth with similar bones of the recent species do not point to any characters available for diagnostic purposes.

The second metacarpal of the Mammoth is represented in the Owles Collection and the Brady and Gunn Collections, the largest being 5·8 inches.

There is a large specimen in the Owles Collection, B. M., from the Dogger Bank, 7·5 inches in length. The proximal articular surface is 5·8 × 3 inches, and the distal 4·4 inches in height by 4·4 in width. The girth midshaft is 8·8 inches.

This digit is not relatively stouter nor longer than in the recent Elephants, and the same character may be said generally to obtain, at all events with the three longest toes, in the fore and hind feet of the Mammoth.

The first phalanx is more even at its proximal or metacarpal articular aspect in both the Asiatic and Mammoth than in the African, in which the foot is relatively broader, but these characters may not be persistent.

Third digit.—The sides of the metacarpal are more flattened in the African than in the Mammoth and Asiatic.

The marginal surface is more concave in the two last-named species, which differ from *E. antiquus* as regards the contours of the central and marginal facets, as seen in Plate XVIII, fig. 7, of the Mammoth, and fig. 6 of *E. antiquus*, on the one hand, whilst

[1] Page 60.

that of *E. meridionalis* (fig. 5) is narrower than either. How far these characters admit of constancy in the three species can only be determined by comparisons of numerous examples. I must state, however, that several specimens referable to *E. meridionalis* maintain the aspect of the proximal extremity shown in fig. 5.

The average length of the third metacarpal in the Mammoth seldom exceeds 8½ inches.

Fourth digit.—There are apparently no characters of a reliable nature in the fourth metacarpal in connection with recent and extinct species to require particular notice. The bone averages from 7 to 8 inches in length in the Mammoth, whereas specimens referable to *E. meridionalis* or *E. antiquus*, from the Norfolk submerged deposits, attain to almost 9 inches, and fragments indicate even longer bones.

Fifth digit.—The fifth metacarpal is not so broad in the Mammoth and Asiatic as in the African Elephant, and the unciform facet is circular in outline in the two former generally, although specimens show an approach to that of the African, which is oval.

The proximal phalanx appears generally more compressed at midshaft in the Asiatic and Mammoth than in Specimen 708n (African) in the British Museum. There are other small points with reference to the distal articular surfaces possibly distinctive of the bone in the recent Elephant of Asia as compared with the African, but these are irregular in the Mammoth.

There is seemingly a wide difference in all these characters in the equivalent bone of *E. meridionalis* (Plate XVIII, figs. 8 and 8 *a*), more especially in the contour of the proximal articular surface, as will be indicated in the sequel.

Phalanges.

The phalanges of the first, second, and fifth digits show apparently several differences in the recent species, more especially the proximal and distal elements, as recorded elsewhere,[1] and as far as I have been enabled to compare them with similar bones of the Mammoth they show closer affinities with the Asiatic than with the African Elephant.

9. FEMUR.

The comparisons of Cuvier and De Blainville in relation to the humerus have the same force with reference to the femora of the two living species. As regards the Mammoth, out of numerous instances from the Arctic region and British strata, it appears to me that the thigh, like the arm, was relatively shorter than in the recent Elephants. But at the same time there is marked variability in individuals of many species of Proboscidea.

1. Comparing the length and direction of the neck in many instances of the

[1] Adams, 'Trans. Zool. Soc. London,' vol. ix, p. 90.

2 3

Mammoth's femur with the same parts in the Asiatic, and with a single example of the African, I find that it is decidedly longer in the Asiatic than in the African, 708n, B. M., and is shorter in the Mammoth than in either; this obtains likewise in a superb specimen from MUNDESLEY, Norfolk coast, which might be fairly referred to *E. meridionalis*. This enormous bone, perfectly entire, is no less than 5 feet in length. It was discovered within a few feet of a radius (3 feet 3 inches in length) and the enormous humerus, No. 200 of the Gunn Collection, Pl. XVI, fig. 2, so as to render it probable that the three bones belonged to the same individual.

2. A rudimentary trochanter minor is often traceable in the Asiatic and Mammoth, and is present in the above-named femur of *E. meridionalis*. This tuberosity is absent in femur 708u of the African. The amount of obliquity of the head is not constant, some specimens being much more inclined than others.

3. The relation of the great trochanter to the head is seemingly subject to variability, but in nearly all perfectly entire specimens of the Mammoth it is almost level with the epiphysial junction of the latter (Pl. XIX, fig. 7), whereas it is considerably below it in the Asiatic. In this respect the MUNDESLEY specimen resembles the Mammoth. Unfortunately the part is not present in 708u, B. M., African; however, according to Cuvier, the summit of the great trochanter is above the level of the apophysial union.[1]

4. The digital pit has a broader outer wall in the Mammoth and colossal Norfolk femurs than in either of the recent species.

5. The position of the nutrient foramen may be considered variable as to position, but it is usually higher up in the Mammoth and Asiatic than in the African. It is undeterminable in the huge thigh-bones from the Norfolk coast, the opening having become filled with matrix.

Surfaces of the Shaft.

Some stress has been put upon the four surfaces of the shaft as distinctive of species, and, although always well marked, there is seemingly individual variability, not only in respect to their evenness, but also the degrees of sharpness or rotundity of their margins. Much, no doubt, depends on the size of individuals and the habits of the species. The colossal Forest-Bed Elephants were evidently less given to active muscular exertions as compared with the feral individuals of recent species and the Mammoth, if we may judge from the absence of pronounced articular surfaces and ridges for muscular attachments.

I have compared many femora of Mammoths with the same bones of recent species and a few examples of the colossal femora from East Anglia, with the following results as regards their shaft. I have not seen an entire femur referable to *E. antiquus*.

1. *The anterior surface* in the Mammoth is broad and flat in many (fig. 7), whilst in other adult specimens it is narrow and round. It is remarkably broad in three

[1] 'Oss. Fossil.,' pl. ii, fig. 6.

enormous bones in the collections of Mr. Gunn, Mr. Johnson, and Mr. Backhouse, from the FOREST BED; but altogether it is slender as compared with them.

2. *The posterior surface* is considerably less flattened in the Mammoth and these huge bones and in the Asiatic than in the African, the external border being more pronounced in the Asiatic than in the other two, whilst it is rounded in the African.

3. *The external surface.*—It is nearly even throughout in the African (708H), whereas it bulges at the third trochanter in the Mammoth and Asiatic. In some femora of the former, such as $\frac{C}{190}$ (fig. 7) and $\frac{C}{197}$ of the Brady Collection, B. M., from ILFORD, this character is pronounced to a greater extent, whereas another femur, $\frac{C}{193}$ in the same collection, the bulging is not so well marked. In the other fossil femora neither character is very evident.

4. *The internal surface.*—It is broader and more even in the Mammoth than in either of the recent species, and more so in the African than in the Asiatic.

Condyles.

The relative dimensions of the condyles do not seem to furnish important distinctions. I have noticed the differences in the width of the inter-condyloid spaces in the recent species,[1] or rather the degrees of convergence, which is greater in the Asiatic than in the African, 708u B. M., and this seems to be the case very generally in the Mammoth (Plate XIX, fig. 7a, and Plate XXII, fig. 6), and the same is shown in the condyles of the femur in Mr. Johnson's possession described in the sequel. Individual differences occur in other specimens of large thigh-bones from the Norwich coast, as seen in Gunn's Collection, and, as before noticed,[2] the condyles referred to *E. antiquus*, from Walton, are not quite so convergent as in the Mammoth.

The patellar surface is broad and shallow in 708n (African), whereas in the Mammoth, and in the huge femora of *E. meridionalis*, it is generally more concave and deeper (see Plate XIX, fig. 7, Plate XXII, figs. 5 and 6, and Plate XXVI, fig. 3b).

In Beechy's ' Voyage of the Blossom'[3] there is represented a femur of the Mammoth from Arctic America. The specimen is in the National Collection. It is remarkable for its long and slender shaft. The following are its dimensions :

Length 39 inches ; to the neck 36 inches.

Girth at midshaft 12 inches.

The smallest width at midshaft $4\frac{1}{2}$ inches.

[1] P. 62. I must here correct a slip of my pen in connection with the degree of convergence of the condyles of the femur in *E. Asiaticus*, where I state that " in the Mammoth and *E. Asiaticus* the condyles are ' more apart,' " which should be *more convergent*.

[2] P. 62.

[3] Plate ii.

Breadth above the condyles 6¾ inches.

Antero-posterior diameter at the distal end 4·4 inches.

Antero-posterior outer condyles 6½ inches.

Antero-posterior inner condyle 8 inches.

Greatest width between inner borders of the condyles 3 inches.

The nutrient foramen is within 15 inches of the head on the inner and posterior surface.

Another left femur, in the same Collection, is 48 inches in length, with the nutrient foramen at the same distance from the head. Various examples are given by authors. Thus, Breyne[1] refers to a femur from Siberia 36 inches in length and 13 inches in girth at midshaft. Cuvier represents a Siberian specimen no less than 42 inches in length without the proximal end, and De Blainville also refers to similar specimens.

With reference to femora from British strata. The Owles Collection from the Dogger Bank contains several thigh-bones of the Mammoth, several of which indicate very large individuals. Thus, No. 46,275 shows an antero-posterior diameter of the inner condyle (by tape) of 11½ inches, and the outer 9½ inches; the breadth across the condyles is 9·2 inches.

The right femur, No. $\frac{C}{100}$ of the Brady Collection, B. M., from Ilford (Plate XIX, fig. 7), is an excellent example of the thigh-bone of the small variety of the Mammoth from the above locality. Its dimensions are given in Davies's Catalogue. The length, however, is less than there stated, being 40 instead of 45·5 inches; its girth midshaft is 14½ inches. The antero-posterior diameter of the inner condyle is 8·3 by callipers, and 15¼ inches by tape; the outer is 7·6 by callipers, and 13½ inches by tape.

There is also another very perfect specimen from the same locality in the possession of Professor Tennant, F.G.S., the length of which is 37½ inches, and least girth 12¾ inches.

A huge left femur in the British Museum, dredged on the Dutch coast, has lost the head and great trochanter, leaving a length of 46 inches; the girth midshaft is 15½ inches. The nutrient foramen is about the junction of the upper with the middle third. Another femur from the same locality, with the head and neck wanting, gives a length of 45 inches. The molars of the Mammoth dredged on the coast of the Netherlands and eastward perfectly correspond with these large bones.[2]

---

[1] 'Phil. Trans.,' vol. xl, p. 124.

[2] I have just lately been shown at Lowestoft, Suffolk, a superb left lower ultimate molar of the Mammoth dredged off Spimlico on the German coast. It is one of the most entire of any molar of this Elephant that has come under my notice. The enamel is very thin, as in the Dogger Bank and Arctic molars. It is 12 inches in length by 3½ in maximum breadth, and holds a formula of x 21 x. The anterior fang is curved backwards, followed by 6 or 7 fangs, and terminating in a hollow shell. Several teeth in the possession of J. J. Colman, Esq., M.P., of Corton, Suffolk, were dredged off Lowestoft, of a precisely similar character. One enormous thin-plated tooth, No. 35 of Mr. Randall Johnson's Collection, was also dredged thirty-five miles to the south-east of Lowestoft. It is in such a state of integrity that it

An abnormal femur, No. 255 of the Gunn Collection, with the ends completely consolidated, is 39 inches in length. The neck, instead of being much inclined, is nearly erect, with the head fully 5½ inches above the level of the great trochanter, thus furnishing a marked exception to the generality of specimens. The girth midshaft is 11½ inches. This bone was dredged off YARMOUTH. With the above exception it agrees in all the foregoing characters. Another femur from the EAST COAST is 41 inches in length, with a girth of midshaft 13·8 inches. The characters agree with typical femora of the Mammoth.

The PATELLA is not common; there are two specimens in Dr. F. Spurrell's Collection from CRAYFORD. One indicates a small individual, as is also represented by several teeth and bones of the Mammoth from the same situation. Neither of the former differ from patellæ of recent Elephants; and they partake of like irregularities in shape. The smaller specimen is 3·5 × 3·4 inches in breadth, and has a girth of 9·4 inches, whilst another is 4 × 4·5, and is 11·5 inches in circumference.

The above instances of the femur in adult individuals sufficiently attest the varieties in size to which the Mammoth was subject—a mutability common also to recent species, and considering the world-wide distribution of the former, it need not be a matter for wonder that it was subject to considerable variability; still, considering the varieties of climate and physical conditions, there is a remarkable persistence of character throughout, as compared with allied forms, showing thereby that the main characters were preserved throughout the Post-Glacial period, whatever may have been the ancestral connections of the Mammoth.

10. TIBIA.

There appears to be in this bone little of importance of a very stable character distinctive of species. The shin is prominent, with a deep cavity for the tibialis, in the generality of leg-bones of the Mammoth (Pl. XIX, fig. 12), and also in the Asiatic. This point is scarcely so pronounced in the African Elephant. Like the other bones of the extremities, the tibia is shorter in the Mammoth than in the two last named.

The facet at the distal end for the fibula is decidedly more oblique in the ILFORD Mammoth (Pl. XIX, fig. 12 b) and in the Asiatic Elephant than in the African; it is less apparent in the huge bones from the EAST COAST, and in several relatively larger and stouter tibiæ from the fluviatile deposits of the Thames Valley referable to E. antiquus, Pl. XIX, fig. 11 b.

The contours of the proximal articular surfaces of E. primigenius and E. antiquus, as shown in figs. 12 a and 11 a, present also differences; the latter being not so circular,

might have tumbled out of the alveolus into the fisherman's trawl. The specimen is an ultimate molar of the upper jaw, left side, and holds x 21 x in 14 × 3½. The highest colline is 8¼ inches.

whilst the distal tarsal surface of *E. antiquus* (Pl. XIX, fig. 11 *b*) is more rounded, and not so defined as in *E. primigenius* (fig. 12 *b*).

There are in London Collections several good examples of this bone from the Thames Valley deposits.

In the Cotton Collection, Museum of Practical Geology, there is a tibia, No. 2, from ILFORD, the dimensions of which are as follows:—Length is 23·5, girth, midshaft, 10·6 inches; girth of the proximal extremity 22·8, and distal 17·5 inches. Breadth of proximal articular surface 7·4 inches, the distal being 4·5 by 3·8 inches.

The above is matched by several specimens from the DOGGER BANK and elsewhere. Two tibiæ in the Beechy Collection from ARCTIC AMERICA are 23 and 20 inches in length respectively.

The bone varies apparently in the adult from about 20 to 25 inches in length.

The above-mentioned tibia from ILFORD, $\frac{C}{213}$, Brady Collection (Pl. XIX, fig. 12), has all the characters of the Arctic specimen, and represents the small-sized animal from that locality. The dimensions are—Length 20 inches, width, proximal end, 7 inches, width, distal end, 5·8 inches.[1]

The measurements of an entire tibia belonging to an adult individual, in connection with other portions of a skeleton of a Mammoth, from SHANDON CAVERN, Waterford, are recorded in my report on that rock cavity.[2] These are as follows:—The length is 22 inches; girth, midshaft, 10·8 inches; the proximal articulation 8 × 6, the outer condyloid cup being 3·5 × 3·5, and the inner 4·4 × 3·7 inches. The distal articulation was 3·8 in the a. p. d. by 4 inches.

The tibiæ from the EAST COAST deposits, as far as I have seen, are of two sorts. A remarkably slender tibia is dredged up occasionally by trawlers, or met with on the strand, and also in Post-Glacial deposits. This bone, by comparison with the Arctic remains of the Mammoth, is clearly inseparable; but occasionally along with the above, in Post-Glacial deposits, or in solitary instances, a much stouter and longer tibia is met with. Whether only a monster individual of the Mammoth, or that of either of the two other species, is not clear. Again, in the FOREST BED we find tibiæ not usually much longer than the equivalent bone of the Mammoth, but relatively much broader, and quite in keeping with the other huge bones of *E. meridionalis*.

There is a tibia, discovered at HAUSWELL, in Yorkshire, now in the Leeds Museum. It is 24 inches in length, the breadth at the proximal end is 7·5 by 5 inches, and that of the distal 4·5 by 3¾ inches, whilst the girth, midshaft, is 13 inches. There is a possibility, however, that it may belong to *E. antiquus*, which was the Elephant of the Kirkdale and other Yorkshire Caverns.

Another unusually stout and large tibia in the Cotton Collection, Jermyn Street

---

[1] Davies, 'Cat. Brady Collection,' p. 24.
[2] 'Trans. Roy. Irish Acad.,' vol. xxvi, p. 214.

Museum, from ILFORD, I am likewise disposed to place with *E. antiquus* for the same reasons. The following are its dimensions:—Length 26·8 inches; girth, midshaft, 13 inches, girth, proximal end, 27·5, and of the distal 22 inches; breadth, proximal articular surface, 8·5 inches, ditto, distal, 5·4 by 4·3 inches. The distal fibular facet is oblique, as in the Mammoth. The remarkable grossness of both these bones is in so much keeping with numerous instances of Mammoths' tibiæ from the Arctic regions and British strata, that I am inclined to place them with the large bone described from CAMBERWELL, Surrey.[1] This tibia is shown in Pl. XIX, fig. 11, for the purpose of comparison with that of the Mammoth (fig. 12).

Another large and very stout tibia, No. 48,134, B. M., ILFORD, shows a prominent incurving shin, with a deep pit for the extensor muscles. The length is 25 inches, the girth, midshaft, is 12·4 inches, and the inferior articular surface 4 (a. p. d.) × 5½ inches. Whether such leg-bones belonged to unusually large individuals of the Mammoth, or its more ponderous ally, the *E. antiquus*, it is difficult to say. The tibia, like the femur, was no doubt subject to considerable individual differences in size.

11. FIBULA.

A noticeable external character in the fibula of the Mammoth is that in several specimens the outer surface of the shaft is decidedly broader in it, the Asiatic, and the huge bones from the East coast, than appears in the single specimen of the African in the National Collection; moreover, as a general rule, the distal tibial facet is more horizontal in the latter than in them. This is seen in Plate XIX, fig. 4, No. $\frac{C}{220}$, Brady Collection from ILFORD, as compared with the huge bone from CROMER (fig. 3). These two bones will be seen to differ also in the contours of their tarsal articular surfaces.

In a large collection of Mammalian remains from the CRAYFORD brick-earths, Kent, belonging to Dr. Flaxman Spurrell, of Belvedere, there is an entire fibula of the Mammoth. The upper facet is oblique, and so is also the distal tibial articular surface. The bone is compressed from side to side at its proximal end, and a prominent external ridge runs down the shaft. There is also an internal ridge, which is sharp, and descends from the head to the internal angle. The bone is almost triquetrous.

The length is 19 inches, and maximum breadth of the distal extremity 3 inches.

12. PES.

The hind foot, like the manus, appears to have been relatively smaller in the Mammoth than in either *E. antiquus* or *E. meridionalis*.

[1] Page 63.

Tarsus.

Astragalus.—1. The posterior border is more even, and the posterior internal angle less pronounced in the African and the gigantic bones from East Anglia (Pl. XIX, fig. 6) than in the Mammoth (fig. 5) and Asiatic Elephant, which are similar in these respects.

2. The tibial aspect is usually more concave from side to side in the Mammoth and Asiatic than in the African and the enormous bones from the Forest Bed.

3. The navicular facet is seemingly not so convex in the Mammoth (fig. 5) and *E. meridionalis* (fig. 6) as in the Asiatic, in which it is more prominent than in the African; the same appertains to the peroneal facet.

4. The calcaneal facets present striking characters; the dividing pit is much broader in the Mammoth (fig. 5) and Asiatic than in the African and the large bones from the Forest Bed (fig. 6), where the articular surfaces are always completely isolated by a deep valley running tortuously across the surface.

5. In *E. meridionalis* (fig. 6) the articular surfaces are more even than in the Mammoth and the two recent species, the inner being crescentic and the outer quadrilateral, as seen in fig. 5, whilst in *E. meridionalis* (fig. 6) the former is triangular and the latter has the inner border more tortuous.

The early ossification of the bones makes it difficult to pronounce on the age of an individual. But generally a large astragal of the Mammoth may be about 5·5 inches in the antero-posterior and lateral directions. The small specimen from Ilford (fig. 5) has a tibial facet of only 4·5 × 4·5 inches.

Another astragal from the Shandon Cave, Waterford, belonging probably to the individual which owned the axis, dorsal vertebræ, and other bones already noticed, is preserved in the Museum of Science and Art, Dublin. It is 3·8 in the a. p. d. diameter by 5·3 in width, the navicular facet is 4·6 in width by 2·5 in height, whilst the calcaneal (outer) is 3·2 × 2·3, and the inner 3·3 × 1·8 inches. These measurements, however, refer to what must have been a rather small individual, as proven, also, by the teeth and bones.

Calcaneum.—The observations on this element of the hind foot of *E. antiquus* at page 64 appears to hold good after a more extended examination of specimens. The only point I observe deserving of further notice is that the upper surface of the heel, generally narrow in *E. Asiaticus* and *E. primigenius* (Plate XIX, fig. 1), and round in 70sn, *E. Africanus*, appears to be occasionally also round in *E. antiquus*, as seen in fig. 2. It is invariably broad in *E. meridionalis*. The dorsal surface of the heel may therefore be subject to individual variability, and can scarcely be accepted as diagnostic of species. The *E. Africanus* shows a relatively larger cuboidal facet, and a more oblique peroneal, and more even astragal facets than *E. primigenius* and *E. Asiaticus*. The points of distinction between the calcaneum of *E. primigenius* and *E. meridionalis* will be noticed in the sequel.

The following may be considered as average dimensions of this bone in the Mammoth. In the British Museum the calcaneum figured in Beechey's 'Voyage of the Blossom,'[1] from the Arctic Regions, is $6\frac{3}{4}$ inches in length by 5 in its maximum breadth. Another large specimen from the same region has a maximum length of 10, and a maximum breadth of $7\frac{1}{2}$, inches. The last displays a broad upper surface, and is therefore exceptional as compared with the generality of Mammoths' calcanea. The calcaneum of *E. antiquus*, No. 27,940, B. M. (Pl. XIX, fig. 2), from GRAYS, Essex, is $7\frac{1}{4}$ by 5 inches in breadth; its facets for the astragal will be seen to differ in their contours as compared with the Mammoth (fig. 1), the outer being nearly four-sided, whilst it is ovoid in *E. antiquus*, and the inner, which is triangular and deeply notched externally in the former, is crescentic in the latter. The interosseous pit is less open anteriorly and posteriorly in the Mammoth (fig. 1) than in *E. antiquus* (fig. 2). The heel is also more prominent in the Mammoth.

Naviculare presents no important diagnostic characters as regards species.

The dimensions of No. 27,931, B. M., from WALTON, in Essex, are 6 in breadth by $3\frac{1}{4}$ inches in height, and most probably represent that of the Mammoth.

Cuboid.—A comparison of several cuboids of the Mammoth with those of the two recent species seems to show that, whilst the external and internal sides are subequal in length in the African, they are about equal in the Mammoth and Asiatic.

The navicular and calcaneal surfaces are separated by a deep furrow in the Asiatic, but not apparently in the African; nor is it the case in three cuboids of the Mammoth, in which the calcaneal facet is perfectly horizontal.

The cuboid, No. $\frac{C}{229}$ Brady Collection, from ILFORD, misprinted in the Catalogue as a meso-cuneiforme, is $3\cdot4 \times 2\cdot2$ in its shorter diameter. It is considerably below the average of Arctic specimens, but adds to the overwhelming evidence, already adduced, of the small race which lived in South-eastern England during the deposition of the brick-earths and gravels of the Thames Valley.

External cuneiforme.—The only point worthy of record in connection with this bone is the absence of the anterior facets for the middle cuneiforme in the majority of specimens of the Asiatic; but there are exceptions, as shown in the cuneiforme, No. 2543, of an old Elephant from India, in the Museum of the Royal College of Surgeons of England, where the two facets are present, as in the African, 708 II, B. M. In the Mammoth, as far as a few instances show, this facet is wanting.

Middle cuneiforme.—This bone varies, as does the next, in configuration and characters of the facets, showing that there is seemingly considerable individual irregularity, both in the recent and extinct species. The points of difference are fully noted in my Monograph on the Maltese Fossil Elephants.[2] These refer to the apex being more

[1] Plate ii, fig. 10.
[2] 'Trans. Zool. Soc. London, vol. vi, p. 87.

round in the young of the Asiatic Elephant and the full-grown Mammoth, as compared with the adult Asiatic and the African, in which the tip is curved, and the greater concavity on the anterior articular surface in the Asiatic and Mammoth as compared with the African. Two cuneiforme bones, from GRAYS, Essex, gave respectively dimensions as follows :—No. 36,612, B. M., is 3½ by 2 inches in breadth, No. 36,613, B. M., is 3¼ by 1½ inches. These, I apprehend, might belong to *E. antiquus.*

I have not seen the *internal cuneiforme* of the Mammoth. A specimen referable to *E. meridionalis* will be noticed in the sequel.

Metatarsus.

First digit.—I have not seen the *first pedal digit* of the Mammoth. There are some apparent differences between the first digits of the two recent species with reference to the configuration of the shafts, the upper surfaces being more convex, and the lower more concave, in the Asiatic than in the African Elephant.

Second digit.—There does not seem much to note in regard to this element of the foot as compared with that of other Elephants. The *second metatarsal* in the Mammoth is usually about 4 inches in length, with a similar girth at the middle of the shaft. Its proximal phalanx has the tarsal union broader and more even in the Mammoth and Asiatic Elephants than in the African, in which it is broad. The bone is more symmetrical in the two former, with the scar for the internal cuneiforme very pronounced in the Mammoth.

Third digit.—The *third metatarsal* is not unfrequently 8 inches in length in the Mammoth. Its characters are much like the recent Elephants, with a few minor distinctions of the shaft in the former, Meridional, and Asiatic, as compared with the African; these, however, may not be persistent.

Fourth digit.—There is little to note of importance as compared with other species. The cuboidal facet of the metatarsal partakes of the character of the Asiatic bone in being less even than in the African. The usual length in the Mammoth is about 4—5 inches.

Fifth digit.—The same characters of the shaft obtained in the *fifth metatarsal* as in the equivalent bone of the fore foot ; but otherwise I can perceive nothing of any very appreciable value, unless that possibly the cuboidal facet, as in the Asiatic, is more circular than in the African, and the same appears to be present in the huge bones from the FOREST BED ; the dorsal surface, however, is broad and rounded, as in the African. The small articular facet on the inner aspect of the distal extremity is not always present.

The first phalanx is apparently larger and more compressed at midshaft in the Mammoth and Asiatic than in the African, and the irregularities as regards the other phalanges referred to in connection with the fore foot seem more or less common to the hind foot.

MOLARS OF *ELEPHAS PRIMIGENIUS* RECENTLY DUG OUT OF THE
FOREST BED.

Since the publication of the last portion of this Monograph on the dentition and
scapula of the Mammoth, I have examined at Cromer several molars in the possession of
Mr. Savin, junr. These teeth, I am assured, were dug out of the FOREST BED at OVER-
STRAND, near Cromer,[1] by his father and himself.

The entire and more important specimens of Mr. Savin's gatherings are—

1. A second or penultimate left lower milk-molar, No. 2 of the Collection. It holds
x 6 x in 2·5 × 1·4 inches. All the plates are well worn. There is very fine crimping of
the machærides, and the spaces between the discs are somewhat wider than ordinarily
appears in Mammoth molars, with a slight tendency to central expansion. Taking the
characters, however, generally, the tooth is undistinguishable from the generality of the
same member of the series in *E. primigenius*.

Admitting the objections to milk-molars generally as suitable for diagnostic purposes,
as formerly indicated, the above, *per se*, might be doubted, but the following, I think,
may be considered as affording more conclusive evidences.

2. A left upper first true molar, the crown and profile views of which, natural size,
are shown in Pl. XXI, figs. 1 and 1 *a*, was removed from the pebbly stratum of the
FOREST BED at Overstrand, Cromer, by Mr. Savin. The hardened matrix is still
seen adhering to its sides (fig. 1 *a*). It is No. 195 of Mr. Savin's Collection, and holds
x 11 x in 5·4 × 2·5 inches, and five ridges in a space of 2·4 inches. The height of the
ninth ridge is 3·8 and of the tenth 4·1 inches, and the eleventh is 4·2 inches. All the
ridges, with the exception of the posterior talon, are in wear, and the crown (fig. 1) shows
the sculpturings very distinctly, although the discs are not fully developed by wear.

The plates are crowded, with no tendency to mesial expansion and angulation of the
enamel, as often seen in the broad-crowned variety of *E. antiquus*. There is, however,
decided crimping of the enamel in the anterior discs, as occasionally appears in undoubted
molars of the Mammoth.[2] Had this tooth been found in Post-Pliocene strata, no competent authority would hesitate in pronouncing it to have belonged to the latter species.
The crown shows rather thin enamel as compared with the Ilford molars, and it is not so
attenuated as in many Arctic and British specimens. The breadth to the height is

---

[1] Mr. Savin deserves the thanks of palæontologists for the zeal with which he prosecutes his
searches after the fossil animal remains along the neighbouring coast, I am, moreover, under obligations
to Mr. Savin for his invariable kindness in permitting me to make use of his specimens for illustration
or description.

[2] See Plates XI, XIII, and XIV.

another character appertaining to the Mammoth; in fact, the diagnosis of its equivalent molar could scarcely be better illustrated than by this specimen.

A deep ragged groove will be seen running along the rim of the crown (fig. 1 *a*), with numerous pits marking the margin of the gum and a "caries" condition, which had commenced early, as the tooth is only about one-third worn.

3. Another specimen (Pl. XX, fig. 3) shows the fragment of a crown on the point of being shed; it confirms the condition of the macherrides observed in Pl. XXI, fig. 1. Here, again, although the plates are nearly worn out, there are none of the pronounced central expansions and angulations which are so generally well developed in teeth of this size in *E. antiquus*. The enamel is very thin and finely crimped.

4. Another entire left lower FIRST true molar, No. 5 of Mr. Savin's Collection, from the same situation as the two preceding, holds *x* 12 *x* in $6\frac{1}{2} \times 2$ inches, and five ridges in 3 inches, and presents all the characters of the foregoing.

The above, when compared with molars of *E. primigenius* from the Norfolk Coast, and supposed to belong to Post-Pliocene deposits, present no appreciable differences whatever. This view is pointedly sustained by the tooth ascribed by Falconer[1] to the *Pre-Glacial* Mammoth, and referred to at p. 118, so that the evidence advanced by him is, to my mind, as fully established as that of any of the other remains belonging to the so-called Forest-Bed Series. Moreover, when the teeth and bones belonging to the other two Elephants are advanced as exponents of their specific distinctions, and the fact that all are met with in the same deposits, one can scarcely admit that they represent individual or race characters of one extremely variable species. Wherever the evolution of these three distinct forms took place it seems to me, as far as materials extend, that the characteristics here pointed out entitle them as much to the rank of species as is claimed by their living representatives. I can now have no hesitation in admitting the Mammoth among the *Pre-Glacial* Mammals of the British Islands. This conclusion, advocated by Falconer and combated by Boyd Dawkins, but ultimately accepted by the latter, clears the ground, it appears to me, for further researches into the chronology of one of the most widely spread Mammals of the Tertiary Period.

FURTHER ADDITIONS TO THE DENTITION OF *ELEPHAS ANTIQUUS*.

The magnificent molars shown in Plate XX, figs. 1 and 2, are two of four entire teeth belonging to the same individual. They were dug out of the submerged FOREST BED at Corton, near Yarmouth, after one of the heavy gales which tear up the deposits and wash bones and teeth ashore. From the perfect state of preservation of the specimens and absence of any rough usage, I apprehend that they were discovered *in situ*.

[1] Op. cit., vol. ii, p. 170.

They are now in the possession of J. J. Colman, Esq., M.P., of the Clyffe, Corton, Lowestoft, to whom I am indebted for his kindness in permitting me to describe and illustrate them in this Monograph.

It will be seen at a glance that they answer in every respect to the characters I have elsewhere laid down as diagnostic of the broad-crowned variety of *E. antiquus*.[1] The contrast between the above and Plate V, fig. 1, of *E. antiquus* (with the exception of the angulations, which, however, as before stated, are often wanting, and not fully developed on newly invaded crowns) is striking; on the other hand, compare the narrow crowns of the same species in the Plates II, III, and IV.

The colossal dimensions of the former owner of these teeth makes the diagnosis of the bones met with in the Forest Bed doubly difficult, seeing that, although *E. meridionalis* appears to have invariably exhibited gigantic proportions as compared with the usual remains of *E. primigenius*, the fact that teeth of *E. antiquus* are not uncommon, even in Post-Glacial deposits, of the dimensions of the largest specimens referable to *E. meridionalis*, must materially affect their diagnosis, not only on the score of size, but to a great extent as regards their specific characters.

Dr. Falconer laid no little stress on the thickness of the plates and enamel as characteristic of *E. meridionalis*; but, as I have shown, and as he admitted by the recantation of the so-called *E. priscus*, these conditions may exist in *E. antiquus*.

Alluding to the above ultimate molars in Mr. Colman's Collection, they represent the right and left upper and lower. All show exactly the same condition of wear and clearly belonged to one individual. The lower molars were accidentally broken across since their removal from the deposit, but can be reunited without any detriment to measurement.

I have selected the right upper and left lower as being in every way the more perfect specimens. The following are their characters:

Upper molars.—The tooth of the right side (fig. 2) is encrusted with matrix, and its substance is in a perfect state of petrifaction. The two anterior talons have been broken across near their middle quite recently. These are followed by another pair, which take their origin about the middle, and are succeeded by the hollow shell, which characterises teeth with crowns one third detrited. The tooth holds *x* 20 *x* in 13×4 inches.

The remarkable breadth of four inches is noteworthy, as compared with *E. meridionalis*.

The posterior talon is a single digitation and an inch in height. There are eight digitations along the inner sides of the last eight ridges, as if the tooth had been bent on itself in the germ state—a condition referred to as existing in the molar of *E. primigenius*.[2]

There are five ridges in three and a half inches.

The height of the thirteenth colline is 7 inches.

[1] Page 32.　　　[2] Page 121.

The tooth of the left side repeats these characters and dimensions, and has the lateral and accessory digitations more pronounced.

Lower molars.—The right lower molar (figs 1 and 1a) is considerably arcuated and tapers towards the heel. It has been recently broken across at the fourteenth plate. The crown holds x 20 x in 16 × 4 inches,[1] and as regards length is the largest molar of any Elephant I have seen from British strata. The same great breadth is likewise exhibited. There are thirteen discs in wear.

The height of the thirteenth colline is also 7 inches, and there are five ridges in 4 inches, with the same number of accessory digitations (8) on the inner side, as seen in the two upper and the other left lower molar.

The left molar appears to have an additional ridge and shows a formula of x 21 x.

Like the other, the anterior fang, which is broken off, was single and curved.

The states of wear are unfortunately not sufficiently advanced to develop the discs to their fullest extent, but they are sufficiently detrited to serve the purposes of comparison with the crowns of the typical *E. meridionalis* as described by Falconer. In the above there is no inordinate excess of cement, so that the plates are closer together, the enamel is fully crimped, and there is a decided disposition to central expansion and angulation of the discs, which doubtless would appear pronounced in a lower transverse section of the teeth.

But the ridge formula of itself shows a difference of fully six ridges over the largest tooth that can be unhesitatingly ascribed to *E. meridionalis*. Falconer has placed the limit of the ridge formula in last molars in that species at x 15 x which he establishes from an Italian specimen,[1] and, on what appears to me questionable grounds, considers that the unusual number of ridges of this specimen may be owing to an abnormal condition of the crown. But I cannot see that there is any reason to establish a limit to a ridge formula, because the ordinary number of ridges seldom exceeds x 13 x. This view, so pertinaciously carried out by him, has been shown in the two previous parts of this Monograph to admit of so many exceptions that I see no reason whatever to doubt that the same may have obtained in *E. meridionalis*. The above addition to the dentition of *E. antiquus* necessarily alters the ridge formula of *E. antiquus* given at page 47 as follows:

I.	II.	III.	IV.	V.	VI.
$x\,2x$—$x\,3x$	$x\,5x$—$x\,7x$	$x\,8x$—$x\,10x$	$x\ \ 9x$—$x\,12x$	$x\,12x$—$x\,13x$	$x\,15x$—$x\,20x$
$x\,3x$—	$x\,6x$—$x\,8x$	$x\,9x$—$x\,11x$	$x\,11x$—$x\,12x$	$x\,12x$—$x\,13x$	$x\,16x$—$x\,21x$

---

[1] In connection with a neighbouring locality, MUNDESLEY, there is a description of a beach specimen by Mr. Henry Baker in the ' Philosophical Transactions' of 1745. The molar referred to was 2 feet 11 inches in longitudinal circumference, linear length 15 inches, height 7 inches, and breadth 3 inches. It contained sixteen ridges with enormous discs " furrowed like a millstone." From its height and ridge formula this may have belonged to the broad-crowned variety of *E. antiquus*. A thigh-bone measured 6 feet in length.

[2] Op. cit., vol. ii, p. 117.

There are in the Norwich Museum two fragmentary specimens of molars of the broad crowns of *E. antiquus* besides those described in p. 32. I refer especially to two lower last molars, Nos. 19 and 20 of Miss A. Gurney's Collection. These two teeth belonged evidently to the same individual, but are unfortunately not quite entire. They were dug out of the Forest Bed, BACTON, and are covered with pebbles cemented to their crown and sides. The right molar has only two ridges invaded with a loss behind of several ridges. The crown is much arcuated, as in the Corton teeth, and holds *x* 18 in 12 inches, with a maximum breadth of 4 inches, and has five ridges in 4 inches.

The height of the eighth colline is 8 inches. The digitations, as in the Corton teeth, are large and numerous, and rival completely anything of the kind found in the teeth of *E. meridionalis*, at all events as met with in British strata.

The resemblances between the crowns of the above and other specimens of the broad-crowned variety of *E. antiquus* and the same tooth in *E. primigenius* I candidly admit are striking; indeed, a comparison between the teeth from the Forest Bed referred to the latter, and the foregoing, as shown in Pls. XX and XXI, complicates the inquiry. Mr. Gunn, F.G.S., long habituated to the discrimination of the Forest Bed remains, has frequently pointed out to me these resemblances in specimens in the Norwich Museum, and were it not from the evidence I have adduced of the connection between the broad-crowned variety of *E. antiquus* and typical molars of that species at p. 31, I feel bound to state that these similitudes between teeth of *E. antiquus* and *E. primigenius* are very close indeed. But, on the other hand, when, as I have shown from abundant material, the narrow, thick-plated, and broad crown of molars of *E. antiquus* can be clearly differentiated among the vast numbers of specimens which have come under my notice, I am constrained to believe that the three varieties belong to one species. That there was any intercourse between the Mammoth and *E. antiquus* in Pliocene or Post-Pliocene we have no proof whatever, and no precedent to establish such a belief, and consequently, after a lengthened and careful survey of the remains of the British fossil Elephants, I feel justified in placing the molars just described with those of *E. antiquus* and the allied teeth described at p. 32.

The thick-plated tooth which puzzled Falconer at first, and caused him to correlate it with *E. priscus*, of Goldfuss, until further instances showed it to be only a variety of *E. antiquus*, and of the broad and thick-plated crown, described at p. 33, is further illustrated by two noteworthy examples I have examined lately. They were dug up on WHITTLESEA MERE, Cambridgeshire, and are now in the Museum of Zoology, Cambridge University. These two lower molars are not quite entire, but evidently belonged to the same individual. The more perfect specimen holds thirteen plates in as many inches; as far as characters and dimensions extend, they are quite undistinguishable from their colossal companion, just referred to, from CULHAM, near Oxford, the enamel being also deeply crimped, with the usual central expansions and angulations of the crown of *E. antiquus*. For comparison with these interesting molars there is a portion of a mandible from Whittlesea, in the

Woodwardian Collection of the above University. It contains two entire ultimate molars, typical of the long narrow crown, the ridge formula of each being x 16 x in 12×3·8 inches. This jaw is stated to have been found " below peat." I have, moreover, examined lately, in Mr. Savin's Collection, a fragment of a very narrow, but very thick-plated first true molar, obtained by him from the FOREST BED, OVERSTRAND, near Cromer. It contains x 12 in 9×2·5 inches. These seem to approach the tooth of *E. Africanus*, as further illustrated by the specimens on which Falconer founded his so-called *E. priscus*,[1] and others recorded at p. 33 *et seq.*, and notably by the interesting molar discovered by Professor Ramsay near TANGIER,[2] in the land of the African Elephant. The reciprocal relations of these links in the chain of evidence are bound together by further instances adduced in this Monograph, and seem to me extremely suggestive as showing the evolutionary characters of *E. Namadicus*, *E. antiquus*, *E. Africanus*, and the Maltese fossil Elephants on the one hand, and of *E. primigenius* and its allies on the other; whilst in *E. meridionalis*, although, as far as yet known, it does not seem to tend so markedly towards any of them, still, as I shall point out, there are indications of a passage between certain molars of this species and the thick and broad crown of *E. Namadicus* and *E. antiquus*.

ELEPHANTS OF THE RED CRAG OF SUFFOLK.

The Proboscidean remains from the Red Crag present more specimens of Mastodon than Elephas; nevertheless fragments of molars of the latter have been found, but seldom more than a few plates in juxtaposition. Like the other animal relics, they show clear traces of having been much rolled, and are usually highly silicified and discoloured by the ferruginous matrix of the bed. These remnants are not uncommon in public collections—to wit, British Museum and Museum of Practical Geology, and in private collections also.

Falconer identified *E. meridionalis* and *E. antiquus*,[3] but I am not aware of any indications of *E. primigenius* having been found ; indeed, as far as my own observations extend, I have been unable to meet with a specimen clearly assignable to *E. meridionalis*, inasmuch as all the transverse sections of discs present thick enamel central expansions and frequently pronounced angulations of the thick-plated (*E. priscus*), variety of *E. antiquus*, as appears from the following :

1. The fragments of crowns (Pl. XXVI, figs. 2 and 4) from Red Crag diggings at

[1] Op. cit., vol. ii, p. 96.
[2] 'Journ. Geol. Soc. London,' vol. xxxiv, p. 515, fig. 9.
[3] Op. cit., vol. ii, p. 206.

TRIMLEY, near Felixstow, Suffolk, were lately presented to the Museum of the Yorkshire Philosophical Society, by Mr. W. Reed, F.G.S., who has kindly forwarded the specimen for description and illustration in this Monograph. Fig. 2 represents three incomplete discs, showing the decidedly central expansions and angulations of the thick-plated crown of *E. antiquus* (p. 33, and Pl. V, fig. 1), but the enamel is free from crimping and all the elements are in excess, as in *E. meridionalis*, in which, as before observed, the two former conditions sometimes occur in individual plates, although rarely on successional discs, as shown in Pl. XXVI, fig. 2.

As in the case of the majority of fragments of thick-plated molars, it is quite impossible to give a decided opinion. However, in consideration of the above characters, I am inclined to place this example with the thick-plated variety (*E. priscus*) of *E. antiquus* rather than with *E. meridionalis*. Each plate is about an inch in thickness at the middle of the disc.

2. The vertical sections of two plates from the same locality (Pl. XXVI, fig. 4) are quite in keeping with the foregoing.

MONOGRAPH

BRITISH FOSSIL ELEPHANTS.

ELEPHAS MERIDIONALIS.

I. INTRODUCTORY.

THE differentiation of a species of fossil Elephant distinct from the *Elephas primi-genius*, to which all teeth and bones referable to the genus were supposed to belong, was first surmised by Nesti from discoveries made in the Valley of the Arno and the neigh-bourhood of Rome.[1] Subsequent researches by Cuvier, Croizet, De Blainville, and Owen, are fully detailed by Falconer,[2] and the more pertinent points are referred to in the previous parts of this Monograph; suffice it to state that, whilst Nesti and Croizet main-tained the specific identity of *E. meridionalis*, the three other palæontologists adhered to the opinion that the evidences he had adduced were not sufficient. It was left to Dr. Falconer, in 1844, when engaged in studying the Proboscidean remains collected by himself and others in Northern India, to correlate certain characters of the molars with those of similar relics from British strata. The result of these comparisons he has embodied in the Essays I have so frequently referred to in this work.

In his classification of the Proboscidea from their forms of dentition, he includes the *E. meridionalis* with *E. planifrons*, of India, *E. priscus* (a species he subsequently with-drew as being only a variety of *E. antiquus*), *E. Africanus*, and *E. Melitensis*, in his sub-genus LOXODON, which he again subdivides into two groups, distinguished by their well-marked dental characters. Thus, *E. meridionalis* and *E. planifrons* have the "colliculi grossè digitati, adamante crasso," and differ in these respects from all other Elephants. The value he attached to the teeth alone as diagnostic of species of Proboscidea is appa-rent throughout all his writings; and, as I have elsewhere observed, his system of taxonomy is formed entirely from dental conditions, as shown by the distinctive cha-racters of the three sub-genera STEGODON, LOXODON, and EUELEPHAS. I have already[3]

[1] 'Annale des Museo di Firenze,' tom. i, et 'Nuovo Giornale de Letterat.,' tom. xi.

[2] 'Palæontological Memoirs,' vol. ii, p. 104.

[3] Page 78 and elsewhere.

expressed a belief, from studies of molars of the *E. antiquus*, *E. primigenius*, and other species, that he often exercised a far too rigorous observance of the characters of these sub-genera in his differentiations of the ridge formulæ of species, thereby reducing the often wide extremes to a mean which cannot fairly be said to express the ridge formula of the tooth in question, as is well exemplified in the case of the ultimate molar of *E. primigenius*,[1] and numerous other instances. Moreover, I find, as far as the materials I have examined are concerned, that the evidences afforded by the teeth of *E. meridionalis* support these inferences deduced from the dental elements appertaining to the other extinct and recent species.

II. DISTRIBUTION.

Both the geological and geographical distribution of *E. meridionalis* generally, and in the British Islands in particular, are much more limited than is the case with either of its two congeners. As far as this so-called Meridional Elephant is concerned, it has only been found hitherto in what is known as the "Forest Bed," or submerged fluviatile and fluvio-marine deposits, which form the bottom of that portion of the North Sea extending along the shores of Norfolk, Suffolk, and Essex, as shown in Map, Pl. XXVII.

The absence of its remains in any British deposits more recent than the Pliocene period accounts for the disparities of distribution between it and the two other extinct species, as shown in Maps, Pls. XXVII and XXVIII.

The contemporaneity of the *E. meridionalis* and *E. antiquus* is generally admitted, from numerous discoveries of their remains in the same bed. Dr. Falconer maintained a similar opinion as regards *E. primigenius*,[2] chiefly on evidences deduced from discoveries in Italy; whilst Boyd Dawkins and others refused to admit that the specimens found along the sea-beaches of Norfolk and Suffolk were derived from the Forest Bed, insisting that they were the products of the Post-pliocene strata overlying the latter, and from which they had been washed by the sea. In support of this view several instances were advanced of molars of the Mammoth having been dug out of these Post-pliocene strata. At page 72 I have alluded to this subject ; and, after a careful survey of the specimens and the writings of authorities, I was of opinion that the existence of the Mammoth prior to the Ice Age had not been clearly proven : but a visit to the coasts of Norfolk and Suffolk during the summer of 1879, and inspections of the specimens described at page 173, together with the evidence of persons who discovered them, leave little doubt on my mind that these teeth and others alluded to cannot be distinguished from typical molars of the Mammoth. The view, therefore, of Falconer, that the three species were contemporaneous, and that the Mammoth was a Pre-glacial Mammal, seems to me more than probable, not only from the

[1] Table, p. 123.
[2] Op. cit., vol. ii, pp. 239 and 587.

late discoveries at Cromer, on the Norfolk coast, but from the proofs adduced previously by Falconer, and the later additions made by Boyd Dawkins.

The geographical distribution of *E. meridionalis*, as far as has been accurately determined, extends from South-Eastern England to France, where it has been found in the northern, middle, and lower Departments.   Its existence in Spain has not been confirmed; and, besides the discoveries in Northern Italy and the determination of remains from South-Eastern Europe by Lartet, I am not aware of any well-authenticated discoveries in other European countries.

The circumstances under which the Proboscidean and other Mammalian remains are met with on the shores of East Anglia may be stated as follows :—Occasionally, after heavy gales, or "scours" as they are locally designated, portions of the overlying cliffs and the littoral zone are laid bare and expose the remains *in situ*.   At other times, usually at low tides, a search over exposed surfaces between high- and low-water mark is rewarded by discoveries; but by far the greater number of finds are picked up casually along the shore-line after the object has been rolled about and often considerably damaged.

The vast quantities of Proboscidean and other Mammalian remains reclaimed from the coast deposits of Norfolk and Suffolk would, if brought together, furnish a very remarkable collection.   Unfortunately, several valuable relics have been dispersed and are not available for study; nevertheless, thanks to the assiduous labours of persons interested in collecting and preserving these specimens for scientific purposes, the Norwich, British, Oxford, Cambridge, and Jermyn-Street Museums, together with several private collections, afford ample evidences of the fauna of the Forest-bed period.

Among numerous benefactors, whose names it seems to me necessary should be placed on record in a Monograph like this, foremost in the ranks stands the honoured name of John Gunn, late of Irstead.   This veteran geologist has enriched the admirable Natural History Museum of his native town with the products of a long lifetime devoted to the study of the later Tertiary deposits of Norfolk; and, with an enthusiasm and scarcely diminished vigour of earlier days, he is still labouring in the field where the father of Norfolk geology, Samuel Woodward, made for himself a well-known reputation.   Among their fellow-workers may be mentioned Miss Anna Gurney, the Rev. J. Layton, the Rev. J. King, the Rev. J. Green, and Robert Fitch, Esq.

III. FAUNA AND FLORA OF THE FOREST-BED.

The Fauna and Flora of the Forest-bed series are highly suggestive of the character and extent of the submerged area of which they are the exponents.   Although the animal remains are in general fragmentary, there is no difficulty in perceiving how very varied were the forms of Mammals which inhabited the land during the deposition of the various strata composing what is termed the Forest Bed.   Unfortunately, the varying nature of the coast-lines of Norfolk and Suffolk, and constant interruptions, interfere very much with attempts to correlate the members of the series, consequently their sequences are by no means accurately determined. Allowing for some diversity of opinion amongst geologists[1] as to the stratigraphical relations, and the fragmentary conditions of the animal remains, the following may be considered a fair summary of the chief Fauna and Flora which existed from the deposition of the lowermost strata up to the commencement of the Glacial formations, as far as has been accurately determined.[2] It is apparent, however, that the list is far from being complete, and that even many of the remains of the Mammals, especially the Ungulates, the most extensive and interesting portion, deserve more attention than has been hitherto bestowed on them.

The Insectivora are represented by *Talpa Europæus, Mygale moschata, Sorex vulgaris, S. fodiens, S. remifer.*

The Rodentia by *Castor fiber, Trogontherium Cuvieri, Arvicola amphibius, A. agrestis, A. glareolus, Sciurus (?).*

The Carnivora by *Canis lupus (?), Canis vulpes (?), Machairodus, Felidæ, Martes sylvatica, Gulo luscus,[3] Ursus spelæus, Ursus ferox, Trichecodon Huxleyi, Phoca.*

Of Proboscidea *Elephas meridionalis, E. antiquus, E. primigenius.*

The Cetacea by *Monodon monoceros,* and two species of *Balænoidea* are represented by vertebræ.

The Ungulata present many difficulties in the way of accurate determinations. The following have been recorded :—*Equus caballus, E. stenonis, Rhinoceros etruscus, R. megarhinus (?), Hippopotamus major, Sus scrofa, Caprovis Savinii.* The Cervidæ are represented by *Cervus megaceros,[4] C. capreolus,[4] C. elaphus,[4] C. polignacus, C. cornutorum, C. verticornis, C. Sedgwickii, C. bovides, C. latifrons,* &c., altogether thirteen species. The majority of the Cervine remains are very fragmentary, and confined to pieces of antlers or portions of the calvarium.

The INVERTEBRATA are represented by *Unio, Cyclas, Paludina, Mya truncata, Leda myalis,* besides Insects, all of recent forms, still met with in East Anglia.

The FLORA of the period, according to the determination of Heer and Hooker, belong to recent genera and species, such as *Quercus, Betula, Alnus, Prunus spinosa, Pinus sylves-*

[1] See Prestwich, 'Journ. Geol. Soc. London,' vol. xxvii. Gunn, vol. xxvi, p. 551.

[2] I am indebted to Mr. E. T. Newton, F.G.S., of H.M. Geological Survey, for a list of the Carnivora and other Mammals. Mr. Gunn has also furnished me with several names. I have also drawn from the writings of Falconer, 'Pal. Mem.,' vol. ii, p. 473.

[3] The Glutton, Marten, and Seal have been lately added to the fauna by Mr. E. T. Newton, 'Geol. Magazine,' vol. vii, 1880.

[4] These species have been retained in lists of the Deer of the Forest Bed on apparently doubtful authority, and seemingly as regards the Irish Elk and Red Deer altogether on the evidences of fragments of antlers, which might have belonged to any of the other large forms. A horn of a capreoloid Deer in the King Collection, Jermyn Street Museum, is said to have been obtained from the coast of East Anglia, but its exact stratigraphical position is not given.

tris et abies, Taxus baccata, and aquatic plants referable to *Potamogeton, Nuphar luteum, Nymphæa alba, Menyanthes trifoliata, Ceratophyllum demersum,* and *Osmunda regalis,* &c.

IV. DENTITION.

The general affinities and distinctions between incisors and molars of *E. meridionalis,* as compared with teeth of *E. antiquus* and *E. primigenius,* have been already noticed,[1] as well as the variations to which they are subject. These comparisons may be summarised as follows :

1. The tusks, in general, present a simple curve, as in the recent species, in both *E. meridionalis* and *E. antiquus,* whilst they are spiral in *E. primigenius,* and generally more slender in proportion.

2. The incisive alveoli are more or less divergent in all, and are variable as to length, breadth, and depth.

3. The molars are very broad in *E. meridionalis* and *E. primigenius,* and are narrow generally in *E. antiquus,* excepting in the broad-crowned variety.

4. The height of the molar has its minimum in *E. meridionalis ;* it is higher in *E. primigenius,* and attains to the maximum height in *E. antiquus.*

5. The enamel is thick in *E. meridionalis* and in varieties of *E. antiquus,* whilst it is thin in *E. primigenius.*

6. The enamel borders are rarely crimped in *E. meridionalis ;* and, when at all, the plaiting is more often confined to only portions of the margins of odd plates, or presents a slight roughening of the external border and surface, as seen in Plates XXIV and XXV. The main feature is the deep channelling and general unevenness of the enamel. In *E. antiquus* the crimping is generally pronounced, and affects the entire thickness of the enamel with a central angular notch. In *E. primigenius* all these characters are generally absent, the borders of the enamel being usually undulating, without plaiting of any sort, or it is confined to parts of the enamel of a disc.

7. The contour of the worn disc in *E. meridionalis* is generally more uniform in breadth throughout, excepting a tendency in odd discs to central expansion and angulation. In *E. antiquus* there are marked central expansions and angulations. The disc is narrow in *E. primigenius,* and rarely shows any tendency to mesial expansion, and no disposition to form the central notch so prominent in many of the teeth of the latter.[2]

8. The cement-wedges are largest in *E. meridionalis,* less so in *E. antiquus,* and much thinner in *E. primigenius.* In consequence the plates are wide apart in the first, more approximated in the second, and crowded in *E. primigenius.*

9. The terms " thick- and thin-plated molars " I have applied to teeth of *E. antiquus*

[1] Pages 7 and 77.

[2] Plates III and V, *E. antiquus.*

and *E. primigenius* is applicable, but in a much smaller degree, to the molars of *E. meridionalis*.[1] These discrepancies, in several instances, as regards the two former species, seem in some cases diagnostic of races and local varieties, such as the small, thick-plated molar of the Mammoth found at Ilford, in the Valley of the Thames, but I apprehend that, as occurs often in the living species, the crown constituents go frequently hand in hand with unusually large developments of the other portions of the skeleton.

The nearest approach to the elements of the molar and its ridge formula in *E. meridionalis* is in the tooth of *E. planifrons*, of Northern India: indeed, a larger assortment of its remains may show a far closer relationship than can be at present admitted with fairness; moreover, Falconer was so impressed with the similarity between the molars of these two Elephants that he correlated them in the classification of his sub-genus Loxodon.[2]

The above are the more general features of the molars of these three forms, but there is much variability, and the most pronounced divergences from typical molars of each species, or of the three conjointly, may be met with in the same deposits.

1. INCISORS.

An enormous tusk in the Norwich Museum, from the Elephant Bed at RUNTON, near Cromer, presented by Sir Thomas Buxton, Bart., is broken across in two places, and the tip is wanting; the contour is, however, preserved throughout, but there has been some desquamation of the outermost layers of dentine. The sides are somewhat compressed, whether a natural condition, or from pressure, or from loss of substance does not appear determinable. The arc is about the same as in the two recent species. A portion of the pulp-cavity is preserved. The entire length lineally is 93 inches, and by tape along the lower border 130 inches. The girth at the proximal extremity is 27 inches, and at the distance of 41 inches from the latter 31 inches.[3]

Seeing that the tusk of *E. antiquus* presents the same configurations, and that individuals of the latter attained to nearly the same colossal dimensions, it is impossible to assign the above with certainty to either species; the probability is, however, that it belonged to *E. meridionalis*.[4]

A portion of a tusk dredged from the North Sea about forty miles off SOUTHWOLD,

[1] The enamel in the generality of well-worn crowns of *E. meridionalis* stands up prominently with both the enclosed dentine and external cement denuded, the latter so much so that the ridges and ribbing of the outer surface of the plate are distinctly seen. This is very apparent in Pl. XXIV, figs. 1 and 2, and in the mandibular teeth in Pl. XXV, fig. 1.

[2] Op. cit., vol. ii, pp. 14 and 108.

[3] This tusk has about the same dimensions and is of the same contour as the specimens of *E. meridionalis* in the Pitti Palace, Florence, recorded by Falconer, 'Pal. Mem.,' vol. ii, p. 120.

[4] A fragment from St. Germain is figured by Logard. It shows also a gentle curve, 'Arch. du Mus. Hist. Nat. de Lyon,' pl. xvii.

on the Suffolk coast, is preserved in the collection of J. J. Colman, Esq., of Corton. It is smaller than the above, but presents precisely the same characters, contrasting in these respects with the more slender and highly arcuated incisor of a Mammoth, in this gentleman's possession, from the submarine deposits close to LOWESTOFT, Suffolk. Considering that the teeth of *E. antiquus* described at page 175, and shown in Pl. XX, figs. 1 and 2, were dug out of the FOREST BED in the neighbourhood, it is just possible that the tusk may have belonged to the same individual.

I have seen no milk-incisors referable to any of the three species.

2. MILK-MOLARS.

Ante-penultimate Milk-Molar.

I can find no reference whatever of this tooth having been found in British strata.

The examples given by Falconer [1] are from the Valley of the Arno. An upper molar is recorded to be 0·95 inches in length by 0·75 in width, and a lower is 0·7 in length, the breadth is not given. Both specimens present a ridge formula of x 3 x. The above dimensions, considered relatively with the successional molars, appear small, and even when compared with the same tooth in *E. antiquus* and *E. primigenius*.[2] The dimensions, however, as already stated in connection with the two latter, vary much, and the crown sculpturing is never so pronounced as to display specific characters. No doubt, however, the plates were thick and the cement in excess as compared with the Mammoth's ante-penultimate milk-molar.

Among the Proboscidean remains from the Sewalik Mountains of India there are numerous molars so closely related in character to teeth of *E. meridionalis*, that had the specimens been found in Europe one would have no hesitation in placing them with the latter; in fact, it was a knowledge of the Sewalik molars, referred by Dr. Falconer to *E. planifrons*, that first led him to surmise the existence of more than one species of fossil Elephant in British strata. In the noble monument of his zeal, and that of his colleague, Colonel Cautley, as evidenced by the fossil remains in the National Collection, and elsewhere, there are several specimens of *E. planifrons* with a small pre-molar in front of the milk and true molars; a condition not, as far as is known to me,[*] yet observed in *E. meridionalis* or any other member of the genus. It is clear, however, from several jaws in the Sewalik Collection, British Museum, that the presence of a pre-molar was not an invariable condition in *E. planifrons*.

---

[1] Op. cit., vol. ii, pp. 110 and 114.
[2] Pages 11, 86, and 88.
[*] Falconer notices the point, op. cit., vol. ii, pp. 93 and 118.

Second or Penultimate Milk-Molar.

The specimens described by Falconer as illustrative of this molar deserve notice. Having examined and compared them carefully with equivalent teeth of allied species, I do not quite agree with the diagnosis established by him.

No. 4, Norwich Museum, is stated by Falconer to belong to the upper jaw.[1] This I am unable to endorse, as the specimen is so much altered from rolling on the beach that the original contour is completely lost, and therefore it would be difficult to say to which jaw it originally belonged. Neither in its ridge formula x 6 x, nor dimensions $2\cdot6\times1\cdot4$ inches, nor in the relations between the crown constituents, are there any confirmatory evidencies to assign it to any particular species. It can therefore scarcely be accepted as diagnostic of the second milk-tooth of *E. meridionalis*.

No. 6, Norwich Museum, is figured and described by Falconer.[2] This tooth, no doubt, is from the lower jaw. The dimensions are $3\times1\cdot4$ inches, and the ridge formula x 6 x. The crown is unusually broad to length. There are, however, *mesial expansions* of the discs, *angulations*, and *crimpings* of the machærides, which are more in keeping with *E. antiquus*. Its large size is its best recommendation, but it appears to me hazardous to accept it as a tooth of *E. meridionalis*, excepting on the score of dimensions.

The fragment of a right ramus and its detached crown, No. 214, Gunn Collection, Norwich Museum, holding an entire second milk-molar *in situ* (Pl. XXII, figs. 3 and 3 *a*), present the following characters :—This tooth is $3\times1\frac{1}{2}$ inches in its greatest breadth, and holds a ridge formula of x 6 x.

Although a label by Dr. Falconer is attached to the jaw, and records its position in the dental series in his own handwriting, I cannot find a reference to it in his works. The crown pattern, as far as the sculpturing of the enamel is concerned, is of no value, seeing that the machærides show crimping; but the excess of cement, large dimensions, and the fragment of jaw are certainly in favour of its belonging to the *E. meridionalis*, or else to a huge individual of *E. antiquus*.

As regards the ramus, there is a small pit in front of the tooth, evidently the remains of the socket of the ante-penultimate molar. The reclination of the dip of the diastenic is also a character of some importance ; it is 4 inches in length. The thickness of the jaw, which is 3 inches in breadth at the heel of the molar, and the height of the ramus, which is $3\frac{3}{4}$ inches in front of the tooth, indicate greater proportions than generally prevails in the Mammoth, and, at all events, in the Post-glacial specimens of *E. antiquus* met with in British strata.

A left lower molar, in Mr. Fitch's Collection, from the "FRESHWATER DEPOSITS" at "MUNDESLEY," holds x 6 x in $2\frac{3}{4}\times1\frac{3}{4}$ inches. The crown is commencing wear, and

---

[1] Op. cit., vol. ii, p. 133.

[2] 'F. A. S.,' pl. xiv B, figs. 3, 3 *a*; 'Pal. Mem.,' vol. ii, p. 134.

although all the ridges, excepting the posterior talon, are invaded, only the first two have their digitations worn out. The enamel has the usual undulations common in such teeth, but there is *no* crimping of their machærides. The posterior fang is very broad, being 1¼ inches; the anterior fang is lost. There are five ridges in 2 inches.

The size is in favour of the tooth being that of a large species of Elephant, the grossness being consequent on thicker wedges of cement than ordinarily obtain in *E. antiquus* and *E. primigenius*, and there is an absence of crimping.

This tooth supports the characters of the true molars of *E. meridionalis* much better than any of the preceding.

Another right lower molar in the above-named gentleman's Collection, from Cromer, has the cement denuded. It is smaller, with a ridge formula of *x* 6 *x* in 2¾ by 1·2 inches in breadth. Here five ridges are contained in a space of 2 inches. The excess of cement and the large dimensions are the important points in the diagnosis; whilst the crimping of the enamel machærides of the discs are, on the other hand, in favour of *E. antiquus*. I repeat, however, that the second milk-molar *per se* is not always a reliable element in the diagnosis of species.

These are all the entire teeth belonging to the above member of the milk-series that have come under my notice.

I have examined several fragmentary specimens; but, with the exception of the foregoing, none are convincing as regards their association with *E. meridionalis*.

The molars, from Tuscan deposits, representing this stage of the dentition of *E. meridionalis* are fully described by Falconer.[1] The ridge formulæ and dimensions of entire penultimate teeth may be thus briefly recapitulated: upper, *x* 6 *x* in 2·5 × 1·6; lower, *x* 6 *x* in 2·4 × 1·5 inches.

The Ultimate Milk-Molar.

This tooth in *E. meridionalis* holds a ridge formula of *x* 8 *x*. Referring to the examples from British strata referred to by Falconer,[2] I find No. 10 of the Norwich Collection is, like No. 4, a previous member of the series, much detrited from rolling in the surf. The formula may have been *x* 7 *x*, but the posterior talon is wanting, and the anterior talon and first plate are not well defined. It is evidently a lower jaw tooth, and of the left side. The length is 3·9 × 2 inches. As a typical example it is defective, and neither in the worn crown nor in its elements do I find sufficient characters to distinguish it from *E. antiquus*.

In the same Collection is a left upper molar (No. 9) nearly entire, from the "IRON PAN, FOREST BED, BACTON," Norfolk coast. The specimen was presented by Miss A. Gurney. It is 4½ × 1¾ inches in breadth, and holds a formula of *x* 7 *x*. All the ridges

[1] Op. cit., vol. ii, pp. 110 and 114.
[2] Op. cit., vol. ii, p. 134, and 'F. A. S.,' pl. xiv u, figs. 4 and 4 a.

27

are in wear, excepting the posterior talon; here the cement is in excess, and the discs have *no* crimping to any very marked extent; for the most part, the latter is confined to the outer borders.

The tooth is decidedly distinct from the usual crowns of *E. antiquus*, with which, I imagine, it could scarcely be confounded. This molar seems to me distinguishable from the equivalent molar of either of the other two British fossil Elephants.

In Mr. Alfred Savin's Collection at CROMER, I examined a left lower molar (No. 12) of nearly the same size as the above, having precisely similar characters. It holds $x7x$ in 4×2 inches, and five ridges in $2\frac{1}{4}$ inches. The first three ridges only are invaded, so that in neither were the digitations worn out. The characters, however, are in keeping with the foregoing, with which it appears to me to claim relationship.

A small lower molar in the King Collection, Jermyn Street Museum, from the FOREST BED, CROMER, shows five discs with irregular outlines. The enamel is thick, uncrimped, with thick wedges of dentine and much intervening cement. The crown widens in front, being 2 inches in breadth, maintaining an increase to the middle of the crown, when it rapidly narrows posteriorly, being 1·4 inches behind. The ridge formula is $x7x$ in 4.8×2.8 inches. In its thick plates, absence of crimping and of central dilatation, with the usual channelling of the enamel border, the above follows its predecessor. On the label is written, "Green band and no gravel," indicating the particular stratum from which it was obtained.

Another, No. $\frac{G}{92}$, in the above Collection, from the same situation, but of the upper jaw, is shown in Pl. XVII, fig. 8. It holds $x8x$ in 4.5×1.4 inches. Here six discs are in wear, with a well-marked pressure-scar in front. It is from the "Green band and gravel of the FOREST BED."

Of foreign specimens of the last milk-molars presenting characters comparable with the foregoing, there is a fragmentary molar, left side, lower jaw, from the Val d'Arno, in the British Museum. It is No. 38,824. The anterior talon appears to be wanting, leaving a formula of $8x$ in 5×1.7 inches, and six ridges in 3 inches. The crown is considerably arched and narrow, with seven discs in wear, showing characters in keeping with the preceding molars. But whether this is an unusually large last milk, or small first true, molar, may be considered doubtful.

The Italian specimens illustrative of the third milk-molar are recorded as follows by Falconer :—Upper, $x8x$ in 4.6×2.5; lower, $x8x$ in 4.6×1.8, $x8x$ in 4.7×1.55, and $x7x$.[1]

---

[1] Op. cit., vol. ii, pp. 111, 115.

3. TRUE MOLARS.

The Ante-penultimate or First True Molar.

The first true molar, according to Falconer, is represented by No. 8 of the Norwich Museum, from MUNDESLEY.[1] It contains *x* 8 *x* in 5·3 × 2·3 inches, and is a left lower molar. Dr. Falconer observes: "The discs of the first three ridges are wide and open, but irregularly indented, with a tendency to mesial expansion, and surrounded by margins of thick enamel, which is vertically channelled externally and slightly crimped." Again, "One of the distinctive characters of the species, namely, the low height of the crown in reference to the breadth, is well exhibited."

With reference to the latter, it must be conceded that the character is important in the diagnosis of these large broad teeth from the Norfolk coast, but in the present instance the crown is about half worn down, consequently the width to height makes the contrast. However looked upon, by comparison with similar molars of *E. antiquus* and *E. primigenius*, the above tooth has a relatively narrow crown for *E. meridionalis*. The enamel of the discs is fully crimped, there is mesial expansion, and the plates are not thick. The most that can be said of it is, that the cement is in excess, and the undulations of the enamel ("vertical channellings" of Falconer) carry with them characters different from the ordinary tooth of *E. antiquus*; but the specimen altogether is not representative of points, which appear much more distinct in other instances, I shall describe presently.

Another instance is adduced[2] from MUNDESLEY. It is No. 7 of the Norwich Collection, and belongs to the lower jaw, left side. It is not entire, having only the anterior talon and seven plates in 5·5 × 2·65 inches, and holds five ridges in 3·2 inches.

Falconer says the enamel ridges are "thick." This appears to me by no means the case; indeed, by comparison with other teeth, I should consider them the reverse. He states that some other plates are "disposed to slight crimping and irregular angular expansions." They appear to me to show decided crimping and angular expansion; which even in typical specimens of *E. antiquus* is not always regular. The tooth has much to recommend it rather for the dental series of the latter species than for *E. meridionalis*.

Another tooth, 33,368, B. M., from the same situation, and much rolled, belonging to the lower jaw, left side, holds what appears to be *x* 7 *x* in 5·5 × 2½ inches, and seven ridges in 4⅔ inches. It is unworn, but the cement wedges are thick, and the general grossness of the crown place it, at all events, with the preceding.

[1] Op. cit., vol. ii, p. 134, and 'P. A. S.,' pl. xiv B, figs. 5 and 5 a.
[2] Op. cit., vol. ii, p. 135; 'P. A. S.,' pl. xiv B, figs. 6 and 6 a.

A highly silicified left upper tooth from CROMER is shown in Pl. XXII, fig. 1. It has been obligingly lent to me by Mr. Fitch, of Norwich, for illustration in this Monograph. It holds *x* 8 *x* in 7×3 inches, and five plates in 3 inches. The parts are highly vitrified and in most perfect states of preservation, but it had evidently been rolled, and is consequently a beach specimen. There is a marked absence of crimping, and the cement is in excess; but, on the other hand, there is a tendency to angular expansion of the discs, as in *E. antiquus*, showing characters intermediate between the two. Now, although I have not seen a first true molar of the latter with a lower ridge formula than *x* 9 *x*, there is, however, the evidence of a last milk-tooth of *E. antiquus* recorded in Note 2, page 127, with as low a ridge formula as *x* 8 *x*. Considering, therefore, the rule of succession in last milk and first true molars, the possibility is that such a formula might be found in first true molars of *E. antiquus*; at the same time, I have no hesitation in asserting that the above specimen presents, in its uncrimped enamel and thick cement wedges, features not observed by me in any teeth referable to the latter Elephant. I would select it, therefore, as a typical instance of the first true molar of *E. meridionalis*.

No. 33,376, B. M., from HAPPISBOROUGH, Norfolk, is a left lower molar, considerably arcuated, with only the first ridge invaded. The plates are thick, with large cement wedges, there being six ridges in 3½ inches. The formula appears to be *x* 8 *x* in 5.8×2 inches.

The first true molar is illustrated, according to Falconer, by the following specimens in the Tuscan Museum at Florence:—Upper, *x* 9 *x* in 6·2 × 2·4 inches, and *x* 8 *x* in 6½ × (?) inches; lower, *x* 8 *x* in 5·5 × 2·6, and *x* 8 *x* in 6·4 × 2·4 inches.[1]

Second True Molar.

Fragmentary specimens are referred to by Falconer;[2] their broken conditions, however, are against any very certain characters with reference to formula. The crown constituents agree with the data he has laid down as diagnostic of *E. meridionalis*, viz. "wide disc," "large rings of the worn digitations," and "thick enamel;" none of which, however, are so pronounced by any means as in thick-plated teeth of *E. antiquus*. The excess of cement, which, of course, makes the ridges more apart, is very well shown. The fragment is 5·2 inches in length, and 2·9 in maximum breadth, and contains seven anterior ridges, the height of the last being 4 inches.

Falconer cites[3] another portion of a crown to show the "angular flexures that are sometimes seen when the plates are ground down low." I perceive in the original specimen

[1] Op. cit., vol. ii, p. 111.
[2] Op. cit., vol. ii, p. 135; 'F. A. S.,' pl. xiv D, figs. 7 and 7 a.
[3] Op. cit.. p. 137 'F. A. S.,' pl. xiv D, figs. 8 and 8 a.

another feature, viz. the crimping of the enamel is not confined to a roughening, or, as Falconer called it, "spurious crimping of the outer border," but invades the entire thickness. In other respects the excess of cement carries it with the above, but the thickness of the enamel shown in pl. xiv b, fig. 8 *a* of the 'F. A. S.' is not of much value when compared with the thick-plated *E. antiquus*; moreover, the "angular flexures" are often seen in crowns of *E. antiquus*, and apart from the central angulations so characteristic of the narrow crown of that Elephant's tooth.[1]

With reference to another fragment in the Norwich Museum,[2] Falconer observes :— "From being worn low down the plate exhibits a greater tendency to crimping than usual." To whichever form of Elephant this portion of a tooth may belong, it is scarcely possible, as far as my experience goes, to make out any well-marked specific characters between it and that of the thick-plated tooth of *E. antiquus*, *i.e. E. priscus* variety, indeed, the excessive crimping is fully as much pronounced as in the Asiatic Elephant. The crown surface is irregularly worn, and contains five ridges in 4·2 inches.

The fragment of a heel (No. 3 of the Norwich Museum), figured by Falconer,[3] and stated by him to belong to the last of the series of *E. meridionalis*, is clearly a fragment of a second true molar, showing a well-marked *pressure-scar posteriorly*. As compared with the thick-plated *E. antiquus* it is now of little value, as *thick* annular discs are often fully as large and wide apart in the latter.

Indeed, certain molars of the Mammoth to which I have referred[4] present these characters; moreover, the crimping of machærides is not always absent in large teeth. For example, No. 22 of Miss A. Gurney's collection in the Norwich Museum shows a crown of the above description, and inseparable from the foregoing. Here the crimping is not only confined to the external margin of the enamel, but also invades the entire thickness. The cement wedges are, however, thick; as is the case likewise with the enamel.

The above tooth is not entire, so its exact position in the series is undeterminable; but from some flattening behind (possibly pressure-marks) there may be a probability that it is a fragment of a second true molar. The crown is well worn, showing confluent fangs, and holds eleven and a half plates in 8 × 3¼ inches. It belongs to the left ramus of the mandible. There are five ridges in 3¾ inches. It is from Iron Pan of the Forest Bed, BACTON.

Another fragment (No. 364, Norwich Museum), from the EAST COAST deposit, belongs to the maxilla, right side. There is a loss of plates in front, and a well-marked pressure-scar on the heel. The tooth is very typical of the *E. meridionalis*, and possesses all the characters already noted. Every ridge is invaded excepting the last two. Eight and a half plates with the posterior talon are contained in 8 × 3·5 inches. No. 320, in the

[1] Plate XX, figs. 1 and 2.
[2] Op. cit., vol. ii, p. 136 ; 'F. A. S.,' pl. xiv b, figs. 9 and 9 *a*.
[3] 'F. A. S.,' pl. xiv b, figs. 12 and 12 *a*.
[4] Page 118.

same collection, from the Iron Pan, Forest Bed, BACTON, is a portion of a right upper tooth, showing a well-marked pressure-scar on the heel, and contains 11 x in $8 \times 3\frac{1}{2}$ inches, and five ridges in $3\frac{1}{2}$ inches. None of the digitations are worn out; nevertheless, the plates are thick, and there is an excess of cement; altogether it may be fairly correlated with the preceding.

No. 33,365, B. M., is a fragment of a right ramus of a mandible from HAPPISBOROUGH. It contains about eight ridges of the first true molar with an entire second true molar behind it; the first four ridges of the latter have been invaded. The diasteme is preserved. This jaw has been broken across at the symphysis in front, and in a line with the heel of the second true molar behind.

The second molar is considerably arcuated and holds x 10 x in $8\frac{1}{2} \times 3\frac{1}{4}$ inches. There is about an inch to every ridge. It is broad behind, being 3·4 inches in width. The crown shows enamel free from crimping, and has the usual excess of cement observed in these uncrimped teeth, whose external margins present some roughening and channelling. The breadth of crown, the length, and the small height are evident characters as compared with the varieties of *E. antiquus*; and the low ridge formula is assuredly significant, inasmuch as I have not met with the same in any second true molar of the latter species.

With reference to the characters of the ramus. The mental foramina are two in number. One at a distance of 1·2 inches from the margin of the diasteme, the other 2·2 inches distant and a short way above the last.

The usual foramen inside the spout is about 1·4 inches from the margin.

The diasteme slopes at about an angle of 45°. The thickness of the jaw at the base of the coronoid is $6\frac{1}{4}$ inches. The rostrum is wanting. In the rather reclinate diasteme the jaw differs from that of *E. antiquus*, and is broadly distinct, of course, from that of *E. primigenius*.

A detached left lower molar (Pl. XXIII, figs. 1 and 1 a), No. 33,343, B. M., also from the NORFOLK COAST, holds apparently a formula of x 9 x. The anterior talon is like a plate, and so is the posterior, excepting a small prominence on its posterior surface. About five or six ridges of this tooth are invaded. It is somewhat arcuated, with a double anterior fang followed by a coalescence posteriorly. The length is $8\frac{1}{4} \times 2\frac{3}{4}$, and contains eight ridges in about 5·2 inches. It presents the same characters as the last, with which it may fairly claim relationship.

A characteristic specimen of evidently a second true molar in a fragment of a jaw was discovered by Mr. Alfred Savin at OVERSTRAND, CROMER; No. 37 of his collection. It is a right upper molar with a well-marked pressure-scar on the heel. All the plates are in wear. The anterior fang is preserved, but the first ridge has been ground away, leaving eleven plates and a posterior talon in $8 \times 3\frac{1}{4}$ inches. There are five plates in $3\frac{1}{4}$ inches. The uncrimped enamel, the channelling of the latter, the excess of cement, its dimensions and low ridge formula, seem to me to place it with the foregoing.

No. $\frac{28,820}{A}$ B. M., from Val d'Arno, is apparently a second true molar of the right side, lower jaw. It holds x 11 x in 10 × 3·2, and six ridges in 5·5 inches. Eight discs are invaded, with large digitations; there is also arcuation of the crown, a character not uncommon in *E. meridionalis*, notwithstanding the usual shortness of its molars as compared with *E. antiquus*.

Falconer gives examples of this tooth in the Tuscan Museum as follows:—Upper, x 9 x in 9×4, and x 10 x in 8·75×3·5 inches; Lower x 9 x in 7·8×3·3 inches.

Logard[1] figures several teeth from Central and Southern France, perhaps referable to *E. meridionalis*, with other crowns decidedly of the type of *E. antiquus*.

Ultimate or Third True Molar.

The fragment of a tooth (No. 7456, B. M.), described and figured by Falconer,[2] is supposed to have come from the "Oyster Beds" of MUNDESLEY or HAPPISBOROUGH, on the Norfolk coast.

This portion of a tooth has all the characters of *E. antiquus* rather than of *E. meridionalis*, to which he has referred it. The anterior fang remains in part with $\frac{1}{2}$ 8 x, or nine and a half ridges. There is pronounced crimping of the middle of the discs with a tendency to central expansion. The specimen at all events is unsatisfactory as a typical instance of the last tooth of *E. meridionalis*.

No. 10 A of the Norwich Museum, recorded by Falconer,[3] is another fragmentary molar. The general features of the crown are well shown in his plates, and the characters faithfully described. The only exception I take to his description is the statement that "the plates of enamel are very thick." To me they appear in no way remarkable in that respect in comparison with *E. antiquus*, seeing that teeth of the latter from the above deposits often show much thicker enamel. There is faint crimping along the external borders of the machœrides, with pronounced undulations of the enamelled cords. This tooth is altogether characteristic of *E. antiquus*, whose dental conditions not unfrequently connect it with *E. meridionalis* by the absence of deep-set crimping, the undulating enamelled borders, and excess of cement between the plates, together with close relationships of breadth to height and length. This example is unfortunately advanced in wear, with several of the anterior ridges worn away, leaving 9 x in 9·2×3·6 inches, so that its original formula is not preserved.

No. 13 A, Norwich Museum, is also described and figured by the same author.[4] The

[1] 'Archives du Mus. Hist. de Lyon,' pl. xv, fig. 4 ; pl. xxi, figs. 2, 3, and 4 ; pl. xx, figs. 4 and 5 ; pl. xix, figs. 1, 2, 3, and 4.
[2] Op. cit., vol. ii, p. 137; and 'F. A. S.,' pl. xiv B, figs. 13 and 13 a.
[3] Op. cit., vol. ii, p. 137, pl. viii, fig. 4. and 'F. A. S.,' pl. xiv B, figs. 14 and 14 a.
[4] Op. cit., vol. ii, p. 138; 'F. A. S.,' pl. xiv B, figs. 15 and 15 a.

remarkable character in this fragment of an upper molar is its breadth of crown, which exceeds any of the broad-crowned variety of *E. antiquus*; the largest of *E. primigenius* I have examined, being 4·9 inches in its maximum breadth.

The bending of the plates backwards contrasts with just the reverse in No. 10 A, although both belong to the same side of the upper jaw. This shows that the character is of little use for diagnostic purposes. The above specimen displays external crimping on the anterior border of the machærides, but not affecting the entire thickness.

The entire lower molar (No. 3, the Norwich Museum) from THORPE, Norwich, was the specimen which first led Falconer to doubt the unity of species of the British Elephants, and is so far interesting.[1] It is a long and bent molar, with the crown scarcely more than touched by wear. The breadth of crown and the thickness of intervening wedges of cement are seldom so pronounced in the thick-plated and broad tooth of *E. antiquus* and its very low ridge formula x 11 x in 11·2×3·8 is quite remarkable as compared with the lowest expression of even the second true molar of *E. antiquus*. The configuration of the tooth appears to indicate the last of the series. There is no pressure-scar, or pronounced flattening posteriorly, which, however, could scarcely appear in its condition of wear. The crown tails off posteriorly, as in all last lower molars. These characters are decidedly in favour of its being that of a distinct form from either of the British species already described, and might well have produced doubts in the mind of one who had already differentiated the characters of its congeners from the Sewalik Hills. The crown fragment, referred to by Falconer,[2] may be correlated with the other teeth with thick cement wedges; but, besides the vertical channellings, it shows some crimping. It has, however, the general appearance of the *E. meridionalis*; but, as in all broken teeth, one cannot always be certain of their diagnostic values, even in such a fragment as that shown in Pl. XVIII, fig. 4, representing a morsel of a huge molar (No. $\frac{G}{102}$) in the Jermyn Street Museum) from MUNDESLEY, where it was dug out of the blue clay of the FOREST BED. Judging from this small portion, the original must have been, indeed, of enormous proportions.

In Mr. Savin's Collection at CROMER, is a large lower left molar (No. 43) holding fourteen ridges; besides a posterior talon there is a loss in front by detrition of not more than a ridge. It is 10×4 inches in breadth, and must have been a stupendous tooth.

No. 12, Norwich Museum, is a superb right lower last molar covered with matrix from the Iron Pan, FOREST BED. It holds x 13 x in 11×3½ inches.

The crown is narrow and considerably arcuated, and has much the aspect of the narrow tooth of *E. antiquus*. The two anterior fangs support the first two ridges. All are invaded excepting the posterior talon. The discs are inseparable in character from the typical crown of *E. meridionalis*. It holds five ridges in 5½ inches.

[1] Op. cit., vol. ii, p. 130, and pl. xiv B, figs. 18 and 18 a.
[2] 'F. A. S.,' pl. xiv D, figs. 11 and 11 a.

In its narrow crown it presents, even although a lower tooth, an exceptional character, compared with the usual molars of *E. meridionalis;* indeed, but for the absence of pronounced crimping of the enamel, it might stand for a thick-plated tooth of *E. antiquus* of the *C* variety, referred to at p. 33. But then for the last of the series it stands apart from that species on account of its low ridge formula.

Another magnificent molar, presented likewise by Miss A. Gurney, is No. 23 of the Norwich Collection. It is from the same locality, and is a left lower, with apparently the loss of only the posterior talon. It holds *x* 13 in 14 inches by 4 in maximum breadth, and has five plates in 4¾ inches. Seven of the anterior plates are invaded.

This molar is quite typical of the broad, uncrimped crown, and channelled enamel of *E. meridionalis,* described by Falconer.

No 21, Norwich Museum, from BACTON, in Miss A. Gurney's Collection, is like No. 12, just referred to, in having a narrow crown. It is also of the lower jaw, right side, and valuable as an aberrant form of tooth. The fangs have coalesced into a keel along the lower surface. The anterior fangs are broken off close to the base. All the ridges, ½ 11 *x*, are in full wear excepting the last plate and posterior talon, and the general contour of detrited surface is concave. Apparently not more than one and a half ridges have disappeared through wear, so that the formula may have been originally *x* 13 *x*, like the above, in 11½ × 3½ inches in breadth. The tooth holds five ridges in 5¼ inches, and has a projecting heel. The same remarks are applicable to this as to the preceding molar.

No. 24 of the Gurney Collection is also from BACTON. It is a fragment, however, showing *x* 7 in 6½ × 3¼ and five in 4½ inches. The tooth has been rolled. It is typical of *E. meridionalis.*

A narrow crown of the type of Nos. 12 and 21, and also in the Norwich Museum, is shown in the fragment of a left lower molar, holding 10 *x* in 8½ × 3, and five ridges in 4·5 inches.

There is a loss of several ridges in front, but eight are in full state of wear, and three with their tips entire. The crimping of the outer borders of enamel is pronounced, and the cement is in excess. A narrow crown seems to have constituted a variety in the dentition of *E. meridionalis* as in *E. antiquus* and rarely in *E. primigenius.*[1]

A typical fragment of *E. meridionalis,* holding 8½ plates in 10 × 3½ inches, is represented by No. 317 of the Gunn Collection. It is a left lower tooth.

Another typical instance is No. 222 of the Gunn Collection, marked by Gunn "from the soil of the Forest Bed, MUNDESLEY." It is encrusted with *débris,* and the discs are obscured by the hard ferruginous cement; nevertheless, it is a fine fragment, and shows fourteen ridges in 12 × 3¼ inches. The same may be said of No. 308 of the same gentle-

---

[1] Mr. Gunn lately directed my attention to a remarkably long narrow molar of *E. primigenius* said to have come from the Norfolk Coast deposits. The tooth (Plate XXVI. fig. 1) is a second true molar, lower jaw, left side, holding *x* 16 *x* in 8½ inches. The discs display all the ridges in wear excepting the posterior talon. The enamel is thin, but the remarkable narrowness of the tooth is noteworthy, being only 2¼ inches broad in front, 2¼ in the middle, and 2¼ posteriorly.

28

man's collection, whilst No. 329, a lower left, holds 8 x in 8×3½ inches.   It shows a long projecting heel which is rare in lower molars of *E. meridionalis*.

No. 330 was dug out of the Iron Pan, Forest Bed, BACTON, by Mr. Gunn, with No. 302, which is a fragment of a tusk showing a gentle curve like that of the recent species. The molar is so encrusted with the Iron Pan as to make it difficult to count the ridges. Apparently there are about fourteen or fifteen, including of course talons, in 13×4 inches. This tooth is of colossal dimensions.

A superb fragment of a left lower molar is shown by No. 311 of the Gunn Collection. The crown is well worn, and displays a depression or fault affecting three central plates in their antero-posterior direction, whereby one half is depressed fully a quarter of an inch below the opposite side, thus indicating a blow when the tooth was fresh.   There is a loss of plates in front by detrition, leaving about an inch of the crown bare, followed by 11 x in 11 inches by 3·8 in breadth.   The channelled border, thick wedges of cement, and general dimensions, show the above to be a typical crown of *E. meridionalis*.

Another instance of such pressure on teeth is well shown on No. 219, being a palate specimen, where fragments of two enormous upper molars, right and left, appear to have been crushed together with great force.   Nos. 220, 221, and 223 are also FOREST BED fragments, undeterminable from the foregoing.

The National Collection contains several very characteristic specimens of the last molar, presenting characters precisely like the foregoing.   The following entire tooth is suggestive.

No. 33,330, in the Layton Collection from HAPPISBOROUGH, is a left upper molar with seven ridges invaded, but none of the digitations worn out.   The crown is somewhat arcuated and short for a last molar of even the upper jaw.   It holds x 13 x in 9¼×3 inches and six ridges in a space of 3·8 inches.   The large wedges of cement, and the breadth as compared with the height and length, are in accord with the foregoing.

No. 46,214, B. M., is a fragment cut across, and the section polished to show the relative proportions of cement to the other elements.   It is very characteristic of *E. meridionalis*.   The specimen is in the Owles Collection, and is reputed to be from the DOGGER BANK,[1] so prolific of remains of *E. primigenius*.

No. 33,354, Plate XXIV, fig. 1, is a right lower entire molar from HAPPISBOROUGH. Nine ridges are invaded, but the digitations are not worn out.   The specimen is considerably arcuated, and holds x 14 x in 12½×3¼ inches, with thick plates and much intervening cement, inasmuch as six plates, including of course their cement, are contained in as many inches or about an inch to each plate.

No. 33,334, B. M., Plate XXIV, fig. 2, is a left upper molar with the anterior talon ground down and a round heel.   It holds x 14 x in 10½×3·8 inches.   The first five discs are fully formed, and show crimping with a tendency to mesial expansion.[2]   Six

---

[1] This statement, however, may be fairly doubted, as I have been informed, on good authority, that the trawlers who furnished specimens for Mr. Owles occasionally trawled on the Norfolk Coast likewise, when on their way to their fishing ground off the Yorkshire coast.

[2] The disposition to central dilatation of the disc, and even the angulations so pronounced in the

ridges are contained in a space of 4·8 inches. The massive size and large quantities of intervening cement maintain its characters with the foregoing, whilst the crimping and central expansion are like the same in the thick-plated variety of *E. antiquus*.

Two last lower molars, right and left, of possibly the same individual, are preserved in the Museum of Practical Geology, Jermyn Street.

The right tooth has the anterior talon and twelve ridges, with a loss of posterior ridges. It is $12 \times 3\frac{1}{2}$ inches.

The left tooth has fourteen of its anterior ridges preserved with anterior talon, but its heel portion is wanting. It is $13 \times 3\frac{1}{4}$ inches.

Each molar holds eight in 7·8 inches.

About five of the anterior ridges are invaded, nevertheless none of the digitations are worn out. The enamel presents the undulatory character of the preceding. The components are all in excess, the cement being conspicuously abundant; but it would be difficult, without a cross section of these teeth, to separate them from the thick-plated molars of *E. antiquus*.

The pebbly matrix of the Iron Pan of the FOREST BED adheres to their sides. These specimens were found by Mr. Andrews in 1860.

Maxillæ and Mandibles containing Molars.

The ramus, Plate XXII, fig. 2, is described, but not figured, by Falconer.[1] It was dug out of the Elephant-bed, or Iron Pan of the Forest Bed, between MUNDESLEY and BACTON, and is No. 215 of the Gunn Collection. It holds portion of the second and the entire ultimate true molar. The ridge formula of the latter is obscured by the cement covering the tooth, which is partly embedded in the jaw. There are four plates remaining of the fifth, and possibly from twelve to thirteen plates besides talons enter into the composition of the ultimate molar.

The enamel of the discs is free from the crimping of *E. antiquus*, and presents an undulating border, but there is a decided tendency to mesial expansion in several discs. The cement is in excess as compared with *E. antiquus* generally, and the ridge formula of the ultimate tooth is far lower than that of either of the other extinct British species.

narrow crown of *E. antiquus*, are met with in *E. meridionalis* from Italian deposits, as is evidenced by a cast (No. 37,337, B. M.) from the Val d'Arno, where a well-worn crown with seven discs shows marked angulations, but the crimping is confined to the anterior borders of the machærides. This tooth presents an excess of cement, so that each plate and its cement occupy about an inch of the basal antero-posterior diameter. Another (No. 37,336, B. M.) upper molar from the same locality has mesial expansion of discs without crimping or angulations; whilst a third (No. 28,820, B. M.) from the same locality contains about ten of the last ridges and a posterior talon in 9×4 inches. It shows not only central expansion of the disc but also pronounced crimping, extending nearly but not quite to the cornua, and is undistinguishable from a well-worn crown of a broad molar of *E. antiquus*. Thus, all these characters of the latter may occasionally appear not only in individual discs, but in several discs of *E. meridionalis*.

[1] 'Pal. Mem.,' vol. ii, pp. 132 and 140.

Add to these the proportions, *i. e.* the length to the breadth and height as compared with them, and the following characters of the mandible, all of which conspire, with the similar fragment to be described, in establishing what may be fairly considered to be characters distinct from *E. antiquus* and *E. primigenius.*[1]

It is unnecessary to detail the measurements of the jaw so accurately laid down by Falconer.[2] I have, however, to offer observations, on, what he observes, are " peculiarities distinctive of this specimen from the lower jaw of the Mammoth,"[3] to which I might add *E. antiquus.* Moreover, these observations are also applicable to fragments to be referred to in the sequel.

1. The lower elevation of the jaw at the anterior extremity as compared with *E. primigenius* and *E. antiquus,* but not *E. planifrons,* with which it agrees.[4]

2. The long and gradual slope of the diasteme into the beak is also a characteristic feature in the above and 215 A, and in *E. planifrons.*[5]

3. The consequent long symphysis resultant of the prolonged diasteme is a good character, but in both these specimens that part is wanting ; the outlines, however, tend to support the diagnosis.

4. The greater length of the horizontal ramus, and the height in proportion to the width of the ascending ramus. This is pronounced and well shown in the above, and is conspicuous in *E. planifrons.*[6]

5. The less sudden curve posteriorly at the angle and margin of the ascending ramus. This character is also distinctive, more especially as compared with the same parts in the Mammoth,[7] and is present also in the jaw of *E. planifrons.*[8]

I observe, further, a flattening on the external border of the ascending ramus, the sharp posterior border of which is similar to that of the African Elephant and *E. planifrons.*

The dental canal is also like that of the African, as it opens upwards and backwards, and not directly upwards, as in the Mammoth.

The usual irregularity in size and position of the mental foramina is shown in this specimen, in which there are two nearly in line with each other. One is 1½ inches, and the other 3 inches from the margin of the diasteme.[9] The internal opening in the gutter is about two inches from the beak.[10]

[1] Pages 52 and 134.   [2] Op. cit., vol. ii, p. 140.   [3] Op. cit., vol. ii, p. 127.
[4] See 'Faun. Ant. Sival.,' pls. xi and xliv.   [5] 'F. A. S.,' pls. xxi and xliv.
[6] 'F. A. S.,' pl. xi, figs. 2 and 3.
[7] 'Ossem. Fossil.,' pl. xv, figs. 5 and 6, taken from Nesti's figs. 1 and 2.   [8] 'F. A. S.,' pl. xi, fig. 3.
[9] Cuvier, in alluding to a mandible from Tuscany (op. cit., vol. ii, p. 213), conceives that the mental foramina being two in line and not above or below one another is distinctive of the Italian fossil ; but, as will be seen in the woodcuts of *E. primigenius,* figs. 4.—12, p. 135, there is no rule as to numbers and position of these openings. He refers also to the contour of the beak, which will be seen to be also exceedingly variable.
[10] The "important specimen" referred to by Falconer ('Pal. Mem.,' vol. ii, p. 132), showing "a longitudinal section" of a molar, is, I am informed by Mr. Gunn, not now in the Norwich Museum.

Another interesting specimen (No. 215 A of the Gunn Collection, Norwich Museum) was, according to a label attached to the jaw, " dug out of the Elephant Bed between the Coal and Cart Gaps, BACTON." It is covered with the *débris* of the Forest Bed, and represents a fragment of a right lower ramus containing the diasteme (injured), with the horizontal ramus entire up to the commencement of the ascending portion.

The jaw holds the last five ridges of the second and the first five ridges of the ultimate tooth, presenting a united worn surface of 10 inches in length. The specimen is described by Falconer.[1] I append, however, several measurements.

The remaining five ridges of the fifth molar, and the five ridges of the sixth, are contained in a space of 4·9 and 6·3 inches respectively. The maximum breadth of the crown of the fifth molar is 4 inches, while that of the ultimate is 3·5 inches; the discrepancy in the latter arises from the tooth being not so much advanced in wear as its predecessors, seeing that only four of the five ridges are detrited. The ridge formula is undeterminable, but the massive dimensions of the teeth and their characters are precisely as in the preceding.

The diasteme is injured, but clearly shows that it was not so erect as in the Mammoth and *E. antiquus*. The mental foramina maintain the same irregularity as to position observed in the preceding, and in all Elephants' mandibles; here one foramen is fully two inches from the margin.

The length from the anterior border of the coronoid to the commencement of the diasteme is 10 inches.

The height of the jaw to the alveolar border in front of the coronoid is 7·5 inches.

Length of the diasteme 8 inches.

Breadth of the ascending ramus at its commencement 7 inches.

Height of the jaw at the commencement of the diasteme 9½ inches. Height at the insertion of the coronoid 7¼ inches.

The characters of this ramus and its teeth are precisely like the foregoing jaw.

The lower jaw described by Falconer[2] was discovered on a cliff near MUNDESLEY, and is now in the Norwich Museum, to which it was presented by R. Barclay, Esq. It is not so well preserved as the preceding, but contains more of the jaw, seeing that portions of the two rami are preserved. The ultimate molars are present, but much mutilated; nevertheless, wherever these and the jaw admit of comparison, they are quite in accord with the two fragments just described, and doubtless represent the mandible of the same species.

A fourth fragment (No. 368 of the Gunn Collection) from the FOREST BED represents a right lower ramus without teeth, but the sockets of both are entire. The last is just commencing wear, with a deep pit in front, possibly for the anterior fang or else a fragment of the second molar. The coronoid is also nearly entire, with an almost perpen-

[1] 'Pal. Mem.,' vol. ii, p. 133.
[2] Op. cit., vol. ii, p. 140.

dicular anterior border. It is a suggestive fragment as compared with the preceding, especially with reference to the absolute and relative heights of the horizontal ramus at the commencement of the diasteme, and of the ascending ramus, as indicated in discussing the characters of jaw (No. 215 A).

In the collection of R. Fitch, Esq., there is a fragment of a right ramus of the lower jaw, with a last true molar in place. The tooth is much worn in front, but its heel is rounded, and there is no mark of pressure, although it is much advanced in wear, seeing that the posterior talon is in line with the anterior border of the coronoid.

There are ten ridges in wear, with a loss by detrition in front. The elements present the same characters as in the foregoing. The molar is $9\frac{1}{4} \times 3$ inches.

These characters are, in fact, even more pronounced than in the jaws in the Gunn Collection, to wit, a gradually descending diasteme into the beak, whilst the height of the horizontal ramus at the commencement of the diasteme is 8 inches, and at the insertion of the coronoid it is 7 inches. But the jaw, although low in height, is of great breadth, being 5 inches in width at the heel of the molar. The length of the symphysial gutter is $4\frac{1}{2}$, and its breadth in front $2\frac{3}{4}$ inches, with an internal foramen near the latter.

Another right ramus of a mandible from BACTON, Norfolk, is in the possession of Randall Johnson, Esq., of Stalham. It displays a fragment of the second, with the last true molar just commencing wear. The fragment is nearly entire, with the loss only of the condyles and coronoid.

Here, again, the diasteme slopes gradually into the beak, and is 6 inches in length.

The height at the commencement of the former is $7\frac{1}{2}$ inches, and at the insertion of the coronoid 6 inches.

The dental canal looks upwards and backwards, as in No. 215 A, Gunn Collection, just described.

The entire characters of this jaw are in accord with the preceding, but the last molar is unfortunately half hidden posteriorly; however, the first fragment of the second molar is undistinguishable from the teeth already noticed as regards the channellings of the enamel, absence of pronounced crimping, and the presence of large wedges of cement.

A specimen (No. 28 of the Woodwardian Collection) is fragmentary. It is a right ramus lower jaw with portion of an ultimate molar in position. There is a loss of substance immediately behind the molar. The diasteme is injured, and has been partly restored with plaster.

The crown of this molar is arcuated; it holds 11 x in $9 \times 3\frac{1}{2}$ inches. There is slight crimping of the machærides, and the cement between the plates is much denuded, so that the discs appear as if raised much above the general level of the crown. The height of the jaw at the commencement of the diasteme is $6\frac{1}{2}$ inches.

The worn discs, as far as they go, are in support of the characters of *E. meridionalis* rather than the broad crown of *E. antiquus*. The specimen was presented by Miss A. Gurney, and is from the NORFOLK COAST.

A third maxilla, showing a portion of the palate with two molars similar to the last, is seen in No. 3 of the same collection. The teeth contain 11 x in $9\frac{1}{2} \times 4$ inches, and converge a little in front, with an intervening space of $3\frac{3}{4}$ inches. The distances between them at the middle and posteriorly being $3\frac{3}{4}$ and 6 inches respectively. The jaw is covered with matrix from the Forest Bed, CROMER, from which it is stated to have been derived. The crowns of the molars are remarkably broad.

The mandible, Plate XXV, fig. 1, was considered by Dr. Falconer to belong to E. *meridionalis*, from a label attached to the jaw with the name in his hand-writing.

It was found in the FOREST BED, CROMER, and now forms one of many treasures in the Woodwardian Museum of Cambridge University. Through the kindness and liberality of my distinguished friend, Prof. McKenny Hughes, I am enabled to furnish an illustration of this interesting jaw. There is a loss of the condyles, neck, and a portion of the under surface of the horizontal ramus posteriorly, otherwise the specimen is nearly entire, and in an excellent state of preservation.

The last molar is in position on either side, with their heels about five inches behind the anterior margin of the coronoid. They converge somewhat in front, the distance between them being 4·5 inches at the first ridge, 5 at the middle, and $10\frac{1}{4}$ at the heels, which are elevated above the margins of their sockets. Both molars have their hinder parts hidden in the jaw, but ten ridges are exposed, all of which are worn. Possibly the formula may have been from eleven to twelve plates with talons; assuredly not more, from the dimensions. The cement having been removed for a short distance down the external sides of the plates (Plate XXV, fig. 1), the ribbing of the plate has become exposed. It is the cross section, through detrition, of these elevated ridges which produces the false or faint crimping of the external border of the unchærides, and distinguishes the character from plaiting or crimping, involving the entire thickness of the enamel. Unfortunately the crowns of the teeth are not worn even, and are here and there encrusted with the Iron Pan, which adheres most pertinaciously to the enamel. There is little of a trustworthy character to be learned from them further than, to all appearances, they are nearly, if not quite, entire. Such being the case, and judging from the exposed ridges, the dental formula does not at the furthest exceed x 14 x. Either tooth, as far as the callipers can extend and along the surface, evidently not the whole length, is $9\frac{1}{4} \times 3\frac{1}{4}$ inches. The cement is in excess, and the enamel, as usual, is thick with slight crimping along the external border.

It is to be regretted that the molars afford so little information. But the mandible is extremely interesting, as it is altogether different from any of the foregoing, and most certainly will not coincide with the descriptions given by Falconer of the mandible of E. *meridionalis*.[1] Indeed, without the molars the jaw is not distinguishable from that of the Mammoth, and, but for one or two characters, might belong to the thick-plated, and

[1] Op. cit., vol. ii, p. 140.

broad-crowned variety of *E. antiquus*. In fact, either the mandible is subject to great variability in the *E. meridionalis*, or else fig. 1 represents another species.

The following characters distinguish it from the preceding jaws, and are for the most part brought out in the figures in Plate XXV.

1. The diasteme is erect or nearly so, as in the Mammoth and *E. antiquus*.

2. The rostrum, instead of being part of the diasteme, projects from the symphysis like a nipple from a breast (Plate XXV, figs. 1 *a* and 1 *b*). These two characters are opposed to the diagnosis of Falconer, who states that the beak in *E. meridionalis* is a prolongation of the inferior margin, into which the diastemal ridges descend with great obliquity ; but, considering the variability in this respect as regards the Mammoth shown in Woodcuts, figs. 19—21, page 138, it may be fairly doubted if any reliance should be placed on the projection in question, to which may be added the numbers or positions of the mental foramina.

3. The chin (Plate XXV, fig. 1 *b*) has the round character of that of the Mammoth, as shown in Woodcuts at page 135, figs. 4—12.

4. The length of the horizontal as compared with the width of the ascending ramus (Plate XXV) is also striking with reference to the other mandibles of *E. meridionalis* just described, and is in keeping with the jaw of *E. antiquus* and *E. primigenius*. How far, indeed, there are any characters of a constant and very reliable nature in connection with the lower jaws of these three species may be questionable from this instance of what is seemingly the mandible of *E. meridionalis*.

5. The great thickness of the ramus just behind the molar (Plate XXV, fig. 1) is assuredly greater in proportion in the jaw in question than I have seen in that of either of the other two species.

The measurements have been already recorded in the table, page 144 ; there are, however, a few additional measurements to be added as follow :

1. Height of coronoid and jaw, 13 inches.
2. Height of jaw in front of coronoid, 9 inches.
3. Thickness at the middle of the molar, 5·5 inches.
4. Thickness at the heel of the molar, 9 inches.
5. Antero-posterior length of symphysial gutter from the tip of the rostrum is 5·5 inches by callipers, and 8 inches by tape line.
6. Breadth of gutter in front below 2·5 inches, and 3·5 inches at its middle.
7. There are four mental foramina on the right, and only two on the left.

The British Museum contains an interesting cast (No. 3733) of a mandible from the VAL D'ARNO.[1] It is entire excepting the coronoids, and holds a fragment of the second, in front of an entire ultimate true molar, of which six discs only are invaded, whilst the

---

[1] Woodcuts of which are shown at p. 136, fig. 14, p. 139, fig. 28, and p. 142, fig. 40 ; its dimensions in the table at p. 144.

posterior portion is hidden in the jaw. The points of interest in this specimen and which correlate it with the preceding mni from East Anglia are :

1. The diasteme is somewhat more erect than in them,[1] but by no means so much as in the Mammoth, and the remarkable mandible from CROMER, just described (Pl. XXV). The diasteme runs into the beak,[2] which seems to have pointed downwards.

2. The horizontal ramus does not bulge out along its external border, especially at the base of the coronoid, as is the case in the Mammoth and *E. antiquus*; indeed, it repeats what I have just indicated of the preceding jaws from British strata, with the exception of Pl. XXV, fig. 1.

3. The condyles, which are rarely preserved in fossil Proboscidean remains, are present in this specimen, these with the contour of the neck are shown (p. 142, fig. 40).

4. The comparatively narrow neck, as seen from behind, and the disposition to compression of the longest sides of the oval condyle with the thicker end inwards, are features in accord rather with the African Elephant than the Mammoth and Asiatic; but the condyle is variable as to its contour in the Asiatic, and may have been so likewise in the extinct species. The dental canal is not well defined in the cast, but it seemingly is small, and directed upwards and backwards. The thickness of the jaw at the base of the coronoid is 7 inches, and the height at the commencement of the diasteme is 9 inches.

The width at the base of the coronoid is 20 inches, and between the condyles $15\frac{1}{4}$ inches. The great breadth of the jaw at the latter is a character shown to be present also in *E. primigenius* and *E. antiquus*.[3]

The crowns of the molars have not been sufficiently impressed on the cast to afford any important data as to sculpturing. The space between them in front is 4 inches, at the middle 3 inches, and posteriorly 9 inches.

The ultimate molar of *E. meridionalis*, as met with in Northern Italy, is represented by the following data, recorded by Falconer :—Upper,[4] *x* 13 *x* in 11×4·3 inches, *x* 12—13 *x*. Lower, *x* 13 *x* in 10·25×3·3; *x* 15 *x* in 13×4·3 inches.

Such are the materials I have been enabled to study referring to the dentition of *E. meridionalis*. In considering the data by which Falconer established the specific characters of this Elephant, as met with in British strata, I have invariably compared the actual specimens, wherever available, with his lucid descriptions ; and although I have seen cause to differ from him on certain structural conditions, yet considering the often fragmentary materials he had to deal with, it must be conceded that the differentiations he formulated are more or less confirmed by the preceding data.

[1] Fig. 11, p. 136, and fig. 28, p. 139.
[2] Fig. 11, p. 136 ; fig. 28, p. 139 ; fig. 40, p. 142.
[3] Page 140.
[4] Op. cit., vol. ii, p. 113.

29

Summary of the Dentition of E. meridionalis.

Incisors.—All the incisor teeth of *E. meridionalis*, hitherto discovered either in British strata or in Northern Italy, appear to differ from the ordinary typical tusk of the Mammoth in being relatively much stouter towards the proximal extremity, and by the absence of the spiral curvature so pronounced in the former. But individual exceptions might have occurred in a tooth so free to pursue an aberrant direction. Even, as has been already shown as regards *E. primigenius*, the upward tendency is not invariable in that species. The relationships between the tusk of *E. meridionalis* and that of *E. antiquus*, to which may be added the two recent species, in contour and direction are so close that, as far as specimens are concerned, it would be difficult to point out any reliable distinctions, excepting in size; moreover, examples of *E. antiquus* might be adduced equal even to the ponderous defensors of *E. meridionalis*.

The ante-penultimate milk-molar.—The very few instances of this member of the series show a tooth easily distinguishable from the same molar in the Mammoth and Asiatic Elephant, not, however, as regards dimensions so much as in thicker plates and more intervening cement. As regards *E. antiquus* and the African Elephant these distinctions are not so pronounced. The ridge formula in one tooth of *E. meridionalis* is $x\ 3\ x$ in 0·95 by 0·75 inch, thus fully bearing out characters confirmed by the true molars; but the exceptional instance of $x\ 3\ x$ in 0·7 inch shows considerable variability, whilst, on the other hand, such a first milk-molar as that of *E. antiquus* referrred to at p. 86, and shown on Pl. XII, fig. 3, embarrasses the diagnosis between their ante-penultimate milk-molars. Moreover, the crown patterns are usually not sufficiently developed to afford reliable data, so that one has to trust to the relative proportion of elements of the crown, which are also variable, as represented by the molars of *E. antiquus* and *E. primigenius* (Pls. I, VIII, IX, and XII). The first milk-tooth is therefore *per se* not reliable for diagnostic purposes.

Penultimate milk-molar.—The previous observations on this tooth, recorded at pp. 15 and 92, receive further confirmation from the more recent researches at p. 188. The sculpturing of the crown is often undistinguishable from that of large second milk-teeth of *E. antiquus*, showing, as in the Mammoth, crimping as well as channelling of the machærides. As regards the ridge formula I have not observed a tooth of a lower figure than $x\ 6\ x$. The instance of "$x\ 5\ x$," alluded to at p. 48, is a mistake on my part from a miscalculation of the ridges. With reference to dimensions, two entire upper molars range from 2·5 to 2·6 inches in length, and are 1·6 in breadth, whilst in five lower teeth the lengths vary from 2·6 to 3 inches, and the breadths from 1·2 to 1·5, three showing the latter measurement. It will be seen, however, that teeth of both *E. antiquus* and *E. primigenius* attain equal measurements.[1] However, a comparison of the crowns of penul-

[1] Pages 13 and 92.

timate milk-molars of the three species, as shown in Pl. I, fig. 3, Pl. V, fig. 2, Pl. XII, fig. 3, Pl. VI, fig. 2, Pl. X, fig. 3, and Pl. XXII, fig. 3 a, are in favour of that of $E.$ *meridionalis* presenting in general a broader crown from the middle posteriorly than in the two other extinct Elephants.

Ultimate milk-molar.—Taking the British and Italian specimens recorded in the foregoing pages, this tooth appears to vary between seven and eight plates, besides talons. Out of eleven examples six show a ridge formula of x 8 x and five of x 7 x. The dimensions vary as follows:—In upper molars the length is from 4·4 inches to 4·6 inches, and the breadth from 1·4 to 2·5 inches; in the mandible these measurements are respectively 3·9 to 4·8 inches, and 1·7 to 2·8 inches in width. The general absence of crimping, the pronounced channelling, thick plates, abundant cement, the low height in proportion to breadth, so pronounced in true molars of $E.$ *meridionalis*, are well shown in this member of the series. These are evident by comparing Pl. XVII, fig. 8, with the same tooth in $E.$ *antiquus* and $E.$ *primigenius* (Pl. I, fig. 4, Pl. XI, fig. 1 a, and Pl. XII, fig. 2), *erroneously* recorded in the explanation of the latter plate as a *penulti- mate* instead of an *ultimate* milk-molar.

First true molar.—Allowing for the difficulty always in discriminating between small- sized first true molars and the last of the milk series, I find that out of three upper and four lower entire teeth, the ridge formula varies from x 7 x to x 9 x. The majority show the figure of x 8 x. The maximum lengths are 7 inches, and the minimum 5·3 inches, whilst the breadths vary from 2 to 3 inches.

This tooth in general displays more distinctly-marked specific characters than the last milk-molar, especially in well-worn crowns, such as shown on Pl. XXII, fig. 1, which may be compared with Pl. III, fig. 2, of $E.$ *antiquus*, and Pl. XI, fig. 2, and Pl. XXI, fig. 1, of $E.$ *primigenius*.

Second true molar.—I have recorded seven entire molars belonging to this member of the series, viz. three upper and four lower. The ridge formula in the above varies from x 9 x to x 11 x in both jaws. The greatest length is 10 inches, and maximum breadth 4 inches, whilst the minimum length is 7·8 inches, and breadth 3·2 inches. Perhaps the majority of second true molars hold about nine plates exclusive of talons.

This tooth, always a valuable exponent of specific distinctions, is represented from British strata by several very characteristic fragmentary or entire specimens.

A comparison of Pl. XXIII, fig. 1, with the same molar of $E.$ *antiquus* (Pl. II, fig. 1, and Pl. IV, fig. 2), shows the absence of crimping, greater breadth in proportion to length and height, and excess of cement, even as compared with the thick-plated variety of that species; whilst as regards $E.$ *primigenius* (Pl. IX, fig. 1, and Pl. XII, fig. 1) these discrepancies are still more pronounced.

Ultimate true molar.—Among the numerous instances of this ponderous tooth met with on the Norfolk Coast, I find eight entire specimens, viz. two upper and six lower, from which the following data are determinable.

The extremes of the ridge formula are $x\,11\,x$ and $x\,14\,x$.   In one upper it is $x\,13\,x$, the other being $x\,14\,x$.   In three lower, perhaps four, it is $x\,13\,x$, one has $x\,14\,x$ and another $x\,11\,x$.   Perhaps, as inferred by Falconer,[1] an additional ridge might be present; but the enormous dimensions attained by the larger specimens render it very improbable that the formula ever exceeded $x\,15\,x$.   The longest molar of which I am cognizant is 13 inches in length, and the shortest, with the same formula, $x\,13\,x$, is 9·4 inches in length. As to width I find it ranges from 3 to 4 inches.   It is true that the colossal teeth of *E. antiquus* (p. 173, Pl. XX, figs. 1 and 2), are much longer, but their plates are crowded together, and the lower molars taper very much posteriorly, which condition seems to be rare in *E. meridionalis*.

It is unnecessary to repeat the characters which distinguish the crown of the latter from that of the other two extinct species.   The only molar with which one is likely to confound it is an unusually thick-plated crown of *E. antiquus*, but the expansion of its disc and the pronounced crimping (not, however, invariably present on every disc), together with a ridge formula not under $x\,15\,x$, will suffice to distinguish such a molar from that in question.[2]   These comparisons are well shown in Pl. XXIV, figs. 1 and 2, as compared with the last molars of *E. antiquus* (Pl. V, fig. 1, Pl. IV, fig. 1, Pl. III, fig. 1, Pl. II, figs. 2 and 3, and Pl. XX, figs. 1 and 2) on the one hand, and of *E. primigenius* on the other (Pl. VIII, fig. 3, Pl. IX, fig. 2, Pl. XIII, figs. 1 and 1 *a*, and Pl. XIV, figs. 1, 2, and 3).

According to the foregoing data the ridge formula of the molar series of *E. meridionalis* will stand as follows:

	Milk-Molars.			True Molars.	
I.	II.	III.	IV.	V.	VI.
$x\,3\,x-?$	$x\,6\,x-?$	$x\,8\,x-?$	$x\,8\,x-x\,9\,x$	$x\,9\,x-x\,11\,x$	$x\,13\,x-x\,14\,x$
$x\,3\,x-?$	$x\,6\,x-?$	$x\,8\,x-!$	$x\,7\,x-x\,9\,x$	$x\,9\,x-x\,11\,x$	$x\,11\,x-x\,14\,x$

These figures, with the exception of my error referred to in regard to the penultimate milk-molar, are substantially the same as were differentiated by Falconer from his researches, with additions consequent on discoveries made since his essays were written.[3]

As compared with *E. planifrons*, whose molars (of all the Sewalik species) come nearest to the above in regard to the dental elements and number of plates, the ridge formula, according to Falconer, is as follows:[4]

	Milk-Molars.			True Molars.	
I.	II.	III.	IV.	V.	VI.
$x\,3\,x$	$x\,6\,x$	$x\,7\,x$	$x\,7\,x$	$x\,8\,x$	$x\,10\,x$
$x\,3\,x$	$x\,6\,x$	$x\,7\,x$	$x\,7\,x$	$x\,8-x\,9\,x$	$x\,10\,x-x\,11\,x$

[1] Op. cit., vol. ii, p. 118.
[2] Page 46.
[3] Op. cit., vol. ii, pp. 118 and 176.
[4] Op. cit., vol. ii, p. 91.

As compared with *E. insignis*, as far as known, and on the same authority—

Milk.			True.		
I.	II.	III.	IV.	V.	VI.
$\frac{x\,2\,x}{x\,2\,x}$	$\frac{x\,5\,x}{x\,3\,x}$	$\frac{x\,7\,x}{x\,7\,x}$	$\frac{x\,7\,x}{7\,x}$	$\frac{x\,8\,x}{x\,8-9\,x}$	$\frac{x\,10-11\,x}{x\,10-13\,x}$

V. OSTEOLOGY.

1. CRANIUM AND MANDIBLE.

The only portions of the skull of *E. meridionalis* hitherto derived from British strata are the fragments of upper and lower jaws just described. The highly suggestive skulls in the Museum of the Piti Palace, Florence, from the Valley of the Arno, furnish very conclusive evidence in connection with the osteological characters of this Elephant, and have been for the most part described by Nesti and Falconer.[1] Having inspected these remains, and compared them with the same parts of other extinct European species, I can endorse the views advanced by Falconer in his excellent descriptions.

As far as the skulls of *E. meridionalis*, *E. antiquus*, and *E. primigenius* are concerned, the lengthened comparisons given at page 128 need not be repeated. These, however, may be briefly summarised as follows:

1. The skull of the Meridional Elephant, from the vertex to the nasal aperture, is relatively shorter than those of the Mammoth and Asiatic Elephant, approaching nearer to that of the African and the short-crowned cranium of *E. planifrons* and other Sewalik species. Unfortunately no skull of *E. antiquus* is available.

2. The posterior border of the vertex is transverse and rounded in the Meridional, although not to the extent apparent in the crown of the African skull; whilst in the Mammoth and Asiatic Elephant it is narrower, and rising higher gives the prominence to the skull which distinguishes at a glance the crania of the two latter from the African.

3. As in all Elephants with ponderous incisors, the premaxillaries are long and broad; and the frontal depression of the Asiatic and Mammoth is more or less apparent also in the Meridional, whereas the same part is flat in the African.

4. The spaces between the temporal fossæ is narrower than in the Asiatic and Mammoth Elephants, contrasting with the relative greater dimensions in the African and *E. planifrons*.

5. The nasal aperture is nearer to the vertex than in the Asiatic and Mammoth, in consequence of the lowness of the crown.

[1] 'Nuova Giornale de Liter.,' 1825, and 'Pal. Mem.,' vol. ii, p. 121.

6. The incisive alveoli are nearly parallel; whilst they diverge considerably in the Mammoth and Asiatic, as seen in Woodcuts, figs. 1, 2, and 3, pages 130 and 131.

7. The lachrymal tubercle is pointed in *E. meridionalis*, and more prominent than in the Mammoth.

8. The zygoma is much below the level of the condyles in the Meridional, as obtains in the African and in the short-crowned fossil Elephants of Northern India, to wit, *E. Namadicus*, *E. planifrons*, &c.; moreover, it inclines to the molars at an angle of 35°, whilst it is nearly parallel to them in the Mammoth and Asiatic Elephant.

In fine, taken with all these and other, but minor, particulars, the skull of the Meridional is broadly distinct from that of the Mammoth and Asiatic Elephant. It is allied to the African, but more so to the other short-crowned species of the Sewalik deposits, with which careful comparisons may establish still closer relationships. To what extent these well-marked distinctions would compare with the skull of *E. antiquus* I am unable to state.

2. CERVICAL VERTEBRÆ.

Atlas.

Numerous entire specimens of this bone are preserved in the British Museum and Norwich Collections.

No. 36,436, B. M., an anterior view of which is shown in Plate XVII, fig. 3, was dredged off the coast of Essex, opposite CLACTON. The transverse processes are injured. Here the odontoid cavity, as formerly pointed out, is much higher than broad as compared with the same in *E. primigenius* and *E. antiquus*, and the upper surface of the arch is curved instead of being flat in them (figs. 1 and 2). It is evidently, however, subject to individual differences, as shown by Davies in the case of the latter species.[1] The above atlas is rivalled by another colossal specimen, also from the NORFOLK COAST, in the possession of R. Johnson, Esq., of Palling, Norfolk. The dimensions, as compared with the huge bone of *E. meridionalis* from Tuscany, figured by Cuvier in the 'Ossemen. Fossil.,' pl. xvii, figs. 3 and 4,[2] are as follows :

Maximum breadth, 18·5, against the Tuscan, which is 19·2 inches.

    ,,   height,   10·5   ditto   9·3   ,,

Vertebral and odontoid canals, 5×4, against the Tuscan, which is 3·6×4·5 inches.

The anterior condyloid articulations in Mr. Johnson's specimen are each 6×4·5 inches by tape along their curves. The foramen for the first cervical nerve is very large, and exposed in all, being 1·8×1·3 inches in breadth.

[1] 'Cat. Brady Collection,' p. 16.
[2] This atlas is also figured by De Blainville, 'Osteographie,' pl. iv.

The general outlines of the condyloid cups will be seen to vary in the three species. They are oval in the Mammoth (fig. 1), more rounded in *E. antiquus* (fig. 2) externally, and less circular in *E. meridionalis* (fig. 3); but the excessive height as compared with the width, so pronounced in the latter specimen, is not the case in the huge atlas from Tuscany, which assimilates best in the relative dimensions of the canal and the condyloid surfaces to the same parts in fig. 2 of *E. antiquus*; the upper surface of the arch, however, is not so flat as in the latter, and assimilates to the Clacton bone in that particular.

Axis.

The vertebral canal in the two recent Elephants differs somewhat. In the Asiatic the opening is larger in the vertical, as compared with the transverse diameter, than in the African. In these respects the Mammoth (Pl. XVII, fig. 6) agrees with the former, whilst that of *E. meridionalis* (fig. 4) is decidedly like that of the latter. Unfortunately the axis of *E. antiquus* (fig. 5) has lost the greater portion of the arch, but it seems to have been very broad, like that of the two last-named species; its anterior articular surfaces are subtriangular, and outer margins projecting with the odontoid process excentral and close to the dorsal border of the centrum.

The huge axis, No. 27,872, B. M. (fig. 4), like the atlas (fig. 3), was dredged off CLACTON, Essex, and, as far as the articulating surfaces are concerned, might have belonged to the same individual.[1]

Several of the other cervical vertebræ in the Norwich Museum, and in Mr. R. Johnson's Collection from the NORFOLK COAST, indicate the enormous dimensions of the animals. They show, however, no diagnostic characters as compared with other species.

An enormous and nearly entire bone, possibly the third cervical, in Mr. R. Johnson's Collection, affords the following measurements:

Entire height 8 inches.

Height of centrum $5 \cdot 5 \times 8 \cdot 5$ inches.

Breadth of circular neural canal $5 \cdot$ inches.

Thickness of the centrum $4 \cdot$ inches.

Another, possibly also a third cervical, has a centrum $7 \cdot 5 \times 8 \cdot 5$ inches in breadth, and is $3 \cdot 4$ inches in thickness.

3. DORSO-LUMBAR VERTEBRÆ.

As far as the other bones of the spinal column are concerned, there is not much to observe of importance beyond size.

[1] Nesti, 'Nuov. Giorn. de Liter.,' No. 24, p. 194, gives the dimensions of an axis from the Val d'Arno as follows:—Height $0 \cdot 325$; breadth of centrum $0 \cdot 268$; anterior articular facet $0 \cdot 162 \times 0 \cdot 107$ mètre.

A centrum of a first dorsal in the above gentleman's possession is 7·4 × 10·4 inches in the transverse direction, and is 3·5 inches in thickness.

There is a large second dorsal, No. 27,878, B. M., covered with barnacles and shells of *Serpulæ*, dredged off CLACTON, Essex.

The tip of the spine is lost, otherwise the bone is entire. It is 22 inches in height, with a maximum breadth of 13 inches. The centrum is 2·2 inches in thickness, and 5·4 in height, by 6·5 in breadth. The vertebral canal is nearly an equilateral triangle, being 2·7 in height, by 2·8 inches at the base.

Other two specimens, one a first dorsal, the other from about the middle of the series, are in the above collection from the same locality. It is just possible, however, that both may belong to *E. antiquus*. The first dorsal has a neural canal 3·6 × 2·8 inches in breadth; the centrum is 5 inches in height and 6 inches broad. The height of spine and neural canal is 14 inches, and thickness 2·4 inches. The middle dorsal shows a less triangular canal, and is 2·5 × 2·8 in breadth, with a centrum 5 inches in height by 6 in breadth. The height, including spine, from the centrum, is 16·5, and thickness of the latter 2·4 inches.

The fragments of RIBS and portions of STERNA in collections are not sufficiently entire for comparative purposes.

4. PELVIC GIRDLE.

The huge pelvic bones from the Norfolk Coast have been already referred to at page 151, in connection with the elements of the pelvis of the Mammoth, with which they agree in general characters but differ remarkably as regards dimensions. At the same time, until similar parts in *E. antiquus* have been described, it seems uncertain whether these huge bones belong to its skeleton or to that of the species under consideration.

5. SHOULDER GIRDLE.

Scapula.

Remains of huge shoulder-blades are represented by several specimens in the Norwich and British Museums, but, with the exception of the glenoid cavity, few other points admit of comparison being made between them and the scapulæ described at page 145. The following table will suffice to show the dimensions attained by the Elephants from the FOREST BED and other deposits along the East Coast of England.

	No. 275, Gunn Collection, Norwich Museum, Pl. xviii, fig. 3 (E. meridionalis?).	Norwich Museum (E. meridionalis?).	Norwich Museum (E. meridionalis?).	275, Gunn Collection, Norwich Museum (E. meridionalis?).	Norwich Museum (E. meridionalis?).	274, Gunn Collection (E. primigenius?).	271, Gunn Collection (E. primigenius?), Pl. xxii, fig. 4.
Height of glenoid cavity[1]	11·5	11	11	11	11	7·5	8·5
Maximum breadth of glenoid cavity	6	6	6	5.5	6	4	4·5
Antero-posterior diameter of neck	12·5	13·8	13	11·5	12·5	9	10
Distance of base of spine from margin of the glenoid cavity	6	6·5	5	4	6	(Lost)	4

In comparison with the Mammoth, it appears that the glenoid cavity is not so compressed laterally and is broader inferiorly in the larger scapula, as shown in Plate XVIII, fig. 3, as opposed to the same parts in the Mammoth (Plate XXII, fig. 4, and Plate XV, fig. 1). The neck, too, is relatively broader in the former.

With reference to the localities where the fragments quoted in the Table were found, No. 271 (Plate XXII, fig. 4) is a left scapula of the Mammoth in the Gunn Collection. It was dredged off YARMOUTH near Kessingland, but only a fragment of the blade, neck, and glenoid cavity is preserved. No. 275 seems to have been dug out of the FOREST BED, as portions of the matrix still adhere to the bone. The second in the Table has a label attached, stating that it was "found at MUNDESLEY, after 'a great run' on the top of the Forest Bed, consisting of nodules of blue clay mixed with red, gravelly pan, and close to a jaw of *Trogontherium*." In the British Museum there is a portion of a glenoid cavity, the maximum width of which is 5·5 inches, and another entire articular surface; both are from HAPPISBOROUGH on the Norfolk coast. The height of the articular surface of the latter is 9 inches by callipers, and 10 inches by tape along the curves of the cavity; width, 4 inches above, 4·5 at the middle, and 4·6 inches below.

6. HUMERUS.

The colossal dimensions of the Elephantine remains met with in the fluviomarine and freshwater deposits of Norfolk and Suffolk coasts receive ample confirmation from the

---

[1] Nesti gives the following dimensions of the glenoid cavity of a scapula from Val d'Arno:—Height 0·291 mètre, maximum breadth 0·170 (11·5 by 6·6 inches), breadth of neck 0·380 mètre=15·0 inches. The entire length of this scapula was 1·080 m., and spine, ·900 m. 'Nuovo Giorn. de Literat.,' No. 24, p. 194.

appendicular as well as the axial elements of skeletons. Taking the complete skeleton of the famous " Choonee " of India in the Museum of the Royal College of Surgeons of England as a standard of the Asiatic Elephant, we find its humerus is 35 inches in length and the height of the skeleton at the commencement of the dorsal region is 103 inches. The huge humerus in Miss A. Gurney's Collection in the Norwich Museum has a maximum length of 53 inches. This specimen, as compared with the above, would give a height of 156 inches or 13 feet, being one foot over that of the largest recorded recent African Elephant, which rarely attains the maximum height of 12 feet at the withers.

Before proceeding to the consideration of the characters of the humerus inferred to belong to *E. meridionalis*, it will be necessary to refer to the humerus of *E. antiquus* as recorded at page 57. In addition to the data there given, I have acquired the following further evidences since the publication of my memoir.

In a valuable collection of Mammalian remains from ILFORD, recently bequeathed to the Jermyn Street Museum by the late Dr. Cotton, are numerous teeth and bones of *E. primigenius* and several relics of *E. antiquus*.

The superb humerus, No. 18, represented on Plate XVI, fig. 6, has lost the greater part of the large tuberosity, and the head is slightly injured, but otherwise it is entire. The dimensions are given in the Table opposite. The noteworthy points in comparison with the humeri of other species may be indicated as follows:

1. The supinator ridge descends more perpendicularly from the shaft (fig. 6 *a*), and is more horizontal towards its apex (fig. 6), than in any of the other species; the nearest approach to it seen is the humerus of *E. meridionalis* (fig. 2).

2. The internal condyloid ridge (fig. 6 *a*), in proportion to the size of the bone, is narrower than in the Mammoth (fig. 1 *a*) and *E. meridionalis* (fig. 2 *a*), but not more so than in the *E. Asiaticus* (fig. 4 *a*).

3. The contours of the external and internal articular surfaces of the condyles (fig. 6 *b*) show more expansive surfaces than in any of the allied species, especially *E. meridionalis* (fig. 3). The concavity of the inferior border of the articular surface (fig. 6 *b*) is deeper and more central than in the other two extinct Elephants and the recent species, whilst the trochlear depression is more circular than in them.

In all these characters the above humerus agrees with the specimens already described at p. 58 and referred to *E. antiquus*, and with which, I think, it may be fairly included.

The following Table represents the dimensions of the humerus in full-grown individuals of the recent and certain extinct Elephants.

	Entire length.	Smallest girth.	Girth proximal extremity.	Girth distal extremity.	Width distal articular surface.	Dimensions of articular surface of head. (by tape).
No. 2744, R. C. S. E., *E. Asiaticus*, Pl. XVI, fig. 4...	36·5	16·5	33·5	27	8·5	7·5 × 7
708n, B. M., *E. Africanus*, Pl. XVI, fig. 5	35·5	13·1	29·5	24	7·8	7·9 × 7
23,151, B. M., *E. antiquus*...............................	41	22·5	Lost	?	?	13 × 10·5
18, Cotton Collection, *E. antiquus*, Pl. XVI, fig. 6 ...	41·4	17½	...	32	8·5	10 × 7·8
36,700, B. M., *E. Namadicus*............................	47	?	45	?	?	
30,531, B. M., *E. primigenius*, Pl. XVI, fig. 1........	34	13·5	...	23·5	8	9 × 6
C/128, B. M., Brady Collection, *E. primigenius*	28·7	11·8	27·8	20·5	6·5	9 × 5
200, Gunn Collection, Norwich Museum, *E. meridionalis*, Pl. XVI, fig. 2 [1]	51	22	45	40	11·5	15 × 9·5
Miss A. Gurney's Collection, Norwich Museum	53	26·6	39	...	13	15 × 10·5
Norwich Museum, *E. meridionalis*	...	...	...	...	...	
Norwich Museum, *E. meridionalis*, Pl. XVI, fig. 3 [2]...	...	...	45	37	10	13·5 × 12
B. M., Val d'Arno; 'Pal. Mem.,' vol. ii, p. 143	47	...	...	32	13	

With reference to *E. meridionalis*, there are other portions of articular surfaces and pieces of shafts in the Norwich Museum, and in several private collections, representing fully as large, if not larger, colossal Elephants than the foregoing. The distal end of an enormous arm-bone, No. 33,396, B. M., from HΑΡΡΙSΠΟΚΟΥΟΙ, Norfolk coast, has a breadth of articular surface of 11 inches. Notably, the inner condyle is proportionally larger than in *E. primigenius* and the humerus in the Cotton Collection. The ginglymus is 6 inches in thickness, and 11½ by tape in the antero-posterior direction; and the inner condyle, by the same appliance, furnishes an antero-posterior length of 16·5 inches against 14·5 of the outer condyle.

One point is very striking in the majority of these enormous bones in comparison with humeri of very old individuals of, at all events, the Mammoth and recent species, that is, the general absence of pronounced ridges, in place of which there is a general smoothness of the surface, as seen in bones of adolescent animals, whilst the epiphyses, which are the last to become anchylosed, are all firmly united. The absence of prominent ridges might tend to the belief that these colossal Proboscideans were tardy in their movements and seldom given to active muscular exertion.

Referring to Pl. XVI, the more distinctive characters of the humerus of the *E. meridionalis* (figs. 2 and 3), as compared with the two extinct and the two recent species, appear to me as follows :

1. It is stouter than that of *E. antiquus*, and rather more so than in *E. primigenius*, and much more so than in either of the recent Elephants.

[1] The external condyle by tape in the antero-posterior measurement is 12½ inches, and the internal 13½ inches; the width of the bicipital groove is 2½ inches.

[2] The antero-posterior measurement by tape of the outer condyle is 9 inches, and the inner 10½ inches, and of the central portion of the ginglymus 9½ inches.

2. The supinator ridge (fig. 2) is shorter and more horizontal than in any of them.

3. The upward continuation of the supinator ridge (fig. 2 *a*) is not nearly so well defined as in them.

4. The contour of the distal articular surface (fig. 2 *a*) is more like that of the Mammoth (fig. 1 *a*) than *E. antiquus* (fig. 6 *a*) and the recent species (figs. 4 and 5). This refers to the configurations of the condyles, the arc on the lower border, and trochlear depression.

5. The internal condyloid ridge is broader (fig. 2) than in any of the above.

6. The deltoid ridge (fig. 2) is not so prominent as in *E. primigenius* and *E. Asiaticus*, and is more in keeping with *E. antiquus* and *E. Africanus*.

Taken collectively, as far as materials enable me to determine, the comparisons already instituted in connection with the humerus in the three extinct and the two living species seem to furnish the following contrasts as regards the former :

1. The bicipital groove is much the same in all the extinct British Elephants.

2. The contour of the head is more circular, and it is less compressed in *E. meridionalis* than, at all events, in the Mammoth.

3. The supinator ridge is shorter, and is the least salient in *E. meridionalis*.

4. The deltoid ridge is prominent in *E. primigenius*, and not nearly so pronounced in the other two.

5. The hollow in front of the supinator ridge is not so deep in *E. primigenius* as in the other two.

6. The trochlear depression is deeper in *E. antiquus* than in the others.

7. The margins of the cubital articular surfaces are not so sharp and defined in *E. meridionalis* as in *E. primigenius* and *E. antiquus*.

8. The contour of the lower border of the cubital articular surface is more central in *E. antiquus* than in the other species.

9. The internal condyloid ridge is broader in *E. meridionalis* than in the other two.

10. The outer condyle is more globose in *E. antiquus* than in either of the two other species.

11. The humerus relatively is not so stout in the *E. antiquus* as in the other two.

7. CUBITUS.

The relations of the two elements of the forearm, to wit, the amount of obliquity of the radius in *E. meridionalis*, as compared with other species, remain to be shown when specimens turn up. At present I have not seen the entire bones of the same individual *in sitû*.

Ulna.

The large ulnæ from the EAST COAST, like the arm-bones, present few prominent ridges for the fasciæ and muscular attachments, as compared with the gnarled humeri and ulnæ of old individuals of the Mammoth. The radial pit is more open and shallow than in the Mammoth, and the shaft is not so flattened nor are the ridges posteriorly so strongly pronounced. The aspects of proximal and distal articulations furnish apparently no characters of importance.

The fragment of the distal extremity, No. 246 of the Gunn Collection, from the "Iron Pan of the Forest Bed," shows a less perpendicular radial facet than I have seen in the Mammoth, but there appears some individual variation in specimens, rendering this character of little value. The dimensions of its carpal articulation is 5·5 inches in the antero-posterior (by tape along the surface), and 7 inches in the transverse diameter.

A proximal fragment, including a little more than half the shaft, in the same Collection, shows a girth of midshaft of 17 inches, and a conjoint breadth[1] of the proximal articular surfaces of 11 inches. Another fragment of the proximal extremity, No. 33,395, B. M., from the East Coast, shows a wide and gaping radial pit. But no entire ulna from the above situation has come under my notice.

Radius

An entire radius of a colossal-sized Elephant, in the possession of Mr. R. Johnson, of Palling, near Stalham, Norfolk, was found at Mundesley, on the coast, along with the humerus (Pl. XVI, fig. 2) and the enormous femur described at page 222. Mr. Johnson was good enough to permit me to take a few measurements of the above and other bones in his collection. With reference to this radius I have taken the following measurements:

Length 30 inches.[2]

Girth, midshaft, 10·4 inches.

Girth, proximal end, 16 inches.

Girth, distal end, 25 inches.

Distal articular surface 9 in the a. p. d. by 6 inches in the transverse.

Proximal articular surface 5¼ by 3·5 inches in the antero-posterior diameter.

The anterior surface of the shaft, as before noticed,[3] is round and prominent down to about the middle third. The outer and inner sides seem flattened as far as a thick coat of matrix would permit inspection. The shape is teetiform, with rather abrupt slopes.

---

[1] Both Cuvier ('Oss. Foss.,' figs. 15, 16, and 17) and De Blainville (' Osteog.,' pl. v) notice large fossil ulnæ, neither of which specimens from their dimensions appear to belong to the Mammoth. The former authority shows that, excepting being a stouter bone, it shows no character distinct from the Indian Elephant. The radial pit, however, is much narrower than in the Pl. XVIII, fig. 1 a. Their lengths are 0·825 and 0·832 mètre respectively. De Blainville's specimen, however, has the distal articulation wanting. Nesti (op. cit.) gives the length of an Italian specimen 0·840 mètre.

[2] Nesti records an instance of a radius of *E. meridionalis* as 0·752 m. in length by 0·111 m. in breadth. 'Nuov. Giorn. de Literat.,' No. 24, p. 194.

[3] Page 158.

8. CARPUS.

Scaphoid.—I have already referred to this bone as met with in the FOREST BED, in comparison with that of the Mammoth.[1] The specimen alluded to is of colossal dimensions, and No. 150 of the Gunn Collection.

The following are its characters:

Extreme length   7 inches.
    „   breadth   6   „
Radial facet   3 × 2·5 inches.
Trapezoidal facet   4·5 (a. p. d.) × 2·2 inches.
Upper lunare facet   2·5 × 1·   „
Lower   „   1·8 × 1·4   „

There is no facet for the trapezium.

The radial facet is nearly erect, as in the Mammoth.

The trapezoidal and magnal facets are continuous, the former is nearly flat with the latter rising gradually upwards from it, as in the African Elephant.[2]

Lunare.—One of the largest lunares I have seen from the EAST COAST is No. 155 of the Gunn Collection. It is covered with barnacles, and is in all probability either a a dredged or a beach specimen.

The length is 7½,[3] and maximum breadth 7 inches.

The radial facet is 5¾ by 5½ inches.

The magnal facet 6 by 6, and maximum thickness 4½ inches.

The characters of the above specimen, as compared with the same parts in the Mammoth, have been already recorded at page 159 along with other large lunares, to wit, the obliquity of the ulnar facet, the slight concavity of the radial aspect, absence of scaphoidal attachments—not uncommon in similar bones of large individuals of both the Mammoth and Asiatic forms—a deep concavity of the marginal surface, especially towards its extremity, from whence it rises up into a plateau on the further extremity of this articular surface. The presence, however, of scaphoidal facets is shown in No. 151 of the Gunn Collection. It does not display so pronounced flattening and concavity of the magnal aspect, otherwise it is of about the same dimensions as the preceding.

In a specimen in the King Collection, Museum of Practical Geology, Jermyn Street, also from the EAST COAST deposits, the same measurements give a length of 6½ by 6 inches in the transverse diameter, the radial facet is 5 × 5¼ inches. The magnal facet shows a deep pit in the same position as in the last, and is 5¾ by 6 inches ; the thickness 4½ inches.

[1] Page 159.

[2] A shorter scaphoid is recorded by Nesti from the Val d'Arno. Its length is 0·165 mètre, and maximum breadth 0·140 mètre.

[3] Nesti gives a lunare not so large from Northern Italy. It is 0·158 mètre in length.

A still smaller bone, No. 33,415, B. M., from the East Coast, is 6×5·8 in breadth, and 3·5 inches in thickness. The characters are not quite so much pronounced, but indeed the lunare furnishes little of a reliable character for diagnostic purposes, and like many of the other bones can only be doubtfully referred to *E. meridionalis.*

Cuneiforme.—The largest specimen from the Norfolk Coast I have seen, and certainly of colossal dimensions, is No. 156 of the Gunn Collection. The following are its dimensions :

Length 10 inches.[1]

Maximum breadth 6 inches.

Ulnar aspect 4 (a. p. d.) by 6¾ inches.

Unciform aspect 6×7 inches.

Thickness 4 inches.

The lunare facets are well developed.

No. 159 of the above Collection, from the same locality, is 7¼×6 inches. Ulnar facet 4×5¾, and the unciform 6×5 inches ; thickness 3¼ inches. Here the lunare facets are also well developed, and the pisiform facet is quite erect and triangular.

A smaller bone, No. 63 of Mr. Savin's Collection, found at Overstrand, Cromer, is 7×5½ ; ulnar facet 4×5½ ; thickness 3 inches.

These cuneiformes have been already referred to[2] in comparison with similar bones of the Mammoth. They show no very distinct characters from the latter, but differ from the African species.

With reference to *E. antiquus*, it will be seen that the admeasurements of this bone[3] rival the largest of the above specimens, otherwise I can see no characters sufficient to separate them.

The *pisiforme* is not represented in any collections examined by me.

Trapezium.—The specimen, No. 33,418, B. M., from East Anglia (Pl. XIX, fig. 10), has been already described[4] in connection with what appears to be the equivalent bones in *E. primigenius* and *E. antiquus* (figs. 8 and 9).[5]

The differences between the three seem pronounced; and, unless subject to variability, this element is diagnostic of the three species.

Trapezoidale.—This bone, referred to[6] in connection with the Mammoth, is represented

---

[1] Nesti records an Italian cuneiforme of much smaller length, and somewhat greater width, being 0·156 by 0·155 m. in width.

[2] Page 160.

[3] Page 60.

[4] Page 161.

[5] None of these seemingly, as regards size, can compare with this bone in the *E. meridionalis* of Northern Italy. Nesti, 'Nuov. Giorn. de Literat.,' No. 24, p. 194, assigns a length of 0·240 m. or 9·4 inches to one specimen.

[6] Page 161.

by No. 160 of the Gunn Collection, Norwich Museum. It is from the FOREST-BED Series, and measures 5 × 2·8 inches.[1] Its scaphoidal surface is 4·8 inches in length, and trapezial 2 × 2·4 inches. In comparison with the foregoing bones of *E. primigenius* and *E. antiquus*, it assimilates more closely to the broad surface of the latter than to that of the former.

Magnum.—The dimensions of this bone in the foot, which I have referred to *E. antiquus*,[2] exceeds the dimensions of the largest specimen I have seen from the EAST COAST, and another, No. 18,244, B. M., from GRAYS, ESSEX, in all probability also belongs to *E. antiquus*. The latter is shown in pl. li, fig. 6, of the 'Fauna Antiqua Sivalensis,' and is 6·4 × 5·8 inches in width. It is undistinguishable from the former in size and characters. Nor does it appear that, unless in rather smaller dimensions, the following from the EAST COAST differ from them, unless in minor points, namely, No. 33,410, B. M., which has the convexities and concavities of the articular surfaces less pronounced, and the metacarpal surface not so broad in proportion.

The dimensions of this specimen from HAPPISBOROUGH, NORFOLK, are—

Maximum (a. p. d.) 6·8 inches.[3]
Breadth[1]   5·0   „
Thickness   5·8   „

A large magnum, scarcely referable to *E. primigenius* on account of size, is shown by No. 164, Gunn Collection. It was dredged off YARMOUTH, NORFOLK. Its

Length is 6 inches.
Breadth 4·5   „
Facets for the three metacarpals 4·5 × 2·4 and 4·5 × 1 inches.
Unciform aspect 5 × 2·5 inches.
Height of the specimen is 5·5 inches.

Unciforme.—This bone in the foot of *E. antiquus*, previously noticed,[4] rivals in size many of the huge bones from the East Coast.

No. 33,407, B. M., from the NORFOLK COAST, has an antero-posterior and transverse diameter of 7 inches, and is 6 inches in thickness.

No. 172, Gunn Collection, from the FOREST BED, gives the following dimensions:

	E. meridionalis.		E. antiquus.	
Maximum length	6·5	inches.	6·8	inches.
Breadth	7	„	7·9	„
Cuneiform facet	5·2 × 5·2	„	5·8 × 4·8	„

[1] Nesti gives a larger specimen from Northern Italy. It is 0·146 × 0·125 m. or 5·7 × 4·8 inches.
[2] Page 60.
[3] Nesti gives one which is 0·160 × 0·120. I have found considerable discrepancies individually in these two dimensions in various species (see "Dentition and Osteology of the Maltese Fossil Elephants," 'Trans. Zool. Soc.,' vol. vi, p. 72).
[4] Page 60.

	E. meridionalis.	*E. antiquus.*
Third metacarpal facet	5 ×2·1 inches.	3×1 inches.
Fourth „ „	4·4×4 „	} 7×4 „
Fifth „ „	4 ×3 „	
Magnal facet	5 ×3·5 „	
Maximum height	5·6 „	6 „

The above contrasts with the same parts of *E. antiquus*, recorded at p. 60. The discrepancies, however, may be the result of specific or individual character, but certainly the relative sizes of the surfaces for the third metacarpal are remarkable.

9. METACARPUS.

The characters of the metacarpals met with on the East Coast, when compared with equivalent bones of the recent species and those of *E. primigenius* and *E. antiquus*, show little that is noteworthy, excepting, perhaps, in the proximal extremities of the third digit, as shown in Pl. XVIII, fig. 5. They, moreover, seem to differ considerably individually in their contours, especially of the two outer toes.

The following are a few of the characters and dimensions of the more characteristic specimens:

A *first* digit from OVERSTRAND, CROMER, in Mr. Savin's possession, is 5 inches in length. The proximal facet is 3×2, and distal 5 inches (by tape) ×2·5 inches; the girth, midshaft, is 8·4 inches. This specimen does not appear to differ from the equivalent bone in the African Elephant, as has been indicated.[1]

Third digit.—The specimen (Pl. XVIII, fig. 5) has been referred to;[2] it is from HAPPISBOROUGH. In this metacarpal (No. 33,428, B. M.) the magnal facet for the fourth metacarpal is not nearly so broad as in *E. antiquus*.

This very large bone is 10·8 inches in length, the height of the proximal extremity being 6 inches, and smallest girth of shaft 11·8 inches. The upper portion of the magnal facet is more concave than in the bone attributed to *E. antiquus*—a character I have observed in all the large third metacarpals from the EAST COAST.

Another specimen in the Gunn Collection is 8·5 inches in length; the breadth of the outer proximal facet for the fourth metacarpal and unciform is 4×3·5 inches; the antero-posterior length of the distal articular surface (by tape) is 5·5×3·8 inches. It displays the same characters of the proximal articular surface as in the former.

Fourth digit.—A metacarpal in the Norwich Museum is 7·5 in length, with an unciform facet of 4×3·5 inches. The surface for the third metacarpal is 3·5×1·4 inches, whilst that for the fifth metacarpal is 4·5×1·8 inches. The distal (a. p. d. by tape) is 5·5 inches, and transverse 2·8 inches. The girth, midshaft, is 10 inches.

[1] Page 162.　　　　[2] Page 163.

Another specimen, also in the Gunn Collection, and from the FOREST BED, is 7 inches in length. The unciform surface is 3·5 in height by 2·8 inches in width; the third metacarpal facet is 2·8 × 1·4 inches.

Distal end 5·8 × 3 inches.

Girth, midshaft, 11 inches.

Fifth digit (Pl. XVIII, figs. 8 and 8 *a*), No. 33,433, B. M., is from HAPPISBOROUGH. It is 7 × 5·2 inches.

As indicated with reference to the Mammoth, the unciform facet (fig. 8 *a*) is much more ovate; otherwise I cannot perceive any peculiarity worth recording.

10. PHALANGES

Are not uncommon in collections, but do not present, excepting in their large dimensions, any points different from the equivalent elements of the feet of allied species.

A first phalanx of possibly the second digit, from OVERSTRAND, Cromer, in Mr. Savin's Collection, is 5 inches in length, with a girth at the middle of 6·4 inches. The proximal articular surface is 3 × 2·5 inches, and the distal 5 × 2·5 inches.

11. FEMUR.

Comparisons between this bone and that of the Mammoth have been already furnished.[1]

As compared with any femur at all referable to European extinct Elephants, the specimen in the possession of Mr. Randall Johnson, of Palling, far outstrips the largest in dimensions. It was discovered at MUNDESLEY, in the FOREST BED, in conjunction with the humerus, No. 200 of the Gunn Collection (Pl. XVI, fig. 2), and the huge radius also referred to.[2] Conjointly they represent a stupendous Elephant only second to the Dinotherium in size. I regret being unable to furnish a representation of this huge thighbone. I was fortunate, however, through the kindness of Mr. Johnson, in being permitted to take the following measurements during a hurried survey of his valuable Collection at Stalham, in the company of my friend, Mr. Gunn.

The specimen is in a perfect state of preservation, without seemingly a chip throughout its vast surface.

The total length is 60 inches.[3]

Breadth of proximal end at the great trochanter 10 inches.

[1] Page 164.   [2] Page 217.

[3] The famous Eppelsheim specimen of the Dinotherium had a femur of 62·7 inches in length.

Girth, midshaft, 20¼ inches.

Breadth across both condyles 12 inches.

Antero-posterior diameter of the outer condyle along the curve, by tape 20, and by callipers 11 inches.

Antero-posterior diameter, by tape, along the curve of the inner condyle 21 inches.

The condyles coalesce more than in the Mammoth, and leave a narrow fissure.[1] The outer condyle is like the African, being more globose than in the Mammoth.

Mr. Johnson possesses, likewise, the distal extremity of another huge femur from PALLING. The antero-posterior diameter of the outer condyle is 17·5 inches, and the inner (both measured along the curve by tape) is 18 inches. The maximum breadth of the intervening sulcus posteriorly is 5·5 inches, and the linear measurement across both condyles 9·5 inches.

Here the intercondyloid space is very *narrow*, as in the Mammoth, and there is considerable bending inwards of the condyles, more so than I have seen in the femur of any other European or fossil Elephant, or, indeed, in either of the recent species.

Another entire femur (Pl. XXVI, figs. 3, 3 *a*, and 3 *b*)[2] was lately discovered by Mr. Savin, at OVERSTRAND, near Cromer, and is now in the possession of Mr. J. Backhouse, West Bank, York, to whom I am under obligations for two excellent photographs of the specimen, and the following data in regard to its dimensions. The bone is nearly entire, excepting the head and neck, which are fractured. This and Mr. Johnson's specimen appear to have belonged to individuals which had perished, like the Irish Elk, by being either mired or drowned, their carcases, in the latter case, floating down a river, and the remains deposited in an estuary or delta.

The total length is 40¾ inches; girth (by tape) at midshaft 18 inches. Breadth at the great trochanter is 14 inches; girth of ditto 36 inches; girth of ball 22 inches. Maximum girth of distal articulation 34 inches. Maximum breadth across the condyles (linear) 10¼ inches. Antero-posterior measurement of the inner condyle (by tape) 16 inches and the outer 18¾ inches.

The general outline of this thigh-bone, judging from figs. 3 and 3 *a*, is quite in keeping with that of Mr. Johnson's specimen. Considering, however, that any points of specific value cannot be determined without careful comparisons, I am constrained to rely altogether on the similarities of contour; whilst as regards dimensions it must be conceded that there are very wide discrepancies. The relation, however, of the CROMER femur with that of the Mammoth would, on the score of size, be quite exceptional, and as regards contour there are the following differences:—In the latter there is a decided bulging about the junction of the middle and lower third externally, as seen in Pl. XIX, fig. 7, and a more general flattening of the shaft in the antero-posterior

[1] This is well seen likewise in pl. xvi, fig. 5, ' Ossem. Fossil,' in a distal fragment from Italy.

[2] Nesti, op. cit., records a femur from the Val d'Arno, 1·400 m., being fully 2 inches longer than the above.

direction; whereas, in both Mr. Johnson's and Mr. Blackhouse's specimens the former is absent, and the shaft is more round, especially about its middle.

The fragment (No. 258 of the Gunn Collection) from the Forest Bed at Walcot, Bacton, described by Falconer,[1] has the head and great trochanter wanting. The distal extremity, although not entire, and the remainder of the shaft, give a length of 47 inches. The girth at midshaft is 20 inches, and the breadth at the point of union of the condyles is 14 inches.

A ball of a femur from the beach of the Norfolk Coast, and No. 237 of the same collection, has a girth of 28 inches.

The distal epiphysis (No. 236) from the above collection, and evidently that of a young animal, as the pitting along the surface for attachment indicates, is represented (Pl. XXII, fig. 5) for the purpose of showing a more gaping intercondyloid fissure than any of the foregoing, or the Italian specimens figured by Cuvier.[2] Moreover, the trochlear depression of fig. 5 will be seen to be much shallower than that of the Mammoth (fig. 6), and the condyles do not converge. How far the discrepancies refer to a youthful condition of *E. meridionalis* or to another species is not easy to determine. That it should be referred to *E. antiquus*, according to the characters of the condyles from Walton,[3] is only in keeping with the appearance in them; but the peculiarity may be inconstant and of less value than a few instances appear to indicate; it is, however, worthy of notice.

As to the dimensions of fig. 5. The inner condyle is 10 inches by tape in the anteroposterior direction, and 4 inches in breadth. The outer is 17 by 4·5 inches, in breadth; the patellar sulcus 9·5 inches in breadth by tape.

12. TIBIA.

The tibia should furnish valuable diagnostic characters, and, supposing the following do not show variability in individuals, there would seem to be some important differences between them and the bones I have referred to *E. primigenius* and *E. antiquus*,[4] more especially as regards the configuration of the articular surfaces and the prominence or otherwise of the shin.

In Mr. Johnson's Collection there is an entire tibia, from Happisborough, of the following dimensions:

Length 24·5 inches.[5]

[1] Op. cit., vol. ii, p. 144.
[2] 'Ossem. Fossil.,' pla. xi, xiv, xvi.
[3] Page 62.
[4] Page 63 and 167.
[5] Nesti gives a tibia of 0·820 m., and Cuvier another Italian specimen of 0·825 m. ('Oss. Fossil.,' vol. ii, p. 226, pl. xvi, fig. 12).

Breadth across the head 8·6 inches.

Diameter of outer condyle (a. p. d.) 4·5 × 3·5 inches.

„ inner 5·5 × 4·5 inches.

Girth of head 25 inches.

„ midshaft 11·8 inches.

Distal articulation (a. p. d.) 5 inches.

Transverse 5·5 inches.

Girth, distal end, 18·8 inches.

Here the spine is prominent, with a pronounced concavity for the extensor muscles, to the extent of 5½ inches broad at the top, with much beetling of the former and deepening of the hollow posteriorly, as shown in the tibia of the Mammoth.

No. 242, Gunn Collection, is an injured tibia from Bacton, of much greater proportions than the last. The transverse diameter of the proximal articular surface is 12 inches, with a girth of head of 35 inches. Here there is also a prominent spine and deep pit for the muscles.

No. 243, Gunn Collection, is a distal end of a large tibia from the "soil of the Forest Bed." The antero-posterior and transverse diameters of the articulations are 5·5 and 6·5 inches respectively. The fibular facet is hollowed out and not erect; it is 4 × 3·5 inches in breadth.

No. 246, Gunn Collection, from the "Iron-pan, Forest Bed," is another enormous distal end, with an articular surface of nearly equilateral dimensions, being 6·5 in the a. p. d. to 6·5 inches in the transverse, consequently like that of E. antiquus (Pl. XIX, fig. 11 a). The fibular facet is small in this specimen as compared with the preceding, but, like it, it is almost horizontal.

No. 247 is a beach specimen, with a tarsal facet of 5 × 6. Here the fibular facet is also nearly horizontal, and large as compared with the last, being 2 × 2 inches.

No. 241 is an entire tibia encrusted with the "Iron Pan" of the Forest Bed. It clearly shows a much smaller animal than any of the foregoing from the same deposit. The length is only 2 feet, and breadth of proximal articulatory surface 8 by 4 inches in the antero-posterior direction. As far as size is a criterion, this bone may have belonged to the Mammoth.

No. 21,305, B. M., is a very large tibia from Ilford, and evidently the leg-bone of an adolescent individual, as the proximal epiphysis is wanting. The shaft is very stout, and altogether too large for the Mammoth. It may possibly belong to E. antiquus. The dimensions are—length 25 inches; girth, midshaft, 12·4 inches; distal articulatory aspect 4 a. p. d. by 5·5 inches in the transverse.

13. FIBULA.

There is a cast of an enormous fibula (No. 26,724, B. M.) from CROMER FOREST BED. The distal end is shown in Pl. XIX, fig. 3, and has been already referred to in connection with that of the Mammoth.[1]

The length is 32·5 inches.

Girth, midshaft, 5·8 inches.

Width, distal end, 5·5 inches.

Malleolar facet 4·5 (transverse) and 4·5 (height) inches.

The tibial articulation is not so erect as in the Mammoth, nor so horizontal as in the African Elephant.

The shaft is broad and flat superiorly, and rounded inferiorly, on its external surface.

No. 240, Gunn Collection, represents the proximal and distal extremities of an enormous fibula from what Mr. Gunn calls the " Soil of the FOREST BED." The tibial facet is a good deal inclined. The astragaloid aspect is 5 inches in breadth by 4 inches in height, and the entire breadth of the distal extremity is 5·5 inches.

No. 256 is nearly an entire fibula from the same situation. Its outer surface is nearly flat and broad, with narrow anterior and posterior sides. The bone is much compressed laterally at its proximal end. The distal articulation is 4·5 inches in breadth. The tibial facet, as in the others, has the articular surface at a low angle ; the dimensions are 3·5 × 3 inches.

The variable character of the shaft of the fibula in Elephants in general leaves little for specific characters, but, as regards dimensions, the above amply support the diagnosis as exhibited by the other elements of the skeleton of *Elephas meridionalis.*

14. TARSUS.

Astragalus.—This element of the foot attains to very large dimensions among the relics from the FOREST BED.

I have elsewhere indicated[2] the chief characters of this bone in relation to that of the Mammoth and recent species. An enormous astragal preserved in the Gunn Collection is 9 × 7 inches in its maximum width and antero-posterior length,[3] with a tibial aspect of 6 × 5½ in the a. p. d. diameter.

No. 254 of Mr. Savin's Collection from the FOREST BED, OVERSTRAND, is 8 by 7 inches in the a. p. d. The tibial facet is 6·4 a. p. d. × 5·5 inches in the transverse direction.

[1] Page 169.
[2] Page 170.
[3] These considerably exceed the dimensions of a Val d'Arno specimen mentioned by Nesti, its length being 0·190 m., and maximum width, 0·163 m.

The external calcaneal facet is 4·5 × 4, and the internal 4·8 × 4 inches; the navicular is 6·4 in breadth, by 3·4 inches in height.

The left astragal, No. 33,425, B. M., from the FOREST BED, HAPPISBOROUGH (Pl. XIX, fig. 6) has the posterior angle almost obsolete, the same being usually pronounced in the Mammoth and Asiatic. The dimensions of the above are—

Length 7·5 inches.
Width 8·4 inches.
Tibial (a. p. d.) 6·4 by 6·4 inches (width).
Navicular facet 3·8 (height) by 7·8 inches (width).
Calcaneal facet (outer) 5 (a. p. d.) by 4 inches (width).
„   „   (inner) 4·8 by 3 inches.

Here, as in the preceding, the interosseous pit between the calcaneal facets is narrow in comparison with the Mammoth and Asiatic, and runs along the entire base.

The absence of pronounced angles and the usual concavities and convexities in the nicely interlocked bones of the recent wild animals, and the majority of the same in the Mammoth, may be another indication of the tardy movements of the colossal denizens of the Pre-glacial forests of East Anglia.

Calcaneum.—One of the largest heel-bones I have seen is in the possession of Mr. Randall Johnson, of Palling, near Stalham. The specimen was obtained at HORGE, in the so-called "Norwich Crag." Its dimensions are—

Length 10 inches.[1]
Width 8 „
Outer astragal facet 5·2 × 2·2 inches.
Inner „   „   5·3 × 2 inches.
Cuboidal facet 4 × 2·4 inches in height.
The girth behind the articulations, or neck of heel, is 14·5 inches.
The tibial facet (by tape) is 4·4 inches.

The National Collection contains two huge calcanea from HAPPISBOROUGH (Nos. 33,420 and 33,425); the former is somewhat injured, but preserves the following measurements:[2]

Length 9·8 inches.
Height 7·5 „
External astragal facet 3·8 (a. p. d.) by 3·4 inches.
Internal „   „   4·5 „
Cuboidal 3 (height) by 5 inches (width).
Fibular facet 4·8 (a. p. d.) by 2 inches (height).
None of the articular surfaces in these two bones present the concavities so

[1] This dimension is exceeded by one recorded by Nesti from Val d'Arno, which was 0·295 m.=11·6 inches in length.
[2] Has been referred to previously at p. 64.

pronounced in the Asiatic Elephant and in the Mammoth; but the fibular facet is convex, as in them, although not to the same extent.

The calcaneum of the Mammoth, No. 33,419, B. M. (Pl. XIX, fig. 1), when compared with the above, shows certain differences, to wit, the prominent posterior and internal angle of that of the Mammoth, the relatively greater convexities of the tibial and perineal facets, which decidedly bulge out more in the Mammoth and (fig. 2) *E. antiquus*,[1] in both of which there is a wider interosseous pit, and in the Mammoth a more concave astragal aspect.

These points seem to prevail generally in the Mammoth and Asiatic Elephant. Again, the dorsal surface of the heel, which is usually narrow (not always, however) in the Mammoth, Asiatic, and *E. antiquus*, is always broad and round in the large bones from the FOREST BED. Moreover, the hollowing out of the inner side of the bone, so evident in the Mammoth generally and in the Asiatic, is not nearly so pronounced in the above and in the African Elephant. How much all these characters may depend on individual peculiarities I cannot say, but, as regards the Asiatic Elephant and the Mammoth, they appear pretty constant.

Naviculare.—Fragments of this bone are met with in collections made on the EAST COAST of Norfolk, but, unless for their huge proportions, they do not present characters of importance.

No. 21,642, B. M., from GRAYS, Essex, exceeds very much the dimensions of any specimen of that of the Mammoth with which I am acquainted. Moreover, seeing that abundant remains of *E. antiquus* have been derived from the fluviatile deposits of the above locality, the probability is that it belongs to this species. The maximum width of the specimen is 9 inches, and the height 5·5.

No instance of a *cuboid* sufficiently large, as compared with the foregoing, has come under my notice.

Internal cuneiforme.—This bone is well represented by the enormous specimen, left side, No. 188 of the Gunn Collection (Pl. XXI, fig. 2), from the NORFOLK COAST. The following are its dimensions:

Extreme length 4·5 inches.

Greatest girth 8·5, the upper end being 8·2 and the lower 7·5 inches in girth.

The navicular facet (fig. 2 *a*) is 2 × 2·5, and the distal articulation (fig. 2 *b*) is 2 (a. p. d.), by 2 inches in width.

Thickness is 3 inches.

The proximal facet inclines gently upwards (fig. 2 *a*), whilst the distal aspect (fig. 2 *b*) is quite even and subtriangular.

There is a small round facet externally for the middle cuneiform.

The variation to which this bone is subject in the recent and extinct Elephants, and possibly also individually, renders its characters, at all events, worthy of record. In the

[1] Pages 64 and 170.

Asiatic and African Elephants, and in the Mammoth, it maintains much the same aspects, being flat and considerably greater in length than in breadth. But the above (Pl. XXI, fig. 2) differs from them in being round, with a more circular outer surface. As compared with the internal cuneiform of any of the above, it is, indeed, widely different.

I have not seen a *middle cuneiforme* of a size sufficiently large to correlate it with the large bones now under consideration.

External cuneiforme.—This element of the foot is well shown in the large bone, No. 187, from the NORFOLK COAST, in the Gunn Collection. The length is 4·4 inches, and maximum breadth 2·5; thickness 1·8 inches. Here the navicular surface shows the usual depression pronounced about the middle of the articular surface.

15. METATARSUS.

There are several examples of the digital proximal bones in the British Museum and in the Norwich Museum, and private collections in Norfolk and Suffolk.

A good illustration of the second metatarsal is afforded by No. 39,465, B. M., from the EAST COAST. It is five inches in length, with a maximum breadth of 3·4 inches.

The third metatarsal of a huge Elephant from MUNDESLEY is preserved in Mr. Fitch's Collection. Its length is 7·4, and girth, midshaft, 8·4 inches.

The facet for the external cuneiform is 3 inches in height, by 3·4 inches in width.

The distal articular surface in the a. p. d. (by tape) is 7·4 inches, whilst the facet for the fourth metatarsal is 3 in height, by 1 inch in breadth.

In general appearance it seems to differ very little from the same bone in the Mammoth.

The fourth metatarsal is represented by a large bone in the British Museum from the East Coast, its maximum length and width being 6 and 3·5 inches respectively.

The fifth metatarsal is well shown by two short and extremely broad specimens in the Norwich Museum from the EAST COAST. One of these (not numbered) has the proximal articulation somewhat injured. The bone is flat on the dorsal aspect, with rounded sides. The length is 4½ inches, and girth, midshaft, 9·4 inches. Another similar bone, No. 195 of the Gunn Collection, is also 4½ inches in length, with a girth of 8·4 at the middle. The proximal articulation is 2·5 × 2·5 (tape), whilst the distal articular surface is 2·5 in the antero-posterior (by tape), and 2·4 inches in the transverse diameter. The upper surface of the articular surfaces are somewhat concave in both bones, with the lower borders protruding.

These two specimens show the circular cuboidal facet of the Mammoth, the same being ovoid in the African.

GENERAL SUMMARY.

The chief morphological characters and comparisons I have inferred from studies of the osseous remains of these three Elephants met with in the British Islands, and similar relics elsewhere, may be epitomised as follows :

As regards their exteriors, nothing is known further than the inference deduced from Arctic specimens of the *E. primigenius*, whose epidermis was clothed with long dark-coloured hair having a dense undergrowth of wool, as appertains to Mammals of cold climates.

As regards the *cranium* of *Elephas primigenius*, the frontal aspect is lengthened; summit narrow; space between the orbits in front narrow; large and long incisive sheaths with diverging alveoli; temporal fossa narrow; depression on the frontal; prominent lachrymal tubercle; zygoma under the level of the condyles, and nearly parallel with the molars; ovoid zygomatic arcade. (Pls. VI and VII.)

Mandible.—Broad, round mental region; small rostrum; erect diasteme, or nearly so; wide symphisial gutter; border of ascending ramus round posteriorly; condyles slightly compressed; neck of ditto narrow behind; dental canal opening upwards; short horizontal ramus; height to width of ascending ramus inconspicuous. (Pls. VIII and X.)

Cranium of E. antiquus.—Characters unknown.

Mandible.—Chin less rounded than *E. primigenius;* diasteme nearly erect; short rostrum; gutter not very wide; dental canal opening inwards; absence of much prominence of posterior border of ascending ramus; horizontal ramus more prolonged than in *E. primigenius;* greater difference between length and breadth of ascending ramus.

Cranium of E. meridionalis.—Shorter than in *E. primigenius;* vertex low and round; nasal aperture nearer to summit than in *E. primigenius;* inter-orbital space narrower; slight frontal depression; pointed lachrymal tubercle; zygoma much below the level of the condyles.

Mandible.—Chin usually less rounded than in either of the other two extinct species; low elevation of jaw at the commencement of the diasteme; long and narrow symphisial gutter; prolonged horizontal ramus, ending in a rather well-developed rostrum; greater height of ascending ramus in proportion to width as compared with the other two forms; absence of conspicuous bulging of ascending ramus posteriorly and at the junction with the horizontal ramus; dental canal directed backwards; narrowness of neck behind and below condyle. (Pl. XXII, fig. 2.)

I have already indicated several points of distinction between the dentitions of the three forms of Elephants,[1] and shall now proceed to a more general epitome of the diagnostic values attached to the dental series of each species.

Dentition of Elephas primigenius.

Permanent incisor very long, spiral, and not remarkably thick near the alveolus; abnormalities not uncommon. (Pls. VI and VII.)

General characters of molar series.—Great breadth as compared with length; narrow and crowded ridges; tenuity of elements; absence of crimping generally; narrow disks; abnormalities pretty common.

Molars.—A pre-antepenultimate milk-molar has been inferred to be occasionally found. The first milk-molar varies from five to six ridges, including talons, the second from eight to eleven ridges, the third from eleven to fourteen ridges; the first true molar from eleven to seventeen ridges, the second from sixteen to eighteen ridges, the third from twenty to twenty-nine, or more, ridges. (Pls. VI—XIV, Pl. XX, fig. 3, and Pl. XXI, fig. 1.)

Dentition of Elephas antiquus.

Permanent incisor curved gently, like the recent species; thick at the alveolus and narrowing gradually towards the tip.[2]

General characters of molar series.—Crown generally narrow compared with the length; high ridges; enamel various, but usually thicker than in *E. primigenius;* crimping of machærides; central expansion and angulation of the disk; all the elements of the crown well developed; discs not aggregated; frequent abnormalities.

Molars.—The first milk-molar varies from four to five ridges, including talons, the second from seven to ten ridges, the third ten to thirteen ridges; the first true molar from eleven to fourteen ridges, the second from fourteen to fifteen ridges, the third from seventeen to twenty-three ridges. (Pls. I—V, Pl. XII, fig. 3, and Pl. XX, figs. 1 and 2.)

[1] Pages 65 and 185.

[2] The large collection of Mammoth's tusks from Ilford, in the Brady Collection, British Museum, shows considerable variability in the degree of curvature, and, as before observed (p. 8), there is one perfectly straight, or nearly so. This solitary specimen, Mr. Davies suggested, in the Catalogue (p. 28), might have appertained to *E. antiquus,* but I have shown that straight tusks are occasionally developed in the recent species, whilst, on the other hand, the only authenticated incisor of *E. antiquus* from Bracklesham Bay seems to show a curvature like that of the recent species; moreover, if the tusk was straight no one would have noted the circumstance sooner than Dr. Falconer, who saw the last-named specimen and another at Syracuse ('Pal. Mem.,' vol. ii, p. 188). I revert to these facts on account of Professor Boyd Dawkins's paper "On the Classification of the Tertiary Period," 'Quart. Journ. Geol. Soc. London,' vol. xxxvi, p. 379, and 'Early Man in Britain,' p. 104, in which he calls *E. antiquus* the "straight-tusked Elephant."

Dentition of Elephas meridionalis.

Permanent incisor enormous; curves gently, like the recent species; thickness maintained for nearly half its length, declining gradually towards the tip. Exceptions rare.

General characters of the molar series.—Crowns very broad; collines short in comparison with *E. antiquus*, and generally as compared with *E. primigenius;* enamel of discs thick and rarely crimped, but usually uneven, looped, or channelled; crown constituents generally in excess; plates wide apart, with thick wedges of cement. Exceptions not common.

Molars.—The first milk-molar has five ridges, including talons, the second has eight ridges, the third ten ridges; the first true molar from nine to eleven ridges, the second from eleven to thirteen ridges, the third from thirteen to sixteen ridges. Exceptions not common, except in the true molars. (Pl. XVII, fig. 8; Pl. XVIII, fig. 4; Pls. XXII —XXV.)

Spinal axis of Elephas primigenius.—The prominent "hog's back," so distinctive of the Asiatic as compared with the African Elephant, seems to have been a character also in the Mammoth.

Atlas.—Anterior articular surfaces semi-lunar; outer margins of the latter even and round; proportions between maximum height and width of neural and odontoid canals as 20 to 15. Exceptions rare. (Pl. XVII, fig. 1.)

Axis.—Neural canal nearly as broad as it is high; anterior articular surfaces subovate, with round external borders; odontoid process central. No exceptions out of several instances. (Pl. XVII, fig. 6.)

Spinal axis of Elephas antiquus : Atlas.—Anterior articular surfaces wider and more rounded than in *E. primigenius;* outer margins more circular; proportions between height and width as 22 to 20 (fig. 2). Differentiations made from a single specimen. (Pl. XVII, fig. 2.)

Axis.—Anterior articular surfaces subtriangular, and nearly as broad as long; outer margins projecting inferiorly and ovoid; odontoid process excentral, and near upper margin of centrum (fig. 5). Characters taken from a single specimen. (Pl. XVII, fig. 5.)

Spinal axis of Elephas meridionalis : Atlas.—Anterior articular surfaces asymmetrical and bulging inferiorly, with uneven external borders; proportions between height and width as 30 to 17. Last-named character not supported by any Italian specimen. (Pl. XVII, fig. 3.)

Axis.—Neural canal circular; anterior articular surfaces subcordate, with projecting external border; odontoid process excentral, and placed on the inferior margin of the centrum. (Pl. XVII, fig. 4.)

Scapula of E. primigenius.—Spine elevated; neck broad; recurved spine nearly central; glenoid cavity compressed laterally. (Pl. XV, fig. 1, and Pl. XXII, fig. 4.) Supported by numerous instances.

Scapula of E. antiquus.—Unknown.

Scapula of E. meridionalis.—Spine high and prominent; neck very broad; glenoid cavity wide inferiorly. (Pl. XVIII, fig. 3.) Supported by several instances.

Humerus of E. primigenius.—Robust; head and tuberosity compressed; deltoid crest prominent; deep and narrow bicipital groove; supinator ridge short and not very salient; border of condyles sharp and well defined; trochlear depression deep, with erect internal side; concavity internal to supinator ridge very pronounced. (Pl. XVI, fig. 1.)

Humerus of E. antiquus.—Not so robust as that of the Mammoth; deltoid crest not so prominent; supinator ridge less salient; hollow in front of supinator ridge very pronounced; trochlear depression deep and circular; outer condyle more globose than in the other two. (Pl. XVI, fig. 6.)

Humerus of E. meridionalis.—Not relatively so robust as in the Mammoth, but stouter than that of *E. antiquus*; head more circular than in the Mammoth; supinator ridge short, with little saliency; deltoid crest not very prominent as compared with the Mammoth; hollow in front of supinator ridge more pronounced in this and the last than in the Mammoth; trochlear depression like that of the Mammoth; margins of cubital articular surface not so defined as in the other two. (Pl. XVI, figs. 2 and 3.)

Cubitus of E. primigenius.—The radius commences to cross the ulna about its middle, and in a more oblique direction than in either of the recent species. The directions in the other two extinct forms are unknown to me.

Ulna.—Radial sulcus often deep; inner articular surface wide at the neck: posterior olecranon ridge rounded; external border well defined.

Radius.—Anterior surface round; upper and outer side of shaft less flattened than in the other two; round inner aspect of shaft. (Pl. XVIII, figs. 1 and 2.)

Cubitus in E. antiquus: Ulna.—Deep radial sulcus; head of olecranon arches more inwards than in the Mammoth.

Radius.—Upper and outer and inner sides of shaft more flat and round than in the Mammoth.

Cubitus of E. meridionalis: Ulna.—Radial sulcus shallow and wide; shaft not so flat as in the Mammoth.

Radius.—Anterior surface of shaft rather round, with outer and inner sides sloping and flat.

Manus of E. primigenius.—Minor distinctions subject to exceptions in *scaphoid, lunare,* and *cuneiforme; trapezium* and *trapezoid* inferred to be diagnostic (Pl. XIX, fig. 8, and Pl. XXI, fig. 3); proximal articular surfaces of the *third metacarpal* are diagnostic. (Pl. XVIII, fig. 7.)

Manus of E. antiquus.—Minor distinctions in *scaphoid, lunare,* and *cuneiforme; trape-*

234   BRITISH FOSSIL ELEPHANTS.

zium and *trapezoid* inferred to be diagnostic (Pl. XIX, fig. 9, and Pl. XXI, fig. 4); proximal articular surfaces of *third metacarpal* are diagnostic.   (Pl. XVIII, fig. 6.)

Manus of E. meridionalis.—Minor distinctions in *scaphoid, lunare,* and *cuneiforme; trapezium* inferred to be diagnostic (Pl. XIX, fig. 10); proximal articular surfaces of *third metacarpal* are diagnostic.   (Pl. XVIII, fig. 5.)

Fifth metacarpal short and broad, with concave proximal articular surface.   (Pl. XVIII, fig. 8.)

Pelvic girdle of E. primigenius.—Foramen ovale ovate, with the smaller end uppermost, and pronounced groove for the nerve and vessels; acetabulum higher than broad; niche of acetabulum wide, and opening on a flat surface; obturator border of ischium narrow, with prominent internal spine.

Pelvis of E. antiqua.—Unknown.

Pelvis of E. meridionalis is apparently like that of *E. primigenius.*

Femur of E. primigenius.—Neck short; great trochanter nearly level with the epiphysial junction of the head; bulging of external side at the commencement of the lower third; convergence of condyles more pronounced than in *E. antiquus,* and less than in *E. meridionalis;* variability of this character not unfrequent.   (Pl. XIX, fig. 7, and Pl. XXII, fig. 6.)

Femur of E. antiquus.—Condyles less convergent than in the other two generally, but subject to considerable variability.

Femur of E. meridionalis.—Shaft more round generally; but more flattening of the upper third anteriorly and posteriorly than in *E. primigenius.*

Crus of E. primigenius.—Prominent beetling spine; oblique fibular facet; circular femoral and tarsal articular surfaces.   (Pl. XIX, figs. 12 and 4.)

Crus of E. antiquus.—Less obliquity of fibular facet; femoral and astragalar articular surfaces subcircular.   (Pl. XIX, fig. 11.)

Crus of E. meridionalis.—Fibular facet nearly horizontal.   (Pl. XIX, fig. 3.)

Pes of E. primigenius: Astragalus.—Posterior border uneven; outer calcaneal facet nearly quadrilateral, inner crescentic; wide intervening fissure.   (Pl. XIX, fig. 5.)

Calcaneum.—Heel prominent; deep hollow internally; dorsal aspect round; outer articular surface four sided, inner nearly triangular.   (Pl. XIX, Fig. 1.)

Cuboid.—Internal and external sides subequal; calcaneal facet horizontal.

Pes of E. antiquus: Calcaneum.—Sides of heel equally compressed, and more round than in *E. primigenius;* peroneal facet large and prominent; outer articular surface ovoid, inner crescentic; intervening pit gaping more anteriorly than in *E. primigenius.*   (Pl. XIX, fig. 2.)

Pes of E. meridionalis: Astragalus.—Posterior border concave; tibial surface even; outer calcaneal facet nearly quadrilateral, with uneven internal side, inner ovoidal; intervening pit wide at the middle.   (Pl. XIX, fig. 6.)

Calcaneum.—Concavity inner side of heel not very pronounced, but more so than in *E. antiquus;* dorsal aspect of heel broad; outer articular surface nearly quadrilateral, inner ovoidal; peroneal surface less prominent than in either of the other two Elephants.

Internal cuneiforme.—Round shaft; proximal articular surface oblique; distal even and subtriangular. (Pl. XXI, fig. 2.)

Fifth metatarsal.—Round dorsal aspect; cuboidal facet circular.

First phalanx compressed laterally.

CONCLUDING OBSERVATIONS.

The osteological distinctions adduced in support of the existence of three species of Elephants in the British Islands during the Pliocene and Post-pliocene Periods suggest certain inferences in relation to their external characters and distributions.

The MAMMOTH seems to have preserved its thick covering of hair in both middle and high latitudes, as inferred from the Arctic specimens and the etching on the piece of tusk found in the cave of La Madelaine in the Dordgne. It was more slender than the other two forms, and apparently more active in its habits.

As regards dimensions there was considerable variability. No doubt there were local races, as with the two living Elephants; and these were characterised by external, as well as internal, distinctions. The small bones and teeth from the Ilford Brick-earths contrast with the larger dental and osseous elements from deposits in the neighbourhood and elsewhere throughout the Islands.

Reverting to the etching from Dordogne, the external ear, like that of the Asiatic, was apparently small as compared with the African; and, like the former, its skull showed a high crown, and the back behind the withers was prominent. These two characters are likewise confirmed by the skeleton.

In its long and dense pile of hair and bristles[1] streaming down face, cheeks, flanks, and quarters, the Mammoth must have presented a far more formidable appearance than might be inferred from its skeleton.

As regards height there seems to have been considerable variability. In comparison with the two recent species it may have averaged about 11 feet at the shoulder, whilst

---

[1] " Referring to the hair from Siberia in the Museum of the Royal College of Surgeons, Owen observes that it differed in length and thickness; some bristles, nearly black, were much thicker than horse-hair, and from twelve to eighteen inches long."—' British Fossil Mammals,' foot-note, p. 266.

individuals stood between 12 and 13 feet high. The smaller races, to wit, the denizens of ancient Ilford and other localities, scarcely equalled the dimensions of an ordinary-sized Asiatic Elephant.

The climate of Siberia does not appear to have caused a diminution in size, seeing that some of the largest teeth and bones have been brought from Polar lands.

The ANCIENT ELEPHANT was both stouter and generally taller than the Mammoth, and presented even greater variability in height.

As to its external appearance, there is no evidence that it possessed a similar epidermic covering, but the probability is that the protection was necessary, at all events, during its sojourn in North-western Europe.

The MERIDIONAL ELEPHANT was proportionally much taller than either of the fore-going; and individuals, judging from bones, must, in comparison with the living species, have attained a height of fully 14 feet at the shoulder. The high prominent crown of the Mammoth was less pronounced in this species; and, being a Pliocene Mammal, the probability is that it was not so densely clad in hair.

During their long struggles with climate and varying conditions, the lighter built Mammoth would have survived where its tardy compeers would have succumbed.

THE ASIATIC ELEPHANT.

The almost naked epidermis of the adult recent Elephants, although general, is not an invariable distinction, even in full-grown individuals, especially among the denizens of the cooler regions of Asia. Indeed, the young often display this character of their ancestors, and the same has been observed in the case of the Rhinoceros of Asia.[1]

In outward appearance the Asiatic Elephant and Mammoth present similar characters, to wit, the high crown, lengthened anterior dorsal spines, and size of ears. The mutability in the size of the Asiatic Elephant is suggestive as regards extinct species, the various races being distinguished by outward characters[2] as well as skeletal differences. Thus, the small-sized race of Central India stands to the taller variety of the North-western Provinces much as the Mammoths of Ilford were to the larger denizens of other localities.

With reference to height there appears to be great variability. The tallest Asiatic Elephant measured by Mr. Sanderson, out of many hundreds, was 10 feet 5 inches at the shoulder; according to Tennent,[3] the Ceylon Elephant seldom exceeds 9 feet, and

[1] This is well shown in youthful individuals of both species at present (1880) in the Gardens of the Zoological Society of London. One of the young Asiatic Elephants lately presented to the Society by H.R.H. the Prince of Wales is more or less clad with hair, which Mr. Bartlett informs me has increased since its arrival.

[2] Falconer, 'Pal. Mem.,' vol. ii, p. 257.

[3] Tennent's 'Ceylon,' vol. iv, p. 291.

the ordinary herds do not average more than 8 feet.[1] The latter is about the height of the Bengal Elephant, which, however, varies considerably, not only in height but in stoutness, as shown by the designations of "slender-built" and "squat-built" Elephants of the Sal Forests. Sanderson asserts that few female Indian Elephants attain to a height of 8 feet at the shoulder.

The statement first advanced by Cuvier, that the Asiatic Elephant has a nail more on both fore and hind foot than in the African, may be pretty generally true; but, as regards the latter species, there are exceptions. Mr. Bartlett informs me that the female African Elephant in the Zoological Gardens has four nails on the hind foot, whilst the male has only three, and that sometimes the Asiatic has five instead of four nails on the hind foot.

It has been asserted, moreover, that the Elephant of Asia displays a greater degree of intelligence and aptitude for instruction. But I am assured by the above-named excellent authority that, as far as the two African individuals now in the Zoological Gardens are concerned, where they have been reared from the time they were calves, they are "quite equal in intelligence to the Asiatic, and far more active, and that the male is as good tempered as it is possible for any animal to be."

THE AFRICAN ELEPHANT.

The natural history of the African Elephant is not so well known as that of its more Eastern congener, at the same time it is easily distinguished from the latter. Neither the crown of the head nor the back is so convex, and the ears are much broader, and it is generally taller. There seems, however, considerable variability in the last-named character. Livingstone, who had seen more Elephants than, perhaps, any African traveller, observes that those living on the banks of the Zambesi averaged about 9 feet 10 inches in height, whilst further south the Elephants attained a height of 12 feet;[2] whilst Sir Samuel Baker considers that the Elephant at the sources of the Nile stands about 10 feet 6 inches. Again, Livingstone speaks of a small race only 5 feet 8 inches in height,[3] which would be about the dimensions of the dwarf *Elephas Mnaidriensis* of Adams.[4]

Distribution.—The view that all the remains of Elephants met with in British and European strata represent the variable conditions of a single species should receive support in the distribution of the animal in space and in time. Now, among the vast quantities of molars and bones from Polar regions, not a trace of teeth referable to the forms to which the names *E. antiquus* and *E. meridionalis* have been given has been

[1] The Cingalese Elephant, although higher at the fore quarters than the Sal Forest Elephant, is otherwise not so bulky.
[2] 'Travels in South Africa,' p. 569. The fine male in the Zoological Gardens, Mr. Bartlett informs me, although not yet full grown, is 11 feet 6 inches; and the female, much younger, is 8 feet 2 inches in height.
[3] 'Last Journals,' vol. ii, p. 29.
[4] 'Trans. Zool. Soc.,' vol. ix, p. 116.

found. Again, the huge teeth and bones referable to the last-named form have not hitherto been found in deposits of a Post-glacial age with those of *E. primigenius* and *E. antiquus.*

The characters so distinctive of the worn crown of *E. primigenius* are maintained throughout its geographical and geological distributions. The close-packed and attenuated wedges of enamel and dentine are preserved equally in molars from the British Isles, German Ocean, European Continent, Arctic Siberia and North America, Canada, and the United States. In Europe they are found often side by side with the teeth and bones of the other two forms, and again, in North America, with a decidedly different form of tooth. But the spiral tusk, so prevalent in all skulls containing grinders of the characters referred to the Mammoth, has not been seen in crania holding molars assigned to the *E. meridionalis*; and, as far as fragmentary instances of the *E. antiquus* are concerned, it is also absent, its place being taken by a defensor similar in outline to that of the two recent Elephants.

Again, if the molars of *E. primigenius*, as stated by a few palæontologists, are seen shading off into thick-plated varieties, provided that such assertions are meant to convey a belief that any two or more of these so-called species can be united by a series of grinders graduating into one another, how is it that this remarkable variability is not present in the teeth from Polar lands?

Then, as to the cranium of *E. primigenius* and *E. meridionalis*—unfortunately, that of *E. antiquus* is unknown—can any two skulls of allied species be more distinct? In the case of the two recent species the cranial characters never vary, and are as broadly specified as are the skulls of the Mammoth, Meridional, and probably that of the Ancient Elephants.

The various physical features and climates with which the Mammoth had to contend throughout its wide distribution in space and in time were well calculated to bring about modifications of its external and internal skeleton. And these, no doubt, took place within certain limits I have indicated; but the ancestral branches from which the *E. primigenius*, *E. antiquus*, and *E. meridionalis* sprang, and the regions in which their evolutions took place, were both geographically and geologically remote from the British Islands, at all events, and from the periods of time represented by the deposits in which the remains of the former are found. No doubt the time will come when the palæontologist can be enabled to bridge over many gaps at present both wide and well defined.

Although a few facts point definitely towards a union of several forms of Proboscideans, at present admitted to be distinct species, it must be conceded that by far the greater number of these are based merely on single characters subject to exceptional cases, and as yet unsupported by other and far more important skeletal elements. It will therefore be granted that the apparent resemblances between certain so-called species, although morphological facts, must be subject to acceptance or rejection in accordance with the advancement of science. At present I see no good—on the contrary, much confusion, in making hasty assumptions without the confirmation of reality. As to persistency of character throughout long periods of time, we find many cotemporaries of the Mammoth, to wit, the Red Deer, Elk, Reindeer, Wolf, and others, maintaining, at all events, their skeletal elements unchanged, however much their Post-pliocene ancestors may have differed from them in external covering.

The association, therefore, of the Mammoth, in North-western, Central, and Southern Europe, with the Ancient and Meridional Elephants, its solitary sojourn in the Arctic and sub-Arctic regions of the Old and New Worlds, and its companionship in the United States with the so-called Columbian Elephant, and maintaining throughout these vast areas the well-marked dental and osseous characters by which it is differentiated from them, are certainly cogent evidences of its claims to be considered a distinct species. As to its range in time, we find the main points connected with, at all events, its dental elements, continuing from the Pliocene Period up to the Neolithic Age.

The Ancient Elephant has left its remains abundantly in North-western, Central, and Southern Europe, also in Northern Africa and probably Hindostan, where, at all events a close ally, if not the same species, existed under the name of the Narbudda Elephant (*E. Namadicus*). The Ancient Elephant displayed far more divergent skeletal characters than either of its congeners, and ranged in time from the Pliocene into the Post-pliocene Periods. It may have become extinct before the Mammoth; at all events the two were cotemporaneous in England during the Cave Period, and the depositions of the drifts, valley-gravels, brick-earths, and possibly the boulder-clays.[1]

The Meridional Elephant has been traced from South-eastern England to the Continent of Europe, including the coast of Holland and Belgium, Northern, Middle, and Southern France, Italy, and South-eastern Europe.[2] Its Eastern congener, the broad-fronted Elephant (*E. planifrons*), claims certain marked relationships.

The differentiations established by Falconer that three well-marked species may be recognised among the fossil remains of Elephants met with in Europe receive further confirmation from the data I have recorded in this Monograph. These, as well as other species, he characterised by the variations in their grinders, which, although valuable as one of the chief means in forming a diagnosis, should, in all cases, go hand in hand with other elements of the skeleton. But, unfortunately, the difficulties in attempts to unite the teeth and bones are frequently embarrassing, owing to the association of remains of two or more species.[3]

No more pointed instance of an involved collection, made, doubtless, under many difficulties, can be adduced than that brought together by Falconer and Cantley in the Sewalik Hills.[3] This may be owing to precise records not having been made during the

[1] Boyd Dawkins, 'Quart. Journ. Geol. Soc.,' vol. xxxv, p. 139.
[2] Lartet, 'Bullet. Sociét. Géol. de France,' 3rd series, t. xvi, p. 500.
[3] Vast quantities of spinal and appendicular elements of Mastodons and Elephants from the above situations, are now in the British Museum, but in the absence of typical examples, it is at present impossible to assign any single bone to its appropriate cranium and molar.

excavations. It must be conceded that until the Asiatic fossil forms have been fully described no sound deductions in connection with the pedigrees of Proboscideans in general are likely to be arrived at.

With reference to the Proboscidean remains from British strata, the abundant materials of the Mammoth skeleton from the Arctic regions in the Museums of this country afford ample means for comparative purposes. In consideration, however, of accidental intrusions, I have invariably, wherever Arctic types were available, preferred them, especially in the cases of the fragmentary elements of the appendicular skeleton. The association of the teeth and bones of the three species in Pre-glacial deposits, and of the Mammoth and *E. antiquus* in Post-pliocene strata, leaves no doubt that they were not only cotemporaneous, but must have often herded together. The same, moreover, was pointedly the case with the Sewalik and Maltese species. Considering, therefore, the marked variability displayed by the skeletal elements of the three extinct British Elephants, we may, I think, fairly suppose that by means of natural selection and its conditions, mutability giving rise to distinct races, and varieties would, in process of time, produce species such as are ordinarily accepted by the term. Referring even to the Mammoth, as compared with *E. antiquus*, there are well-marked distinctions between the teeth and bones met with in the brick-earths of Ilford and typical molars from neighbouring localities and the Arctic regions. These two pronounced varieties are easily recognised from each other by their dimensions and characters. Now, although any one who will take the trouble to examine the Brady Collection in the British Museum, and compare the teeth and bones from the same parts from other British localities and foreign countries, cannot doubt that they represent one species; at the same time it must be admitted that they present considerable variability. This mutability is very much more apparent in the remains of *E. antiquus*, and to a small extent with *E. meridionalis*, as far as remains of the latter are at present known. These mutabilities, more especially in the case of the Mammoth, I cannot help believing were never fully recognised by Falconer.[1]

The following relationships between the extinct and recent Elephants, indicated either solely by their dentitions, or in combination with the skeleton generally and distribution, must be considered, for the most part, as merely approximations subject to the corrections and additions of a progressive branch of scientific research.

[1] I refer especially to one of the last sentences he wrote on this subject, where he states that the Mammoth retained its "organs of locomotion and digestion all but unchanged through an enormous lapse of ages." Posthumous essay on "Primeval Man and his Contemporaries," 1863, 'Pal. Mem.,' vol. ii, p. 587.

Elephas primigenius.

The correlation by Falconer of *E. Hysudricus*, a Miocene form, with *E. primigenius* and other allies in his subgenus *Euelephas*, on account of similarities in the ridge formula of their grinders, indicates an alliance of some kind with the Asiatic Elephant and the Mammoth; but this is as much as can be advanced at present.

The nearest approach to the latter, established by the ridge formula and general osteological characters, is presented by the skeleton of the living denizen of Asia. The disagreements displayed in the tusks, crown patterns of the grinders, and epidermic coverings, are assuredly very pronounced, and require further evidences of relationship before one can break down the barrier existing between them, inasmuch as there must have been considerable intermediate modifications of these parts in either direction.

The molars of *E. Armeniacus*, described by Falconer, and placed by him as intermediate in character between the Mammoth and the Asiatic Elephant,[1] present assuredly broader crowns than ordinarily appertain to the grinders of the latter. Consequently, this is one step towards the union of the two; otherwise the Armenian form, as far as the specimens in the British Museum are concerned, have failed in my hands, after repeated comparisons, to show any appreciable differences between them and grinders of the Asiatic Elephant. Indeed, should the Italian specimens,[2] referred to by Falconer, turn out identical with the Armenian molars, it might be a matter for speculation whether or not we should look to the evolvement of the Mammoth from *E. Asiaticus*, rather than the opposite. The plaited enamel of the living species has numerous homologies among fossil teeth of the Sewalik Elephants, whereas the typical molar of the Mammoth stands widely apart from any Eastern form.

The grinders of *Elephas Columbi*, Falconer,[3] represented by the specimens in the British Museum and the Royal College of Surgeons of England, occupy a similar position to the Mammoth's grinders met with in North America as do those of the Asiatic and Armenian Elephants to the teeth of that form found in Europe and boreal Asia. Moreover, the extreme breadth of the crowns of certain molars of *E. Columbi*—and there seems to be considerable variability—are in keeping with that of the Armenian Elephant,[4] from which it would be difficult to make out any differences of importance. In North America we find the Mammoth's remains restricted to the Arctic and temperate regions, whilst the plaited tooth of *E. Columbi* predominates in the more southern and warm, temperate climates. Again, in Asia the thin-plated molar of the Mammoth is restricted to Siberia, whilst the fluted enamel of the disc is repeated in the living denizen of subtropical Asia.

[1] Op. cit., vol. ii, p. 247.
[2] Op. cit., vol. ii, p. 249.
[3] Op. cit., vol. ii, p. 219.
[4] Falconer, 'Nat. His. Review,' 1863, plates i and ii. Same reduced, 'Pal. Mem.,' vol. ii, plate x.

Elephas antiquus.

If I am correct in assigning the three well-marked varieties of teeth[1] to *E. antiquus*, the following inferences may be drawn in connection with their relations to the molars and other remains of allied forms hitherto regarded as distinct species :

1st. The massive broad crown of *E. antiquus*, with its ridges closely approximated, and not unfrequently devoid of, or only partially displaying, angulations, central expansions, and crimping of the enamel discs, so characteristic of the long narrow tooth, coupled with the characters of the bones, appears to assimilate closely to the same elements of the skeleton of *E. Namadicus* of India. Molars and bones of the above description are plentiful in collections from British and European Pliocene and Postpliocene strata. But these affinities do not end here, for on comparing the above with the fluted crowns of *E. Asiaticus*, *E. Armeniacus*, *E. Columbi*,[2] and certain teeth assigned to *E. primigenius*, very close relationships are likewise traceable. These are most apparent in crowns of the latter, in which all the characters of the broad massive molar of *E. antiquus* are represented. Hypothetically, one might argue that from the Miocene *E. Hysudricus* sprang the *E. Namadicus* and *E. antiquus*, from which *E. Asiaticus*, *E. Armeniacus*, *E. Columbi*, and *E. primigenius* branched off.

2nd. The long narrow, and often arcuated crown of *E. antiquus*, on which the species was first differentiated, although the most common variety, as far as British specimens are concerned, can be, without difficulty, traced in a series towards the third variety, to which Falconer assigned the name of *E. priscus*, from its close agreement with the tooth of *E. Africanus*. It was only after a more extended experience, that he withdrew that name and placed it in the same category with *E. antiquus*. The instances recorded elsewhere of the variety in question[3] include several colossal teeth of Elephants whose dimensions must have rivalled those of the broad crown, and even the tooth of *E. meridionalis*, whilst other grinders and bones belonging to animals with the narrow crown must be referred to much smaller individuals.

The discs of these molars generally display well-marked angulations and expansions (Pl. V, fig. 1), although these are not always on every disc.

The degrees of crimping and thickness of the enamel, dentine, and cement are variable. Again, when the elements are in excess, and the crimping very feeble, or nearly absent, and the central expansions and angulations pronounced,[4] the sculpturing of the

[1] Page 31, and elsewhere.
[2] The molar of *E. Columbi*, 'Pal. Mem.,' vol. ii, p. 222, and in vol. v, plate iv, of the 'Geologist,' and No. 33,218 of the Palæontological Collection, B. M.; also No $\frac{20,792}{\Lambda}$, B. M. The characters of their crowns closely resemble the following examples of the broad variety of *E. antiquus*. The molar from Happisborough, No. 33,327, B. M., alluded to at p. 37, and No. 27,907, B. M., from Clacton, at p. 33, plate IV, fig. 1, and also plates V, fig. 1, and XX, figs. 1 and 2.   [3] Page 33.
[4] See molar 39,370, B. M., from GRAY's, Essex, 'Pal. Mem.,' vol. ii, pl. xvii, fig. 1, and part i, p. 34.

tooth is scarcely to be differentiated from crowns of *E. Africanus*; but this agreement is not confined to it alone, innsmuch as their bones have been shown to present many affinities.

Again, one of the most remarkable resemblances in connection with this description of molar, and, in no small degree, the bones likewise, is presented by their relations to the same elements in the dwarf Elephants of Malta, as pointed out in my Monograph on these pigmy forms.[1]

From these data it might be conjectured that the African and Maltese Elephants were evolved from the narrow-crowned variety of *E. antiquus*.

Elephas meridionalis.

Frequent allusions have been made in preceding pages to the relations of the dental elements of the above with those of the *E. planifrons* of the Sewalik Hills of Northern India. The materials of this Miocene Elephant, although somewhat scanty, at all events, as far as the grinders are concerned, show a decided relationship with *E. meridionalis*. Both were of stupendous dimensions, and show by no means such tendencies to variability as displayed in the dental and osseous structure of *E. antiquus*. The only striking resemblances between certain molars of the former and the latter are furnished by such enormous and thick-plated molars as the remarkable tooth from Culham,[2] in the Oxford University Museum, and another from Whittlesea, in the Museum of Zoology of Cambridge University,[3] and the largest ultimate molars of *E. meridionalis*. But whilst these agree as to the thickness of the dental elements, they differ in the sculpturings of the crowns; indeed, the disposition to thick- and thin-plated varieties in all the British, Maltese, and, to a less extent, the recent species, shows that these conditions alone are not trustworthy diagnostic characters. The presence of a pre-molar in *E. planifrons* and its suppression in *E. meridionalis* constitute an important distinction, but, like the pre-antepenultimate milk-molar, may not be an invariable condition.

The passage from the sub-genus *Stegodon* towards *Loxodon* has been thus indicated by Falconer :—"The ciphers yielded by the 'ridge formula' of *E. (Stegodon) insignis* place the species in close affinity with the Loxodons, and more particularly with the species named *E. (Lox.) planifrons*."[4] The former, according to this authority, is of both Miocene and Pliocene, and the latter Miocene.

Again, the natural affinities between the Mastodons and the Stegodons are shown by

Also, and the very suggestive example discovered by Ramsay a few years ago in a deposit near Tangier, 'Quart. Journ. Geol. Soc.,' vol. xxxiv. p. 514, fig. 9.

[1] 'Trans. Zool. Soc. London,' vol. ix, p. 109, and plates iii—ix inclusive.
[2] Page 33.
[3] Page 177.
[4] Op. cit., vol. ii, p. 86.

Falconer in the teeth of *Mastodon longirostris* and *M. latidens* as compared with *Stegodon Cliftii, St. bombifrons,* and *St. insignis.*[1]

All these and other allied Proboscidean and Mammalian affinities, as far as they go, might be arranged in the following manner :

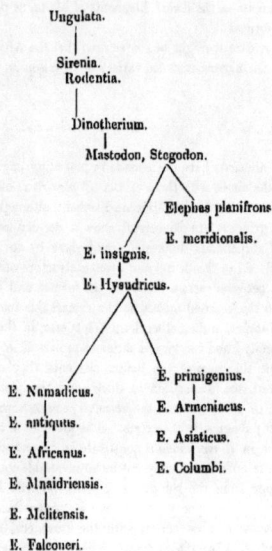

Ungulata.
|
Sirenia.
Rodentia.
|
Dinotherium.
|
Mastodon, Stegodon.

Elephas planifrons
|
E. meridionalis.
E. insignis.
|
E. Hysudricus.

E. Namadicus.   E. primigenius.
| |
E. antiquus.   E. Armeniacus.
| |
E. Africanus.   E. Asiaticus.
| E. Columbi.
E. Mnaidriensis.
|
E. Melitensis.
|
E. Falconeri.

[1] Op. cit., vol. ii, p. 82.

INDEX.[1]

---

[1] The author is indebted to the Rev. T. Wiltshire, M.A., F.G.S., Secretary of the Palæontographical Society, for the pains he has taken in the compilation of this Index.

34

[1] The letter (a) following a locality intimates that the bones of Elephas antiquus have been found in that neighbourhood; (m) or (p), shows that Elephas meridionalis or Elephas primigenius has been discovered.

¹ The letter (a) following a locality intimates that the bones of Elephas antiquus have been found in that neighbourhood; (m) or (p), shows that Elephas meridionalis or Elephas primigenius has been discovered.

[1] The letter (a) following a locality intimates that the bones of Elephas antiquus have been found in that neighbourhood; (m) or (p), shows that Elephas meridionalis or Elephas primigenius has been discovered.

[1] The letter (a) following a locality intimates that the bones of Elephas antiquus have been found in that neighbourhood; (m) or (p), shows that Elephas meridionalis or Elephas primigenius has been discovered.

---

[1] The letter (a) following a locality intimates that the bones of Elephas antiquus have been found in that neighbourhood ; (m) or (p), shows that Elephas meridionalis or Elephas primigenius has been discovered.

[1] The letter (a) following a locality intimates that the bones of Elephas antiquus have been found in that neighbourhood; (m) or (p), shows that Elephas meridionalis or Elephas primigenius has been discovered.

---

[1] The letter (a) following a locality intimates that the bones of Elephas antiquus have been found in that neighbourhood; (m) or (p), shows that Elephas meridionalis or Elephas primigenius has been discovered.

PRINTED BY J. E. ADLARD, BARTHOLOMEW CLOSE.

37

PLATE XVI.

Figs. 1, 1 *a*, and 1 *b*. Anterior, posterior, and inferior views of a humerus of *E. primigenius*, No. 30,531, British Museum, from the Bay of Galway. (About ⅛ natural size.)

Figs 2 and 2 *a*. Anterior and posterior views of a humerus of *E. meridionalis*, No. 200, Gunn Collection, Norwich Museum, from the Forest Bed, coast of Norfolk. (About ₁₁ natural size.)

Fig. 3. Inferior view of the distal extremity of a humerus of *E. meridionalis*, Norwich Museum, from the Forest Bed, Rockland. (About ₁₁ natural size.)

Figs. 4, 4 *a*, and 4 *b*. Anterior, posterior, and inferior views of a humerus of *E. Asiaticus*, No. 2744 E, in the Museum of the Royal College of Surgeons, London. (About ⅛ natural size.)

Figs. 5, 5 *a*, and 5 *b*. Anterior, posterior, and inferior views of a humerus of *E. Africanus*, No. 708 n, British Museum. (About ⅛ natural size.)

Figs. 6, 6 *a*, and 6 *b*. Anterior, posterior, and inferior views of a humerus of *E. antiquus*, in the Cotton Collection, Jermyn Street Museum, from the brick-earths of Ilford, Essex. (About ⅛ natural size.)

The expenses connected with the drawing of the specimens upon the stone in connection with Plates XVI, XX, XXI, XXII, and XXV, were defrayed by a grant allocated by the Government Grant Committee of the Royal Society for the Promotion of Scientific Research.

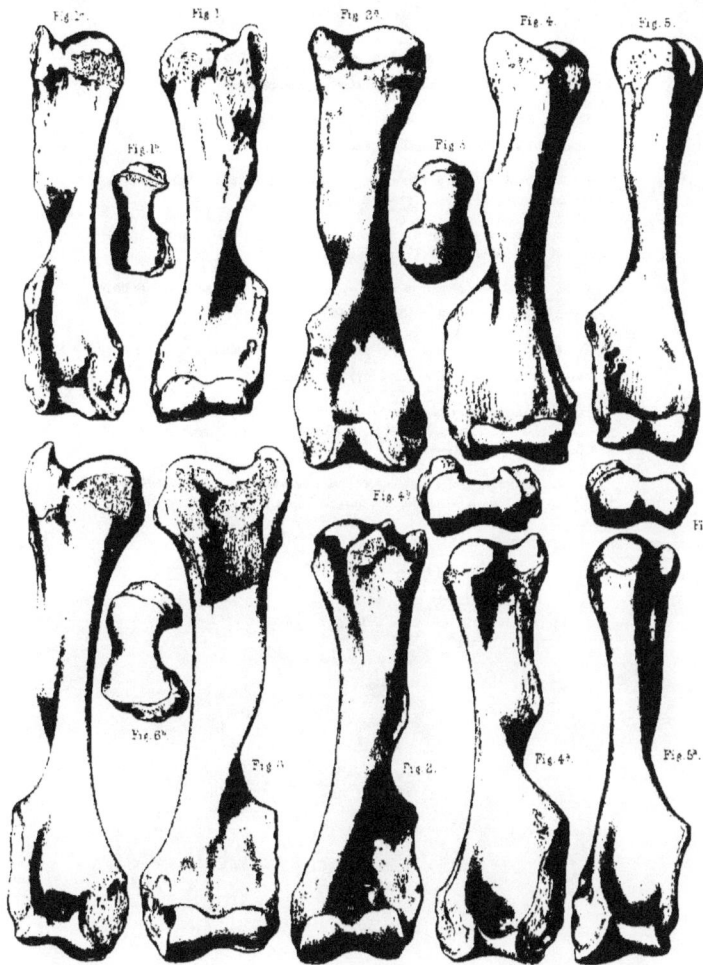

Fig. 1ᵃ. Fig. 1. Fig. 2ᵃ. Fig. 4. Fig. 5.

Fig. 1ᵇ. Fig. 3.

Fig. 4ᵇ. Fi

Fig. 6ᵇ. Fig. 6. Fig. 2. Fig. 4ᵃ. Fig. 5ᵃ.

PLATE XVII.

Fig. 1. Front view of an atlas of *E. primigenius*, Nos. 45,025 and $\frac{C}{93}$ of the Brady Collection, British Museum, from Ilford, Essex. ($\frac{1}{4}$ natural size.)

Fig. 2. Front view of an atlas of *E. antiquus*, Nos. 45,200 and $\frac{D}{9}$ of the Brady Collection, British Museum, from Ilford, Essex. ($\frac{1}{4}$ natural size.)

Fig. 3. Front view of an atlas of *E. meridionalis*, No. 36,436, British Museum, dredged off the coast of Essex. ($\frac{1}{4}$ natural size.)

Fig. 4. Front view of an axis of *E. meridionalis*, No. 27,872, British Museum, dredged off the coast of Essex. ($\frac{1}{4}$ natural size.)

Fig. 5. Front view of an axis of *E. antiquus*, Nos. 45,201 and $\frac{D}{10}$ of the Brady Collection, British Museum, from Ilford. ($\frac{1}{4}$ natural size.)

Fig. 6. Front view of an axis of *E. primigenius*, Nos. 45,030 and $\frac{C}{98}$ of the Brady Collection, British Museum, from Ilford. ($\frac{1}{4}$ natural size.)

Fig. 7. Anterior view of a first dorsal vertebra of *E. primigenius* (?), in the possession of J. J. Colman, Esq., M.P., of Corton, Suffolk, dredged off Lowestoft, Suffolk. (About $\frac{1}{4}$ natural size.)

Fig. 8. Crown view of a right upper last milk molar of *E. meridionalis*, in the King Collection, Jermyn Street Museum, from the Forest Bed, Norfolk. (Natural size.)

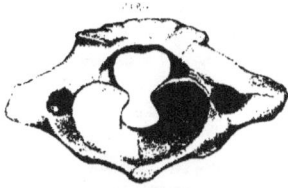

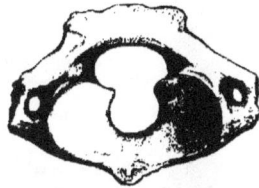

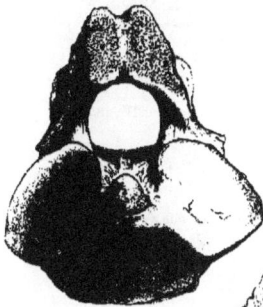

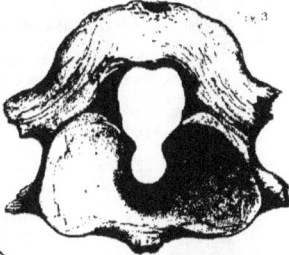

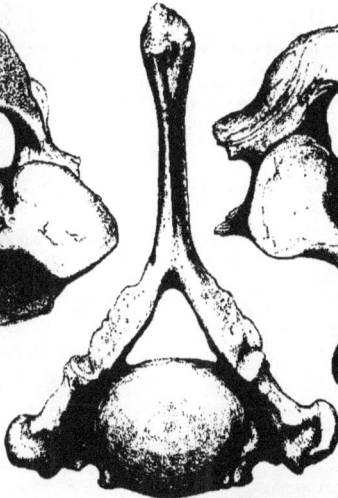

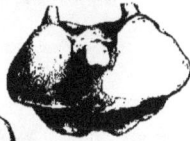

PLATE XVIII.

Fig. 1. A right cubitus of *E. primigenius*. Fig. 1 *a*. Proximal end of the ulna. Fig. 1 *b*. Distal aspect. No. 38,011, British Museum.

Fig. 2. Radius, No. 38,012, detached from fig. 1. Fig. 2 *a*. Distal aspect. Fig. 2 *b*. Proximal aspect. Both from Ilford, Essex. ($\frac{1}{4}$ natural size.)

Fig. 3. Glenoid cavity of a left scapula of *E. meridionalis*, No. 275, Gunn Collection, Norwich Museum, from the Forest Bed, Norfolk coast. ($\frac{1}{4}$ natural size.)

Fig. 4 Fragment of a true molar of *E. meridionalis*, No. $\frac{G}{103}$, Jermyn Street Museum, from the Forest Bed at Mundesley, Norfolk coast. (Natural size.)

No. 5. Proximal articular aspect of a third metacarpal of *E. meridionalis*, No. 33,428, British Museum, from Happisborough, Norfolk Coast. ($\frac{1}{4}$ natural size.)

Fig. 6. Proximal articular surface of a third metacarpal of *E. antiquus*, No. 18,248, British Museum, from Grays, Essex. ($\frac{1}{2}$ natural size.)

Fig. 7. Proximal articular surface of a third metacarpal of *E. primigenius*, No. 36,232, British Museum, from Ilford, Essex. ($\frac{1}{2}$ natural size.)

Figs. 8 and 8 *a*. Fifth metacarpal, with proximal articular surface, of *E. meridionalis*, No. 33,433, British Museum, from Happisborough, coast of Norfolk. ($\frac{1}{4}$ natural size.)

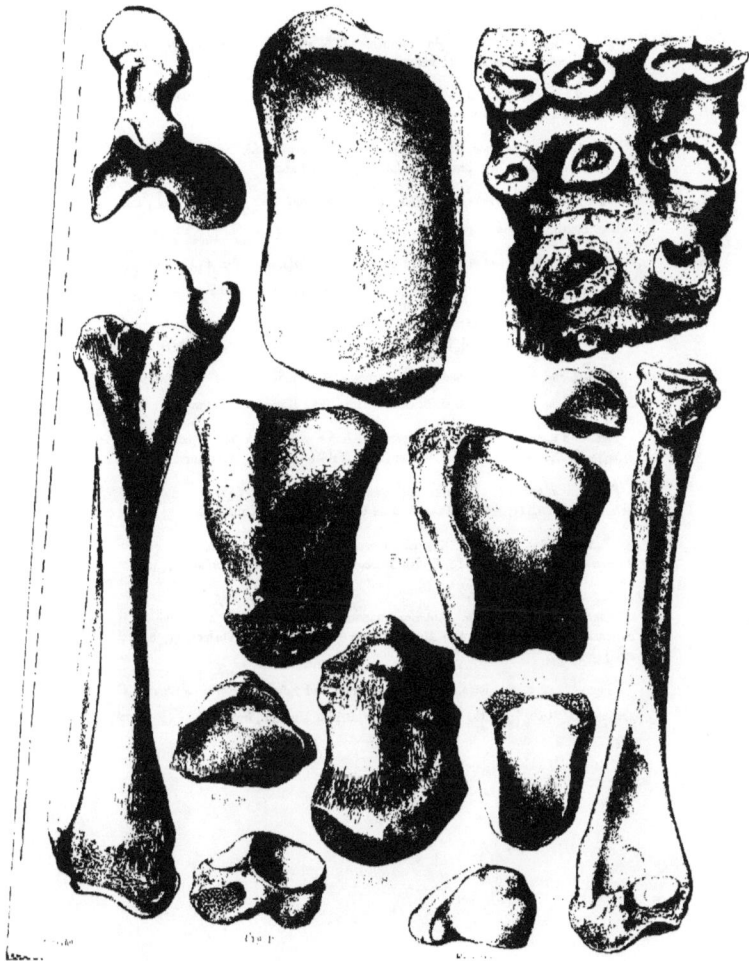

PLATE XIX.

Fig. 1. Upper view of a right calcaneum of *E. primigenius*, Nos. 33,410, British Museum, from Ilford, Essex. ($\frac{1}{3}$ natural size.)

Fig. 2. Upper view of a left calcaneum of *E. antiquus*, No. 27,040, British Museum, from Grays, Essex. ($\frac{1}{2}$ natural size.)

Fig. 3. Distal internal view of a fibula of *E. meridionalis*, No. 26,724, British Museum, from Forest Bed, Cromer, Norfolk. ($\frac{1}{4}$ natural size.)

Fig. 4. Distal internal view of fibula of *E. primigenius*, No. $\frac{C}{220}$ of the Brady Collection, British Museum, from Ilford. ($\frac{2}{3}$ natural size.)

Fig. 5. Inferior view of a right astragalus of *E. primigenius*, Nos. 45,171 and $\frac{C}{221}$ of the Brady Collection, British Museum, from Ilford. ($\frac{1}{3}$ natural size.)

Fig. 6. Inferior view of a left astragalus of *E. meridionalis*, No. 33,425, British Museum, from the Forest Bed, Happisborough, Norfolk coast. ($\frac{1}{3}$ natural size.)

Figs. 7 and 7a. Front and inferior aspects of a right femur of *E. primigenius*, No. $\frac{C}{190}$ of the Brady Collection, British Museum, from Ilford. ($\frac{1}{8}$ natural size.)

Figs. 8, 8 *a*, and 8 *b*. External, upper, and lower views of a left trapezium of *E. primigenius*, No. 36,611, British Museum, from Maidstone, Kent. ($\frac{1}{3}$ natural size.)

Figs. 9, 9 *a*, and 9 *b*. External, upper, and lower views of a right trapezium of *E. antiquus*, No. 20,821, British Museum, from Grays, Essex. ($\frac{1}{2}$ natural size.)

Figs. 10, 10 *a*, and 10 *b*. External, upper, and lower views of a right *trapezium* of *E. meridionalis* (?), No. 33,418, British Museum, from East Coast, Norfolk. ($\frac{1}{4}$ natural size.)

Figs. 11, 11 *a*, and 11 *b*. Anterior, superior, and inferior views of a tibia of *E. antiquus* (?), No. 40,134, British Museum, from the Valley of the Thames. ($\frac{1}{5}$ natural size.)

Figs. 12, 12 *a*, and 12 *b*. Anterior, superior, and inferior views of a tibia of *E. primigenius*, No. $\frac{C}{218}$ of the Brady Collection, British Museum, from Ilford. ($\frac{1}{5}$ natural size.)

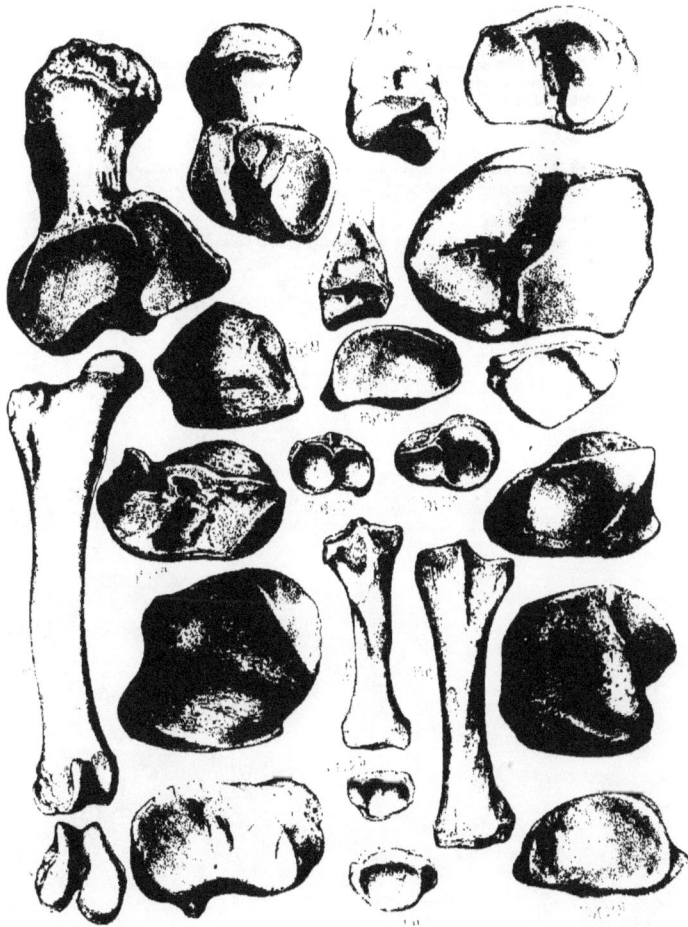

PLATE XX.

Fig. 1.   Profile view of a right lower last true molar of the broad-crowned variety of *E. antiquus*, in the possession of J. J. Colman, Esq., M.P., from the Forest Bed at Corton, Suffolk.   (Much reduced.)

Fig. 1 *a.*   Crown view of fig. 1.   ($\frac{1}{4}$ natural size.)

Fig. 2.   Crown view of a right upper last true molar of the broad-crowned variety of *E. antiquus* from the same locality.   ($\frac{1}{4}$ natural size.)

Fig. 3.   Fragment of a crown of a true molar of *E. primigenius* (?), in the possession of A. Savin, Esq., from the Forest Bed, Overstrand, near Cromer, Norfolk.   (Natural size.)

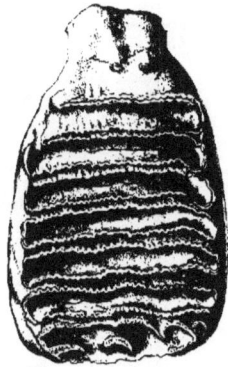

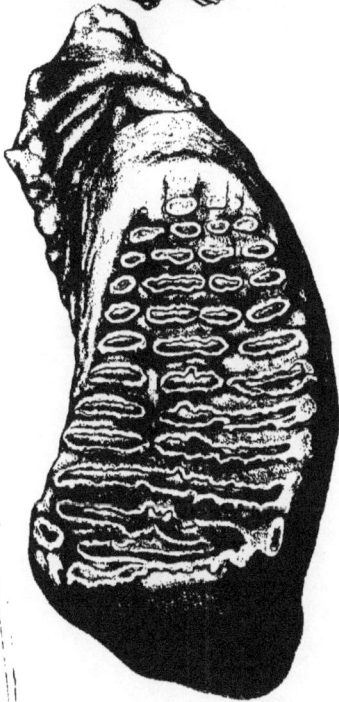

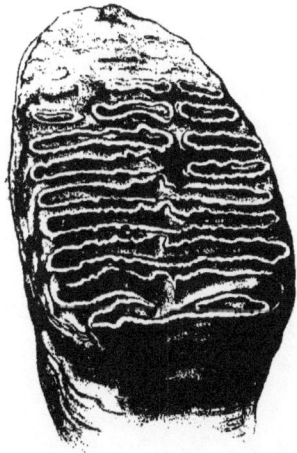

PLATE XXI.

Figs. 1 and 1 *a*.   Crown and profile views of a left upper first true molar of *E. primigenius*, in the possession of Mr. A. Savin, from the Forest Bed, Overstrand, near Cromer.   (Fig. 1 natural size, fig. 1 *a* $\frac{2}{3}$ natural size.)

Figs. 2, 2 *a*, and 2 *b*.   External, superior, and inferior aspects of a left internal cuneiforme of *E. meridionalis*, No. 188, of the Gunn Collection, from the Norfolk coast. (About natural size.)

Fig. 3.   Scaphoidal and metacarpal articular surfaces of No. 23,119, British Museum, a left trapezoid of *E. primigenius*, from Maidstone, Kent.   ($\frac{1}{2}$ natural size.)

Fig. 4.   Scaphoidal and metacarpal articular surfaces of No. 36,609, British Museum, a left trapezoid of *E. antiquus*, from Grays, Essex.   ($\frac{1}{2}$ natural size.)

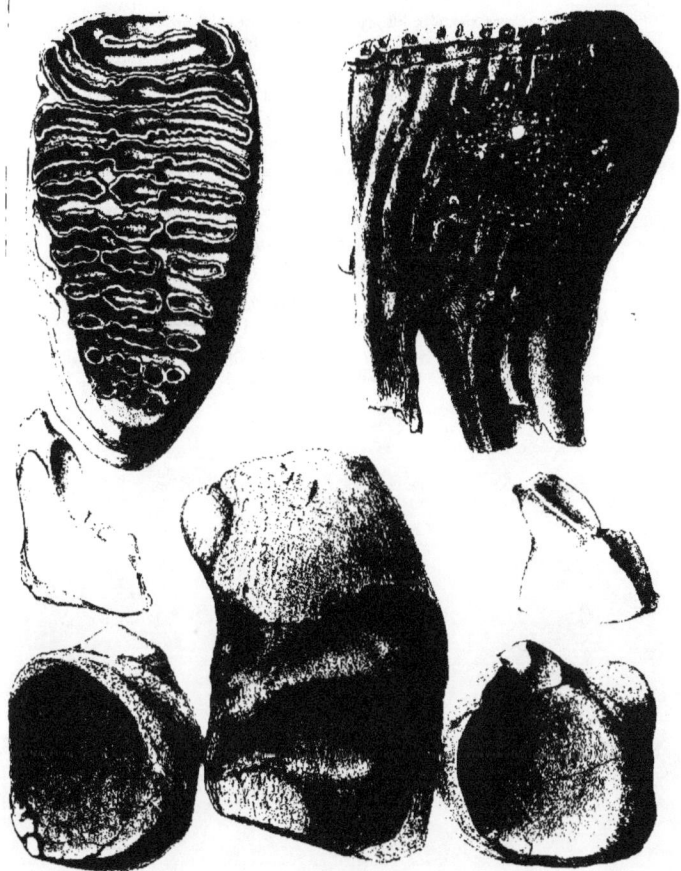

PLATE XXII.

Fig. 1. Crown view of a left upper first true molar of *E. meridionalis*, in the possession of R. Fitch, Esq., of Norwich, from the Forest Bed, Cromer, Norfolk. (Natural size.)

Fig. 2. Portion of the right ramus of a mandible of *E. meridionalis*, containing the two last true molars, No. 215, Gunn Collection, Norwich Museum, from near Mundesley, Norfolk coast. (⅓ natural size.)

Figs. 3 and 3 *a*. Fragment of a right ramus of a mandible, with crown view of the penultimate milk molar of *E. meridionalis*, No. 214, Gunn Collection, Norwich Museum, from the Forest Bed, Norfolk coast. (Fig. 3 ⅓ natural size, fig. 3 *a* natural size.)

Fig. 4. Glenoid cavity of a scapula of *E. primigenius*, Gunn Collection, Norwich Museum, from the Norwich Coast. (Much reduced.)

Fig. 5. Inferior aspect of a femur of *E. antiquus* (?), No. 236, Gunn Collection, Norwich Museum, from the Forest Bed, Bacton, Norfolk. (Much reduced.)

Fig. 6. Inferior aspect of a femur of *E. primigenius*, No. 271, Gunn Collection, Norwich Museum, from the Norfolk coast. (Much reduced.)

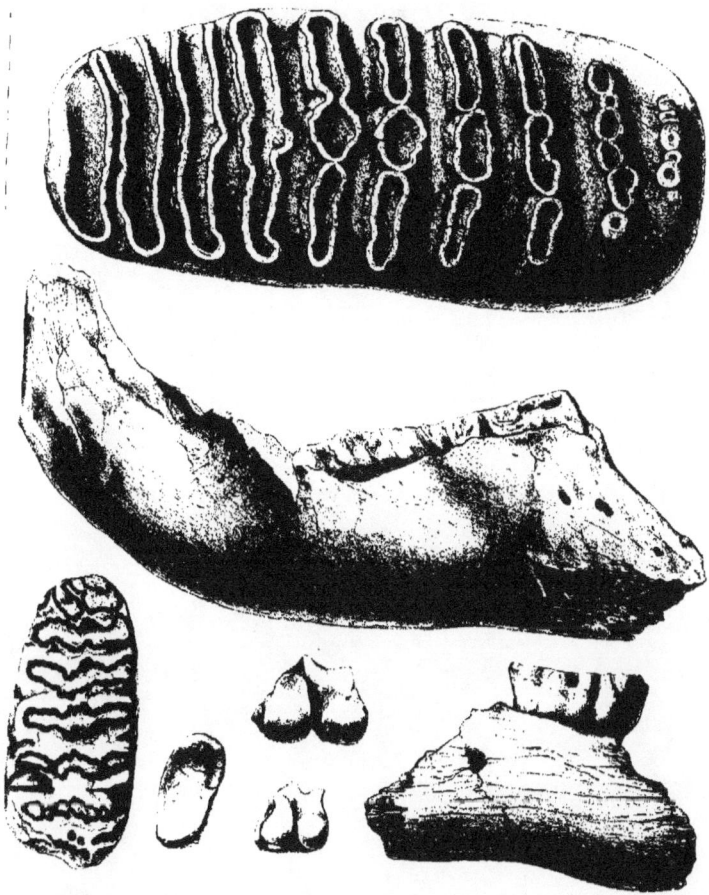

PLATE XXIII.

Figs. 1 and 1 *a*. Crown and profile views of a left lower second true molar of *E. meridionalis*, No. 33,343, British Museum, from the Norfolk coast.   (Natural size.)

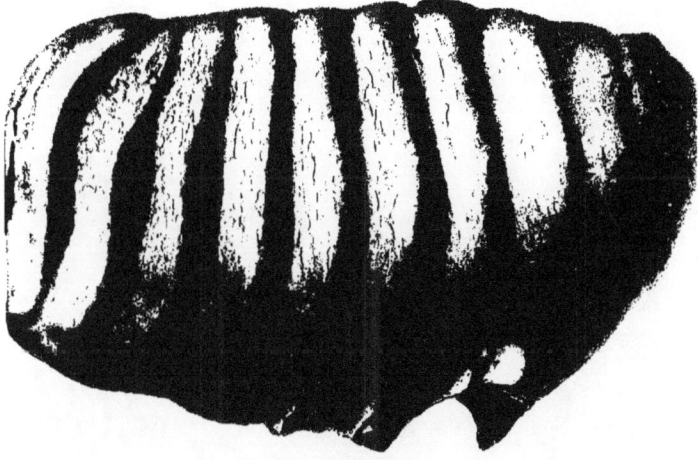

Fig. 1. A right lower last true molar of *E. meridionalis*, No. 33,354, British Museum, from Happisborough, Norfolk coast. (Considerably reduced.)

Fig. 2. A left upper last true molar of *E. meridionalis*, No. 33,334, British Museum, from the Norfolk coast. (Somewhat reduced.)

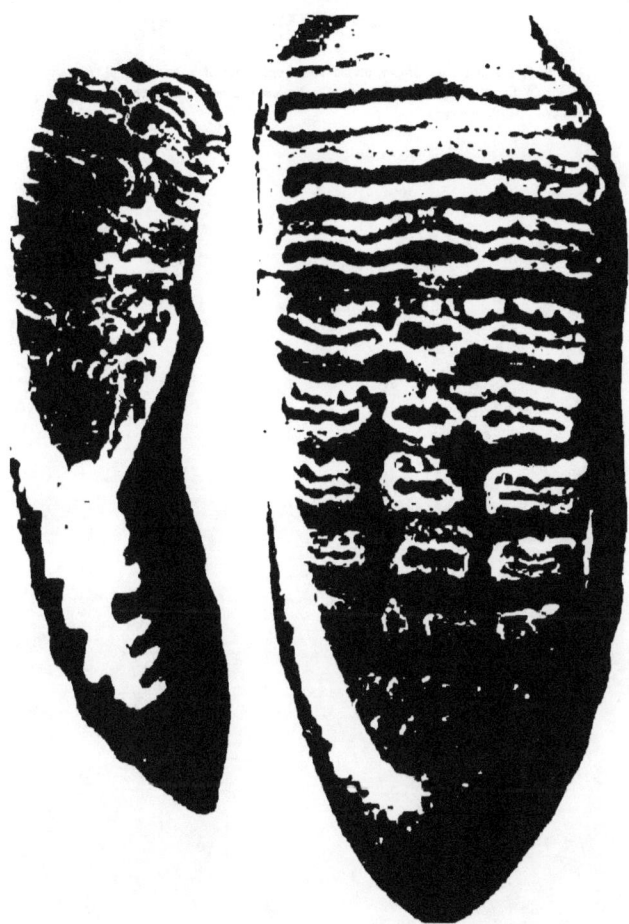

Figs. 1, 1 *a*, and 1 *b*. Upper, profile and front views of a mandible of *E. meridionalis*, in the Woodwardian Museum, Cambridge University, from the Forest Bed, Cromer. (Much reduced.)

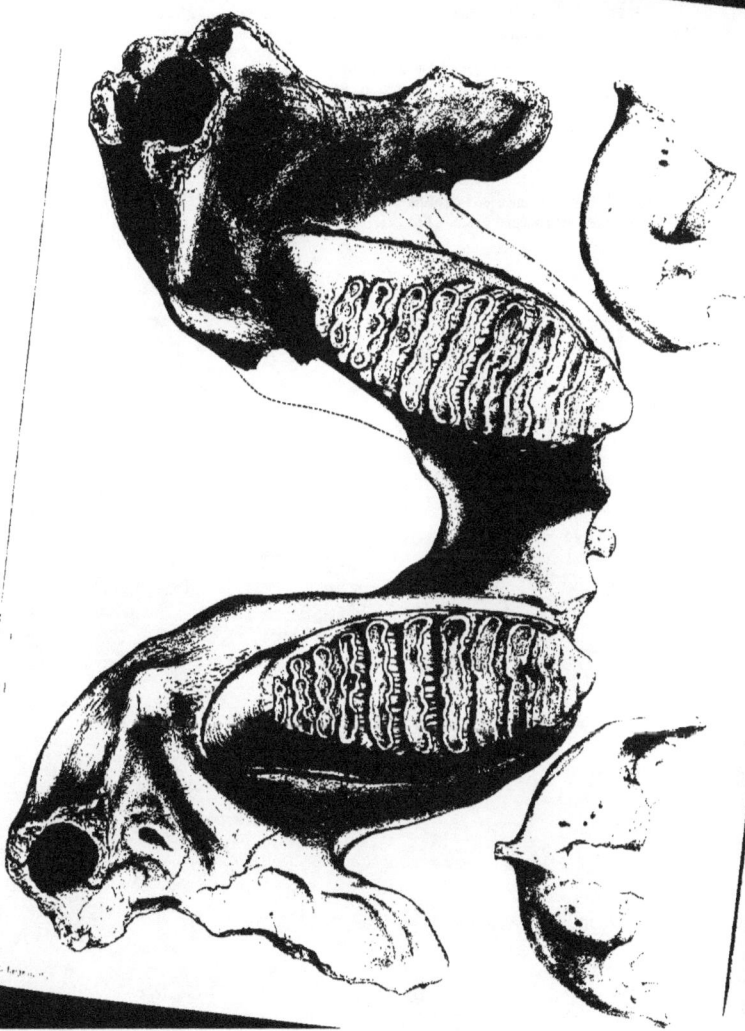

PLATE XXVI.

Fig. 1. Crown view of an abnormal second true molar of *E. primigenius*, from the Norfolk coast. (Natural size.)

Fig. 2. Fragment of the crown of a true molar of *E. antiquus* (?), in the Leeds Philosophical Museum, from the Red Crag, Trimley, Suffolk. (Natural size.)

Figs. 3, 3 *a*, and 3 *b*. Anterior, profile, and inferior views of a left femur of *E. meridionalis*, in the possession of J. Backhouse, Esq., West Bank, York, from Overstrand, Norfolk coast. (about ½ natural size.)

Fig. 4. Vertical section of two plates of a true molar of *E. antiquus* (?), in the Leeds Philosophical Museum, from the Red Crag, Trimley, Suffolk. (Natural size.)

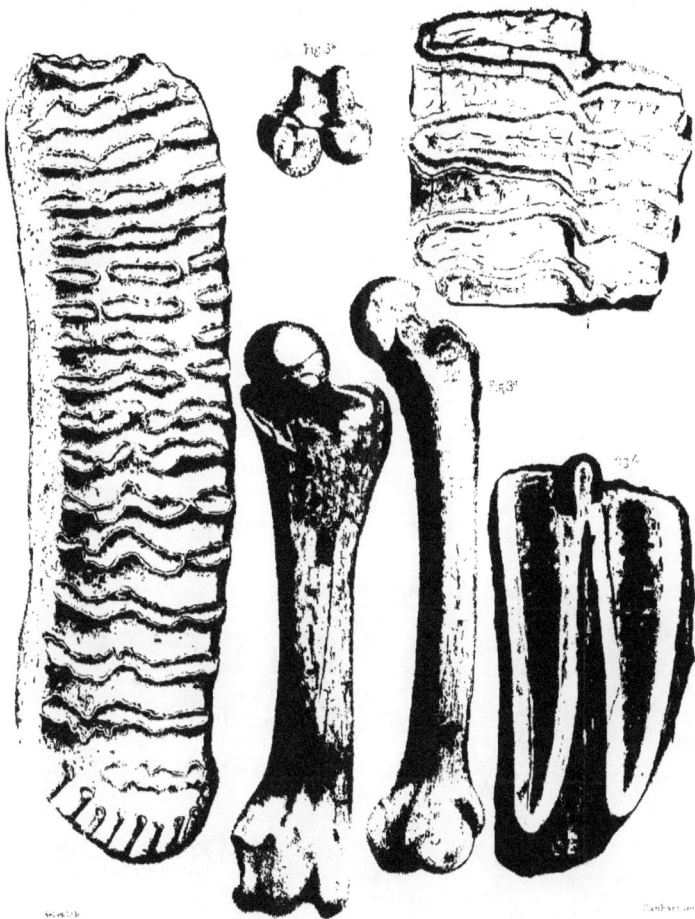

Fig. 3.ª

Fig 4.ª

PLATE XXVII.

Map of the distribution of Elephas antiquus and Elephas meridionalis in England and Wales.

The marks ⊟ and ◇ refer solely to *Elephas antiquus*; no traces of *E. meridionalis* having hitherto been discovered on dry land. In both cases the finds have been most plentiful when either land or trawling operations have been extensively prosecuted.

PLATE XXVII.

DISTRIBUTION OF ELEPHAS ANTIQUUS & MERIDIONALIS IN ENGLAND & WALES.

ENGLAND & WALES.

Reference

London: John Murray, Albemarle Street.

Map of the distribution of Elephas primigenius in England, Wales, Scotland and Ireland.

The most abundant discoveries of *Elephas primigenius* will be seen to prevail in districts where the surface deposits have been most disturbed, to wit, the Valley of the Thames and the chief railway routes. The same is applicable to the dredgings and trawlings along the East coast.

PLATE XXVII.

DISTRIBUTION of ELEPHAS PRIMIGENIUS in ENGLAND, WALES & SCOTLAND

DISTRIBUTION IN IRELAND

IRELAND

Dogger Bank

References.

Reference.

London. Published

www.ingramcontent.com/pod-product-compliance
Lightning Source LLC
Chambersburg PA
CBHW021117270326
41929CB00009B/918